The JED editor and all the programs from A
Square One are also available on diskette for th
been given to many major national IBM PC user groups
Group. These groups will provide this diskette as part of their own ongoing
software library programs. Contact your local user group or TUG for current prices
and ordering information.

Or, you can order this diskette directly from the author for $10.00, using the order
form below.

Order Form
Shipping information—please print

Name _____

Street _____

City _____ State _____ Zip _____

Date _____

Please send me

_____ diskettes to accompany **Assembly Language from Square One**
(includes both the JED editor and all listings)

at $10.00 each; $15 each outside U.S. and Canada.

Check method of payment

☐ check ☐ money order ☐ cash
(Credit cards and C.O.D. payments are not accepted.)

Amount enclosed $ _____

Mail to: Jeff Duntemann
103 Hidden Drive
Scotts Valley, CA 95066

Price includes postage and handling and applicable sales tax. Price and availability subject
to change without notice.

Assembly Language
from Square One

For the PC AT and Compatibles

◆◆

Scott, Foresman
Assembly Language Programming Series

Jeff Duntemann, Editor

Assembly Language from Square One

For the PC AT and Compatibles

Jeff Duntemann

Scott, Foresman and Company
Glenview, Illinois   London

Cover photo: Courtesy of The Image Bank

Turbo Assembler is a trademark of Borland International, Inc. Microsoft
Macro Assembler is a trademark of Microsoft Corporation. IBM, IBM PC, IBM
PC/AT, and IBM PS/2 are trademarks of IBM Corporation.

Library of Congress Cataloging-in-Publication Data

Duntemann, Jeff.
    Assembly language from square one for the PC AT and compatibles / Jeff Duntemann.
       p.   cm. — (Scott, Foresman assembly language programming series)
     ISBN 0-673-38590-6
     1. Assembler language (Computer program language) 2. IBM Personal Computer
AT—Programming. I. Title. II. Series.
    QA76.73.A8D86   1990
    005.265—dc20   89-10944
                                            CIP

1 2 3 4 5 6 MVN 94 93 92 91 90 89

ISBN 0-673-38590-6

Copyright © 1990 Scott, Foresman and Company.
All Rights Reserved.
Printed in the United States of America.

Notice of Liability

The information in this book is distributed on an "As Is" basis, without warranty. Neither
the author nor Scott, Foresman and Company shall have any liability to customer or any
other person or entity with respect to any liability, loss, or damage caused or alleged to be
caused directly or indirectly by the programs contained herein. This includes, but is not
limited to, interruption of service, loss of data, loss of business or anticipatory profits, or
consequential damages from the use of the programs.

Scott, Foresman professional books are available for bulk sales at quantity discounts. For
information, please contact Marketing Manager, Professional Books Group, Scott,
Foresman and Company, 1900 East Lake Avenue, Glenview, IL 60025.

For Kathleen M. Duntemann, Godmother . . .
. . . who gave me books
when all I could do was put teeth marks in them.
It was a good investment.

Acknowledgments

◆◆

To Carol, for patience;

To Mr. Byte, who curled up around my feet;

To Michael Abrash, who taught most of it to me;

To Irene Governale, for proofing the manuscript; and

To Amy Davis of Scott, Foresman and Company, the invisible power who noodged the series from fantasy into reality.

Foreword to the Scott, Foresman Assembly Language Programming Series

◆◆

There is really only one kind of book on 8086/8088 assembly language today; one that contains a chapter on the central processing unit (CPU) registers, perhaps a chapter on memory addressing modes, which is then followed by a long tour of the instruction set with (at most) a few two- or three-line examples of how the instructions are put together. Few of these books mention the PC at all, and those that do generally stop after demonstrating a few BIOS calls that are too slow to be useful anyway.

This is no way to teach assembly language.

Assembly language is, after all, the language of the machine. This means that it is the language of a specific, particular machine; the use of assembly language on that machine is inextricably tied to the architecture and peculiarities of that machine. Teaching assembly language on the PC requires teaching the PC as well or what is taught won't be especially useful.

This realization led to one of the two design goals of this series: to teach assembly language in the context of the PC standard so that those learning assembler will be able to apply it immediately without also having to bury themselves in books about the PC. At an advanced level (as Michael Abrash brilliantly demonstrates in *Zen of Assembly Language*) the border between machine code and the machine itself begins to blur. Hidden performance thieves (Michael calls them "the cycle eaters") like DMA refresh and video memory wait states lurk behind every instruction. Arcana such as the difference between 8-bit and 16-bit I/O ports can mean the difference between slow software and fast software or in extreme cases, between software that works and software that crashes and burns. Without understanding the PC's hardware, the assembly language programmer is at the mercy of such villains—the more sophisticated the program becomes, the more it is exposed to such dangers.

The second design goal addresses both the nature of the subject and the nature of the audience: no single book can turn a green programmer into a Zen-level expert. The subject is large and complex; what's worse, the details of assembly language are an interconnected web that make serial discussion of any assembly language topic without "forward references" to more advanced topics almost impossible. This means that the same broad set of topics must be taught in each book, but that the level of detail be gradually increased in moving from beginner to expert.

The goal, then, was to define a series of books that gradually moves from absolute beginner level to world-class programmer, covering the same old CPU and assembly language each time, but covering it in a fashion appropriate to the gradually escalating skills that the reader is building. This is what we have done.

Assembly Language from Square One takes the bold step of treating assembly language as a programmer's *first* language. In doing so, it must explain not only what assembly language is, but what *programming* is, and it does so without apology. As the ground-level book on the topic, *Assembly Language from Square One* lays the groundwork for assembly language programming on the PC, which includes considerable discussion of the PC itself. The idea is to get the newcomer to become familiar with the jargon and the concepts behind the language, both of which bewilder the newcomer far more often than assembly language itself.

The journeyman's course in assembly language lies in *Assembly Language Magic,* which assumes that the programmer has the jargon and context for assembly language and needs to work at the considerable spread of the instruction set itself. *Assembly Language Magic* provides a great many short but complete demonstration programs that exercise the full range of the instruction set of the 8086/8088 microprocessors. Most books fail to adequately address how instructions work together and tend to treat instructions in isolation. Programs do not consist of one instruction, and any intermediate-level assembly language book that does not provide numerous complete and working programs simply will not do the student any lasting good.

Finally, there is the difference between assembly language programs that work and assembly language programs that work *well.* Writing in assembler is difficult compared with writing in C or Pascal, and if the resulting assembly language programs are no smaller or no faster than an equivalent program in C or Pascal, there's very little point to the extra effort. I have yet to see any assembly language book make this point, much less dwell on it. *Zen of Assembly Language* carries the theme that assembly language, which offers a higher level of control than any other language, must be written with a knowledge of the machine, the individual instructions, and the relationships among instructions that transcend all three. Without this second-level understanding, the programmer might as well return to C or Pascal, because the payback will not be enough to justify the effort.

Zen of Assembly Language assumes that the programmer understands the general principles of assembly language and shows how to melt the program into the machine in a way calculated to get the very most out of both. Wait states, DMA, the prefetch queue, planning for and measuring performance—these are the topics that await the Zen programmer in assembly language, Master *Zen of Assembly Language* and you will have mastered assembly language.

Until, like Michael Abrash, you discover some new unturned stone in the garden.

With these books, and other books to come, we hope to put the subject of assembly language for the PC at your fingertips. The subject deserves better than it has gotten at the hands of the computer book industry, and with the Scott, Foresman Assembly Language Programming Series we hope to put that situation aright.

The Books in the Scott, Foresman Assembly Language Programming Series

Assembly Language from Square One
by Jeff Duntemann
ISBN 0-673-38590-6

Assembly Language Magic
by William H. Murray and Chris H. Pappas
ISBN 0-673-38766-6

Zen of Assembly Language Volume I, Knowledge
by Michael Abrash
ISBN 0-673-38602-3

Zen of Assembly Language Volume H, The Flexible Mind
by Michael Abrash
(To be published in 1990)

Introduction: Agony in the Key of AX

What astonishes me about learning how to program is not that it's so hard, but that it's so *easy*. Am I nuts? Hardly. It's just that my curse is the curse of a perfect memory, and I remember *piano lessons*.

My poor mother paid six hundred 1962 dollars for a beautiful cherrywood spinet, and every week for two years I trucked off to Wilkins School of Music for a five-dollar lesson. It wasn't that I was a reluctant student; I loved music and I genuinely wanted to master the damned thing. But after two years the best I could do was play *Camelot* well enough to keep the dog from howling. I can honestly say that nothing I ever tried and failed to achieve after that (including engineering school and sailboarding) was anything close to that difficult.

That's why I say, if you can play the piano, you can learn to program in assembly language. Even if you can't play the piano, I hold that you can learn to program in assembly language if:

◆ you've ever done your own long-form taxes
◆ you've earned a degree in medicine, law, or engineering
◆ you've ever put together your average kid's swing set
◆ you've ever cooked a five-course dinner for eight and gotten everything to the table, hot, at all the right times

Playing the piano, however, is the acid test; there are lots more similarities than there are differences. To wit:

In both cases, you sit down in front of a big, expensive machine with a keyboard, you try to memorize a system of notation that seems to have originated on Mars, you press the keys according to incomprehensible instructions in stacks of books, and ultimately, you sit there and grit your teeth while making so many mistakes your self-confidence dribbles out of your pores and disappears into the carpet padding. In many cases it gets so bad that you hurl the books against the wall and stomp off to play Yahtzee with your little brother.

The differences are fewer: mistakes committed while learning assembly language won't make the dog howl. More crucially, what takes *years* of agony in front of a piano can be done in a couple of months in front of your average PC.

Furthermore, I'll do my best to help.

That's what this book is for: to get you started as an assembly language programmer from a dead stop. I'll assume that you know how to run your machine. That is, I won't go through all that nonsense about flipping the big red switch and inserting a disk in a drive and holding down the Ctrl key while pressing the C key. Von Wolverton can teach you all that.

On the other hand, I won't assume that you know *anything* about programming or very much about what happens inside the box itself. That means the first few sections will be the kind of necessary groundwork that will start you nodding off if you've been through it already. There's no helping that. Skip to Chapter 3 or so if you get bored.

I also have to come clean here and admit that this book is not intended to be a complete tutorial on assembly language, or even close to it. What I want to do is let you become familiar enough with the jargon and the assumptions of assembly language so that you can pick up a typical "introduction" to assembly language and not get lost by page six. Specifically, Bill Murray and Chris Pappas have taken pains to dovetail their book, *Assembly Language Magic,* to the end of this one so that once you finish this book you can pick up theirs and keep that comfortable sense of being on familiar territory.

Assembly language is almost certainly the most difficult kind of computer programming, but keep in mind that we're speaking in relative terms here. Five pushups are harder to do than five jumping jacks—but compared with running the marathon, both amount to almost nothing. Assembly language is more difficult to learn than Pascal, but compared to raising an average American child from birth to five years, it's a cakewalk.

So don't let the mystique get you. Assembly language programmers feel pretty smug about what they've learned to do, but in our workaday lives we are forced to learn and do things that put even assembly language to shame. If you're willing to set aside a couple months' worth of loose moments, you can pick it up too. Give it a shot. Your neighbors will thank you.

And so will the dog.

Jeff Duntemann
Scotts Valley, CA
April 1989

A Note to People Who Have Never Programmed Before . . .

◆◆◆

More than anyone else, this book was written for you. Starting with assembly language would not be most people's first choice in a computer language, but it's been done; it *can* be done, and it can be done with less agony than you might think. Still, it's a novel aim for a computer book, and I'd like you to do a little quality control for me and tell me how I'm doing.

While you're going through this book, ask yourself once in a while, "Is it working?" and, "If not, why not?"

If I lose you somewhere in the discussion, jot a note in the margin. Tell me where I lost you. If possible, tell me why. (Saying, "I just don't get it" is perfectly acceptable as long as you tell me where in the book you were when you started to *not* get it.)

As with all my books, I hope to keep this one in print well into the twenty-first century, revising it as needed to hone my technique and to follow the technology. Telling me how the book works or doesn't work will, in time, help me make a better book.

Write to me at *103 Hidden Drive, Scotts Valley, CA 95066.*

I can't reply individually to all letters (not if I ever intend to get another book written!) but you'll have my eternal gratitude nonetheless.

How to Get the Most from This Book

By design, this is a serial-access book. I wrote it to be read like one of those bad, wonderful novels, starting at page one and moving right along to the end. Virtually all the chapters depend on the chapters that came before them, and if you read a chapter here and a chapter there, there's some danger that the whole thing won't gel.

If you're already familiar with programming, you could conceivably skip Chapters 0, 1, and 2, but why not assume there's a hole or two in parts of your experience and a little rust on the rest? Skill is not simply knowledge but the resonance that comes from seeing how different facets of knowledge reinforce one another.

Do it all. Get the big picture.

Contents

◆◆

4   Learning and Using JED   *108*

A Programming Environment for Assembly Language

5   An Uneasy Alliance   *144*

The 8086/8088 CPU and Its Segmented Memory System

6   Following Your Instructions   *167*

Meeting Machine Instructions up Close and Personal

Assembly Language from Square One

For the PC AT and Compatibles

Chapter 0

Another Pleasant Valley Saturday

Understanding What Computers Really Do

"Quick, get the kids up, it's past 7! Nicky's got Little League at 9 and Dione's got ballet at 10. Mike, give Max his heartworm pill!"

"We're out of them, ma, remember?"

"Your father picked a great weekend to go fishing . . . here, let me give you ten bucks and go get more pills at the vet's . . . my God, that's right, Hank needed gas money and left me broke. There's a teller machine over by K-Mart, and I if I go there I can take that stupid toilet seat back and get the right one. *I guess I'd better make a list.*"

It's another Pleasant Valley Saturday, and 30-odd million suburban housewives sit down with a pencil and pad at the kitchen table to try to make sense of a morning that would kill and pickle any lesser being. In her mind she thinks of the dependencies and traces the route.

'Drop Nicky at Rand Park, go back to Dempster—it's about ten minutes to Golf Mill Mall. Do I have gas? I'd better check first—if not, stop at Del's Shell or I won't make it to Milwaukee Avenue. Bleed the teller machine at Golf Mill, then cross the parking lot to K-Mart to return the toilet seat that Hank bought last weekend without checking what size it was. Gotta remember to throw the toilet seat in the back of the van—write that at the top of the list.

'By then it'll be half past, maybe later. Ballet is all the way down Greenwood in Park Ridge. No left turn from Milwaukee, but there's the sneak path around behind the Mall. I have to remember not to turn right onto Milwaukee like I always do—jot that down. While I'm in Park Ridge I can check to see if Hank's new glasses are in—should call but they won't be open until 9:30. Oh, and groceries—can do that while Dione dances. On the way back I can cut over to Oakton and get the dog's pills.'

In about ninety seconds flat the list is complete:

Throw toilet seat in van

Check gas—if empty, stop at Del's Shell

Drop Nicky at Rand Park

Stop at Golf Mill teller machine

Return toilet seat at K-Mart

Drop Dione at ballet (remember back path to Greenwood)

See if Hank's glasses are ready—if they are, make sure they remembered the extra scratch coating

Get groceries at Jewel

Pick up Dione

Stop at vet's for heartworm pills

Drop off groceries at home

If it's time, pick up Nicky. If not, collapse for a few minutes, then pick up Nicky.

Collapse!

In what we often call a *laundry list* (whether it involves laundry or not) is the perfect metaphor for a computer program. Without realizing it, our intrepid housewife has written herself a computer program and then set out (acting as the computer) to execute it and be done before noon.

Computer programming is nothing more than this. You, the programmer, write a list of steps and tests. The computer then performs each step and test in sequence. When the list of steps has been executed, the computer stops.

A computer program is a list of steps and tests, nothing more.

Steps and Tests

Think for a moment about what I call a *test* in the laundry list shown above. A test is the sort of either/or decision we make dozens or hundreds of times on even the most placid of days, sometimes nearly without thinking about it.

Our housewife performed a test when she jumped into the van to get started on her adventure. She looked at the gas gauge. The gauge would tell her one of two things: (1) She has enough gas, or (2) she doesn't. If she has enough gas, she takes a right and heads for Rand Park. If she doesn't have enough gas, she takes a left down to the corner and fills the tank at Del's Shell. (Del takes credit cards.) Then, with a full tank, she continues the program by making a U-turn and heading for Rand Park.

In the abstract, a test consists of two parts:

♦ First you look at something that can go one of two ways.
♦ Then you do one of the two things, depending on what you saw when you took a look.

Toward the end of the program, our housewife got home, took the groceries out of the van, and looked at the clock. If it wasn't time to get Nicky back from Little League, she has a moment to collapse on the couch in a nearly empty house. If it *is* time to get Nicky, there's no rest for the ragged: she sprints for the van and heads back to Rand Park.

(Any guesses as to whether she really gets to collapse when the "program" is complete?)

More Than Two Ways?

You might object that many or most tests involve more than two alternatives. Sorry, but you're dead wrong—in every case. Furthermore, you're wrong whether you think you are or not.

> **Except for totally impulsive behavior, every human decision comes down to the choice of one of two alternatives.**

What you have to do is look a little more closely at what goes through your mind when you make decisions. The next time you buzz down to Moo Foo Goo for fast Chinese, observe yourself while you're poring over the menu. The choice might seem, at first, to be of one item out of 26 Cantonese main courses. Not so—the choice, in fact, is between choosing one item and *not* choosing that one item. Your eyes rest on chicken with cashews. Naw, too bland. *That was a test.* You slide down to the next item. Chicken with black mushrooms. Hmmm, no, had that last week. *That was another test.* Next item: kung pao chicken. Yeah, that's it! *That was a third test.*

The choice was not among chicken with cashews, chicken with black mushrooms, or chicken with kung pao. Each dish had its moment, poised before the critical eye of your mind, and you turned thumbs up or thumbs down on it, individually. Eventually, one dish won, but it won in that same game of *to eat or not to eat.*

Many of life's most complicated decisions result from the fact that 99% of us are not nudists. You've been there, standing in the clothes closet in your underwear, flipping through the rack of pants. The tests come thick and fast. This one? No. This one? No. This one? No. This one? Yeah. You pick a pair of blue pants, say. (It's a Monday, after all, and blue seems appropriate.) Then you stumble over to your sock drawer and take a look. Whoops, no blue socks. *That was a test.* So you stumble back to the clothes closet, hang your blue pants back on the pants rack, and start over. This one? No. This one? No. This one? Yeah. This time it's brown pants, and you toss them over your arm and head back to the sock drawer to take another look. Nertz, out of brown socks, too. So it's back to the clothes closet . . .

What you might consider a single decision, or perhaps two decisions inextricably tangled (like picking pants and socks of the same color, given the stock on hand) is actually a series of small decisions, always binary in nature: pick 'em or don't pick 'em, find 'em or don't find 'em. The Monday morning episode in the clothes closet is a good analogy of a programming structure called a *loop;* you keep doing a series of things until you get it right, and then you stop. (Assuming you're not the kind of guy who wears blue pants with brown socks.) Whether or not you get everything right always comes down to a sequence of simple, either/or decisions.

Computers Think Like Us

I can almost hear what you're thinking: 'Sure, it's a computer book, and he's trying to get me to think like a computer.' Not at all. Computers think like *us.* We designed them; how else could they think? No, what I'm trying to do is get you to take a long hard look at how *you* think. We run on automatic for so much of our lives that we literally do most of our thinking without really thinking about it.

The very best model for the logic of a computer program is the very same logic we use to plan and manage our daily affairs. No matter what we do, it comes down to a matter of confronting two alternatives and picking one. What we might think of as a single large and complicated decision is nothing more than a messy tangle of many smaller decisions. The skill of looking at a complex decision and seeing all the little decisions in its tummy will serve you well in learning how to program. Observe yourself the next time you have to decide something. Count up the little decisions that make up the big one. You'll be surprised.

And, surprise! You'll be a programmer.

0.2 ◆ Had This Been the Real Thing . . .

DO NOT BE ALARMED. What you have just experienced was a metaphor. It was not the real thing. (The real thing comes later.)

I'll be using metaphors a lot in this book. A metaphor is a loose comparison drawn between something familiar (like a Saturday morning laundry list) and something unfamiliar (like a computer program). The idea is to anchor the unfamiliar in the terms of the familiar so that when I begin tossing facts at you you'll have someplace comfortable to lay them down. The facts don't start until Section 1. (That's why I call this Section 0, metaphors only, please.)

The most important thing for you to do right now is keep an open mind. If you know a little bit about computers or programming, don't pick nits. Yes, there are important differences between a housewife following a scribbled laundry list and a computer executing a program; I'll mention those differences all in good time.

For now, it's still Section 0. Take these initial metaphors on their own terms. Later on, they'll help a lot.

0.3 ◆ Do Not Pass GO

"There's a reason 'bored' and 'board' are homonyms," my best friend Art said one evening, as we sat (two super-sophisticated 12-year-olds) playing some game in his basement. (He may have been unhappy because he was losing.) Was it *Mille Bornes?* Or *Stratego?* Or *Monopoly?* Or something else entirely? I confess I don't remember. I simply recall hopping some little piece of plastic shaped like a pregnant bowling pin up and down a series of colored squares that told me to do dumb things like go back two spaces or put $100 in the pot or nuke Outer Mongolia.

Outer Mongolia notwithstanding, there are strong parallels to be drawn between that peculiar American obsession, the board game, and assembly-language programming. First of all, everything we said before still holds: board games, by and large, consist of a progression of steps and tests. In some games, like *Trivial Pursuit, every* step on the board is a test to see if you can answer, or not answer, a question on a card. In other board games, each little square on the board contains some sort of instruction like, "Lose One Turn," "Go Back Two Squares," "Take a Card From Community Chest," and, of course, "Go to Jail."

Certain board games made for some lively arguments between Art and myself (it was that or be bored, as it were) concerning what it meant to "Go Forward" or "Backward Five Steps." It seemed to me that you should count the square you were already on, and Art, traditionalist always, thought you should start counting with the first step in the direction you had to go. This made a difference in the game, of course. (I conveniently forgot to press my point when doing so would land me on something like Park Place with 15 of Art's hotels on it . . .)

The Game of Big Bux

To avoid getting in serious trouble, I have invented my own board game to continue with this particular metaphor. In the sense that art mirrors life, the game *Big Bux* mirrors life in Silicon Valley, where money seems to be created spontaneously (generally in somebody else's pocket) and the three big black holes for money are fast cars, cocaine, and messy divorces.

A portion of the *Big Bux* game board is shown Figure 0.1. The line of rectangles on the left side of the page continues around the board. In the middle of the board are cubbyholes to store play money and game pieces, stacks of cards to be read occasionally, and short detours with names like "Messy Divorce" and "Start a Business," which are brief sequences of the same sort of action rectangles as those forming the path around the edge of the board.

Unlike many board games, you don't throw dice to determine how many steps around the board you take. *Big Bux* requires that you move *one* step forward on each turn, *unless* the square you land on instructs you to move forward or backward or go somewhere else, like through a detour. This makes for a considerably less random game. In fact, *Big Bux* is a pretty deterministic game, meaning that whether you win or lose is far less important than just going through the ringer and coming out the other side. (Again, this mirrors Silicon Valley, where you come out either bankrupt or ready to flee to Peoria and open a hardware store. That *other* kind of hardware.)

There is some math involved. You start out with one house, a cheap car, and $50,000 in cash. You can buy CDs at a given interest rate, payable each time you make it once around the board. You can invest in stocks and other securities whose value is determined by a changeable index in economic indicators, which fluctuates based on cards chosen from the stack called "The Fickle Finger of Fate." You can sell cars on a secondary market, buy and sell houses, and wheel and deal with the other players. Each time you make it once around the board you have to evaluate your net worth. All of

THE GAME OF "BIG BUX!" -- By Jeff Duntemann

THE BANK
Mortgage: $153,000 11% adj.
Car loan: $ 15,000 10% fixed

YOUR PORTFOLIO
CD's: $100,000

YOUR CHECKING ACCOUNT
Balance: $12,255.00
Line of credit: $ 8,000.00

OTHER ASSETS
Salary: $1000/week

MARKET VALUES
Posches: $48,000   Chevies: $10,000
BMWs: $28,000   Used Fords: $2700
Cocaine: $5000/oz.
2br Palo Alto condo: $385,000
4br Palo Alto house: $742,000

Buy put option on Pomegranite Computer. Look out the window—if you can see the moon, stock falls. Make $50,000.

PAYDAY! Deposit salary into checking acct.

Take a card from: The Fickle Finger of Fate.

Did you get laid off? If so, detour thru Start Your Own Business.

Are you married? If not, marry chief programmer for $10,000. If so, detour through Messy Divorce.

Friday night. Do you have any cocaine? If so, snort some and jump back 3 squares.

Total car on Highway 101. Buy another one of equal value.

Is your job boring? (Prosperity Index > 0.6 but less than 1.2) If not, jump ahead 3 squares.

Get promoted. Salary rises by 25%. (If unemployed, get new job at salary of $800/week.)

Have an affair with the Chief Programmer. Jump back 5 squares.

Holiday. NOTHING HAPPENS AT ALL!

Vest 5,000 stock options. Sell at $10 X economic indicator.

Buy condo in Palo Alto for 15% down.

Are you bankrupt? If so, move to Peoria. If not, detour through Start a Business.

Spend $10,000 on something. Anything.

Do you have any cocaine? If not, jump ahead 2 squares.

Sell 2 oz. cocaine to Nick at market value. An error—Nick is a cop. Wave at Peoria. Move to Joliet. End of game.

Messy Divorce
Start Here:

She moves out, rents $2000/mo. apartment

Are you bankrupt? If so, get cheap lawyer. Jump ahead 4.

Hire expensive lawyer. Pay $50,000 from checking.

Lawyer proves in court that wife is a chinchilla.

Wife is sent to Brookfield Zoo. Return to whence you came.

Lawyer proves in court that you are a chinchilla.

Court and wife skin you alive. Lose 50% of everything.

Start paying wife $5000/mo. for the rest of your life.

Go back to where you came from.

Start a Business
Start Here:

Draw up a business plan and submit it to a venture firm

Venture firm requires $50,000 matching capital.

Have it? If not, return to where you came from.

Add $850,000 to checking account.

Hire 6 people. Subtract $100,000 from checking acct.

Work 18 hours a day for a year. Spend $200,000.

Spend $300,000 launching the new product.

Take a card from: The Fickle Finger of Fate.

First year's sales: $500,000 x economic ind.

Are you bankrupt? If not, jump ahead 2 squares.

Go through messy divorce.

Return to where you came from.

Sell company for $10,000,000. Buy another $65,000 Porsche.

Go back to where you came from.

The Fickle Finger of Fate

Major Bank Failure!
Decrement Economic Indicators line by thirty percent. Bonds tumble by 20%; housing prices by 5%. Re-valuate your portfolio. Bank cuts your line of credit by $2000. Have a good cry.

1000
100
50
30
20
Prosperity
12.0
7.0
4.0
2.0
1.0
0.5
0.4
0.3
0.2
Recession
0.1
0.0

$
ECONOMIC INDICATORS

PEORIA →

FIGURE 0.1   The game of "Big Bux!"

this involves some addition, subtraction, multiplication, and division, but there's no math more complex than compound interest. Most of *Big Bux* involves nothing more than taking a step and following the instructions at each step.

Is this starting to sound familiar?

Playing Big Bux

At one corner of the *Big Bux* board is the legend "Move In," because that's how people start life in California—no one is actually *born* here. Once moved in, you begin working your way around the board, square by square, following the instructions in the squares.

Some of the squares simply tell you to do something like, "Buy a condo in Palo Alto for 15% down." Many of the squares involve a test of some kind. For example, one square reads, "Is your job boring? (Prosperity index 0.3 but less than 4.0). If not, jump ahead 3 squares." The test is actually to see if the prosperity index has a value between 0.3 and 4.0. Any value outside those bounds (e.g., runaway prosperity or Four Horsemen—class recession) are defined as "Interesting Times," and cause a jump ahead by three squares.

You always move one step forward at each turn, unless the square you land on directs you to do something else, like jump forward three squares or back five squares.

The notion of taking a detour is an interesting one. Two detours are shown in the portion of the board I've provided. Taking a detour means leaving the main run of the game board and stepping through a series of squares elsewhere on the board. The detours involve some specific process such as starting a business or getting a divorce.

You can work through a detour step by step until you hit the bottom. At that point you simply pick up your journey around the board right where you left it. You may also find that one of the squares in the detour instructs you to go back to where you came from. Depending on the logic of the game (and your luck and finances) you may completely run through a detour, or get thrown out somewhere in the middle.

Also note that you can take a detour from within a detour. If you detour through "Start a Business" and your business goes bankrupt, you leave "Start a Business" temporarily and detour through "Messy Divorce." Once you leave "Messy Divorce" you return to where you left "Start a Business." Ultimately, you also leave "Start a Business" and return to wherever you were when you took the detour.

The same detour (for example, "Start a Business") can be taken from any of several different places along the game board.

Assembly Language Programming as a Board Game

Now that you're thinking in terms of board games, take a look at Figure 0.2. What I've drawn is actually a fair approximation of assembly language as it was used on some of our simpler microprocessors about ten to twelve years ago. The column labeled "PROGRAM INSTRUCTIONS" is the main path around the edge of the board, of which only a portion can be shown here. This is the assembly language computer program, the actual series of steps and tests that, when executed, cause the computer to do something useful. Setting up this series of program instructions is what programming in assembly language actually is.

Everything else is odds and ends in the middle of the board that serve the game in progress. You're probably noticing (perhaps with sagging spirits) that there are a *lot* of numbers involved. (They're weird numbers, too—what, for example, does "004B" mean? I'll deal with that issue in Chapter 1, Alien Bases.) I'm sorry, but that's simply the way the game is played. Assembly language, at its innermost level, is nothing *but* numbers, and if you hate numbers the way many people hate anchovies, you're going to have a rough time of it.

I should caution you that the *Game of Assembly Language* represents no real computer processor like the Intel 8088. Also, I've made the names of instructions more clearly understandable than the names of the instructions in 8086 assembly language. In the real world, instruction names are typically things like **STOSB, DAA, INC, SBB,** and other crypticisms that cannot be understood without considerable explanation. We're easing into this stuff sideways, and in this chapter I have to sugar-coat certain things a little to draw the metaphors clearly.

Code and data.   Like most board games (including *Big Bux*) the assembly language board game consists of two broad categories of elements: game steps and places to store things. The game steps are the steps and tests I've been speaking of all along. The places to store things are just that: cubbyholes where you can place numbers with the confidence that those numbers will remain where you put them until you take them out or somehow change them.

In programming terms, the game steps are called *code,* and the numbers in their cubbyholes (as distinct from the cubbyholes themselves) are called *data.* The cubbyholes themselves are usually called *storage.*

The game *Big Bux* works the same way. Look back to Figure 0.1 and note that in the "Start a Business" detour, there is an instruction reading, "Add $850,000 to checking account." The checking account is one of several

The Game of Assembly Language

PROGRAM INSTRUCTIONS

0040	MOVE 0 to B
0041	MOVE data at B to C
0042	INCREMENT B
0043	MOVE data at B to A
0044	PUSH Program Counter onto the Stack
0045	CALL UpCase
0046	MOVE A to data at B
0047	DECREMENT C
0048	COMPARE C to 0
0049	JUMP BACK 7 if C > 0
004A	MOVE 5 to B
004B	MOVE data at B to A
004C	PUSH Program Counter onto the Stack
004D	CALL UpCase
004E	MOVE A to data at B
004F	ADD 5 to A
0050	Etc...
0051	

DATA IN MEMORY

0000	3
0001	l
0002	b
0003	m
0004	4
0005	c
0006	a
0007	r
0008	l

PROGRAM COUNTER

0046	

PROCEDURE

UpCase

0081	COMPARE data at A with 'a'
0082	JUMP AHEAD 5 if data < 'a'
0083	COMPARE data at A with 'z'
0084	JUMP AHEAD 1 if data > 'z'
0085	ADD 32 to data at A
0086	POP program counter from stack

REGISTERS

0	B	A
CARRY		
	2	B
	2	C
	0	D

THE STACK

0000	00
0001	45
0002	
0003	
0004	
0005	
0006	

STACK POINTER | 0000 |

FIGURE 0.2   The Game of Assembly Language

different kinds of storage in *Big Bux,* and money values are a type of data. Conceptually, it's no different from an instruction in the *Game of Assembly Language* reading "ADD 5 to Register A." An **ADD** instruction in the code alters a data value stored in a cubbyhole named Register A.

Code and data are two very different kinds of critters, but they interact in ways that make the game interesting. The code includes steps that place data into storage (**MOVE** instructions) and steps that alter data that is already in storage (**INCREMENT** and **DECREMENT** instructions). Most of the time you'll think of code as being the master of data, in that the code writes data values into storage. Data do influence code as well, however. Among the tests that the code makes are tests that examine data in storage, the **COMPARE** instructions. If a given value of the data exists in storage, the code may do one thing and if that value does not exist in storage, the code will do something else, as in the **JUMP BACK** and **JUMP AHEAD** instructions.

The short block of instructions marked **PROCEDURE** is a detour off the main stream of instructions. At any point in the program you can duck out into the procedure, perform its steps and tests, and then return to the very place from which you left. This allows a sequence of steps and tests that is generally useful and used frequently to exist in only one place rather than exist as a separate copy everywhere it is needed.

Addresses. Another critical concept lies in the funny numbers at the left side of the program step locations and data locations. Each number is unique, in that a location with that number appears only once inside the computer. This location is called an **address.** Data are stored and retrieved by specifying the data's address in the machine. Procedures are called by specifying the address at which they begin.

The little box (which is also a storage location) marked **PROGRAM COUNTER** keeps the address of the next instruction to be performed. The number inside the program counter is increased by one (we say "incremented") each time an instruction is performed *unless an instruction tells the program counter to do something else.*

Notice the **JUMP BACK 7** instruction at address 0049. When this instruction is performed, the program counter will back up by seven counts. This is analogous to the "go back three spaces" concept in most board games.

Metaphor Check!

That's about as much explanation of the *Game of Assembly Language* as I'm going to offer for now. This is still Chapter 0, and we're still in metaphor territory. People who have had some exposure to computers will recognize and understand more about what Figure 0.2 is doing. (There's a real, traceable program going on in there—I dare you to figure out what it does, and how!) People with no exposure to computer innards shouldn't feel left behind for being utterly lost. I created the *Game of Assembly Language* solely to put across the following points:

♦ *The individual steps are very simple.* One single instruction rarely does more than move a single byte from one storage cubbyhole to another, or compare the value contained in one storage cubbyhole to a value contained in another. This is good news, because it allows you to concentrate on the simple task accomplished by a single instruction without being overwhelmed by complexity. The bad news, however, is that

♦ *It takes a lot of steps to do anything useful.* You can often write a useful program in Pascal or BASIC in five or six lines. A useful assembly language program cannot be implemented in fewer than about fifty lines, and anything challenging takes hundreds or thousands of lines. The skill of assembly language programming lies in structuring these hundreds or thousands of instructions so that the program can be read and understood. Finally,

♦ *The key to assembly language is understanding memory addresses.* In languages like Pascal and BASIC, the compiler takes care of *where* something is located. You simply have to give that something a name and call it by that name when you want it. In assembly language, you must always be cognizant of where things are in your computer's memory. So, in working through this book, pay special attention to the concept of *addressing*, which is nothing more than the art of specifying where something is. The *Game of Assembly Language* is peppered with addresses and instructions that work with addresses such as, "**MOVE data at B to C,**" which means move the data stored at the address specified by register **B** to the address specified by register **C**.) Addressing is by far the trickiest part of assembly language, but master it and you've got the whole thing in your hip pocket.

Everything I've said so far has been orientation. I've tried to give you a taste of the big picture of assembly language and how its fundamental principles relate to the life you've been living all along. Life is a sequence of steps and tests; so are board games, and so is assembly language. Keep those metaphors in mind as we proceed to get real by confronting the nature of computer numbers.

◆◆

Chapter 1

Alien Bases

Getting Your Arms around Binary and Hexadecimal

1966—perhaps you were there. New Math burst upon the grade school curricula of the nation, and homework became a turmoil of number lines, sets, and alternate bases. Parents scratched their heads with their children over questions like, "What is 17 in base 5?" and "Which set does the null set belong to?" In very short order (I recall a period of about two months) the whole thing was tossed in the trash as quickly as it had been concocted by addle-brained educrats with too little to do.

That was a pity, actually. What nobody seemed to realize at the time was that, granted, we were learning New Math—except that Old Math had never been taught at the grade school level either. We kept wondering of what possible use it was to know what the intersection of the set of squirrels and the set of mammals was. The truth, of course, was that it was of no *use* at all. Mathematics in the U.S. has always been taught as *applied* mathematics (arithmetic), which was heavy on word problems. If it won't help you balance your checkbook or proportion a recipe, it ain't real math, man. Little or none of the logic of mathematics has *ever* made it into the elementary classroom, in part because elementary school in the U.S. historically has been a sort of trade school for everyday life. Getting the little beasts fundamentally literate is difficult enough. Trying to get them to appreciate the beauty of alternate number systems simply went over the line for much of the practical American populace.

I was one of the few who enjoyed fussing with math back in 1966, but I gladly laid it aside when the whole thing blew over. I didn't have to pick it up again until 1976, when, after working like a maniac with a wire-wrap gun for several weeks, I fed power to my COSMAC ELF computer, and was greeted by an LED display of a pair of numbers in *base 16!*

Mon dieu, New math *redux . . .*

This chapter exists because at the assembly-language level, your computer does not understand numbers in our familiar base 10. Computers, in a slightly schizoid fashion, work in base 2 *and* base 16—all at the same time. If you're willing to confine yourself to BASIC or Pascal, you can ignore these alien bases altogether, or perhaps treat them as an advanced topic once you get the rest of the language down pat. Not here. *Everything* in assembly language depends on your thorough understanding of these two number bases. So, before we do anything else, we're going to learn how to count all over again—in Martian!

1.2 ◆ Counting in Martian

There is intelligent life on Mars.

That is, the Martians are intelligent enough to know from watching our TV programs these past 40 years that a thriving tourist industry would not be to their advantage. So they've remained in hiding, emerging only briefly to carve big rocks into the shape of Elvis's face to help the *National Enquirer* ensure that no one will ever take Mars seriously again. The Martians do occasionally communicate with us science fiction writers, knowing full well that *nobody* has ever taken *us* seriously. Hence the information in this section, which involves the way Martians count.

Martians have three fingers on one hand, and only one finger on the other. Male Martians have their three fingers on the left hand, while females have their three fingers on the right hand. This makes waltzing and certain other things easier.

Like human beings or any other intelligent race, Martians started counting by using their fingers. Just as we used our ten fingers to set things off in groups and powers of ten, the Martians used their four fingers to set things off in groups and powers of four. Over time, our civilization settled on a set of ten digits to serve our number system. Similarly, the Martians standardized on a set of four digits for their number system. The four digits follow, along with the names of the digits as the Martians pronounce them: ө (xip), ſ (foo), ∩ (bar), ≡ (bas).

Like our zero, xip is a placeholder representing no items, and while Martians sometimes count from xip, they usually start with foo, representing a single item. So they start counting: *Foo, bar, bas* . . .

Now what? What comes after bas? Table 1.1 demonstrates how the Martians count to what we would call twenty-five.

With only four digits (including the one representing zero) the Martians can only count to bas without running out of digits. The number after bas has a new name, *fooby*. Fooby is the base of the Martian number system, and probably the most important number on Mars. Fooby is the number of fingers a Martian has. We would call it *four*.

The most significant thing about fooby is the way the Martians write it out in numerals: ſө . Instead of a single column, fooby is expressed in two columns. Just as with our decimal system, each column has a value that is a power of fooby. This only means that as you move from the rightmost column toward the left, each column represents a value fooby times the column to its right.

TABLE 1.1   Counting in Martian, base fooby

Martian Numerals	Martian Pronunciation	Earth Equivalent
ө	Xip	0
ſ	Foo	1
∩	Bar	2
≡	Bas	3
ſө	Fooby	4
ſ ſ	Fooby-foo	5
ſ∩	Fooby-bar	6
ſ≡	Fooby-bas	7
∩ө	Barby	8
∩ſ	Barby-foo	9
∩∩	Barby-bar	10
∩≡	Barby-bas	11
≡ө	Basby	12
≡ſ	Basby-foo	13
≡∩	Basby-bar	14
≡≡	Basby-bas	15
ſөө	Foobity	16
ſөſ	Foobity-foo	17
ſө∩	Foobity-bar	18
ſө≡	Foobity-bas	19
ſ ſө	Foobity-fooby	20
ſ ſ ſ	Foobity-fooby-foo	21
ſ ſ∩	Foobity-fooby-bar	22
ſ ſ≡	Foobity-fooby-bas	23
ſ∩ө	Foobity-barby	24
ſ∩ſ	Foobity-barby-foo	25

The rightmost column represents units, in counts of foo. The next column over represents fooby times foo, or (given that arithmetic works the same way on Mars as here, New Math notwithstanding) simply fooby. The next column to the left of fooby represents fooby times fooby, or foobity, and so on. This relationship should become clearer through Table 1.2.

Dissecting a Martian Number

Any given column may contain a digit from xip to bas, indicating how many instances of that column's value are contained in the number as a whole.

TABLE 1.2   Powers of fooby

⌈	Foo	X Fooby =
⌈θ	Fooby	X Fooby =
⌈θθ	Foobity	X Fooby =
⌈θθθ	Foobidity	X Fooby =
⌈θθθθ	Foobididity	X Fooby =
⌈θθθθθ	Foobidididity	and so on. . .

Let's work through an example. Look at Figure 1.1, which is a dissection of the Martian number ∩≡⌈θ≡, pronounced "Barbididity-basbidity-foobity-bas." (A visiting and heavily disguised Martian precipitated the doo-wop craze while standing at a Philadelphia bus stop in 1954, counting his change.)

The rightmost column tells how many units are contained in the number. The digit there is bas, indicating that the number contains bas units. The second column from the right carries a value of fooby times foo (essentially fooby times one or fooby). A xip in the fooby column indicates that there are no foobies in the number. The xip digit in ∩≡⌈θ≡ is a placeholder, just as zero is in our numbering system. Notice also that in the columnar sum shown to the right of the digit matrix, the foobies line is represented by a double xip. Not only is there a xip to tell us that there are no foobies, but there is also a xip holding the foos' place as well. This pattern continues in the columnar sum as we move toward the more significant columns to the left.

Fooby times fooby is foobity, and the ⌈ digit tells us that there is foo foobity (a single foobity) in the number. The next column, in keeping with the pattern, is foobity times fooby, or foobidity. In the columnar notation, foobidity is written as ⌈θθθ. The ≡ digit tells us that there are bas foobidities in the number. Bas foobidities is a number with its own name, basbidity, which can be written as ≡θθθ. Note the presence of basbidity in the columnar sum.

The next column to the left has a value of fooby times foobidity, or foobididity. The ∩ digit tells us that there are bar foobididities in the number. Bar foobididities (written ∩θθθθ) is also a number with its own name, barbididity. Note also the presence of barbididity in the columnar sum, and the four xip digits that hold places for the empty columns.

The columnar sum expresses the sense of the way a number is assembled—the number contains barbididity, basbidity, foobity, and bas. Roll all that together by simple addition and you get ∩≡⌈θ≡. The

Consider the Martian number ∩≡ſθ≡

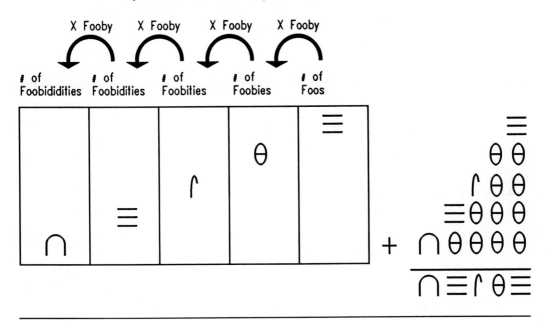

FIGURE 1.1   The anatomy of "barbididity-basbidity-foobity-bas"

name is pronounced simply by hyphenating the component values: barbididity-basbidity-foobity-bas. Note that there is no part in the name representing the empty fooby column. We don't, for example, pronounce the number 401 as "four hundred, zero tens, one." We simply say, "four hundred one." In the same manner, rather than say "xip foobies" the Martians just leave it out.

As an exercise, given what I've told you so far about Martian numbers, figure out the Earthly value equivalent to ∩≡ſθ≡.

The Essence of a Number Base

Because tourist trips to Mars are unlikely to begin any time soon, of what Earthly use is knowing the Martian numbering system? Just this: It's an excellent way to see the sense in a number base without getting distracted by familiar digits and our universal base 10.

In a columnar system of numeric notation like both ours and the Martians', the *base* of the number system is the magnitude by which each column of a number exceeds the magnitude of the column to its right. In our base 10 system, each column represents a value ten times the column to its right. In a base fooby system, each column represents a value fooby times that of the column to its right. (In case you haven't already caught on, the Martians are actually using base 4—but I wanted you to see it from the Martians' own perspective.) Each has a set of digit symbols, the number of which is equal to the base. In our base 10, we have ten symbols, from 0 to 9. In base 4, there are four digits, from 0 to 3. *In any given number base, the base itself can never be expressed in a single digit!*

1.3 ◆ Octal: How the Grinch Stole 8 and 9

Farewell to Mars. Aside from lots of iron oxide and some terrific *a capella* groups, they haven't much to offer us ten-fingered folk. There are some similarly odd number bases in use here, and I'd like to take a quick detour through one that occupies a separate world right here on Earth; the world of Digital Equipment Corporation, better known as DEC.

Back in the Sixties, DEC invented the minicomputer as a challenger to the massive mainframes pioneered by IBM. To ensure that no software could possibly be moved from an IBM mainframe to a DEC minicomputer, DEC designed its machines to understand only numbers expressed in base *eight.*

Let's think about that for a moment, given our experience with the Martians. In base 8, there must be eight digits. DEC was considerate enough not to invent their own digits, so what they used were the traditional digits from 0 to 7. *There is no digit 8 in base 8!* That always takes a little getting used to, but it's part of the definition of a number base. DEC gave a name to its base 8 system: **Octal.**

A columnar number in octal follows the rule we encountered in thinking about the Martian system. Each column has a value 8 times that of the column to its left.

Who Stole 8 and 9?

Counting in octal starts out in a very familiar fashion: One, two, three, four, five, six, seven . . . *ten.* This is where the trouble starts. In octal, ten comes after seven. What happened to eight and nine? Did the Grinch steal them? (or the Martians?) Hardly. They're still there—but they have different names. In octal, when you say "ten" you mean "eight." Worse, when you say "eleven" you mean "nine."

Unfortunately, what DEC did *not* do was invent clever names for the column values. The first column is, of course, the units column. The next column to the left of the units column is the tens column, just as it is in our own decimal system. But there's the rub, and the reason I dragged Mars into this: *Octal's tens column actually has a value of 8.*

A counting table will help. Table 1.3 counts up to thirty octal, which has a value of 24 decimal. I dislike the use of the terms eleven, twelve, and so on in bases other than ten, but the convention in octal has always been

TABLE 1.3	Counting in Octal, base 8	
Octal Numerals	**Pronunciation (Follow with Octal)**	**Decimal Equivalent**
0	Zero	0
1	One	1
2	Two	2
3	Three	3
4	Four	4
5	Five	5
6	Six	6
7	Seven	7
10	Ten	8
11	Eleven	9
12	Twelve	10
13	Thirteen	11
14	Fourteen	12
15	Fixteen	13
16	Sixteen	14
17	Seventeen	15
20	Twenty	16
21	Twenty-one	17
22	Twenty-two	18
23	Twenty-three	19
24	Twenty-four	20
25	Twenty-five	21
26	Twenty-six	22
27	Twenty-seven	23
30	Thirty	24

to pronounce the numbers as we would in decimal, only with the word *octal* after them.

Remember, each column in a given number base has a value base times the column to its right, so the tens column in octal is actually the eights column. (They call it the tens column because it is written 10, and pronounced "ten.") Similarly, the column to the left of the tens column is the hundreds column (because it is written 100) but the hundreds column actually has a value of 8 times 8, or 64. The next column over has a value of 64 times 8, or 512, and the column left of that has a value of 512 times 8, or 4096.

This is why if someone talks about a value of "ten octal" they mean 8; "one hundred octal" they mean 64, and so on. Table 1.4 summarizes the octal column values and their decimal equivalents.

A digit in the first column, the units or 1s column, tells how many units are contained in the octal number. A digit in the next column to the left, the tens column, tells how many 8s are contained in the octal number. A digit in the third column, the hundreds column, tells how many 64s are in the number, and so on. For example, 400 octal means that the number contains 4 64s, or 256 in decimal.

It is confusing. The best way to make it all gel is to dissect a middling octal number, just as we did with a middling Martian number. This is what's happening in Figure 1.2: The octal number 76225 is pulled apart into columns and added up again.

It works the same way it does in Martian, or decimal, or any other number base. In general, each column has a value consisting of the number base raised to the power represented by the ordinal position of the column minus one. The value of the first column is the number base raised to the $1-1$, or 0 power. Because any number raised to the 0 power is 1, the first column in *any* number base always has the value of one and is called the

TABLE 1.4	Octal Columns as Powers of 8			

Octal		Power of 8		Decimal	
1	=	8^0	=	1	X 8 =
10	=	8^1	=	8	X 8 =
100	=	8^2	=	64	X 8 =
1000	=	8^3	=	512	X 8 =
10000	=	8^4	=	4096	X 8 =
100000	=	8^5	=	32768	X 8 =
1000000	=	8^6	=	262144	X 8 =

Consider the Octal number 76225

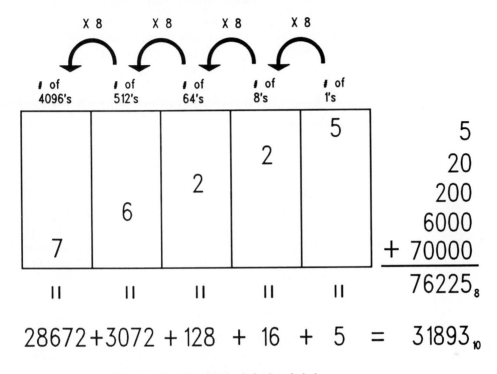

Each column carries a value
eight times the column on its right.

FIGURE 1.2   The anatomy of 76225 octal

units column. The second column has the value of the number base raised to the 2−1, or first power, which is the value of the number base itself. In octal this is 8; in decimal, 10; in Martian base fooby, fooby. The third column has a value consisting of the number base raised to the 3−1, or second power, and so on.

Within each column, the digit holding that column tells how many instances of that column's value is contained in the number as a whole. Here, the 6 in 76225 octal tells us that there are six instances of its column's value in the total value 76225 octal. The six occupies the fourth column, which has a value of 8^{4-1}, which is 8^3, or 512. This tells us that there are six 512s in the number as a whole.

You can convert the value of a number in any base to decimal (base 10) by determining the value of each column in the alien base, then multiplying the value of each column by the digit contained in that column, (to create the decimal equivalent of each digit) and then finally taking the sum of the decimal equivalent of each column. This is done in Figure 1.2, and the octal number and its decimal equivalent are shown side by side.

Now that we've looked at columnar notation from both a Martian and an octal perspective, make sure you understand how columnar notation works in any arbitrary base before we go on.

Log in Please

You may use an octal number every day. You may, in fact, have it memorized. This number is your ID number on the CompuServe timesharing system. CompuServe runs on a large bank of DEC computers, and their user ID numbers are all in octal. Notice, if you use CompuServe, that *nowhere* in *any* of the ID numbers attached to the messages you read will you find either the digit 8 or the digit 9.

1.4 ◆ Hexadecimal: Solving the Digit Shortage

Octal is unlikely to be of use to you unless you choose to become a minicomputer programmer, which is about as exciting as blowing packing peanuts into boxes on someone else's shipping dock. As I mentioned earlier, the *real* numbering system to reckon with in the microcomputer world is base 16, which we call *hexadecimal* or, more affectionately, simply *hex.*

Hexadecimal shares the essential characteristics of any number base, including both Martian and octal. It is a columnar notation, in which each column has a value *sixteen* times the value of the column to its right. It has sixteen digits, running from 0 to . . . what?

We have a shortage of digits here. From zero through nine we're in fine shape. Ten, eleven, twelve, thirteen, fourteen, and fifteen, however, need to be expressed as single digits. Without any additional numeric digits, the people who developed hexadecimal notation in the early 1950s borrowed the first six letters of the alphabet to act as the needed digits.

Counting in hexadecimal, then, goes like this: 0, 1, 2, 3, 4, 5, 6, 7, 8, 9, A, B, C, D, E, F, 10, 11, 12, 13, 14, 15, 16, 17, 18, 19, 1A, 1B, 1C and so on. Table 1.5 restates this in a more organized fashion, with the decimal equivalents up to 32.

One of the conventions in hexadecimal that I favor is the dropping of words like *eleven* and *twelve* that are too tied to our decimal system and only promote gross confusion. Confronted by the number 11 in hexadecimal (usually written 11H to let us know what base we're speaking) we would

TABLE 1.5   Counting in Hexadecimal, base 16

Hexadecimal Numerals	Pronunciation (Follow with Hex)	Decimal Equivalent
0	Zero	0
1	One	1
2	Two	2
3	Three	3
4	Four	4
5	Five	5
6	Six	6
7	Seven	7
8	Eight	8
9	Nine	9
A	A	10
B	B	11
C	C	12
D	D	13
E	E	14
F	F	15
10	Ten (or, One-oh)	16
11	One-one	17
12	One-two	18
13	One-three	19
14	One-four	20
15	One-five	21
16	One-six	22
17	One-seven	23
18	One-eight	24
19	One-nine	25
1A	One-A	26
1B	One-B	27
1C	One-C	28
1D	One-D	29
1E	One-E	30
1F	One-F	31
20	Twenty (or, Two-oh)	32

say, "one-one hex." Don't forget to say *hex* after a hexadecimal number, again to avoid gross confusion. This is unnecessary with the digits 0 to 9, which represent the exact same values in both decimal and hexadecimal.

Some people still say things like "twelve hex," which is valid, and means 18 decimal. I don't care for it, however, and advise against it. This business of alien bases is confusing enough without giving the aliens Charlie Chaplin masks.

Each column in the hexadecimal system has a value 16 times that of the column to its right. (The rightmost column, as in *any* number base, is the units column and has a value of 1.) As you might imagine, the values of the individual columns go up frighteningly fast as we move from right to left. Table 1.6 shows the values of the first seven columns in hexadecimal. For comparison, note that the seventh column in decimal notation has a value of 1,000,000, while the seventh column in hexadecimal has a value of 16,777,216.

To help you understand how hexadecimal numbers are constructed, I've dissected a middling hex number in Figure 1.3, in the same fashion that I dissected numbers earlier in both Martian base fooby and in octal base 8. Just as in octal, zero holds a place in a column without adding any value to the number as a whole. Note in Figure 1.3 that there are zero 256s present in the number 3C0A9H.

As in Figure 1.2, the decimal values of each column are shown beneath the column, and the sum of all columns is shown in both decimal and hex.

1.5 ◆ From Hex to Decimal and from Decimal to Hex

Most of the manipulation of hex numbers you'll be performing will be simple conversions between hex and decimal, in both directions. The easiest way to perform such conversions is by way of a hex calculator,

TABLE 1.6　　　　Hexadecimal columns as powers of 16

Hexadecimal		Power of 16		Decimal	
1	=	16^0	=	1	X 16 =
10	=	16^1	=	16	X 16 =
100	=	16^2	=	256	X 16 =
1000	=	16^3	=	4096	X 16 =
10000	=	16^4	=	65536	X 16 =
100000	=	16^5	=	1048576	X 16 =
1000000	=	16^6	=	16777216	etc. . .

Consider the Hexadecimal number 3C0A9

Each column carries a value sixteen times
that of the column on its right.

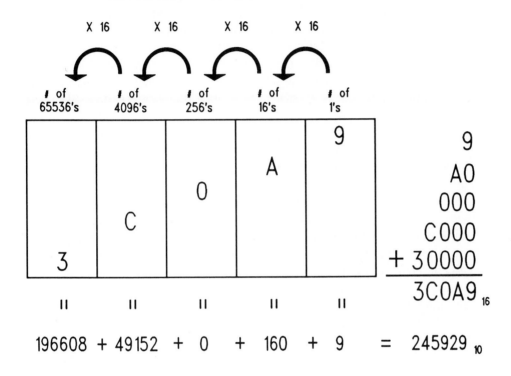

The sum of each column's decimal equivalent
is the value of the hex number in decimal.

FIGURE 1.3 The anatomy of 3C0A9 hex

either a "real" calculator like the venerable TI Programmer (which I still have, wretched battery-eater that it is) or a TSR software calculator like Sidekick. This demands nothing of your gray matter, of course, and won't help you understand the hexadecimal number system any better. So while you're a green student, lay off anything that understands hex—hardware, software, or human associates.

In fact, the best tool is a simple four-function memory calculator. The conversion methods I'll describe here all make use of such a calculator, because what I'm trying to teach you is number base conversion, not decimal addition or long division.

From Hex to Decimal

As you'll come to understand, converting hex numbers to decimal is a good deal easier than going the other way. The general method is to do what we've been doing all along in the dissection figures: derive the value represented by each individual column in the hex number, and then add up the total of all the column values in decimal.

Let's try an easy one. The hex number is 7A2. Start at the right column. This is the units column in any number system. You have 2 units, so enter 2 into your calculator. Now store that 2 into memory (or press the SUM button, if you have one).

So much for units. Keep in mind that you're keeping a running tally of the values of the columns in the hex number. Move to the next column to the left. Remember that each column represents a value 16 times the value of the column to its right. So the second column from the right is the 16s column. (Refer to Table 1.6 if you lose track of the column values.) The 16s column has an A in it, and A in hex is decimal 10. The total value of that column, therefore, is 16 × 10, or 160. Perform that multiplication on your calculator, and add the product to the 2 that you stored in memory. (Again, the SUM button is a handy way to do this if your calculator has one.) Remember that you're evaluating each column in decimal and keeping a running total. Now, move to the third column from the right, which contains a 7. The value of the third column is 16 × 16, or 256. Multiply 256 × 7 on your calculator, and add the product to your running total. You're done. Retrieve the running total from your calculator's memory. The total should be 1954, which is the decimal equivalent of 7A2 hex.

Let's try it again, with a little less natter and a much larger number: C6F0DB.

Evaluate the units column. B × 1 = 11 × 1 = 11. Start your running total.

Evaluate the 16s column. D × 16 = 13 × 16 = 208. Add 208 to your running total.

Evaluate the 256s column. 0 × 256 = 0. Move on.

Evaluate the 4096s column. F × 4096 = 15 × 2096 = 61,440. Add it to your running total.

Evaluate the 65536s column. 6 × 65536 = 393,216. Add it to the running total.

Evaluate the 1048576s column. C × 1048576 = 12 × 1048576 = 12,582,912. Add it to your total.

The running total should be 13037787.

Finally, try it yourself with the following number: 1A55BE.

From Decimal to Hex

The lights should be coming on about now. This is good, because going in the other direction, from hex to our familiar base 10 is *much* harder and involves more math. What we have to do is find the hex column values within a decimal number, and that involves some considerable use of that fifth-grade boogeyman, long division.

But let's get to it; again, starting with a fairly easy number: 449. The calculator will be handy in spades. Tap in the number 449 and store it in the calculator's memory.

What we need to do first is find the *largest* hex column value that is contained in 449 at least *once*. Remember grade-school "gazintas"? (12 gazinta 855 how many times?) It's something like that. Looking back at Table 1.6, we can see that 256 is the largest power of 16, and hence the largest hex column value that is present in 449 at least once.

So we start with 256, and determine how many times 256 "gazinta" 449. $449 \div 256 = 1.7539$. At least once, but not quite twice. So 449 contains only one 256. Write down a 1 on paper. *Don't enter it into your calculator.* We're not keeping a running total here; if anything, we could say we're keeping a running remainder. The *1* is the leftmost hex digit of the hex value equivalent to decimal 449.

We know that there is only one 256 contained in 449. What we must do now is *remove* that 256 from the original number, now that we've "counted" it by writing a 1 down on paper. Subtract 256 from 449. Store the difference, 193, into memory.

The 256 column has been removed from the number we're converting. Now we move to the next column to the right, the 16s. How many 16s are contained in 193? $193 \div 16 = 12.0625$. This means the 16s column in the hex equivalent of 449 contains a . . . 12? Hmmmm . . . remember the digit shortage, and the fact that in hex, the value we call 12 is represented by the letter C. From a hex perspective, we have found that the original number contains C in the 16s column. Write a C down to the right of your 1 so we have 1C. So far, so good.

We have the 16s column, so just as with the 256s, we have to remove the 16s from what's left of the original number. The total value of the 16s column is $C \times 16 = 12 \times 16 = 192$. Bring the 193 value out of your calculator's memory, and subtract 192 from it. A lonely little 1 is all that's left.

So we're down to the units column. Obviously, there is only one unit in one. Write that 1 down to the right of the C in our hexadecimal number: 1C1. Decimal 449 is equivalent to hex 1C1. Now, perhaps, you'll begin to understand why Sidekick is so popular.

Let's glance back at the big picture of the decimal-to-hex conversion. We're looking for the hexadecimal columns hidden in the decimal value. We find the largest column contained in the decimal number, find that column's value, and subtract that value from the decimal number. Then we look for the next smallest hex column, and the next smallest, and so on, removing the value of each column from the decimal number as we go. In a sense, we're dividing the number by consecutively smaller powers of 16, and keeping a running remainder by removing each column as we tally it.

Let's try it again. The secret number is 988,664.

The largest column contained in 988,664 from Table 1.6 is 65536. 988,664 ÷ 65536 = 15 and change. Ignore the change. 15 = F in hex. Write down the F.

Remove F × 65536 from 988,664. Store the remainder: 5624.

Move to the next smallest column. 5624 ÷ 4096 = 1 and change. Write down the 1.

Remove 1 × 4096 from the remainder: 5625 − 4096 = 1528. Store the new remainder: 1528.

Move to the next smallest column. 1528 ÷ 256 = 5 and change. Write down the 5.

Remove 5 × 256 from the stored remainder: 1528. Store 248 as the new remainder.

Move to the next smallest column. 248 ÷ 16 = 15 and change. 15 = F in hex. Write down the F.

Remove F × 16 from stored remainder: 248. The remainder, 8, is the number of units in the final column. Write down the 8.

There you have it. 988,664 decimal = F15F8H.

Note the presence of the *H* at the end of the hex number. From now on, every hex number in the text of this book will have that H affixed to its hindparts. It's important, because not *every* hex number contains letter digits. There is a 157H as surely as a 157 decimal, and the two are *not* the same number. Don't forget that H in writing your assembler programs, as I'll be reminding you later on.

Practice. Practice! PRACTICE!

The best (actually, the only) way to get a gut feel for hex notation is to use it a lot. Convert *each* of the following hex numbers to decimal. Lay each number out on the dissection table and identify how many 1s, how many 16s, how many 256s, how many 4096s, and so on, are present in the number, and then add them up in decimal.

CCH	157H	D8H	BB29H	7AH	8177H
A011H	99H	2B36H	FACEH	8DB3H	9H

That done, now turn it inside out, and convert each of the following decimal numbers to hex. Remember the general method: from Table 1.6, choose the largest power of 16 that is *less* than the decimal number to be converted. Find out how many times that power of 16 is present in the decimal number, and write it down as the leftmost-converted hex digit. Then subtract the total value represented by that hex digit from the decimal number. Repeat the process, using the next smallest power of 16 until you've subtracted the decimal number down to nothing.

39	413	22	67,349	6,992	41
1,117	44,919	12,331	124,217	91,198	307
		112,374,777			

(Extra credit for that last one. . . .)

If you need more practice, choose some decimal numbers, convert them to hex, and then convert them back to decimal.

This is a good place to point out the convention of preceding any hex number beginning with a hex digit from A to F with a 0 digit, as in 0FH rather than FH. This is primarily for the convenience of the assembler (as I'll explain in a later chapter) but it's a good habit to get yourself into.

1.6 ◆ Arithmetic in Hex

As you become more and more skilled in assembly language, you'll be doing more and more arithmetic in base 16. You may even (good Lord) come to do it in your head. (I tend to do most of mine on my Sidekick hex calculator.) Still, it takes some practice.

Addition and subtraction are nothing more than what we know in decimal, with a few extra digits tossed in for flavor. The trick is nothing more than knowing your addition tables to 0FH + 0FH. This is best done not by thinking to yourself, 'Now, if C is twelve and F is fifteen, then C + F is twelve plus fifteen, which is 27 decimal but 1BH.' Instead, you should simply say inside your head, 'C + F are 1BH.'

Yes, that's asking a lot. But I ask you now, as I will ask you again on this journey, "do you wanna hack DOS, or do you just wanna fool around?" It takes practice to learn the piano, and it takes practice to get really greased up on the foundation concepts of assembly language programming.

So let me sound like an old schoolmarm and tell you to memorize the following. Make flash cards if you must.

9	8	7	6	5
+ 1	+ 2	+ 3	+ 4	+ 5
0AH	0AH	0AH	0AH	0AH

A	9	8	7	6
+ 1	+ 2	+ 3	+ 4	+ 5
0BH	0BH	0BH	0BH	0BH

B	A	9	8	7	6
+ 1	+ 2	+ 3	+ 4	+ 5	+ 6
0CH	0CH	0CH	0CH	0CH	0CH

C	B	A	9	8	7
+ 1	+ 2	+ 3	+ 4	+ 5	+ 6
0DH	0DH	0DH	0DH	0DH	0DH

D	C	B	A	9	8	7
+ 1	+ 2	+ 3	+ 4	+ 5	+ 6	+ 7
0EH	0EH	0EH	0EH	0EH	0EH	0EH

E	D	C	B	A	9	8
+ 1	+ 2	+ 3	+ 4	+ 5	+ 6	+ 7
0FH	0FH	0FH	0FH	0FH	0FH	0FH

F	E	D	C	B	A	9	8
+ 1	+ 2	+ 3	+ 4	+ 5	+ 6	+ 7	+ 8
10H	10H	10H	10H	10H	10H	10H	10H

F	E	D	C	B	A	9
+ 2	+ 3	+ 4	+ 5	+ 6	+ 7	+ 8
11H	11H	11H	11H	11H	11H	11H

F	E	D	C	B	A	9
+ 3	+ 4	+ 5	+ 6	+ 7	+ 8	+ 9
12H	12H	12H	12H	12H	12H	12H

F	E	D	C	B	A
+ 4	+ 5	+ 6	+ 7	+ 8	+ 9
13H	13H	13H	13H	13H	13H

F	E	D	C	B	A
+ 5	+ 6	+ 7	+ 8	+ 9	+ A
14H	14H	14H	14H	14H	14H

F	E	D	C	B
+ 6	+ 7	+ 8	+ 9	+ A
15H	15H	15H	15H	15H

F	E	D	C	B
+ 7	+ 8	+ 9	+ A	+ B
16H	16H	16H	16H	16H

F	E	D	C
+ 8	+ 9	+ A	+ B
17H	17H	17H	17H

F	E	D	C
+ 9	+ A	+ B	+ C
18H	18H	18H	18H

F	E	D
+ A	+ B	+ C
19H	19H	19H

F	E	D
+ B	+ C	+ D
1AH	1AH	1AH

```
     F          E
   + C        + D
   -----      -----
    1BH        1BH


     F          E
   + D        + E
   -----      -----
    1CH        1CH


     F
   + E
   -----
    1DH


     F
   + F
   -----
    1EH
```

If nothing else, this exercise should make you glad computers don't work in base 64.

Columns and Carries

With all of the single-column additions committed (more or less) to memory, you can tackle multicolumn addition. It works pretty much the same as it does with decimal. Add each column starting from the right, and carry into the next column anytime a single column's sum exceeds 0FH.

For example:

```
     1              1
     2   F   3   1   A   DH
 +   9   6   B   A   0    7H
   --------------------------
     C   5   E   B   B    4H
```

Work this one through, column by column. The sum of the first column (the rightmost) is 14H, which cannot fit in a single column, so we must carry the one into the next column to the left. Even with the additional 1, however, the sum of the second column is 0BH, which fits in a single column and no carry is required.

Keep on adding toward the left. The second-to-last column will again overflow, and you will need to carry the one into the last column. As long as you have your single-digit sums memorized, it's a snap. . . . Well, more or less.

> **The most you can ever carry out of a single-column addition of two numbers is *1*.**

It doesn't matter whether it is base 16, base 10, Fooby, or base 2. You will either carry a 1 out of a column or carry nothing at all. This is important when you add numbers on paper or within the silicon of a CPU, as we'll learn a few chapters on.

Subtraction and Borrows

If you have your single-column sums memorized, you can usually grind your way through subtraction with a shift into a sort of mental reverse: 'if E plus 6 equals 14H, then 14H minus E must equal 6.' The alternative is memorizing an even larger number of tables and because I haven't memorized them, I won't ask you to memorize them.

Over time, however, that's what tends to happen. In hex subtraction, you should be able to dope out any given single-column subtraction by turning a familiar hexadecimal sum inside-out. And just as with base 10, multicolumn subtractions are done column by column, one column at a time:

```
  F76CH
 —A05BH
 ———————
  5711H
```

During your inspection of each column, you should be asking yourself, 'What number added to the bottom number yields the top number?' Here, you should know from your tables that B + 1 = C, so the difference between B and C is 1. The leftmost column is actually more challenging: what number added to A gives you F? Chin up; even I have to think about it on an off day.

The problems show up, of course, when the top number in a column is smaller than its corresponding bottom number. Then, like the federal government on a bomber-buying binge, you have no recourse but to borrow.

Borrowing is one of those grade-school, rote-learned processes that very few people really understand. (To understand it is tacit admittance that something of New Math actually stuck—horrors!) From a height, what happens in a borrow is that one count is taken from a column and applied to the column on its right. I say "applied" rather than "added to" because in moving from one column to the column on its right, that single count is multiplied by "ten," where "ten" represents the number base. (Remember that "ten" in octal has a value of 8, while "ten" in hexadecimal has a value of 16.)

It sounds worse than it is. Let's look at a borrow in action, and you'll get the idea.

```
 9   2 H
-4   F H
_____
```

Here, the subtraction in the rightmost column can't happen as-is because F is larger than 2, so we borrow from the next column to the left.

More than twenty-five years out of the past, I can still hear Sister Marie Bernard toughing it out on the blackboard, albeit in base 16. "Cross out the nine; make it an eight. Make the two a twelve. And twelve minus F is what, class?"

"Three, Sister."

And that's how a borrow works. (I hope the poor dear will forgive me for putting hex bytes in her mouth. . . .)

Think about what happened here functionally. *We subtracted 1 from the 9 and added 10H to the 2.* One obvious mistake is to subtract 1 from the 9 and add 1 to the 2, which, needless to say, won't work. Think of it this way: We're moving part of one column's surplus value over to its right, where some extra value is needed. The overall value of the upper number doesn't change (which is why we call it a "borrow" and not a "steal") but the recipient of the loan is increased by *10,* not *1.*

After the borrow, what we have looks something like this:

```
 8   ¹2 H
-4    F H
_____
```

Of course, once we're here, the columnar subtractions all work out, and we discover that the difference is 43H.

People sometimes ask if they ever have to borrow more than 1. The answer, plainly, is *no.* If you borrow 2, for example, you would add 20 to the recipient column, and *20 minus any single digit remains a 2-digit number;* that is, the difference won't fit into a single column. Subtraction contains an important symmetry with addition:

> **The most you ever need to borrow in any single-column subtraction of two numbers is *1*.**

Borrows across Multiple Columns

Understanding that much about borrows gets you most of the way there. But, as life is wont, you will *frequently* come across a subtraction similar to this:

```
 F   0   0   0H
-3   B   6   CH
────────────────
```

Column 1 (from the right) needs to borrow, but neither column 2 nor column 3 have anything at all to lend. Back in grade school, Sister Marie Bernard would have rattled out with machine-gun efficiency: "Cross out the F, make it an E. Make the zero a ten, then cross it out and make it an F. Make the next zero a ten, cross it out and make it an F. Then make the last zero a ten."

Got that?

What happens is that the middle two 0s act as loan brokers between the F and the rightmost 0, keeping their commission in the form of enough value to allow their own columns' subtractions to take place. Each column to the right of the last column borrows 10 from its neighbor to the left, and loans 1 to the neighbor on its right. After all the borrows trickle through the upper digits, what we have looks like this (minus all those cross-outs):

```
 E   F   F   ¹0H
-3   B   6    CH
────────────────
```

At this point, each columnar subtraction can take place, and the difference is B494H.

In remembering your grade-school machinations, don't fall into the old rut of thinking, 'cross out the 10, make it a 9.' In the world of hexadecimal, $10H - 1 = F$. Cross out the 10, make it an *F*.

What's the Point?

What's the point if you have a hex calculator or a hex-capable screen calculator? The point is *practice*. Hexadecimal is the *lingua franca* of assemblers, to multiply-mangle a metaphor. The more you burn a gut-level understanding of hex into your reflexes, the easier assembly language will be. Furthermore, understanding the internal structure of the machine itself will be much easier if you have that intuitive grasp of hex values. We're laying important groundwork here. Take it seriously now and you'll lose less hair later on.

1.7 ◆ Binary

Hexadecimal is excellent practice for taking on the strangest number base of all—binary. Binary is base 2. Given what we've learned about number bases so far, what can we surmise about base two?

◆ Each column has a value two times the column to its right.

◆ There are only two digits (0 and 1) in the base.

Counting is a little strange in binary, as you might imagine. It goes like this: 0, 1, 10, 11, 100, 101, 110, 111, 1000. . . . Because it sounds absurd to say, "zero, one, ten, eleven, one hundred . . ." it makes more sense to simply enunciate the digits, followed by the word "binary." For example, most people say "one zero one one one zero one binary" instead of "one million, eleven thousand, one hundred one binary" when pronouncing the number 1011101—which sounds enormous until you consider that its value in decimal is only 93.

Odd as it may seem, binary follows all of the same rules we've discussed in this chapter regarding number bases. Converting between binary and decimal is done using the same methods described for hexadecimal in Section 1.5.

Because counting in binary is as much a matter of counting columns as it is counting digits (because there are only two digits in binary) it makes sense to take a long, close look at Table 1.7, which shows the values of the binary number columns out to 32 places.

One look at that imposing pyramid of zeroes implies that it's even hopeless to think of pronouncing the larger columns as strings of digits: "One zero zero zero zero zero zero zero . . ." and so on. There's a crying

TABLE 1.7   Binary columns as powers of 2

Binary		Power of 2		Decimal
1	=	2^0	=	$1 \times 2 =$
10	=	2^1	=	$2 \times 2 =$
100	=	2^2	=	$4 \times 2 =$
1000	=	2^3	=	$8 \times 2 =$
10000	=	2^4	=	$16 \times 2 =$
100000	=	2^5	=	$32 \times 2 =$
1000000	=	2^6	=	$64 \times 2 =$
10000000	=	2^7	=	$128 \times 2 =$
100000000	=	2^8	=	$256 \times 2 =$
1000000000	=	2^9	=	$512 \times 2 =$
10000000000	=	2^{10}	=	$1024 \times 2 =$
100000000000	=	2^{11}	=	$2048 \times 2 =$
1000000000000	=	2^{12}	=	$4096 \times 2 =$
10000000000000	=	2^{13}	=	$8192 \times 2 =$
100000000000000	=	2^{14}	=	$16394 \times 2 =$
1000000000000000	=	2^{15}	=	$32768 \times 2 =$
10000000000000000	=	2^{16}	=	$65536 \times 2 =$
100000000000000000	=	2^{17}	=	$131072 \times 2 =$
1000000000000000000	=	2^{18}	=	$262144 \times 2 =$
10000000000000000000	=	2^{19}	=	$524288 \times 2 =$
100000000000000000000	=	2^{20}	=	$1048576 \times 2 =$
1000000000000000000000	=	2^{21}	=	$2097152 \times 2 =$
10000000000000000000000	=	2^{22}	=	$4194304 \times 2 =$
100000000000000000000000	=	2^{23}	=	$8388608 \times 2 =$
1000000000000000000000000	=	2^{24}	=	$16777216 \times 2 =$
10000000000000000000000000	=	2^{25}	=	$33554432 \times 2 =$
100000000000000000000000000	=	2^{26}	=	$67108864 \times 2 =$
1000000000000000000000000000	=	2^{27}	=	$134217728 \times 2 =$
10000000000000000000000000000	=	2^{28}	=	$268435456 \times 2 =$
100000000000000000000000000000	=	2^{29}	=	$536870912 \times 2 =$
1000000000000000000000000000000	=	2^{30}	=	$1073741824 \times 2 =$
10000000000000000000000000000000	=	2^{31}	=	$2147483648 \times 2 =$
100000000000000000000000000000000	=	2^{32}	=	4294967296 etc . . .

need for a shorthand notation here, so I'll provide you with one in a little while—and its identity will surprise you.

You might object that such large numbers as the bottommost in the table aren't likely to be encountered in ordinary programming. Sorry, but a 32-bit microprocessor like the 80386 can swallow numbers like that in one electronic gulp and eat billions of them for lunch. You *must* become accustomed to thinking in terms of numbers like 2^{32}, which, after all, is only a trifling four billion in decimal. You can't even run NASA on numbers like that, and it's the poor orphan at the federal trough.

Just as with hexadecimal, there can be identity problems when using binary. The number 101 in binary is not the same as 101 in hex, or 101 in decimal. For this reason, always append the suffix *B* to your binary values to make sure people reading your programs (including you, six weeks after the fact) know what base you're working from.

Values in Binary

Converting a value in binary to one in decimal is done the same way it's done in hex—more simply in fact, for the simple reason that you no longer have to count how many times a column's value is present in any given column. In hex, you have to see how many 16s are present in the 16s column, and so on. In binary, a column's value is either present (1 time) or not present (0 times).

Running through a simple example should make this clear. The binary number 11011010B is a relatively typical binary value in small-time computer work (it's on the small side, actually—many common binary numbers are twice its size.) Converting 11011010B to decimal comes down to scanning it from right to left with the help of Table 1.7 and tallying any column's value where that column contains a 1 while ignoring any column containing a 0.

Clear your calculator and let's get started:

Column 0 contains a zero; skip it.

Column 1 contains a 1. That means its value, 2, is present in the value of the number. So we punch 2 into the calculator.

Column 2 is 0. Skip it.

Column 3 contains a 1. The column's value is 2^3, or 8; add 8 to our tally.

Column 4 also contains a 1. 2^4 is 16, which we add to our tally.

Column 5 is 0. Skip it.

Column 6 contains a 1. 2^6 is 64, so add 64 to the tally.

Column 7 also contains a 1. Column 7's value is 2^7, or 128. Add 128 to the tally, and we have 218. It's as easy as that.

Converting from decimal to binary, while more difficult, is done *exactly* the same way as converting from decimal to hex. Go back and read that section again, searching for the *general method* used. In other words, see what was done and separate the essential principles from any references to a specific base like hex.

I'll bet by now you can figure it out without much trouble.

As a brief aside, perhaps you noticed that I started counting columns from 0 rather than 1. A peculiarity of the computer field is that we always begin counting things from 0. Actually, that's unfair; the computer's method is the reasonable one, because 0 is a perfectly good number and should not be discriminated against. The rift occurred because in our world, counting things tells us *how many* things are there, while in the computer world counting things is more generally done to *name* them. For example, we need to deal with bit 0 and then bit 1, and so on, far more than we need to know how many bits there are.

This is not a quibble, by the way. The issue will come up again and again in connection with memory addresses, which as I have said and will say again are the key to understanding assembly language.

In programming circles, *always* begin counting from 0!

This is a good time to get some practice in converting numbers from binary to decimal and back. Cut your teeth on these:

110   10001   11111   11   101   1100010111010010   11000   1011

When that's done, convert these decimal values to binary:

77   42   106   255   18   6309   121   58   18,446

Why Binary?

If it takes eight digits (11011010) to represent an ordinary 3-digit number like 218, binary as a number base would seem to be a bad intellectual investment. Certainly for us it would be a waste of mental bandwidth; even aliens with only two fingers would probably have come up with a better system.

The problem is, lights are either on or they're off.

This is just another way of saying (as I'll discuss in detail in the next chapter) that at the bottom of it, *computers are electrical devices.* In an electrical device, voltage is either present or it isn't; current either flows or it doesn't. Very early in the game, computer scientists decided that the presence of a voltage in a computer circuit would indicate a 1 digit, while lack of a voltage at that same point in the circuit would indicate a 0 digit. This isn't many digits, but it's enough for the binary number system. This is the only reason we use binary, but it's a pretty compelling one, and we're stuck with it. You will not necessarily drown in ones and zeroes, however, because I've already taught you a form of shorthand.

1.8 ♦ Hexadecimal as Shorthand for Binary

The number 218 expressed in binary is 11011010B. Expressed in hex, however, the same value is quite compact: DAH. The two hex digits comprising DAH merit a closer look. AH (or 0AH as your assembler will require for reasons I'll explain later) represents 10 decimal. Converting any number to binary simply involves detecting the powers of 2 within it. The largest power of 2 within 10 decimal is 8. Jot down a 1 digit and subtract 8 from 10. What's left is 2. Now, 4 is a power of 2, but there is no 4 hiding within 2, so we put a 0 to the right of the 1. The next smallest power of 2 is 2, and there is a 2 in 2. Jot down another 1 to the right of the 0. 2 from 2 is 0, so there are no 1s left in the number. Jot down a final 0 to the right of the rest to represent the 1s column. What you have is 1010. Look back at the binary equivalent of 218, which is 11011010. The last four digits are 1010. 1010 is the binary equivalent of 0AH.

The same will work for the upper half of DAH. 0DH, if you work out the binary equivalence as we just did (and it would be good mental exercise) is 1101. Look at the binary equivalent of 218 this way:

	218	decimal
1101	1010	binary
D	A	hex

It should be dawning on you that you can convert long strings of binary 1s and 0s into more compact hex format by converting every four binary digits (starting from the right, *not* from the left!) into a single hex digit.

As an example, here is a 32-bit binary number that is not the least bit remarkable. In fact, it's a pretty typical memory address on the PC:

11110000000000001111101001101110

This is a pretty obnoxious collection of bits to remember or manipulate, so let's split it up into groups of four from the right:

1111 0000 0000 0000 1111 1010 0110 1110

Each of these groups of four binary digits can be represented by a single hexadecimal digit. Do the conversion now. What you should get is the following:

1111	0000	0000	0000	1111	1010	0110	1110
F	0	0	0	F	A	6	E

In other words, the hex equivalent of that mouthful is

F000FA6E

In use, of course, you would append the *H* on the end, and also put a 0 at the beginning, so the number would actually be written 0F000FA6EH.

This is still a good-sized number, but such 32-bit addresses are the largest quantities you would typically encounter in journeyman-level assembly language programming. Most hexadecimal numbers you will encounter would be either four or two hex digits long instead. Furthermore, the PC's CPU likes to deal with 32-bit addresses 16 bits at a time, so most of the time you will look upon enormous hex numbers like 0F00FA6EH as the pair 0F00H and 0FA6EH. Suddenly, this business starts looking a little more graspable.

> **Hexadecimal is the programmer's shorthand for the computer's binary numbers.**

This is why I said earlier that computers use base 2 (binary) and base 16 (hexadecimal) both at the same time in a rather schizoid fashion. What I didn't say is that the computer isn't really the schizoid one; *you* are. At their very heart (as I'll explain in the next chapter) computers use *only* binary. Hex is a means by which you and I make dealing with the computer easier. Fortunately, every four binary digits may be represented by a hex digit, so the correspondence is clean and comprehensible.

Prepare to Compute

Everything up to this point has been necessary groundwork. I've explained conceptually what computers *do* and given you the tools to understand the slightly alien numbers they use. But I've said nothing so far about what computers actually *are*, and it's well past that time. We'll return to hexadecimal numbers again and again in this book; I've said nothing about hex multiplication or bit-banging. The reason is plain: Before you can bang a bit, you must know where the bits live, so let's lift the hood and see if we can catch a few in action.

Chapter 2

Lifting the Hood
Discovering What Computers Actually *Are*

In 1970 I was a senior in high school, and the Chicago public schools had installed a computer somewhere. A truckful of these fancy typewriter gimcracks was delivered to Lane Tech, and a bewildered math teacher was drafted into teaching computer science (they had the nerve to call it) to a high school full of rowdy males.

I figured it out fairly quickly. You pounded out a deck of these goofy computer cards on the card punch, dropped them into the hopper of one of the typewriter gimcracks, and watched in awe as the typewriter danced its little golfball over the greenbar paper, printing out your inevitable list of error messages. It was fun; I got straight As. I even kept the first program I ever wrote that did something useful: a little deck of cards that generated a table of parabolic correction factors for hand-figuring telescope mirrors.

The question that kept gnawing at me was exactly what sort of beast RAX (the computer's wonderfully appropriate name) actually was. What we had were ramcharged typewriters that RAX controlled over phone lines. But what was RAX?

I asked the instructor. In brief, the conversation went something like this:

ME: "Umm, sir, what exactly *is* RAX?"

HE: "Eh? Um, a computer. An electronic computer."

ME: "That's what it says on the course notes. But I want to know what RAX is made of and how it works."

HE: "Well, I'm sure RAX is all solid-state."

ME: "You mean, there's no levers and gears inside."

HE: "Oh, there may be a few. But no radio tubes."

ME: "I wasn't worried about tubes. I suppose it has a calculator in it somewhere. But what makes it remember that A comes before B? How does it know what FORMAT means? How does it tell time? What does it have to do to dial the phone?"

HE: "Now, come on, that's why computers are so great! They put it all together so that we don't have to worry about that sort of thing! Who cares what RAX is? RAX knows FORTRAN, and will execute any correct FORTRAN program. That's what matters, isn't it?"

He was starting to sweat. So was I. End of conversation.

That June I graduated with 3 inches of debugged and working FORTRAN punch cards in my bookbag but I still had absolutely no clue as to what RAX was. It has bothered me to this day.

Gus to the Rescue

I was thinking about RAX six years later while on the Devon Avenue bus heading for work with the latest copy of *Popular Electronics* in my lap. The lead story involved a little thing called the COSMAC ELF, which consisted of a piece of perfboard full of integrated circuit chips, all wired together, plus some toggle switches and a pair of LED numeric displays.

It was a computer (it said so right on the label). The article told us how to put it together and that was about all. What did those chips do? What did the whole thing do? It was driving me nuts.

As usual, my friend Gus Flassig got on the bus at Ashland Avenue and sat down beside me. I asked him what the damned thing did. He was the first human being to make the concept hang together for me.

"Those are memory chips. You load numbers into the memory chips by flipping these switches in different code patterns. Each number means something to the CPU chip. One number makes it add, another number makes it subtract, another number makes it write different numbers into memory, and lots of other things. A program consists of a bunch of these instruction numbers in a row in memory. The computer reads the first number, does what the number instructs it to do, then reads the second one, does what *that* number says to do, and so on until it runs out of numbers."

If *you* don't find that utterly clear, don't worry. I had the advantage of being an electronics hobbyist (so I knew what some of the chips did) and had already written some programs in RAX's FORTRAN. But for me, my God, everything suddenly hit critical mass and exploded in my head until the steam started pouring out of my ears.

No matter what RAX was, I knew that he had to be something like the COSMAC ELF but on a larger scale. I built an ELF. It was quite an education, and it allowed me to understand the nature of computers at a very deep level. I don't recommend that anybody but total crazies wirewrap their own machines out of loose chips anymore, although it was a common enough thing to do in the late Seventies. In this chapter I'll try to provide you with some of the insights that I obtained while assembling my own machine the hard way. (You wonder where the *hard* in hardware comes from? Not from the sound it makes when you bang it on the table, I promise . . .)

2.2 ◆ Switches, Transistors, and Memory

Switches remember.

Think about it. You flip the switch by the door, and the light in the middle of the ceiling comes on. It stays on. When you leave the room, you flip the switch down again, and the light goes out. It stays out. Poltergeists notwithstanding, the switch will remain in the position you last left it until you or someone else comes back and flips it to the other position.

In a sense, the switch remembers what its last command was until you change it and overwrite that command with a new one. In this sense, a light switch represents a sort of rudimentary memory element.

Light switches are more mechanical than electrical. This does not prevent them from acting as memory; in fact, the very first computer, Babbage's nineteenth-century difference engine, was entirely mechanical. In fact, the far larger version he designed but never finished was to have been *steam-powered*. Babbage's machine had lots of little cams that could be flipped by other cams from one position to another. Numbers were encoded and remembered as patterns of cam positions.

One If by Land . . .

Whether a switch is mechanical, electrical, hydraulic, or something else is irrelevant. What counts is that a switch contains a pattern: on or off, up or down, flow or no flow; to that pattern can be assigned a meaning. Paul Revere told his buddy to set up a code in the old north church: "One if by land, two if by sea." Once lit, the lamps in the steeple remained lit (and thus remembered that very important code) long enough for Paul to call out the militia and whup some British butt.

In general, then, what we call *memory* is an aggregate of switches that will retain a pattern long enough for that pattern to be read and understood by a person or a mechanism. For our purposes, those switches will be electrical, but keep in mind that both mechanical and hydraulic computers have been proposed and built with varying degrees of success.

> **Memory consists of containers for alterable patterns that retain an entered pattern until someone or something alters the pattern.**

Transistor Switches

One problem with building a computer memory system of light switches is that light switches are pretty specialized; they require fingers to set them and their output is a current path for electricity. Ideally, a computer memory switch should be operated by the same force it controls. This allows the patterns in memory locations to be passed on to other memory locations. In the gross electromechanical world, such a switch is called a *relay.*

A relay is a switch that is operated by electricity and also controls electricity. You flip a relay by feeding it a pulse of electricity, which powers a little hammer that whaps a lever to one side or another. This lever then opens or closes a set of electrical contacts, just as your garden-variety light switch does. Computers have been made out of relays, although as you might imagine (with a typical relay being about the size of an ice cube) they weren't especially powerful computers.

Fully electronic computers are made out of transistor switches. Transistors are tiny crystals of silicon that use the peculiar electrical properties of silicon to act as switches. I won't try to explain what those peculiar properties are, because that would take an entire (fat) book unto itself. Let's consider a transistor switch as a sort of electrical black box and describe it in terms of inputs and outputs.

Figure 2.1 shows a transistor switch. When an electrical current is fed through pin 1, current flows between pins 2 and 3. When the current ceases flowing through pin 1, current ceases to flow between pins 2 and 3.

In real life, a tiny handful of other components (typically diodes and capacitors) are necessary to make things work smoothly in a computer's memory. These are not necessarily little gizmos connected by wires to the outside of the transistor (although in early transistorized computers they were) but are now cut from the same silicon crystal the transistor itself is cut from, and they occupy almost no space at all. Taken together, the transistor switch and its support components are called a *memory cell.* I've hidden the electrical complexity of the memory cell within an appropriate black-box symbol in Figure 2.1.

A memory cell keeps current flow through it to a minimum, because electrical current flow produces heat, and heat is the enemy of electrical components. The memory cell's circuit is arranged so that if you put a tiny voltage on its input pin and a similar voltage on its *select* pin, a voltage will appear *and remain* on its output pin. That output voltage will remain in its set state until you take away the voltage from the cell as a whole, or else remove the voltage from the input pin while putting a voltage on the select pin.

A voltage on the transistor's input causes current to flow through its output.

A transistor switch

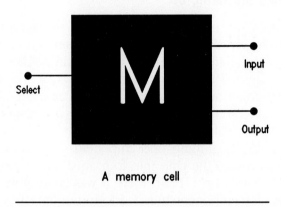

A memory cell

FIGURE 2.1   Transistor switches and memory cells

The voltage being applied to all these pins is never varied. In other words, you don't put 12 volts on the input pin and then change that to 6 volts or 17 volts. The computer designers pick a voltage and stick with it. (Most memory cells operate at a constant 5 volts, although many operate at 12 volts.) The pattern is a binary one: You either put a voltage on the input pin or you take the voltage away. The output pin echoes that: it either holds a fixed voltage or no voltage at all.

We apply a code to that state of affairs. *The presence of voltage indicates a binary 1, and the lack of voltage indicates a binary 0.* This code is arbitrary. We could as well have said that the *lack* of voltage indicates a binary 1 and vice versa (computers have been built this way for obscure reasons) but the choice is up to us. Having the *presence* of something indicate a binary 1 is more natural, and that is the way things have evolved in the computing mainstream.

A single computer memory cell such as the transistor-based one we're speaking of here holds one binary digit: either a 1 or a 0. This is called a *bit*. A bit is the indivisible atom of information. There is no half-a-bit, and no bit-and-a-half. (This has been tried, and it works badly; but that didn't stop it from being tried.)

A bit is a single binary digit, either 1 or 0.

The Incredible Shrinking Bit

One bit doesn't tell us much. To be useful, we need to bring a lot of memory cells together. Transistors started out small (the originals from the Fifties looked a lot like stove-pipe hats for tin soldiers) and decreased in size from there. The first transistors were created from little chips of silicon crystal about an eighth of an inch square. The size of the crystal chip hasn't changed much since then, but the *transistors* themselves have shrunk almost incredibly.

Where in the beginning one chip held one transistor, in time the designers crisscrossed the chip into four equal areas and made each area an independent transistor. From there it was an easy jump to adding the other minuscule components needed to turn a transistor into a computer memory cell.

The chip of silicon was a tiny and fragile thing, and was encased in an oblong molded-plastic housing, like a stick of Dentyne gum with metal legs for the electrical connections.

What we had now was a sort of electrical egg carton: four little cubby-holes, each of which could contain a single binary bit. Then the shrinking process began. First 8 bits, then 16, then multiples of 8 and 16, all on the same tiny silicon chip. By the late Sixties, 256 memory cells could be made on one chip of silicon, usually in an array of 8 cells by 32. In 1976, my COSMAC ELF computer contained two memory chips. On each chip was an array of memory cells 4 wide and 256 long (picture a *very* long egg carton). Each chip could thus hold 1024 bits.

This was a pretty typical memory chip capacity at that time. We called them "1K RAM chips," because they held roughly 1000 bits (the K stands for kilobit) of *random access memory* (RAM). We'll get back to the notion of what "random access" means shortly. Toward the mid-70s, the great memory-shrinking act was kicking into high gear. 1K chips were criss-cross divided into 4K chips containing 4096 bits of memory. The 4K chips were almost immediately divided into 16K chips. (16,384 bits of memory.) These 16K chips were the standard when the IBM PC appeared in 1981. By 1982 the chips had been divided once again, and 16K became 64K, with 65,536 bits inside that same little gumstick. Keep in mind that we're talking about more than 65,000 transistors (plus other components) formed on a square of silicon about a quarter-inch on a side.

Come 1985 and the 64K chip had been pushed aside by its drawn-and-quartered child, the 256K chip. (262,144 bits.) Chips always increase in capacity by a factor of 4 simply because the current-generation chip is divided into 4 equal areas, and onto each quadrant is then placed the same number of transistors that the previous generation of chip had held over the whole silicon chip.

By 1989 that 256K chip is almost history. It was subdivided into 4 a couple of years ago, and now for our mainstream memory container we have the 1M chip. The *M* means *mega* (Greek for million) and the critter has a grand total of 1,048,576 bits in its tummy, and still is no larger than that stick of Dentyne gum.

Will it stop here? Ha! The Japanese, patrons of all things small, have begun making quantities of 4M chips containing 4,194,304 bits, and in November 1988 broke ground on a new facility for manufacturing 16M chips containing 16,777,216 bits. Some physicists think that even the Japanese will have trouble dividing that little wafer one more time because the transistors are now so small that it gets hard to push more than one electron through them at a time. At that point some truly ugly limitations of life called quantum mechanics begin to get in the way. More likely the next generation of chips will be stacked vertically for greater capacity. Many people are off in their labs looking for other tricks, and don't make the oft-made mistake of assuming they won't find any.

Random Access

These chips are called RAM chips because they contain random access memory. Newcomers sometimes find this a perplexing and disturbing word, because *random* often connotes chaos or unpredictability. What the word really means is "at random," meaning you can reach into a one megabit memory chip and pick out any of those million-plus bits without disturbing any of the others, just as you might select one book at random from a library's many shelves of thousands of books without sifting through them in order.

Memory didn't always work this way. Before memory was placed on silicon chips, it was stored on magnetic gadgets of some kind, usually rotating drums or disks that are distantly related to the Winchester hard disk drives we use today. Rotating memory sends a circular collection of bits beneath a magnetic sensor. The bits pass beneath the sensor one at a time, and if you miss the one you want, like a Chicago bus in January, you simply have to wait for it to come by again. These are *serial access devices;* they present their bits to you in a fixed order, one at a time, and you have to wait for the one you want to come up in its order.

There is no need to remember that; we've long since abandoned serial-access devices for main computer memory. We still use such systems for *mass storage,* which I'll describe later.

Random access works like this: inside the chip, each bit is stored in its own memory cell, identical to the memory cell diagrammed in Figure 2.1. Each of the however-many memory cells in each chip has its own unique number. This number is the cell's (and hence a bit's) *address.* It's like the addresses on a street: The bit on the corner is number 0 Silicon Alley, the bit next door is number 1, and so on. You don't have to knock on the door of bit number 0 and ask which bit it is, then go to the next door and ask there too, until you find the bit you want. If you have the address, you can zip right down the street and park square in front of the bit you intend to visit.

Each chip has a number of pins coming out of it. (This is the computer room's equivalent of the killer rake: don't step on one in the dark!) The bulk of these pins are called *address pins.* One pin is called a *data pin.* (See Figure 2.2.) The address pins are electrical leads that carry the binary address code. The address is a binary number expressed in 1s and 0s only. This address is applied to the address pins by encoding a binary 1 as five volts and a binary 0 as zero volts. Special circuits inside the RAM chip decode this address to one of the select inputs of the numerous memory cells inside the chip. For any given address applied to the address pins, only *one* select input will be raised to five volts, thereby selecting that particular cell.

Depending on whether you intend to read a bit or write a bit, the data pin is switched between the memory cell's input or its output, as shown in Figure 2.2. That is all done internally to the chip. As far as you on the outside are concerned, once you've applied the address to the address pins, *voila!* The data pin will contain a voltage representing the value of the bit you requested. If that bit contained a binary 1, the data pin will contain a five volt signal; otherwise, the binary 0 bit will be represented by zero volts.

Memory Access Time

Chips are graded by how long it takes for the data to appear on the data pin after you've applied the address to the address pins. Obviously, the

Data pin

Address pins

FIGURE 2.2   A megabit memory chip

faster the better, but some chips (for electrical reasons that are difficult to explain) are faster than others.

The access times seem so small as to be insignificant—100 nanoseconds is a typical memory chip access time. A nanosecond is a *billionth* of a second, so 100 nanoseconds is one ten-millionth of a second. Great stuff, but to accomplish anything useful, a computer needs to access memory hundreds of thousands or millions of times and this time adds up. If you become an expert assembly language programmer, you will jump through hoops to shave the number of memory accesses your program needs to perform because memory access is the ultimate limiting factor in a computer's performance. Michael Abrash, in fact, has published two whole books on doing exactly that. *Zen of Assembly Language,* Volumes I and II, can be (badly) summarized in just these few words: *Stay out of memory whenever you can!* (You'll discover just how difficult this is soon enough . . .)

Bytes, Words, and Double Words

The days are long gone when a serious computer can exist on only one memory chip. My poor 1976 COSMAC ELF needed at least two memory chips. Today's computers need dozens, or even hundreds, regardless of the fact that today's chips hold megabits rather than the ELF's paltry 2,048 bits. Understanding how a computer gathers its memory chips together into a coherent memory *system* is critical when you want to write efficient assembly language programs. Whereas there is an infinity of ways to hook memory chips together, the system I'll describe here is that of the IBM PC computer, which includes the PC, XT, AT, PS/2 and a veritable plethora of clones.

Our memory system must store our information. How we organize a memory system out of a hatful of memory chips will be dictated largely by how we organize our information.

The answer begins with this thing called a *byte*. The fact that the grandaddy of all computer magazines took this word for its title indicates its importance in the computer scheme of things. From a functional perspective, memory is measured in bytes; a byte is 8 bits. Two bytes side by side are called a *word,* and two words side-by-side are called a *double word*. There are other terms like *nybble* and *quad word,* but you can do quite well with bits, bytes, words, and double words.

A bit is a single binary digit, 0 or 1.

A byte is bits side-by-side.

A word is 2 bytes side-by-side.

A double word is 2 words side-by-side.

Computers were designed to store and manipulate human information. The basic elements of human discourse are built from a set of symbols consisting of letters of the alphabet (two of each letter, for upper and lower case), numbers, and symbols like commas, colons, periods, exclamation marks. Add to these the various international variations on letters like ä and ò plus the more arcane mathematical symbols, and you'll find that human information requires a symbol set of well over 200 symbols. (The symbol set used in all PC-style computers is given in Appendix A.)

Bytes are central to this scheme because one symbol out of that symbol set can be neatly expressed in one byte. A byte is 8 bits, and 2^8 is 256. This means that a binary number 8 bits in size can be one of 256 different values, measured from 0 to 255. Because we use these symbols, most of what we do in computer programs is done in byte-sized chunks. In fact, except for the very odd and specialized kind of computers we are now putting into intelligent food processors and the like, *no* computer processes information in chunks smaller than one byte. Most computers today, in fact, process information either a word or a double word at a time.

Pretty Chips All in a Row

One of the more perplexing things for beginners to understand is that today's standard 1 megabit RAM chip does not even contain *one* byte, although it has 1,048,576 bits. Remember that a RAM chip has only *one* data pin. To store a byte you would have to store 8 bits in sequence at eight consecutive addresses, and to retrieve that byte you would have to retrieve 8 bits in sequence. Because it takes 100 nanoseconds at the very least to store a bit in one of those chips, storing a byte would take at least 800 nanoseconds, and in practical terms, nearly a microsecond, which is (believe it or not) far, far too slow to be useful.

What actually is done is that a single stored byte is distributed across eight separate RAM chips, with one bit from the stored byte in each chip at the same address across all chips. This way, when a single address is applied to the address pins of all eight chips, all 8 bits appear simultaneously on the eight output pins, and a full byte can be retrieved in 100 nanoseconds instead of 800 nanoseconds (see Figure 2.3).

We call this row of eight chips a *bank* of memory; how much memory is contained in a bank depends on the type of chips incorporated in the bank. A row of eight 64K chips contains 64K *bytes*. (It contains 8 × 64K or 512K *bits*, however. Remember, computers deal with information a minimum of 8 bits at a time.) A row of eight 256K chips contains 256K bytes, and so on.

This is the system used in the IBM PC, the XT, and their clones. The IBM AT and its clones process information a word at a time, so their memory systems use a row of 16 memory chips to store and retrieve a full 16-bit word at once. Furthermore, the newest generation of IBM-compatible machines using the 80386 processor handles memory at a double word at a time, so those machines access a row of 32 memory chips at a time. (A double word consists of 4 bytes, or 32 bits.)

Actual computers combine various combinations of memory banks in

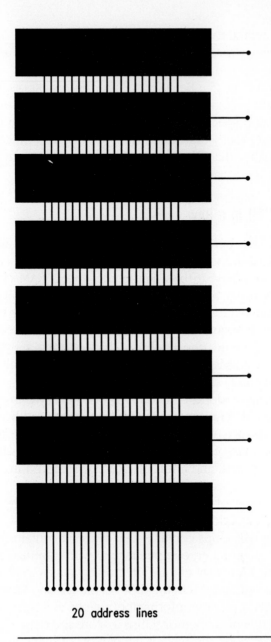

Each black box is
a chip like that shown
in Figure 2.2.

Each of eight chips
contains 1,048,576 bits.
The eight chips taken
together contain
1,048,576 bytes, with
each chip contributing
one bit to every byte.
Bytes of data may be
written to and read
from the eight data
lines shown here.

20 address lines

FIGURE 2.3   A memory bank containing one megabyte

various ways to produce different amounts of memory. I'll take up the subject again when we begin talking specifically about the IBM PC in Chapter 6.

2.3 ◆ The Shop Foreman and the Assembly Line

The gist of the previous section was only this: electrically, your computer's memory consists of one or more rows of memory chips, each chip containing a *large* number of memory cells consisting of transistors and other minuscule electrical components. Most of the time, it's just as useful, to avoid confusion, to forget about the transistors and even the rows of chips. (My high school computer science teacher was not *entirely* wrong . . . but he was right for the wrong reasons.)

It's better in most cases to envision a very long row of byte-sized containers, each with its own address. Don't assume that in computers that process information a word at a time that only *words* have addresses; it is a convention with the PC architecture that *every* byte has its own address regardless of how many bytes are pulled from memory at one time.

> **Every byte of memory in the computer has its own unique address, even in computers that process 2 bytes or even 4 bytes at a time.**

If this seems counterintuitive, yet another metaphor will help. When you go to the library to take out the three volumes of Tolkien's *The Lord of the Rings,* you'll find that each of the three volumes has its own card catalog number (essentially that volume's address in the library) but that you take all three down at once and process them as a single entity. If you really *want* to, you can take only one of the books out at a time, but to do so will require yet another trip to the library to get the next volume, which is wasteful of your time and effort.

So it is with 16-bit or 32-bit computers. Every byte has its own address, but when a 16-bit computer accesses a byte, it actually reads *2* bytes, starting at the address of the requested byte. You can use the second byte or ignore it if you don't need it—but if you later decide you do need the second byte you'll have to access memory again to get it. It is best to save time and get it all at one swoop. (There is an additional complication here involving whether addresses are odd or even or divisible by 4 or 16, but we'll cover that in detail later on.)

The Honcho Chip

All of this talk about reading things from memory and writing things to memory has thus far carefully skirted the question of *who* is doing the reading and writing. The who is almost always a single, remarkable chip, the *central processing unit* (CPU). If you are the president and CEO of your personal computer, then the CPU is the shop foreman who sees that your orders are carried out down in the chips where the work gets done.

Some would say that the CPU is what actually does the work, but that's an oversimplification. Plenty of real work is done in the memory system, and especially in what are called *peripherals,* like video display boards, serial and parallel ports, and modems. While the CPU does do a good deal of the work, it also parcels out quite a bit to other components within the computer. I think its role of foreman outweighs its role as assembly line grunt.

The CPU chips used in IBM-compatible computers all come from a company called Intel, which pretty much invented the single-chip CPU back in the early 1970s. Intel's first big success was the 8080, which helped trigger the personal computer revolution by being chosen for the seminal MITS Altair 8800 computer, which was introduced in Popular Electronics in late 1974. The 8080 was an 8-bit computer because it accessed memory 8 bits (1 byte) at a time. The 8080 is now pretty well extinct, but it gave birth to a pair of next-generation CPU chips called the 8086 and the 8088. These two chips are nearly identical except that the 8088 is an 8-bit CPU, while the 8086 is a 16-bit CPU that accesses memory 2 bytes (one word) at a time. IBM chose the 8088 for its original 1981 IBM PC and later the XT, but the 8086 never made it into a true IBM computer until the PS/2 models 25 and 30 appeared in 1987.

Intel produced yet another generation of CPU chip in 1983, and by 1984 the 80286 became the beating heart of the enormously successful PC/AT. The 80286 is a more powerful 16-bit CPU, capable of everything the 8086 can do plus numerous additional things. Early 1986 brought Intel's 80386 CPU chip to market. The 80386 upped the ante by being a 32-bit machine. It reads and writes memory a double word (4 bytes) at a time. The 80386 is enormously more powerful, and a great deal faster, than the 80286.

By the end of 1989 or early 1990 we may see quantity production of Intel's newest wonder, the 80486, but what we will do with it is anybody's guess. As good as it is, the 80486 is not a 64-bit CPU. Many experts think that 32 bits is an ideal format for CPU memory access, and increasing memory access beyond 32 bits at a time would begin to slow things down.

And in this business, you do *not* want to slow things down.

Talking to Memory

All the various Intel CPUs operate at varying speeds with various features, but they are conceptually identical, and this discussion will apply to all of them.

The CPU's most important job is to communicate with the computer's memory system. Like a memory chip, a CPU chip is a small square of silicon onto which a great many transistors have been placed. This fragile chip is encased in a plastic or ceramic housing with a large number of protruding pins. Like the pins of memory chips, the CPU's pins transfer information encoded as voltage levels. Five volts indicate a binary 1, and zero volts indicate a binary 0.

Like the memory chips, the CPU has a number of pins devoted to memory addresses, and these pins are connected directly to the computer's banks of memory chips. When the CPU reads a byte (or word or doubleword) from memory, it places the memory address of the byte to be read on its address pins, encoded as a binary number. 100 nanoseconds or so later, the byte appears (also as a binary number) on the data pins of the memory chips. The CPU also has data pins, and it slurps up the byte presented by the memory chips through its own data pins (see Figure 2.4).

This process, of course, also works in reverse. To write a byte into memory, the CPU first places the memory address of where it wants to write onto its address pins. Nanoseconds later, it places the byte it wishes to write into memory on its data pins. The memory chips obediently store the byte inside themselves at the requested address.

Riding the Bus

This give-and-take between the CPU and the memory system represents the bulk of what happens inside your computer. Information flows from memory, into the CPU, and back again. Information flows in other paths as well. Your computer contains additional devices called *peripherals* that are either sources or destinations (or both) of information.

Video display boards, disk drives, printer ports, and modems are the most common peripherals in PC-type computers. Like the CPU and memory, they are all ultimately electrical devices. Most modern peripherals consist of one or two large chips and several smaller chips that support the larger chips. Like both the CPU and the memory chips, these peripheral devices have both address pins and data pins. Some peripherals, video boards in particular, have their own memory chips.

Peripherals "talk" to the CPU (i.e., pass data to the CPU or take data from

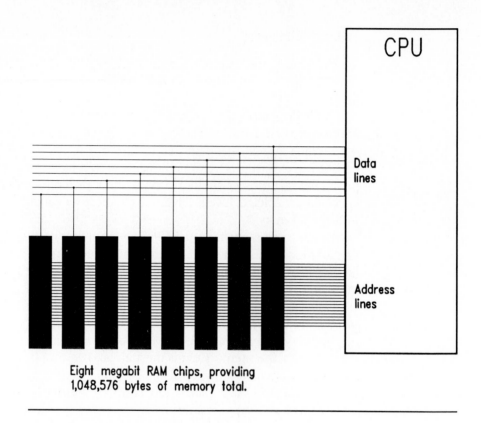

CPU

Data
lines

Address
lines

Eight megabit RAM chips, providing
1,048,576 bytes of memory total.

FIGURE 2.4   The CPU and memory

the CPU) and sometimes to one another. These conversations take place across the electrical connections linking the address pins and data pins that all devices in the computer have in common. These electrical lines are called a *data bus,* and they form a sort of party line linking the CPU with all of the other parts of the computer. There is an elaborate system of electrical arbitration that determines when and in what order the different devices can use this party line to talk with one another, but it always happens the same way: an address is placed on the bus, followed by a byte (or word or double word) of data. Special signals go out on the bus with the address to indicate whether the address is a location in memory or of one of the peripherals attached to the data bus. The address of a peripheral is called an *I/O address* to differentiate between it and a *memory address* such as we've been discussing all along.

The data bus is the major element in the *expansion slots* present in most PC-type computers, and most peripherals are boards that plug into these slots. The peripherals talk to the CPU and to memory through the data bus connections, which are the electrical pins in the expansion slots.

The Foreman's Pockets

Every CPU contains a small number of data storage cubbyholes called *registers*. These registers are at once the foreman's pockets and the foreman's workbench. When the CPU needs a place to tuck something away for awhile, an empty register is just the place. The CPU could always store the data out in memory, but that takes a lot of time. Because the registers are actually inside the CPU, placing data in a register and reading it back again is *fast*.

More important than their use as storage, registers are the foreman's workbench. When the CPU needs to add two numbers, the easiest and fastest way to do this is to place the numbers into two registers and then add the two registers together. The sum can then be placed in yet another register, or added to yet another number in another register, or stored out in memory, or be used in any of a multitude of other operations.

> **The CPU's immediate work-in-progress is held in temporary storage containers called *registers*.**

Work involving registers is always fast because the registers are within the CPU and very little movement of data is necessary. Like memory cells and, indeed, like the entire CPU, registers are made out of transistors. Rather than having numeric addresses, however, registers have names like AX or DI. To make matters even more complicated, while all CPU registers have certain common properties, most registers have unique special powers not shared by other registers. Understanding the ways and the limitations of CPU registers is something like following the Watergate hearings: there are partnerships, alliances, and always a bewildering array of secret agendas that each register follows. I'll be devoting most of a chapter to registers later in this book.

Most peripherals also have registers, and peripheral registers are even more limited in scope than CPU registers. Their agendas are quite explicit and in no way secret. This does not prevent them from being confusing, as anyone who has tried programming the EGA video board at a register level will attest.

The Assembly Line

If the CPU is the shop foreman, then the peripherals are the assembly line workers, and the data bus is the assembly line itself. (Unlike most assembly lines, however, the foreman works the line as hard or harder than the rest of his crew!)

As an example, information enters the computer through a modem peripheral, which assembles bits received from the telephone line into bytes of data representing characters and numbers. The modem then places the assembled byte onto the bus, where the CPU picks it up, tallies it, and then places it back on the data bus. The video board then retrieves the byte from the bus and writes it into video memory so that you can see it on your screen.

Obviously, a lot is going on inside the box. Continuous, furious communication along the data bus between CPU, memory, and peripherals is what accomplishes the work that the computer does. The question then arises, who tells the foreman and crew what to do? You do. How do you do that? You write a program. Where is the program? It's in memory, along with all the rest of the data stored in memory. In fact, the program *is* data, and that is the heart of the whole idea of programming as we know it.

2.4 ◆ The Box That Follows a Plan

We finally come to the essence of computing: the nature of programs and how they direct the CPU to control the computer. We've seen how memory can be used to store bytes of information. These bytes are all binary codes, patterns of 1s and 0s stored as minute electrical voltage levels and making up binary numbers. We've also spoken of symbols and how certain binary codes can be interpreted as meaning something to us humans, things like letters, digits, punctuation, and so on.

Just as the table in Appendix A contains a set of codes and symbols that mean something to us, there is a set of codes that mean something to the CPU. These codes are called *machine instructions,* and their name is evocative of what they actually are: instructions to the CPU.

Let's take an example or two from the venerable 8088 CPU. The binary code 01000000 (40H) has meaning to the 8088 chip. It is an order: *Add 1 to register AX.* That's about as simple as they get. Most machine instructions occupy more than a single byte. The binary codes 11010110 01110011 (0B6H 73H) comprise another order: *load the value 73H into register DH.* On the other end of the spectrum, the binary code 11110011 10100100

(0F3H 0A4H) direct the CPU to do the following (take a deep breath): *begin moving the number of bytes specified in register CX from the 32-bit address stored in registers DS and SI to the 32-bit address stored in registers ES and DI, updating the address in both SI and DI after moving each byte.*

The rest of the several hundred instructions understood by the Intel CPUs fall in and among those three in terms of complication and power. There are instructions that perform arithmetic operations (addition, subtraction, multiplication, and division) logical operations (AND, OR, etc.; see Chapter 3), and instructions that move information around memory or exchange information with peripherals.

Fetch and Execute

A computer program is nothing more than a table of machine instructions stored in memory. There's nothing special about the table nor where it is positioned in memory; it could be anywhere, and the bytes in the table are nothing more than binary numbers.

The binary numbers comprising a computer program are special only in the way that the CPU treats them. When the CPU is started, it *fetches* a byte from an agreed-upon address in memory. This byte is read from memory and loaded into the CPU. The CPU then examines the byte and begins performing the task that the fetched machine instruction directs it to do. In many cases, this means fetching another byte (or another two or three) from memory to complete the machine instruction before the real work begins.

For example, if it fetches the binary code 40H (as mentioned above), it immediately adds one to the value stored in register AX. But if it fetches the binary code 0B6H, it knows it must go back out to memory and fetch an additional byte to complete the instruction. When both bytes are in memory, *then* the CPU takes the required action, which is to load the second byte into register DH.

As soon as the CPU finishes executing an instruction, it goes out to memory and fetches the next byte in sequence. Inside the CPU is a register called the *instruction pointer* that quite literally contains the address of the next instruction to be executed. Each time an instruction is completed, the instruction pointer is updated to point to the next instruction in memory.

Thus, the process is fetch and execute, fetch and execute, etc. The CPU works its way through memory, with the instruction pointer register leading the way. As it goes it works: moving data around in memory, moving values around in registers, passing data to peripherals, and crunching data in arithmetic or logical operations.

> **Computer programs are lists of binary machine instructions stored in memory. They are no different from any other list of data bytes stored in memory *except* in how they are treated when fetched by the CPU.**

The Foreman's Innards

I made the point earlier that machine instructions are *binary* codes. This is something we often gloss over, yet to understand the true nature of the CPU we have to step away from the persistent image of machine instructions as *numbers.* They are *not* numbers, they are binary patterns designed to throw electrical switches.

Inside the CPU there are a *very* large number of transistors. A small number of those transistors go into making the foreman's pockets, the machine registers that hold information. The vast bulk of the remaining transistors (which now number over a million in a CPU like the 80386) are switches connected to other switches, which are connected to still more switches in a mind-numbingly complex network.

As we discussed, the machine instruction 01000000 (40H) directs the CPU to add one to the value stored in register AX. It's very instructive of the true nature of computers to think about the execution of machine instruction 01000000 in the following way. The CPU fetches a byte from memory that contains the code 01000000. Once the byte is fully within the CPU, the CPU, in essence, lets the machine instruction byte push eight transistor switches. The lone 1 digit pushes its switch up electrically; the rest of the digits, all 0's, push their switches down.

In a chain reaction, those eight switches flip the states of first dozens, then hundreds, then thousands, and finally tens of thousands of tiny transistor switches within the CPU. This isn't random—this furious moment of electrical activity within the CPU operates strictly according to patterns etched into the silicon of the CPU by Intel's teams of engineers. Ultimately, perhaps after hundreds of thousands of individual switch throws, the value contained in register AX is suddenly one greater than it was before.

How this happens is difficult to explain, but you must remember that *any* number within the CPU can also be looked at as a binary code, including the numbers stored in registers. Also, most switches within the CPU contain more than one "handle." These switches, called *gates,* work according to the rules of logic. Perhaps two, three, or even more "up" switch throws have to arrive at a particular gate at the same time in order for one "down" switch throw to pass through that gate.

These gates are used to build the complex internal machinery within the CPU. Collections of gates can add two numbers in a device called an *adder,* which again is nothing more than a crew of dozens of little switches working together as gates; a number of gates then work together to form an adder.

As part of the cavalcade of switch-throws kicked off by the binary code 01000000, the value in register AX was dumped trapdoor style into an adder, while at the same time the number 1 was fed into the other end of the adder. Finally, rising on a wave of switch-throws, the new sum emerges from the adder and ascends back into register AX and the job is done.

The foreman of your computer, then, is made of switches, just like all the other parts of the computer. The chip contains a mind-boggling number of such switches, which are interconnected in even more mind-boggling ways. The important thing is that whether you are boggled or, like me on off-days, merely jaded by it all, the CPU, and ultimately the computer, *does what we tell it to.* We set up a list of machine instructions as a table in memory, and then, by God, that mute iron brick comes alive and starts earning its keep.

Changing Course

The first piece of genuine magic in the nature of computers is that a string of binary codes in memory tells the computer what to do, step-by-step. The second piece of that magic is really the jewel in the crown: *there are machine instructions that change the order in which machine instructions are fetched and executed.*

In other words, once the CPU has executed a machine instruction that does something useful, the next machine instruction may tell the CPU to go back and play it again—and again, and again, as many times as necessary. The CPU can keep count of the number of times that it has executed that particular instruction or list of instructions, and keep repeating them until a prearranged count has been met. The CPU also can arrange to skip certain sequences of machine instructions entirely if they don't need to be executed at all.

What this means is that the list of machine instructions in memory does not necessarily begin at the top and run without deviation to the bottom. The CPU can execute the first fifty or a hundred or a thousand instructions, then jump to the end of the program, or jump back to the start and begin again. It can skip and bounce up and down the list like a stone tossed over a calm pond. It can execute a few instructions up here, then zip down somewhere else and execute a few more instructions, then zip back and pick up where it left off, all without missing a beat or even wasting too much time.

How is this done? Recall that the CPU contains a register that always contains the address of the next instruction to be executed. This register, the instruction pointer, is not essentially different from any of the other registers in the CPU. Just as a machine instruction can add 1 to register AX, another machine instruction can add or subtract some number from the address stored in the instruction pointer. Add 100 to the instruction pointer, and the CPU will *instantly* skip one hundred bytes down the list of machine instructions before it continues. Subtract one hundred from the address stored in the instruction pointer, and the CPU will *instantly* jump *back* one hundred bytes up the machine instruction list.

And finally, the third piece of magic: *the CPU can change its course of execution based on the work it has been doing.* The CPU can "decide" whether or not to execute a given instruction or group of instructions based on values stored in memory, or based on the state of special one-bit CPU registers called *flags*. The CPU can count up how many times it needs to do something, and then do that something that number of times.

So, not only can you tell the CPU what to do, you can tell it where to go. Better, you can sometimes let the CPU, like a faithful bloodhound, sniff out the best course forward in the interest of getting the work done in the quickest possible way.

Back in Chapter 0, I spoke of a computer program being a sequence of steps and tests. Most of the machine instructions understood by the CPU are steps, but others are tests. The tests are always two-way tests, and in fact the choice of what to do is always the same, jump or don't jump. *That's all.* You can test for any of numerous different conditions, but the choice is always one of jumping to another place in the program, or just keep truckin' along.

The Plan

I can sum it all up by borrowing one of the most potent metaphors for computing ever uttered: *"The computer is a box that follows a plan."* These are the words of Ted Nelson, author of the uncanny book *Computer Lib/Dream Machines* and one of those very rare people who have the infuriating habit of being right most of the time.

You write the plan, and the computer follows it by passing the instructions, byte by byte, to the CPU. At the very bottom level, the process is a hellishly involved electrical chain reaction involving tens of thousands of switches composed of hundreds of thousands, or even millions, of transistors.

This plan, this list of machine instructions in memory, is your assembly language program. The whole point of this book and the books that follow it in this series is to teach you to correctly arrange machine instructions in memory for the use of the CPU.

With any luck at all, by now you'll have a reasonable conceptual understanding of both what computers do and what they are. It's time to start looking more closely at the nature of the operations that machine instructions force the CPU to do.

Chapter 3

The Right to Assemble

The Process of Making Assembly Language Programs

Years ago (back in the Sixties, it had to be!) I recall reading about a comely female artist who produced her oil paintings by the intriguing process of rolling naked on a tarp splattered with multicolored oil paint, and then throwing herself against a canvas taped to the studio wall. (I can see the headline now: 'NUDE WITH BRUISES' FETCHES RECORD PRICE AT NY AUCTION.)

I've seen people write programs this way. The BASIC language makes it easy: you roll in an intoxicating collection of wild and powerful program statements, and then smear them about on the screen until something works. Something invariably *does* work, no matter how little thought goes into the program's design. BASIC is like that. It's moron-friendly, and will stoop to whatever level of carelessness goes into a program's preparation.

The programs that result, while workable in that they don't crash the machine, can take seven seconds to paint a screen, or an hour and a half to sort a database with 150 check records in it.

You can't paint "Nude with Bruises" in assembly language. Trust me.

The Sears Catalog Fallacy

There are other perfectly proper programming paradigms that won't work with assembly language, either. One is commonly used with my own beloved Turbo Pascal: Decide what you want to do, sketch out a design based on a reasonable amount of forethought, and then go hunting through a veritable Sears catalog of toolbox products looking for stock procedures like

```
SearchDataFileForFirstRecordBeginningWithStringAndDisplayInRed
```

Basically, this method glues together canned procedures created by others into programs that aren't exactly canned but are more or less polybagged, which is OK—I do it all the time. I also eat at Burger King a couple of times a week because it's quick and cheap, and because I get hungry no matter how hard I try not to. When I need a software tool in a bad way and just can't get around not having it, I look for the quickest possible way to produce it.

As an interesting sidenote, I once produced a necessary utility, my **JRead** utility, by starting with Borland's **FirstEd** example editor from their Editor Toolbox and cutting things out of it until the program did what I needed. All told, I ended up writing only about twenty lines of new code. It was programming in reverse—you can't do it all the time, but this time it allowed me to make a solid, useful tool in about an hour and a half. Keep your eyes open for opportunities like that.

There is an occasional toolbox of assembly language routines, but hardly enough to avoid having to think too much about the task at hand, which is what many people end up doing with the Sears catalog fallacy.

I started this chapter this way as a warning that you can't write assembly language programs by trial and error, nor can you do it by letting other people do your thinking for you. It is a complicated and tricky process compared to either BASIC or we-do-it-all-for-you languages like Turbo Pascal. You have to pay attention. You have to read the sheet music. And most of all, you have to practice.

3.2 ◆ DOS and DOS Files

In the previous chapter, I defined what a computer program is from the computer's perspective. It is, metaphorically, a long journey in very small steps. A *long* list of binary codes direct the CPU to do what it must to accomplish the job at hand. These codes are, even in their hexadecimal shorthand form, gobbledegook to us here in the land of the living:

    FE FF A2 37 4C 0A 29 00 91 CB 60 61 E8 E3 20 00 A8 00 B8 29 1F FF 69 55
    7B F4 F8 5B 31

Is this a real program or isn't it? You'd probably have to ask the CPU, unless you were a machine-code maniac of the kind that hasn't been seen since 1977. (It isn't.)

The CPU, however, has no trouble with programs presented in this form. In fact, the CPU can't handle programs any other way. The CPU simply isn't equipped to understand a string of characters like

    LET X = 42

or even something we out here would call assembly language:

    MOV AX,42

To the CPU, it's binary only and hold the text, please, ma'am.

While it is possible to write computer programs in pure binary (I have done it, but not since 1977), it's unpleasant work, and will take you until the next Ice Age to accomplish anything useful.

The process of developing assembly language programs is a path that runs from what we call *source code* that you can read to something called *machine code* that the CPU can execute. In the middle is a resting point called *object code* that we'll take up a little later.

The process of creating true machine code programs is one of translation. You must start with something you and the rest of us can read and understand, and then somehow convert that to something the CPU can understand and execute. Before examining either end of that road, however, we need to understand a little more about the land on which the road is built.

The God Above; the Troll Below

Most of all, we need to understand DOS. Some people look upon DOS as a god; others as a kind of troll. In fact, DOS is a little of both. Mostly what you must put behind you is the common notion that DOS is a part of the machine itself and somehow resides in the same sort of silicon as the CPU. Not so! DOS is a computer program of an only slightly special nature, called an *operating system.*

In part, an operating system is a collection of routines that do nothing but serve the components of the computer itself. By components I mean things like disk drives, printers, and so on. DOS acts something like a troll living under the bridge to your disk drive. You tell the troll what you want to do with the disk drive, and the troll does it, *his* way, and at some cost (in machine cycles) to you.

You could write a program that handled every little aspect of disk operation itself (many game programs do exactly that) but it would be more trouble than it was worth because *every* program that runs on a computer needs to access the disk drives. Regardless of how grumpy the troll is, he *does* get the job done, and (assuming your disk drives aren't falling-down damaged) does it right every time. Can *you* guarantee that you know all there is to know about running a disk drive? (Forgive me if I have my doubts.) That is, in my opinion, what trolls are for.

The other (and more interesting thing) that operating systems do is run programs. It is here that DOS seems more godlike than troll-like. When you want to run a program on your computer, you type its name at the DOS command line. DOS goes out and searches one or more disk drives for the named program, loads it into memory at a convenient spot, sets the instruction pointer to the start of the program, and boots the CPU in the rear to get it going.

DOS then patiently waits for the program to run its course and stop. When the program stops, it hands the CPU obediently back to DOS, which again lifts a hand to its ear and listens for your next command from the command line.

As programmers, we use DOS two ways. The first is as a sort of toolkit; an army of trolls, each of which can perform some service for your program, saving your program that effort. The other is as a means of loading a program into memory and getting it going, and then catching the machine gracefully on the rebound when your program is through.

I'll be mentioning DOS again and again in this book. Everywhere you look in assembly language, you're going to see the old troll's face, so get used to it.

DOS Files: Magnetic Memory

Very simply, DOS files are memory banks stored on a magnetic coating rather than inside silicon chips. A DOS file contains a certain number of bytes stored in a specific order. One difference from RAM memory is that DOS files stored on disk are sequential-access memory banks.

A disk (floppy or hard) is a circular platform coated with magnetic plastic of some sort. In a floppy disk drive, the platform is a flexible disk of tough plastic; in a hard disk the platform is a rigid platter of aluminum. Data are stored as little magnetic disturbances on the plastic coating in a fashion similar to that used in audio cassettes and VCRs. A sensor called a *read/write head* sits very close beside the rotating platform and waits for the data to pass by.

A simplified illustration of a rotating disk device is shown in Figure 3.1. The area of the disk is divided into concentric circles called *tracks*. The tracks are further divided radially into *sectors*. A sector (typically containing 512 bytes) is the smallest unit of storage that can be read or written at one time. A DOS disk file consists of one or more sectors containing the file's data.

The read/write head is mounted on a sliding shaft that is controlled by a solenoid mechanism. The solenoid can move the head horizontally to position the head over a specific track. (In Figure 3.1, the head is positioned over track 2—counting from 0, remember!) Once the head is over a particular track, however, it has to count sectors until the sector it needs passes beneath it. The *tracks* can be accessed at random, just like bytes in the computer's memory banks, but the sectors within a track must be accessed sequentially.

The solenoid moves the read/write head horizontally to the requested track;

The head then waits for the requested sector to pass beneath it.

FIGURE 3.1   Rotating disk storage

Perhaps the single most valuable service DOS provides is handling the headache of distributing data onto the empty sectors of a disk. Programs can hand sectors of data to DOS, one at a time, and let DOS worry about where on the disk they can be placed. Each sector has a number, and DOS keeps track of what sectors belong together as a file. The first sector in a file might be stored on track 3, sector 9; the second sector might be stored on track 0, sector 4, and so on. You don't have to worry about that. When you ask for sector 0 of your file, DOS looks up its location in its private tables, and goes directly to track 3, sector 9 and brings the sector's data back to you.

Binary Files

The data stored in a file are just binary bytes and can be anything at all. Files like this, where there are *no* restrictions on the contents of a file, are called *binary files,* because they can legally contain any binary code. Like all files, a binary file consists of some whole number of sectors, with each sector (typically) containing 512 bytes. The least space any file on your disk occupies is 512 bytes; when you see the DOS DIR command tell you a file has 17 bytes in it, that's the count of how many bytes were *stored* in that file. But like a walk-in closet with only one pair of shoes in it, the rest of the sector is still there, empty but occupying space on the disk.

A binary file has no structure, but is simply a long series of binary codes divided into numbered groups of 512 bytes and stored out on the disk in a scheme that is best left to DOS to understand.

Text Files

If you've ever tried to use the TYPE command to display a binary file (like an .EXE or .COM file) to the screen, you've seen some odd things indeed. There's no reason for such files to be intelligible on the screen; they're intended for other eyes, typically the CPU's.

There is a separate class of files that is specifically restricted to containing human-readable information. These are *text files,* because they contain the letters, digits, and symbols of which printed human information (text) is composed.

Unlike binary files, text files have a particular structure. The characters in text files are divided into *lines;* a line in a text file is defined not so much by what it contains as by how it ends. A special series of invisible characters called *end-of-line markers* (EOL) tags the end of a line. The first line in a text file runs from the first byte in the file to the first EOL marker; the second line starts immediately after the first EOL marker and runs to the second EOL marker, and so on. The text characters falling between two sequential EOL markers is considered a single line.

The EOL marker is in truth not one character but two: the carriage return character (called CR by those who know and love it) followed by the linefeed character (similarly called LF). You don't see these characters on the screen as separate symbols, but you see what they do: they end the line. Anywhere a line ends in an ordinary DOS text file, you'll find a mostly invisible partnership of one CR character and one LF character hanging out.

Why two characters to end a line? Long ago, there was (and still is at hamfests, lordy) an incredible mechanical nightmare called a teletype machine. These were invented during World War II as robot typewriters that could send written messages over long distances through electrical signals that could pass over wires. It was a separate mechanical operation to return the typing carriage to the left margin of the paper (carriage return) and another to feed the paper up one line to expose the next clean line of paper to the typing carriage (line feed). A separate electrical signal was required to do each of these operations, and while I don't know why that was necessary, it has carried over into the solid-state autumn of the twentieth century in the form of those two characters, CR and LF. Not only is this a case of the tail wagging the dog, it is a case of the tail walking around twenty years after the poor dog rolled over and died.

Figure 3.2 shows how CR and LF divide what might otherwise be a single meaningless string of characters into a structured sequence of lines. It's important to understand the structure of a text file because that structure dictates how some important software tools operate, as I'll explain a little later.

The CR character is actually character 13 in the ASCII character set summarized in Appendix A. The LF character is character 10. They are two of a set of several invisible characters called *white space,* indicating their role in positioning text characters within the white space of a text page. The other whitespace characters include the space character itself (character 32)

Samwasaman.

These eleven characters by themselves
form one meaningless group.

Sam⟦CR⟧⟦LF⟧was⟦CR⟧⟦LF⟧a⟦CR⟧⟦LF⟧man.

Adding structure requires adding pairs
of invisible carriage return (CR) and
line feed (LF) characters.

Sam

was

a

man.

Displayed on your screen,
the invisible characters divide
the text into lines.

FIGURE 3.2   Structuring text into lines

the tab character (character 9) and the form feed character (character 12), which can, optionally, divide a text file further into *pages*.

Another character, the *bell character* (BEL) falls in between binary and text characters. When displayed or printed, it signals that a tone should be sounded. Back in the old teletype days, the BEL character caused the teletype machine to ring its bell. BEL characters are allowed in text files, but more and more are considered sloppy practice.

One more invisible character plays an important role in the structure of a text file, the *end of file* (EOF) marker character. Unlike EOL, EOF is a single character, ASCII character 26, sometimes written as Ctrl-Z because you will generate the EOF character by holding the control key down and pressing the Z key.

By convention, the EOF character is considered the last significant character in a text file, and DOS will ignore any characters following it, *even if the file goes on for thousands of additional bytes.* Those additional bytes will be ignored by the assembler and by most text editors.

An EOF marker can be mistakenly placed in the middle of a text file by some utilities. The most frequent source of these false EOF markers is from saving a text file to disk in a word processor program's native mode, which may write EOF characters and many other "unprintable" characters into a text file. Such native mode document files are not actually text files, but are binary files intended to be read *only* by that particular word processor.

Text Editors

Manipulating a text file is done with a program called a *text editor*. A text editor is a word processor for a program's source code files. In its simplest form, a text editor works like this: you type characters at the keyboard and they appear on the screen. When you press the Enter key, an EOL marker (the two characters CR and LF) are placed at the end of a line, and the cursor moves down to the next line.

The editor also allows you to move the cursor back up into text you've already entered in order to change it. You can delete words and whole lines and replace them with newly entered text.

Ultimately, when you decide that you're finished, you press some key like F2, or some combination of keys like Ctrl-KD, and the text editor saves the text you entered from the keyboard as a text file. This text file is the source code file you'll later present to the assembler for processing. Later, you can load that same text file back into the editor to make repairs on faulty lines that cause errors during assembly or bugs during execution.

A great many people still use their word processors as program text editors. WordStar, Word Perfect, and most of the others make acceptable text editors, as long as you remember to write your text file to disk in nondocument mode or ASCII text mode. Most true word processors embed countless strange little codes in their text files to control things like margin settings, font selections, headers and footers, soft page depth, and line breaks. These codes are not recognized ASCII characters but are binary values and actually turn the document file from a text file to a binary file. The codes will give the assembler fits. *If you write a program source code file to disk as a document file, it will not assemble.* See the word processor documentation for details on how to export a document file as a pure ASCII text file.

There are numerous text editor products on the market specifically for use by assembly language programmers. Two of the best are Brief and Epsilon. Another very good editor, Point, is often sold as an accessory with the Logitech mouse. The Sidekick notepad editor makes a perfectly reasonable text editor for assembly language work, as do the editors built into Microsoft's Quick language compilers and Borland's Turbo language compilers.

If you have no other editor, I have put one together and given it to various user groups around the country. If you can't find my JED editor anywhere, you can order it directly from me through the address on the flyleaf. JED works very much like the editor in the Turbo language products, because I produced it with the Turbo Pascal Editor Toolbox and Turbo Pascal 5.0.

Because there are so many different text editors in use among programmers, I'll be using JED as the example editor in this book. When you see a command line incorporating the name JED, keep in mind that you will have to substitute the name and command suite for whatever editor you may be using if you're not using JED.

Chapter 4 describes JED in detail. JED has the advantage (over editors like Brief and Epsilon) of being simple. I designed it for beginning assembly language programmers, and if you've ever used any of the Turbo language products, JED will feel just like home.

3.3 ◆ Compilers and Assemblers

With the understanding of DOS files and text editors under your belt, you can come to understand the nature of two important kinds of programs, *compilers* and *assemblers*. Both fall into a category of computer program that we call *translators*.

A translator is a program that accepts human-readable source code files and generates some kind of binary file. The binary file could be an executable program file that the CPU can understand, or it can be a font file, a compressed binary data file, or any of a hundred other types of binary file.

Program translators are translators that generate machine instructions that the CPU can understand. A program translator reads a source code file line by line and writes a binary file of machine instructions that accomplishes the computer actions that the source code file describes. This binary file is called an *object code file*.

A compiler is a program translator that reads source code files written in higher-level languages like C and Pascal and outputs object code files.

An assembler is a special type of compiler. It, too, is a program translator that reads source code files and outputs object code files for the CPU. An assembler, however, is a translator designed specifically to translate what we call *assembly language* into object code. In the same sense that a language compiler for Pascal or C compiles a source code file to an object code file, we say that an assembler *assembles* an assembly language source code file to an object code file. The process, one of translation, is similar in both cases. Assembly language, however, has an overwhelmingly important characteristic that sets it apart from compilers: *total control over the object code.*

Assembly Language

Some people define assembly language as a language in which one line of source code generates one machine instruction. This has never been literally true because some lines in an assembly language source code file are instructions to the translator program and do not generate machine instructions.

> **Assembly language is a language that allows total control over *every individual machine instruction* generated by the translator program.**

Pascal or C compilers, on the other hand, make a multitude of invisible and unalterable decisions about how a given language statement will be translated into a machine instruction. For example, the following single Pascal instruction assigns a value of 42 to a numeric variable called **I:**

```
I := 42;
```

When a Pascal compiler reads this line, it outputs a series of four or five machine instructions that take the value 42 and store it in memory at a location encoded by the name **I.** Normally, the programmer has *no idea* what these four or five instructions actually are, and you have utterly no way of changing them, even if you happen to know a sequence of machine instructions that is faster and more efficient than the sequence the compiler uses. The Pascal compiler has its own method of generating machine instructions and you have no choice but to accept what it writes to disk to accomplish the Pascal statements in the source code file.

An assembler, however, has at least one line in the source code file for every machine instruction it generates. It has more lines than that to handle numerous other things, but *every* machine instruction in the final object code file is controlled by a corresponding line in the source code file.

Each of the CPU's many machine instructions has a corresponding *mnemonic* in assembly language. As the word suggests, these mnemonics began as devices to help programmers remember a particular machine instruction. For example, the mnemonic for machine instruction 9CH, which pushes the flags register onto the stack, is **PUSHF.**

When you write your source code file in assembly language, you will arrange series of mnemonics, typically one mnemonic to a source code file text line. A portion of a source code file might look like this:

```
MOV  AH,12H      ; 12H is Motor Information Service
MOV  AL,03H      ; 03H is Return Current Speed function
XOR  BH,BH       ; Zero BH for safety's sake
INT  71H         ; Call Motor Services Interrupt
```

Here, the words **MOV, XOR,** and **INT** are mnemonics. The numbers and other items to the immediate right of each mnemonic are that mnemonic's *operands*. There are various kinds of operands for the various machine instructions, and some instructions (like **PUSHF** mentioned above) have no operands at all. We'll thoroughly describe each instruction's operands later.

Taken together, a mnemonic and its operand or operands are called an *instruction*. This is the word we'll be using most of the time in this book to indicate the human-readable equivalent of one of the CPU's pure binary machine code instructions. To talk about the binary code specifically, we'll always refer to a *machine* instruction.

The assembler's most important job is to read lines from the source code file and write machine instructions to an object code file (see Figure 3.3).

Mnemonic   Operands   Comment

MOV AX,BX	; Put byte count into AX

The assembler reads a line like this one from the source code file
and writes the equivalent machine instruction to the object code file:

8BH 0C3H

FIGURE 3.3   What the assembler does

Comments.   To the right of each instruction is some information starting
with a semicolon. This information is called a *comment,* and its purpose
should be obvious: to cast some light on what the associated assembly
language instruction does. The instruction **MOV AH,12H** places the value
12H in register AH—but *why?* The comment provides the why.

Far more than in any other programming language, comments are critical to the success of assembly language programs. My own recommendation
is that *every* instruction in the source code file should have a comment to
its right.

Structurally, a comment starts with the first semicolon on a line and
continues to the EOL marker at the end of that line. This is one instance
where understanding how a text file is structured is very important, because
in assembly language, a comment ends at the end of a line. In most other
languages, comments are placed *between* pairs of comment delimiters like
(***** and ***)**, and EOL markers are ignored.

> **Comments begin at semicolons and end at EOL.**

Beware write-only source code! This is as good a time as any to point out a serious problem with assembly language. The instructions themselves are almost vanishingly terse, and while each instruction states what it does, there is *nothing* to indicate a context within which that instruction operates. With some skill and discipline, you can build that context into your Pascal or BASIC code, but in assembly language you can *only* add context through comments.

Without context, assembly language starts to turn into what we call write-only code. It can happen like this: on November 1, in the heat of creation, you crank out about 300 instructions in a short utility program that does something important. On January 1 you go back to add a feature to the program and discover that *you no longer remember how it works!* The individual instructions are all correct, but knowledge of how it all came together and how it works from a height have vanished under Christmas memories and eight weeks of doing other things. In other words, you *wrote* it, but you can no longer read it or change it. Voila! Write-only code.

Comment like crazy. Each individual line should have a comment, and every so often in a sizeable source code file, take a few lines out and make entire lines into comments, explaining what the code is up to at this point in its execution.

While comments do take room in your source code disk files, they are *not* copied into your object code files, and a program with loads of comments runs *exactly* as fast as the same program with no comments at all.

You will be making a considerable investment in time and energy when you write assembly language programs. It's more difficult than just about any other way of writing programs, and if you don't comment you may end up having to simply toss out hundreds of lines of inexplicable code and write it again, *from scratch.*

Work smart. Comment 'til you drop.

Object Code and Linkers

There's no reason at all why an assembler could not read a source code file and write out a finished, executable program file as its object code file. Most assemblers don't work this way, however. Object code files produced by the major assemblers are a sort of intermediate step between source code and executable program. This intermediate step is a type of binary file called a *relocatable object module,* or (more simply) an .OBJ file, after the file extension used by the assembler when it creates the file. For example, a source code file called FOO.ASM would be assembled into an object file called FOO.OBJ. (The relocatable portion of the concept is crucial, but a little too advanced for this chapter. More on this later.) .OBJ files cannot be run as programs. An additional step, called *linking,* is necessary to turn .OBJ files into executable program files.

The reason for .OBJ files as intermediate steps is that a single large source code file may be cut up into numerous smaller source code files to keep them manageable in size and complexity. The assembler assembles the various component fragments separately, and the several resulting .OBJ files are woven together into a single, executable program file. This process is shown in Figure 3.4.

When you're first starting out, it's unlikely that you will be writing programs spread out across several source code files. Even if you only have one source code file, however, you must still use the linker to change the single .OBJ file into an executable program file, as I'll explain a little later.

The larger your programs become, however, the more time can be saved by cutting them up into components. There are two reasons for this.

1. You can move tested, proven routines into separate libraries and link them into any program you write that might need them. This way, you can reuse code over and over again and not build the same old wheels every time you begin a new programming project in assembly language.

2. Once portions of a program are tested and found to be correct, there's no need to waste time assembling them over and over again along with newer, untested portions of a program. Once a major program gets into the tens of thousands of lines of code (and you'll get there sooner than you might think) you can save an *enormous* amount of time by only assembling the portion of a program that you are currently working on, and linking the finished portions into the final program without reassembling the whole thing every time.

Executable Program Files

The linker program can be seen as a kind of translator program but its major role is in combining multiple object code files into a single executable program file. This executable file is sometimes called an .EXE file, from the file extension that the linker appends to the file's name. For example, a source code file named FOO.ASM would be assembled to an object code file named FOO.OBJ, which would then be processed by the linker to an executable program file called FOO.EXE. The executable file can be run by typing its name at the DOS prompt.

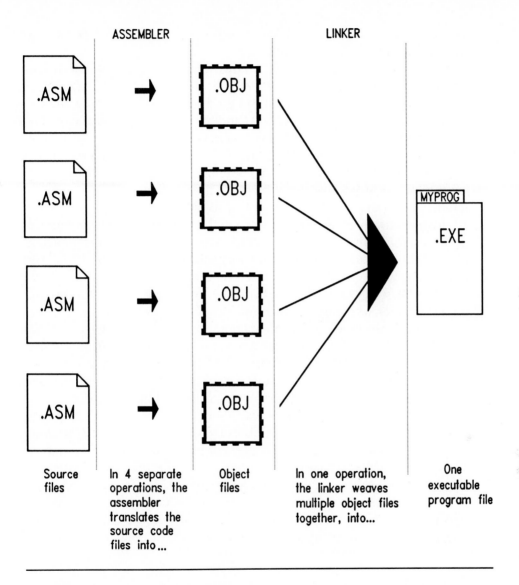

ASSEMBLER   LINKER

.ASM

.ASM

.ASM

.ASM

.OBJ

.OBJ

.OBJ

.OBJ

MYPROG

.EXE

Source
files

In 4 separate
operations, the
assembler
translates the
source code
files into...

Object
files

In one operation,
the linker weaves
multiple object files
together, into...

One
executable
program file

FIGURE 3.4   The assembler and linker

Real Assembler Products: MASM and TASM

For quite a few years there was only one assembler product in general use
for the PC, Microsoft's Macro Assembler, which is better known as MASM.
MASM is an enormously popular program and has established a standard

for assembler operation on the PC. The source code in this book is all designed to be assembled by MASM.

MASM is by no means perfect, however, and in 1988 Borland International released their answer to MASM in the form of Turbo Assembler, which was quickly christened *TASM* by syllable-conserving programmers. TASM is a great deal faster than MASM and has numerous advanced features that I won't be able to describe in this book. At the level we're describing in this book, however, MASM and TASM are totally compatible in that they will assemble identical source code files identically. MASM and TASM are the two most popular assemblers for the '86 family of CPUs, and the information in this book can be applied to either assembler.

I won't, however, attempt to describe the two assemblers' operation in detail. There are many differences in the way the two assemblers function, and you'll have to delve into the manuals to get the full story. Very fortunately, when you're first starting out, there isn't a whole lot to using either TASM or MASM, and I'll describe the simple commands for invoking each assembler where appropriate.

The most recent releases of MASM now come with their own text editor, but for years MASM was editorless and you had to supply your own editor. TASM currently does not come with a text editor, so if you're a TASM user you'll have to come up with a text editor on your own. I recommend using something simple like my JED editor described in Chapter 4.

Both MASM and TASM come with their own special debugging tools called *debuggers.* MASM's debugger is called *CodeView,* and TASM's debugger is called *Turbo Debugger.* Both are enormously sophisticated programs, and I won't be discussing either in this book, in part because of their complexity but mostly because there is a debugger shipped with every copy of PC DOS. This debugger, simply named DEBUG, is more than enough debugger to cut your teeth on and will get you familiar enough with debugger theory to move up to CodeView or Turbo Debugger later on. I'll describe DEBUG much more fully in Section 3.5.

Setting up a Working Subdirectory

The process of creating and perfecting assembly language programs involves a lot of different kinds of DOS files and numerous separate software tools. Unlike the tidy, fully-integrated environments offered by the Turbo and Quick languages, assembly language development comes in a great many pieces with (as it were) some assembly required.

I recommend setting up a development subdirectory on your hard disk and putting all of the various pieces in that subdirectory. Create and move into a subdirectory called ASM by using these DOS commands:

```
MD ASM
CD ASM
```

Then, from within ASM, copy the following files or groups of files in the subdirectory:

1. Your text editor. If you're using JED (see Chapter 4) you need only copy the file JED.EXE. If you're using a memory-resident editor like Sidekick's notepad, you may not need to copy any editor program at all into your development subdirectory because it will be memory resident at boot-time. For other editors like Brief, you'll need to consult the editor's vendor documentation.

2. Your assembler. Again, consult the vendor's documentation to see what files are necessary to assemble a source code file. Usually, there is a single executable file like MASM.EXE or TASM.EXE and perhaps some help files or configuration files. The older versions of MASM stood alone as MASM.EXE and needed nothing else in the subdirectory to operate. Similarly, the first release of TASM allows the file TASM.EXE to work alone.

3. Your linker. Both MASM and TASM include their own linkers. MASM's linker program is LINK.EXE. TASM's linker is TLINK.EXE. Copy the appropriate file. Both linkers stand alone.

4. DEBUG. On your DOS distribution disk (or in your DOS subdirectory, if you have a DOS subdirectory) should be a file called DEBUG.COM. Files with a .COM extension are, like .EXE files, executable programs. The .COM programs are slightly old fashioned and not used much anymore since Turbo Pascal 3.0 was supplanted by version 4.0 in 1987. Copy DEBUG.COM into your development subdirectory.

5. Odds and ends. A listing program for printing your source code files to paper, while not essential, can be very helpful. Add anything else that may be helpful, keeping in mind that a *lot* of files are generated during assembly language development, and you should strive to keep unnecessary clutter to a minimum.

3.4   ◆ The Assembly Language Development Process

As you can see, there are a lot of different file types and a fair number of programs involved in the cycle of writing, assembling, and testing an assembly language program. The cycle itself sounds more complex than it is. I've drawn you a map to help you keep your bearings during the discussions in this chapter. Figure 3.5 shows the assembly language development process in a "view from a height." At first glance it may look like a map of the Los Angeles freeway system, but in reality the flow is fairly straightforward. Follow along on a quick tour.

Assembling the Source Code File

The text editor first creates a new text file, and later changes that same text file as you modify and perfect your assembly language program. As a convention, most assembly language source code files are given a file extension of .ASM. In other words, for a program named FOO, the assembly language source code file would be named FOO.ASM.

It is possible to use file extensions other than .ASM, but I feel that using the .ASM extension can eliminate some confusion by allowing you to tell at a glance what a file is for just by looking at its name. All told, about nine different kinds of files can be involved during assembly language development. (We're only going to speak of four or five in this book.) Each type of file will have its own standard file extension. Anything that will help you keep all that complexity in line will be worth the (admittedly) rigid confines of a standard naming convention.

As you can see from the flow in Figure 3.5, the editor produces a text file, which we show as having the .ASM extension. This file is then passed to the assembler program itself for translation to a relocatable object module file with an extension of .OBJ.

Invoking the assembler is very simple. For simple stand-alone assembly language programs in Turbo Assembler, it's nothing more than the name of the assembler followed by the name of the program to be assembled

    C:\ASM>TASM FOO

For Microsoft's MASM, you must put a semicolon on the end of the command. This tells MASM that no further prompts are necessary

    C:\ASM>MASM FOO;

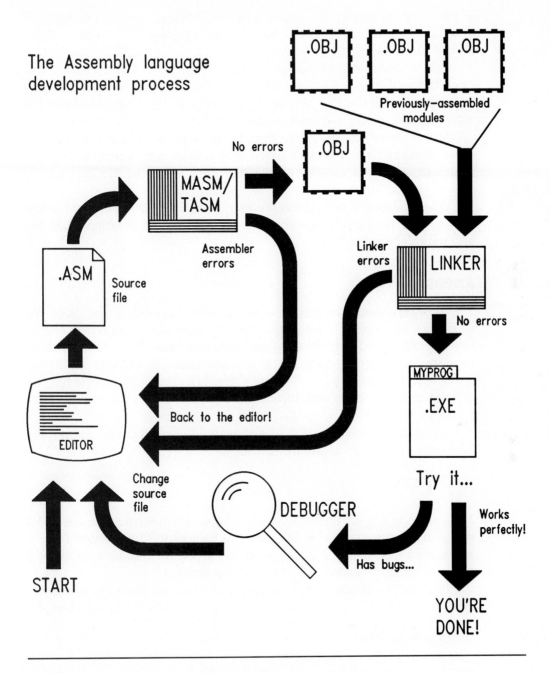

FIGURE 3.5   The assembly language development process

If you omit the semicolon, nothing bad will happen, but MASM will ask you for the names of several other files and you will have to press Enter several times to select the defaults.

DOS will load the assembler from disk and run it. The assembler will open the source code file you named after the name of the assembler and begin processing the file. Almost immediately, it will create an object file with the same name as the source file, but with an .OBJ extension.

As the assembler reads lines from the source code file, it will examine them, construct the binary machine instructions the source code lines represent, and then write those machine instructions to the object code file.

When the assembler detects the EOF marker signalling the end of the source code file, it will close both source code file and object code file and return control to DOS.

Assembler Errors

The previous three paragraphs describe what happens if the .ASM file is *correct*. By correct, I mean the file is completely comprehensible to the assembler and can be translated into machine instructions without the assembler getting confused. If the assembler encounters something it doesn't understand when it reads a line from the source code file, we call the misunderstood text an error and the assembler displays an *error message*.

For example, the following line of assembly language will confuse the assembler and summon an error message,

    MOV AX,VX

The reason is simple: there's no such thing as a *VX*. What came out as *VX* was actually intended to be *BX*, which is the name of a register. (The *V* key is right next to the *B* key and can be struck by mistake without your fingers necessarily knowing that they done wrong.)

Typos are by far the easiest kind of error to spot. Others that take some study to find involve transgressions of the assembler's rules. For example

    MOV ES,0FF00H

This looks like it should be correct because ES is a real register and 0FF00H is a real 16-bit quantity that will fit into ES. However, among the multitude of rules in the fine print of the '86 family of assemblers is the one that you cannot directly move an immediate value (any number like 0FF00H) directly into a segment register like ES, DS, SS, or CS. It simply isn't part of the CPU's machinery to do that. Instead, you must first move the immediate value into a register like AX, and *then* move AX into ES.

You don't have to remember these details here; we'll go into the rules later on. For now, simply understand that some things that look reasonable are simply against the rules and are considered an error.

There are much, *much* more difficult errors that involve inconsistencies between two otherwise legitimate lines of source code. I won't offer any examples here, but I want to point out that errors can be truly ugly, hidden things that can take a lot of study and torn hair to find. Toto, we are definitely *not* in BASIC anymore.

The error messages vary from assembler to assembler, but they may not always be as helpful as you might hope. The error TASM displays upon encountering the "VX" typo follows:

```
Turbo Assembler Version 1.0   Copyright (c) 1988 by Borland International

Assembling file:      FOO.ASM
**Error** FOO.ASM(74) Undefined symbol: VX
Error messages:       1
Warning messages:     None
Remaining memory:     395k
```

This is pretty plain, assuming you know what a *symbol* is. The error message TASM will present when you try to load an immediate value into ES is less helpful:

```
Turbo Assembler Version 1.0   Copyright (c) 1988 by Borland International

Assembling file:      IBYTECPY.ASM
**Error** IBYTECPY.ASM(74) Illegal use of segment register
Error messages:       1
Warning messages:     None
Remaining memory:     395k
```

The assembler will let you know you're guilty of performing illegal acts with a segment register, but that's it. *You* have to know what's legal and what's illegal to really understand what you did wrong. As in running a stop sign, ignorance of the law is no excuse.

> **Assembler error messages do not absolve you from understanding the CPU's or the assembler's rules.**

I hope I don't frighten you too terribly by warning you that for more abstruse errors, the error messages may be almost no help *at all*.

You may make (or *will* make; let's get real) more than one error in writing your source code files. The assembler will display more than one error message in such cases, but it may not necessarily display an error for *every* error present in the source code file. At some point, multiple errors confuse the assembler so thoroughly that it cannot tell right from wrong anymore. While it's true that the assembler reads and translates source code files line by line, there is a cumulative picture of the final assembly language program that is built up over the course of the whole assembly process. If this picture is too shot full of errors, in time the whole picture collapses.

The assembler will stop and return to DOS, having printed numerous error messages. *Start at the first one* and keep going. If the following ones don't make sense, fix the first one or two and assemble again.

Back to the Editor

The way to fix errors is to load the .ASM file back into your text editor and start hunting up the error. This loopback is shown in Figure 3.5.

The error message will almost always contain a line number. Move the cursor to that line number and start looking for the false and the fanciful. If you find the error immediately, fix it and start looking for the next.

Here's a little logistical snag: how do you make a list of the error messages on paper so that you don't have to memorize them or scribble them down on paper with a pencil? You may or may not be aware that you can *redirect* the assembler's error message displays to a DOS text file on disk.

It works like this: invoke the assembler just as you normally would, but add the *redirection operator* > and the name of the text file to which you want the error messages sent. If you were assembling FOO.ASM with TASM and wanted your error messages written out to a disk file named ERRORS.TXT, you would invoke TASM this way:

```
C:\ASM>TASM FOO > ERRORS.TEXT
```

Here, error messages will be sent to ERRORS.TXT in the current DOS directory C:\ASM. When you use redirection, the output is *not* displayed on the screen. The stream of text from TASM that you would ordinarily see is quite literally steered in its entirety to another place, the file ERRORS.TXT.

Once the assembly process is done, the DOS prompt will appear again. You can then print the ERRORS.TXT file on your printer and have a handy summary of all that the assembler discovered was wrong with your source code file.

Assembler Warnings

As taciturn a creature as an assembler may appear to be, it genuinely tries to help you any way it can. One way it tries to help is by displaying *warning messages* during the assembly process. These warning messages are a monumental puzzle to beginning assembly language programmers. Are they errors or aren't they? Can I ignore them or should I fool with the source code until they go away?

There is no clear answer—sorry about that.

Warnings are the assembler acting as an experienced consultant and hinting that something in your source code is a little dicey. Now, in the nature of assembly language, you may fully *intend* that the source code be dicey. In an '86 CPU, dicey code may be the only way to do something fast enough or to do it at all. The critical factor is that you had better know what you're doing.

The most common generator of warning messages is doing something that goes against the assembler's default conditions and assumptions. If you're a beginner doing ordinary, 100% by-the-book sorts of things, you should crack your assembler reference manual and figure out why the assembler is tut-tutting you. Ignoring a warning *may* cause peculiar bugs to occur later on during program testing or, ignoring a warning message may have no undesirable consequences at all. I feel, however, that it's always better to know what's going on.

> **Ignore a warning message only if you know *exactly* what it means.**

In other words, until you understand why you're getting a warning message, treat it as though it were an error message. Only once you fully understand why it's there and what it means should you try to make the decision whether to ignore it or not.

In summary, the first part of the assembly language development process (as shown in Figure 3.5) is a loop. You must edit your source code file, assemble it, and return to the editor to fix errors until the assembler spots no further errors. *You cannot continue until the assembler gives your source code file a clean bill of health.*

When no further errors are found, the assembler will write an .OBJ file to disk, and you will be ready to go on to the next step.

Linking

Theoretically, an assembler could generate an .EXE executable program file directly from your source code .ASM file. Some obscure assemblers have been able to do this, but it's not a common assembler feature.

What actually happens is that the assembler writes an intermediate object code file with an .OBJ extension to disk. You can't run this .OBJ file, even though it contains all the machine instructions that your assembly language source code file specified. The .OBJ file needs to be processed by another translator program, the linker.

The linker performs a number of operations on the .OBJ file, most of which would be meaningless to you at this point. The most obvious task the linker does is to weave several .OBJ files into a single .EXE executable program file. Creating an assembly language program from multiple .ASM files is called *modular assembly.*

Why create multiple .OBJ files when writing a single executable program? One of two major reasons is size. A middling assembly language application might be 50,000 lines long. Cutting that single monolithic .ASM file up into multiple 8,000 line .ASM files would make the individual .ASM files smaller and much easier to understand.

The other reason is to avoid assembling completed portions of the program every time any *part* of the program is assembled. One thing you'll be doing is writing assembly language *procedures,* small detours from the main run of steps and tests that can be taken from anywhere within the assembly language program. Once you write and perfect a procedure, you can tuck it away in an .ASM file with other completed procedures, assemble it, and then simply link the resulting .OBJ file into the working .ASM file. The alternative is to waste time by reassembling perfected source code over and over again every time you assemble the main portion of the program.

This is shown in Figure 3.5. In the upper right corner is a row of .OBJ files. These .OBJ files were assembled earlier from correct .ASM files, yielding binary disk files containing ready-to-go machine instructions. When the linker links the .OBJ file produced from your in-progress .ASM file, it adds in the previously assembled .OBJ files, which are called *modules.* The single .EXE file that the linker writes to disk contains the machine instructions from all of the .OBJ files handed to the linker when the linker is invoked.

Once the in-progress .ASM file is completed and made correct, its .OBJ module can be put up on the rack with the others and added to the next in-progress .ASM source code file. Little by little you construct your application program out of the modules you build one at a time.

A very important bonus is that some of the procedures in an .OBJ module can be used in a future assembly language program that hasn't even been begun yet. Creating such libraries of toolkit procedures can be an extraordinarily effective way to save time by reusing code over and over again, without even passing it through the assembler again!

It should be kept in mind that the linker must be used even when you have only *one* .OBJ file. Connecting multiple modules is only one of many essential things the linker does. To produce an executable .EXE file, you *must* invoke the linker, even if your program is a little thing contained in only one .ASM and, hence, one .OBJ file.

Invoking the linker is again done from the DOS command line. Each assembler typically has its own linker. MASM's linker is called LINK and TASM's is called TLINK. Like the assembler, the linker understands a number of commands and directives that I can't describe exhaustively here. Read your assembler manuals carefully.

For single-module programs, there's nothing complex to be done. Linking our hypothetical FOO.OBJ object file into an .EXE file using TLINK is done like this:

```
C:\ASM>TLINK FOO
```

If you're using MASM, using LINK is done much the same way. Again, as with MASM, you need to place a semicolon at the end of the command to avoid a series of questions about various linker defaults.

```
C:\ASM>LINK FOO;
```

Linking multiple files involves naming each file on the command line. With TLINK, you simply name each .OBJ file on the command line after the word TLINK, with a space between each file name. You do *not* have to include the .OBJ extension—TLINK assumes that all modules to be linked end in .OBJ:

C:\ASM>TLINK FOO BAR BAS

Under MASM, you do the same thing, except that you place a plus sign (+) between each of the .OBJ file names:

C:\ASM>LINK FOO+BAR+BAS

In both cases, the name of the .EXE file produced will be the name of the first .OBJ file named, with the .EXE extension replacing the .OBJ extension.

Linker Errors

As with the assembler, the linker may discover problems as it weaves multiple .OBJ files together into a single .EXE file. Linker errors are subtler than assembler errors and are usually harder to find. Fortunately, they are rarer and not as easy to make.

As with assembler errors, when you are presented with a linker error you have to return to the editor and figure out what the problem is. Once you've identified the problem (or *think* you have) and changed something in the source code file to fix the problem, you must reassemble and relink the program to see if the linker error is solved. Until it does, you have to go back to the editor, try something else, and reassemble and relink again.

If possible, avoid doing this by trial and error. Read your assembler and linker manuals. Understand what you're doing. The more you understand what's going on within the assembler and the linker, the easier it will be to determine what is giving the linker fits.

Testing the .EXE File

If you receive no linker errors, the linker will create and fill a single .EXE file with the machine instructions present in all of the .OBJ files named on the linker command line. The .EXE file is your executable program. You can run it by simply naming it on the DOS command line:

C:\ASM>FOO

When you invoke your program in this way, one of two things will happen: the program will work as you intended, or you'll be confronted with the effects of one or more program *bugs*. A bug is anything in a program that doesn't work the way you want it to. This makes a bug somewhat more subjective than an error. One person might think red characters displayed on a blue background is a bug, while another might consider it a clever New Age feature and be quite pleased. Settling bug versus feature conflicts like this is up to you. Consensus is called for here, with fistfights only as a last resort.

There are bugs and there are *bugs*. When working in assembly language, it's quite common for a bug to completely blow the machine away, which is less violent than some think. A *system crash* has occurred when the machine sits there mutely and will not respond to the keyboard. You may have to press Ctrl-Alt-Delete to reboot the system, or, worse, power down and then power up again by flipping the power switch off, waiting ten seconds, and switching it on again. Be ready for this—it *will* happen to you, sooner and more often than you will care for.

Figure 3.5 announces the exit of the assembly language development process as happening when your program works perfectly. A very serious question is, how do you know when it works perfectly? Simple programs assembled while learning the language may be easy enough to test in a minute or two. But any program that accomplishes anything useful at all will take *hours* of testing at *minimum*. A serious and ambitious application could take weeks—or months. A program that takes various kinds of input values and produces various kinds of output should be tested with as many different combinations of input values as possible and every possible output should be examined every time.

Finding every last bug is considered by some to be an impossible ideal. Perhaps—but you should strive to come as close as possible, as efficiently as possible. I'll have a lot more to say about bugs and debugging throughout the rest of this book.

Errors versus Bugs

In the interest of keeping the Babel effect at bay, I think it's important to carefully draw the distinction between errors and bugs. An *error* is something wrong with your source code file that either the assembler or the linker kicks out as unacceptable. An error prevents the assembly or link process from going to completion and will thus prevent a final .EXE file from being produced.

A bug, by contrast, is a problem discovered during the *execution* of a program under DOS. Bugs are not detected by either the assembler or the linker. Bugs can be benign, such as a mispelled word in a screen message or a line positioned on the wrong screen row, or a bug can make your DOS session run off into the bushes and not come back.

Both errors and bugs require that you go back to the text editor and change something in your source code file. The difference here is that most errors are reported with a line number telling you where to go in your source code file to fix the problem. Bugs, on the other hand, are left as an exercise for the student. You have to hunt them down and neither the assembler nor the linker will give you much in the line of clues.

Debuggers and Debugging

The final, and almost certainly the most painful part of the assembly language development process is debugging. *Debugging* is simply the systematic process by which bugs are located and corrected. A *debugger* is a utility program designed specifically to help you locate and identify bugs.

Debugger programs are among the most mysterious and difficult to understand of all programs. Debuggers are part x-ray machine and part magnifying glass. A debugger loads into memory with your program and remains in memory, side-by-side with your program. The debugger then puts tendrils down into both DOS and into your program, and enables some truly peculiar things to be done.

One of the problems with debugging computer programs is that they operate so quickly. Thousands of machine instructions can be executed in a single second, and if one of those instructions isn't quite right, it's past and gone long before you can identify which one it is by staring at the screen. A debugger allows you to execute the machine instructions in a program *one at a time,* allowing you to pause indefinitely between each one to examine the effects of the last instruction on the screen. The debugger also lets you look at the contents of any location in memory, and the values stored in any register, during that pause between instructions.

As mentioned previously, both MASM and TASM are packaged with their own advanced debuggers. MASM's CodeView and TASM's Turbo Debugger are brutally powerful (and hellishly complicated) creatures that require manuals considerably thicker than this book. For this reason, I won't try to explain how to use either CodeView or Turbo Debugger.

Very fortunately, every copy of DOS is shipped with a more limited but perfectly good debugger called DEBUG. DEBUG can do nearly anything that a beginner would want from a debugger, and in this book we'll do our debugging with DEBUG.

3.5 ◆ DEBUG and How to Use It

The assembler and the linker are rather single-minded programs. As translators, they do only one thing: translate. This involves reading data from one file and writing a translation of that data into another file.

That's all a translator needs to do. The job isn't necessarily an easy thing for the translator to do, but it's easy to describe and understand. Debuggers, by contrast, are like the electrician's little bag of tools; they do lots of different things in a great many different ways, and take plenty of explanation and considerable practice to master.

In this chapter I'll introduce you to DEBUG, a program that will allow you to *single-step* your assembly language programs and examine both the program's and the machine's innards between each and every machine instruction. This section is only an introduction—DEBUG is learned best by doing, and you'll be both using and learning DEBUG's numerous powers all through the rest of this book. By providing you with an overview of what DEBUG does here, you'll be more capable of integrating its features into your general understanding of the assembly language development process as we examine it through the rest of the book.

DEBUG's Bag of Tricks

It's well worth taking a page or so simply to describe what sorts of things DEBUG can do before actually showing you how they're done. It's actually quite a list:

◆ **Display or change memory and files.** Your programs will both exist in and affect memory and DEBUG can show you *any* part of memory, which implies that it can show you any part of any program or binary file as well. It displays memory as a series of hexadecimal values, with a corresponding display of any printable ASCII characters to its right; I'll show you some examples a little later on. In addition to seeing the contents of memory, you can change those contents as well, and if the contents of memory represent a file, you can write the changed file back out to disk.

◆ **Display or change the contents of all CPU registers.** CPU registers allow you to work *very* quickly and you should use them as much as you can. This means that you need to see what's going on in the registers while you use them, and with one command DEBUG can display the contents of all machine registers and flags at one time. If you want to change the contents of a register while stepping through a program's machine instructions, you can do that as well.

♦ **Fill a region of memory with a single value.** If you have an area of memory that you want blanked out, DEBUG will allow you to fill that area of memory with any character or binary value.

♦ **Search memory for sequences of binary values.** You can search any area of memory for a specific sequence of characters or binary values. These could include names stored in memory or sequences of machine instructions. This allows you to examine or change something that you know exists somewhere in memory without first knowing where it is located.

♦ **Assemble new machine instructions into memory.** DEBUG contains a simple assembler that does much of what MASM and TASM can do, one machine instruction at a time. If you want to replace a machine instruction somewhere within your program, you can type **MOV AX,BX** rather than having to look up and type 8BH 0C3H.

♦ **"Un-assemble" binary machine instructions into their mnemonics and operands.** The flip side of the last feature is also possible. DEBUG can take the two hexadecimal values 8BH and 0C3H and tell you that they represent the assembly language mnemonic **MOV AX,BX.** This feature is utterly essential when you need to trace a program in operation and understand what is happening when the next 2 bytes in memory are read into the CPU and executed. If you don't know what machine instruction those 2 bytes represent, you'll be totally lost.

♦ **Single-step a program under test.** Finally, DEBUG's most valuable skill is to run a program one machine instruction at a time, pausing between each instruction. During this pause you can look at or change memory, look at or change registers, search for things in memory, patch the program by replacing existing machine instructions with new ones, and so on. This is what you'll do most of the time with DEBUG.

Taking DEBUG for a Spin

DEBUG can be a pretty forbidding character; it is terse to the point of being mute. You'll be spending a lot of time standing on DEBUG's shoulders and looking around, however, so you'd best get used to it now.

The easiest way to start is to use DEBUG to load a file into memory and examine it. On the listings disk associated with this book is a file called SAM.TXT. It's an ordinary DOS text file whose contents are used to demonstrate the line structuring of text files with CR and LF (see Figure 3.1). If you don't have the listings disk, you can simply load your text editor and enter the following lines:

```
Sam
was
a
man.
```

Make sure you press Enter after the period at the end of *man,* then save the file to disk as SAM.TXT.

Let's lay SAM.TXT out on DEBUG's dissection table and take a look at his innards. DEBUG will load itself and the file of your choice into memory at the same time with only one command. Type DEBUG followed by the name of the file you want to load.

```
C:\ASM>DEBUG SAM.TXT
```

Make sure you use the full file name. Some programs like MASM and TASM will allow you to use only the first part of the file name and assume a file extension like .ASM, but DEBUG requires the full file name.

Like old Cal Coolidge, DEBUG doesn't say much and never more than he has to. Unless DEBUG can't find SAM.TXT, all it will respond with is a single dash character (–) as its prompt, indicating that all is well and that DEBUG is awaiting a command.

Looking at a Hex Dump

Looking at SAM.TXT's interior is easy. Just type a D at the dash prompt (think *D*ump). DEBUG will obediently display a hex dump of the first 128 bytes of memory containing the contents of SAM.TXT read from disk. The hexadecimal numbers will probably look bewilderingly mysterious, but to their right you'll see the comforting words *Sam was a man* in a separate area of the screen. To help a little, I've taken the hex dump of SAM.TXT as you'll see it on your screen and annotated it in Figure 3.6.

This is a *hex dump.* It has three parts: The leftmost part on the screen is the address of the start of each line of the dump. Each line contains 16 bytes. An address has two parts, and you'll notice that the left part of the address does not change while the right part is 16 greater at the start of each succeeding line. The '86 family's two-part addresses are a source of considerable confusion and aggravation, and I'll examine them in detail in Chapter 5. For now, ignore the unchanging part of the address and consider

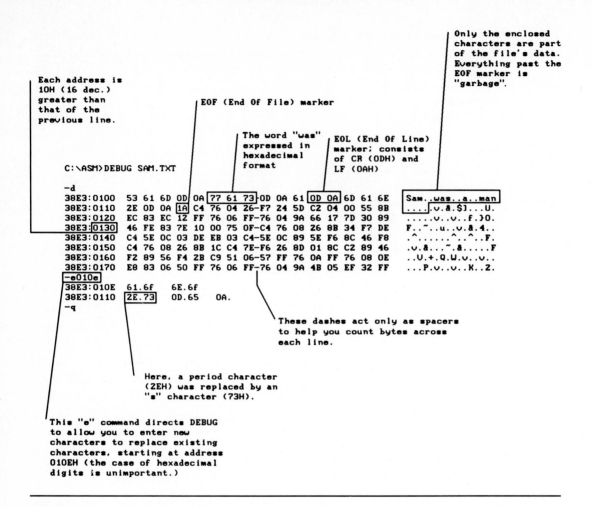

FIGURE 3.6   A hex dump of SAM.TXT

the part that changes to be a count of the bytes on display, starting with 100H.

The part to the right of the address is the hexadecimal representation of the 128 bytes of memory being displayed. The part to the right of the hexadecimal values are those same 128 bytes of memory displayed as ASCII characters. Now, not all binary values have corresponding printable ASCII characters. Any invisible or unprintable characters are shown as period (.) characters.

This can be confusing. The last displayable character in SAM.TXT *is* a period, and is actually the very first character on the second line of the hex dump. The ASCII side shows four identical periods in a row. To find out what's a period and what's simply a nondisplayable character, you must look back to the hexadecimal side and recognize the ASCII code for a period, which is 2EH.

This is a good place to point out that an ASCII table of characters and their codes is an utterly essential thing to have. Borland's Sidekick includes a very good table, and it's always waiting in memory only a keystroke away. If you don't have Sidekick, I'd advise you to take a photocopy of the ASCII table provided in Appendix B and keep it close at hand.

Memory "Garbage"

Take a long, close look at the hexadecimal equivalents of the characters in SAM.TXT. Notice that SAM.TXT is a very short file (20 bytes), but that 128 bytes are displayed. Look for the EOF (end of file) marker on the second line. Character 1AH is always considered the last byte of any text file. All the other bytes after the EOF marker are called *garbage*, and that's pretty much what they are: random bytes that existed in memory before SAM.TXT rode in from disk. DEBUG works only from memory and displays hex dumps of memory only in 128-byte chunks. Only the first 20 bytes of SAM.TXT are significant information, but DEBUG obligingly shows you what's in memory well beyond the end of SAM's data.

The bytes are probably not entirely random, but instead may be part of the code or data left over from the last program to be loaded and executed in that area of memory. Because the garbage bytes fall after the EOF marker, you can safely ignore them, but you should know just what they are and why they appear in your hex dump. You might occasionally see recognizable data strings from other programs in memory garbage and wonder how they got into your current program. *They didn't get into your current program.* They were just there and now show through beyond the end of the file you last loaded under DEBUG. Knowing where legitimate information ends and where garbage begins is always important and not usually as clear-cut as here.

Changing Memory with DEBUG

DEBUG can easily change bytes in memory, whether they are part of a file loaded from disk or not. The DEBUG command to change bytes is the E command. (Think, *E*nter new data.) You can use the E command to change some of the data in SAM.TXT. Part of this process is shown in Figure 3.6.

Notice the command line

```
-e 010e
```

To taciturn Mr. Debug, this means "begin accepting entered bytes at address 010EH." I show the lower-case *es* used in the command to make the point that DEBUG is not sensitive to case, *even for letters used as hexadecimal digits.* In other words, there is nothing sacred about using upper case A to E for hex digits. They can be lowercase or uppercase as you choose and you don't even have to be consistent about it.

What DEBUG does in response to the E command shown in Figure 3.6 is display the following prompt:

```
38E3:010E   61.
```

The cursor waits after the period for your input. What DEBUG has done is show you what value is *already* at address 010EH so that you can decide whether you want to change it. If not, just press Enter and the dash prompt will return.

Otherwise, enter a hexadecimal value to take the place of value 61H. In Figure 3.6, I used 6FH. Once you enter a replacement value, you have two choices: (1) that's all you wish to change; press Enter and return to the dash prompt. (2) You wish to change the byte at the *next* address. In this case, press the space bar instead. DEBUG will display the byte at the next highest address and wait for your replacement value, just as it did the first time.

This is shown in Figure 3.6. In fact, Figure 3.6 shows *four* successive replacements of bytes starting at address 010EH. Notice the lonely hex byte 0A followed by a period. What happened there is that I pressed Enter *without* typing a replacement byte, ending the E command and returning to the dash prompt.

You'll also note that the next command typed at the dash prompt was *q,* for Quit. Typing *Q* at the dash prompt will return you immediately to DOS.

The Dangers of Modifying Files

Keep in mind that what I've just demonstrated was not changing a file, but simply changing the contents of a file loaded into memory. A file loaded into memory through DEBUG as we did with SAM.TXT is called a *memory image* of that file. *Only the memory image of the file was changed.* SAM.TXT remains on disk, unchanged and unaware of what was happening to its döppelganger in memory.

You can save the altered memory image of SAM.TXT back to disk with a simple command: type *W* and then Enter. (Think, *Write*.) DEBUG remembers how many bytes it read in from disk, and it writes those bytes back out again. It provides a tally as it writes:

```
Writing 0014 bytes
```

The figure is given in hex, even though DEBUG does not do us the courtesy of displaying an *H* after the figure. In hex, 14H is 20 decimal, and there are exactly 20 bytes in SAM.TXT, counting the EOF marker. DEBUG writes out *only* the significant information in the file. It does not write out anything that it didn't load in *unless* you explicitly command DEBUG to write out additional bytes beyond the end of what was originally read.

If you haven't already figured out what was done to poor SAM.TXT, you can dump it again and take a look. If you simply press D for another dump, however, you're in for a surprise: the new dump does not contain any trace of SAM.TXT at all. (Try it!) If you're sharp you'll notice that the address of the first line is not what it was originally, but instead is

```
38E3:0180
```

(The first four digits will be different on your system, but that's all right—look at the second four digits instead during this discussion.) If you know your hex, you'll see that this is the address of the *next* eight lines of dumped memory, starting immediately after where the first dump left off.

The D command works that way. Each time you press D, you get the next 128 bytes of memory, starting with 0100H. To see SAM.TXT again, you need to specify the starting address of the dump, which was 0100H:

```
-d 0100
```

Enter that command, and you'll see a dump of the altered memory image of SAM.TXT:

```
38E3:0100  53 61 6D 0D 0A 77 61 73-0D 0A 61 0D 0A 6D 6F 6F   Sam..was..a..moo
38E3:0110  73 65 0A 1A C4 76 04 26-F7 24 5D C2 04 00 55 8B   se...v.&.$]...U.
38E3:0120  EC 83 EC 12 FF 76 06 FF-76 04 9A 66 17 7D 30 89   .....v..v..f.}0.
38E3:0130  46 FE 83 7E 10 00 75 0F-C4 76 08 26 8B 34 F7 DE   F..~..u..v.&.4..
38E3:0140  C4 5E 0C 03 DE EB 03 C4-5E 0C 89 5E F6 8C 46 F8   .^......^..^..F.
```

```
38E3:0150  C4 76 08 26 8B 1C C4 7E-F6 26 8D 01 8C C2 89 46   .v.&...˜.&.....F
38E3:0160  F2 89 56 F4 2B C9 51 06-57 FF 76 0A FF 76 08 0E   ..V.+.Q.W.v..v..
38E3:0170  E8 83 06 50 FF 76 06 FF-76 04 9A 4B 05 EF 32 FF   ...P.v..v..K..2.
```

Sam, as you can see, is now something else again entirely.

Now, something went a little bit wrong when you changed Sam from a man to a moose. Look closely at memory starting at address 0111H. After the *e* (65H) is *half* of an EOL marker. The carriage return character (0DH) is gone, because you wrote an *e* over it. Only the line feed character (0AH) remains.

This isn't fatal, but it isn't right. A lonely line feed can cause trouble or not, depending on what you try to do with it. If you load the altered SAM.TXT into the JED editor, you'll see a ghostly "J" after the word "moose." This is how JED indicates certain invisible characters that are not EOL or EOF markers, as I'll explain in the next chapter, which describes JED in detail. The "J" tells you an LF character is present at that point in the file.

The lesson here is that DEBUG is a gun without a safety catch. There are no safeguards. You can change *anything* inside a file with it, whether it makes sense or not, or whether it's dangerous or not. All safety considerations are up to you. You must be aware of whether or not you're overwriting important parts of the file.

This is a theme that will occur again and again in assembly language: *Safety is up to you.* Unlike BASIC, which wraps a protective cocoon around you and keeps you from banging yourself up, assembly language lets you hang yourself without a whimper of protest.

Keep this in mind as we continue:

Examining and Changing Registers

If you saved SAM.TXT back out to disk in its altered state, you created a damaged file. Fixing SAM.TXT requires reconstructing the last EOL marker by inserting the CR character that you overwrote using the E command. Unfortunately, this means you'll be making SAM.TXT larger than it was when DEBUG read it into memory. To save the corrected file back out to disk, we need to somehow tell DEBUG that it needs to save more than 14H bytes out to disk. To do this we need to look at and change a value in one of the CPU registers.

Registers, if you recall, are special-purpose memory cubbyholes that exist inside the CPU chip itself rather than in memory chips outside the CPU. DEBUG has a command that allows us to examine and change register values as easily as we examined and changed memory.

At the dash prompt, type R. (Think, *R*egisters.) You'll see a display like this:

```
-r
AX=0000  BX=0000  CX=0014  DX=0000  SP =FFEE   BP=0000  SI=0000  DI=0000
DS=1980  ES=1980  SS=1980  CS=1980  IP=0100   NV UP EI PL NZ NA PO NC
1980:0100 53       PUSH   BX
```

The bulk of the display consists of register names followed by equal signs, followed by the current values of the registers. The cryptic characters **NV UP EI PL NZ NA PO NC** are the names of *flags,* and we'll discuss them later in the book.

The line beneath the register and flag summaries is a *disassembly* of the byte at the address contained by the *instruction pointer.* (The instruction pointer is a register that is displayed by the DEBUG R command, under the shorter name IP. Find IP's value in the register display above—it should be 0100H, which is also the address of the *S* in Sam.) This line will be useful when you are actually examining an executable program file in memory. In the case of SAM.TXT the disassembly line is misleading, because SAM is *not* an executable program and contains nothing we intend to be machine instructions.

The hexadecimal value 53H, however, *is* a legal machine instruction as well as the ASCII code for upper case *S.* DEBUG doesn't know what kind of file SAM.TXT is. SAM could be a program file as well as a text file; DEBUG makes no assumptions based on the file's contents or its file extension. DEBUG examines memory at the current address and displays it as though it were a machine instruction. If memory contains data instead of machine instructions, the disassembly line should be ignored.

This is once again an example of the problems you can have in assembly language if you don't know exactly what you're doing. Code and data look the same in memory; they are only different in how you interpret them. In SAM.TXT, the hex value 53H is the letter *S*; in an executable program file, 53H would be the instruction **PUSH BX**. We'll be making good use of the disassembly line later in the book when we get down to examining real assembly language programs. For now, just ignore it.

When DEBUG loads a file from disk, it places the number of bytes contained in the file in the CX register. CX is a general-purpose register, but it is often used to contain such count values and is therefore sometimes called the *count register.*

Notice that the value of CX is 14H—just the number DEBUG reported when it wrote the altered SAM.TXT out to disk in response to the W command. If we change the value in CX, we change the number of bytes DEBUG will write to disk.

So let's fix SAM.TXT. In changing the word *man* to *moose* we wrote over two characters: the period at the end of the sentence and the CR character portion of the last EOL marker. We could start at address 0112H and enter a period character (2EH—use your ASCII table!) followed by a CR character (0DH). In doing so, however, we would overwrite the LF character and the EOF marker character, which is just as bad or worse.

Unlike a text editor, DEBUG will not just shove over the values to the right of the point where you wish to insert new values; DEBUG has no insert mode. You have to enter all four characters: the period, the CR, the LF, and the EOF.

Use the E command to enter them, and then display a dump of the file again:

```
-e 0112
1980:0112    0D.2e    0A.0d    1A.0a    0D.1a

-d 0100
38E3:0100 53 61 6D 0D 0A 77 61 73-0D 0A 61 0D 0A 6D 6F 6F   Sam..was..a..moo
38E3:0110 73 65 2E 0D 0A 1A 04 26-F7 24 5D C2 04 00 55 8B   se.....v.&.$]...U.
38E3:0120 EC 83 EC 12 FF 76 06 FF-76 04 9A 66 17 7D 30 89   .....v..v..f.}0.
38E3:0130 46 FE 83 7E 10 00 75 0F-C4 76 08 26 8B 34 F7 DE   F..~..u..v.&.4..
38E3:0140 C4 5E 0C 03 DE EB 03 C4-5E 0C 89 5E F6 8C 46 F8   .^......^..^..F.
38E3:0150 C4 76 08 26 8B 1C C4 7E-F6 26 8D 01 8C C2 89 46   .v.&...~.&.....F
38E3:0160 F2 89 56 F4 2B C9 51 06-57 FF 76 0A FF 76 08 0E   ..V.+.Q.W.v..v..
38E3:0170 E8 83 06 50 FF 76 06 FF-76 04 9A 4B 05 EF 32 FF   ...P.v..v..K..2.
```

Now the file is repaired, and we can write it back to disk—except that the version of SAM.TXT in memory is now 2 bytes longer than the SAM.TXT version on disk. We need to tell DEBUG that it needs to write 2 additional bytes to disk when it writes SAM.TXT back out.

DEBUG keeps its count of SAM's length in the BX and CX registers. The count is actually a 32-bit number split between the two 16-bit registers BX and CX, with BX containing the "high" half of the 32-bit number. Adding 2 to the count only changes the low half of the number, which is contained in CX. Changing the value of CX is done with the R command, by specifying CX after R:

```
-r cx
```

DEBUG responds by displaying the name *CX,* its current value, and a colon prompt on the next line:

```
CX 0014
:
```

Add 2 to the value of CX and enter 0016 at the prompt. Press Enter. DEBUG simply returns the dash prompt—remember, it's a utility of few words.

Now, however, when you enter a W command to write SAM.TXT back to disk, DEBUG displays this message:

```
Writing 0016 bytes
```

The new, longer SAM.TXT has been written to disk in its entirety—problem solved.

One final note on saving files back out to disk from DEBUG: if you change the values in either BX or CX to reflect something other than the true length of the file, and then execute a W command to write the file to disk, DEBUG will write as many bytes to disk as are specified in BX and CX. This could be 20,000 bytes more than the file contains, or it could be 0 bytes, leaving you with an empty file. You can destroy a file this way. Either leave BX and CX alone while you're examining and patching a file with DEBUG, or write the initial values in BX and CX down and enter them back into BX and CX just before issuing the W command.

The Hacker's Best Friend

There is a *great* deal more to be said about DEBUG, but most of it involves concepts we haven't yet covered. DEBUG is the single most useful tool you have as an assembly language programmer, and I'll be teaching you more of its features as we get deeper and deeper into the programming process itself.

The next chapter describes JED, a simple program editor and development environment I created for people who have not purchased a commercial editor product like Brief or Epsilon. If you do not intend to use JED, you can skip right over Chapter 4 and meet us on the other side in Chapter 5, where we begin our long trek through the '86 family instruction set.

Chapter 4

Learning and Using JED

A Programming Environment for Assembly Language

"Give me a lever long enough, and a place to stand, and I will move the Earth."

Archimedes was speaking literally about the power of the lever, but behind his words there is a larger truth about work in general: to get something done, you need a place to work with access to tools. My radio bench in the garage is set up that way—a large, flat space to lay ailing transmitters and a shelf above where my oscilloscope, VTVM, frequency counter, signal generator, and dip meter are within easy reach.

Much of the astonishing early success of Turbo Pascal was grounded in that truth. For the first time, a compiler vendor assembled the most important tools of software development and put them together in an intuitive fashion so that the various tasks involved in creating software flowed easily from one step to the next. From a menu that was your place to stand, you pressed one key, and your Pascal program was compiled. You pressed another key and the program ran. It was simple, fast, and easy to learn. Turbo Pascal literally took Pascal from a backwater language favored by academicians to the most popular compiled language in history, BASIC not excluded.

What Borland so boldly introduced in 1983 was adopted (reluctantly at times) by their major competitor, Microsoft. Today, Turbo Pascal, Turbo C, Turbo Basic, Turbo Prolog, Quick C, and Quick BASIC are what we call *integrated development environments.* They provide well-designed menus to give you that place to stand and a multitude of tools that are only one or two keystrokes away.

A little remarkably, there is no true equivalent to Turbo Pascal in the assembly language field. Neither MASM nor Borland's own Turbo Assembler have that same comfortable place to stand. The reasons for this may seem peculiar to you, the beginner: seasoned assembly language programmers either create their own development environments (they are, after all, the programming elite) or they simply work from the naked DOS prompt. The appeal of a Turbo Pascal–type environment is not as strong to them as it is to you. An integrated development environment for MASM and TASM may happen in time, but you must understand that both Microsoft and Borland are catering to their most important audience, the established assembly language programmer.

That doesn't do much good for you. One glance at Figure 3.5 on page 87 can give you the screaming willies. Assembly language development is not a simple process and grabbing all the tools from the DOS prompt is complicated and error-prone, rather like standing on a swiveling bar stool to get the shot glasses down from a high shelf.

So, to make things a little easier for you, I've created a program called JED. JED is a beginner's development environment for either MASM or TASM. It's nowhere near as powerful as the environments provided with the Turbo or Quick languages, but it's powerful enough to get you started on the long road toward assembly language proficiency.

Laying Hands on JED

JED.EXE is written in Turbo Pascal 5.0. You can get a copy from many of the larger user groups around the country. Perhaps your friends have a copy; ask around. I've allowed people to copy it freely in the hopes that it will be widely used. If you can't find it anywhere, you can order the listings diskette from me through the coupon on the flyleaf. Both source code and .EXE versions of JED are included on the listings diskette. You don't need Turbo Pascal to run JED.EXE. It's fully compiled and ready to run.

I must emphasize that not quite all of the source code for JED is on the listings diskette. JED contains a powerful text editor that is provided with Borland's Turbo Pascal Editor Toolbox. You can get JED's source code from the listings diskette, but keep in mind that it's not all there; you *must* buy the Turbo Pascal Editor Toolbox *and* own Turbo Pascal 5.0 in order to compile or modify JED.

I must also emphasize right now that you don't *need* to have JED to work with assembly language or to use this book. JED smooths access to your tools like TASM and TLINK, and provides a very good text editor to boot, but you can work very well from the DOS prompt using some other text editor. I'll be speaking of JED during the descriptions of the assembly language process in this book, because there are a multitude of ways to work with assembly language and I have to settle on something. But the information on assembly language itself is independent of the text editor and programming environment you may choose to use.

4.2 ◆ JED's Place to Stand

Like Turbo Pascal and the other integrated development environments from both Borland and Microsoft, JED's most visible part is a text editor. If you'll look back once again to Figure 3.5, you'll see that all roads seem to lead back to the text editor in good time. In general, you do most of your *thinking* while staring at the text editor screen, so it seems a logical location to put your place to stand.

Running JED is easy. The first time you want to work on a particular source code file, you type the name JED followed by the name of the source code file:

C:\ASM>JED EAT2.ASM

In this example, EAT2.ASM is the name of an assembly language source code file described a little later in this book. JED will be loaded from disk and run by DOS and then JED will load the text file EAT2.ASM from disk into its editor workspace. You'll get a view like that shown in Figure 4.1.

The Status Line

Apart from the very top line, everything on the screen is a display of your text file. This top line, the *status line,* contains several important items of information about the file JED loaded at startup, which is called the *current file.* The first two items tell you the position of the cursor in terms of line

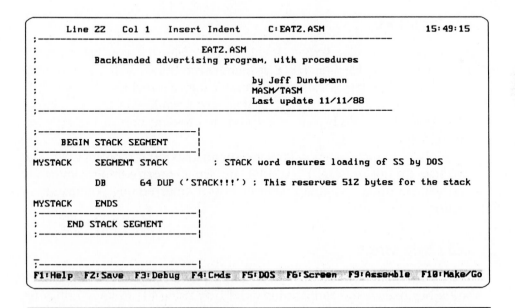

```
       Line 22    Col 1    Insert Indent      C:EAT2.ASM              15:49:15
;---------------------------------------------------------------
;                              EAT2.ASM
;             Backhanded advertising program, with procedures
;
;                                      by Jeff Duntemann
;                                      MASM/TASM
;                                      Last update 11/11/88
;---------------------------------------------------------------


;--------------------------------|
;     BEGIN STACK SEGMENT         |
;--------------------------------|
MYSTACK      SEGMENT STACK           ; STACK word ensures loading of SS by DOS

            DB        64 DUP ('STACK!!!') ; This reserves 512 bytes for the stack

MYSTACK     ENDS
;--------------------------------|
;     END STACK SEGMENT           |
;--------------------------------|


;--------------------------------|
F1:Help  F2:Save  F3:Debug  F4:Cmds  F5:DOS  F6:Screen  F9:Assemble  F10:Make/Go
```

FIGURE 4.1   JED's edit screen

number and column number. In case you're unfamiliar with such things, the line numbers run from top to bottom with line 1 at the top and the column numbers run from left to right with column 1 at the left margin. As you move the cursor around the file using the cursor control keys (see Section 4.4) the position of the cursor will be constantly updated in the status line.

The word **Insert** will be present in the status line if JED's editor is in *insert mode,* meaning that characters typed at the keyboard will be inserted at the cursor position, pushing aside the characters to the right of the cursor position. When the word **Insert** is *not* present, JED's editor is in *overwrite mode,* meaning that characters typed at the cursor position will be placed atop characters that already exist on the screen and that those underlying characters will be lost. I'll say more on this item later in this chapter.

Similarly, the word **Indent** indicates that the editor is in *indent mode.* In indent mode, indenting one line by spacing over from the left margin will cause subsequent lines to automatically indent to the same number of spaces from the margin. Again, more on this later in this chapter.

The name of the current file is also present in the status line. Finally, the current time of day as present in DOS's clock is shown in the upper right hand corner of the screen.

The Prompt Bar

At the bottom of the screen, highlighted in blue (if you have a color monitor) is a single line bar that summarizes most of JED's important commands. This bar is called the *prompt bar.* It provides always visible reminders as to which tools are at your grasp while you are standing at JED's edit screen. Each tool is invoked by pressing one of the PC's ten function keys.

Eight of the ten function keys are summarized in the prompt bar. The two that are not present, F7 and F8, are actually text editing commands and will be discussed along with all of the other editing commands in Section 4.4.

JED's Help Screen

Perhaps the single most important command to remember while you're still a beginner is the Help command, F1. Pressing F1 instantly brings up a 24-line help display of all JED commands and most of the text editing commands. If you ever forget a command or are unsure what one of the prompt bar reminders means (like **F4:Cmds,** which is something less than obvious) simply press F1 and read the available information. JED's help screen is shown in Figure 4.2.

Once the help screen is displayed, you can put it away and return to the editing screen by pressing any nonshift key. (That is, any key but the Shift, Ctrl, or Alt keys.)

4.3 ◆ Using JED's Tools

The very best way to explain JED's commands and how they are used is to run through a simple JED session with a real assembly language program and explain what happens as we go. The program we'll use is EAT2.ASM, which is shown in Section 8.2 on page 236. It's not much of a program, and exists only to get you started in understanding the internal mechanisms of a real, working assembly language program. When run from the DOS prompt, EAT2.EXE displays this simple message on your screen:

Eat at Joe's...
...ten million flies can't ALL be wrong!

```
 _  _  _        Version 1.0 — Released 1/8/89  —  ALT-X EXITS!
| || || |
|_||_||_|       (c) 1988, 1989  Jeff Duntemann — ALL RIGHTS RESERVED
─────────────────────────── COMMAND SET ───────────────────────────
F1:  Display this screen            ^KD: Quit and save file
F2:  Save current source code file  ^KQ: Quit without saving
F3:  Invoke DEBUG on current .EXE file ^KW: Write marked block to disk
F4:  Update assemble/link command lines ^KR: Read a file to cursor position
F5:  Shell out to DOS               ^KH: Hide/unhide the marked block
F6:  Show last assemble/link screen ^KY: Delete marked block
F7:  Mark beginning of block        ^KV: Move marked block
F8:  Mark end of block              ^KC: Copy marked block
F9:  Assemble only                  ^QL: Undo changes to line
F10: Assemble/link (if needed) and Go! Alt-F: Change current source code file

^QR: Move to start of file   ^Y: Delete line   ^T: Delete word  ^QY: Del. to EOL
^QC: Move to end of file     ^QF: Find  ^QA: Find/Replace  ^L: Find/repl. again
^A:  Move 1 word left         Options: N: Without asking  W: Whole words only
^F:  Move 1 word right              G: Global  U: Ignore case  B: Backwards

   <<REMEMBER!!>> If your .ASM file is not a standalone program, but a device
   driver or a library of procedures, pressing F10 may lock up your system!!
                  Press any key to return to JED...
```

FIGURE 4.2   JED's help screen

After it displays those two lines, it ends and returns control to DOS.

EAT2.ASM is the source code file from which the executable program file EAT2.EXE is assembled and linked. EAT2.ASM is present on the disk with JED. If you have somehow obtained JED without the rest of the example files from this book, you can type EAT2.ASM into JED after running JED.

If, as I have suggested earlier, you have created a subdirectory on your hard disk called ASM, copy all of the files on the JED disk into subdirectory ASM. In order for JED to operate correctly, the following files must be present in the subdirectory with JED:

1. Your assembler. This can be any command line–oriented assembler, but will typically be either MASM.EXE (Microsoft's Macro Assembler) or TASM.EXE (Borland's Turbo Assembler.)
2. Your assembler's linker. Assemblers are usually shipped with their own linker. This is certainly true of MASM and TASM. Some assemblers may not use their own linker, but will use the DOS linker LINK.EXE instead.
3. The DOS debugger, DEBUG.COM. Some versions of DOS are no longer shipped with DEBUG, which is offered as part of an additional utilities disk. Prior to DOS 3.2, all versions have DEBUG.COM. If you don't have DEBUG.COM, you will find it slow going, since nearly all of the debugging skills I'll be teaching in this book center on DEBUG.COM.

Of course, other files can be present without any hindrance to your work.

Invoking JED

Make the current directory your working assembly language subdirectory, which I have suggested you call ASM. From the DOS prompt, invoke JED with the file name EAT2 after it:

        C:\ASM>JED EAT2

Notice that you don't have to type the .ASM at the end of the file name EAT2. JED has a *default file extension* of .ASM. In other words, if you don't enter a file extension, JED will append the file extension .ASM on the end of the name you enter on the command line. You could, of course, have entered the full file name including extension if you chose:

        C:\ASM>JED EAT2.ASM

JED will in either case consider the name of the *current file* to be EAT2.ASM.

Now, either EAT2.ASM exists on your disk or it doesn't. JED won't mind if the file doesn't exist—new files have to start somewhere! If JED can't find the filename you enter on the command line, it will display the words *new file* in the upper left corner of the screen while it creates an empty text file on your hard disk. When you type text into the text editor screen, JED will save the text into that new file.

The file may well exist on disk, however, and if it does, JED will load the file into the editor screen and display it for you. Assuming you entered the name EAT2, the screen should look almost identical to that shown in Figure 4.1.

You might wonder what will happen if you simply type JED at the DOS command line without specifying any file name at all for it to work on. One of two things will happen:

1. JED will load the file that you last worked on from within JED. JED keeps a record of the last file it loads and saves it in a small file on disk named JED.CFG. If it can find JED.CFG, and if the file named in JED.CFG is in your working subdirectory, JED will load that file. JED updates JED.CFG automatically so you don't need to worry about updating JED.CFG.

2. If there is no JED.CFG on your disk, JED will create a file imaginatively named NONAME.ASM and store your text into a new file with that name. NONAME.ASM is a pretty rank name for any assembly language program, so while it will be saved as a perfectly good file, you might as well think of a better name and enter that when invoking JED.

JED's remembering the name of the last file you worked on makes it unnecessary for *you* to remember what project you were in the middle of when you pulled the plug and went to bed. Furthermore, JED also remembers where the cursor position was when you saved your file and exited from JED. Simply type JED, and JED will bring up the correct file and allow you to continue at the exact cursor position where you left off.

Moving around within the editor.   Your place to stand is JED's text editor, and when nothing else is going on (like assembling, linking, debugging, or running your program) you'll be in the text editor.

When you're in the text editor, any characters you type on the keyboard will be inserted into the current file and displayed on your screen. You can move the cursor around within the current file by using any of a number of cursor movement keys.

The easiest to remember are the PC's cursor keypad keys. The four arrow keys will move the cursor one character position in the direction the arrow points. The **PgUp** key will move the cursor one page (i.e., the size of your screen; typically 25, 43, or 50 lines) up, whereas **PgDn** will move the cursor one page down. The **Home** key will move the cursor immediately to the left screen margin, and the **End** key will move the cursor immediately to the end of the current line. (The end of the line is defined as the character *after* the rightmost *non-blank* character in the line.)

There are numerous other cursor movement keys that you can use within JED. I'll describe them all in detail in Section 4.4. Take a few moments scooting around inside EAT2 until you feel comfortable with it.

Making changes to the file.   The simplest way to change the file is simply to type something at the keyboard. All such characters will appear at the cursor and the cursor will move one position to the right for each character.

You can insert a new line beneath the current line by pressing Enter.

Getting rid of unwanted text is as important as adding new text. Deleting one character at a time can be done simply by moving the cursor to the immediate right of the offending character and using the backspace key to back the cursor over it. The character will disappear.

You can delete an entire line by placing the cursor on the line and pressing Ctrl-Y. This can be done all too easily by accident, and you can lose a line that may or may not be in your head or written down on paper. Be careful!

JED contains numerous other ways to delete text, all of which are described in Section 4.4. For the sake of the current guided tour through JED, move the cursor to the blank line immediately beneath EAT2's comment header (line 9 in the file) and type the word *FOO*. That done, press Enter and add a new line beneath it.

Saving changes to a file.   As they say in Chicago, that grand old (and cold) town where I grew up, "Vote early and often." The same philosophy applies to saving the changes you make to your current file under JED.

Every so often, perhaps when you kick back in your chair to think for a bit, save your work. It's easy: one keystroke, function key F2. JED will display the word "Saving . . ." in the status line at the top of the screen while it saves your file to disk. If you have a fast hard disk this will rarely take more than a second. If you're still working on diskettes, the process may take a few seconds more, especially if the current file is a good size.

Get into the habit of pressing F2 once in a while. Keep in mind that if you save your work every five minutes, you will never lose more than five minutes of work!

JED keeps an eye on things and does its level best to keep you from losing any of your work. If you try to exit JED without saving your file to disk, JED will remind you with the following prompt:

> File modified. Save it? (Y/N)

If you press "Y," Jed will save your work to disk. Pressing "N" will allow you to exit JED without saving your work. All keys other than *Y* and *N* will be ignored.

JED also automatically saves your work every time you go out to use the assembler, linker, or debugger, or when you run the program you're developing, as I'll explain a little later.

Changing the current file.
If you want to change the current file while you're in JED and working, simply press Alt-F (think: *F*ile). A window will appear in the center of the screen and display the name of the current file above a field where you can enter the name of the new file.

The name of the current file will be in the field. You can do one of two things to the name:

1. Begin typing a new name. The old name will vanish as soon as you press a printable character key.
2. Backspace over some portion of the old name. This will allow you to change the name of the current file from EAT2.ASM to EAT3.ASM without typing the whole name.

When you press Enter, JED will attempt to load the file of the name you typed. If the file does not exist, or if the name field was blank, JED will create a new file called NONAME.ASM according to the rules summarized in the previous section.

Checking and Changing the Assemble and Link Commands

The whole point of JED is to help your work in assembly language, and the central task in assembly language work is processing a correct file through an assembler. JED can execute your assembler program and assemble your current file with only one keystroke. That keystroke is function key F9, as you'll see from the prompt bar at the bottom of the screen. Before you press F9 on our tour, however, we'd better make sure JED has your assembler and linker commands straight.

As programs go, JED is pretty clever, but it doesn't read minds. It can make use of any assembler that operates from the DOS command line, but you have to tell JED how to invoke the assembler you've chosen. MASM and TASM are invoked in different ways, and JED must know which assembler you're using to be able to call the assembler program from disk and make use of it. This is done with yet another JED command. Press function key F4, and a whole new screen will appear, as shown in Figure 4.3. JED contains two command lines, one that invokes your assembler, and another that invokes your linker. I've set JED up to assume the use of Borland's Turbo Assembler TASM, which is faster and in many ways more sophisticated than Microsoft's MASM. If you are using TASM, you needn't change JED's built-in default command lines. Figure 4.3 shows the default command lines for TASM.

To use MASM or some other assembler, however, you'll need to change both command lines. This will require some knowledge of how your assembler and linker operate. I'll provide you with some basic information about MASM and TASM; for other assemblers (or for using specialized features of MASM and TASM) you're on your own.

```
        \\JED\\  Assemble/link command edit screen


                        Assemble command:
TASM ~.....................................................................


                        Link command:
TLINK ~


Line editing commands:

CR:      Accepts changes and continues
ESC:     Abandons changes and continues
Ctrl-X:  Clears entire field to empty string
BS:      Destructive backspace
```

FIGURE 4.3   Changing JED's assembler and link command lines

The line beneath the prompt, "Assemble command" is the line JED will use to invoke your assembler. The default is

TASM˜

which will invoke Borland's Turbo Assembler with all default conditions in force. The tilde character (˜) is used to indicate where in the line JED is to substitute the name of the current file. In other words, when JED goes out to DOS to execute TASM on the file EAT2.ASM, it will substitute the name *EAT2.ASM* for the tilde and use this actual line for invoking TASM:

TASM EAT2.ASM

If you're using MASM instead, the assemble command line must be changed. Invoking MASM with all defaults in force (using the tilde to indicate the position of the file name) requires this command line:

MASM˜ ;

Again, in our example this would be expanded to

MASM EAT2.ASM;

The semicolon is very important and prevents MASM from going into interactive mode. If you omit the semicolon, MASM will stop and begin asking questions through the keyboard. JED is not equipped to answer these questions, and while you yourself could answer MASM's questions from the keyboard, there's no point to it if all we want to do is use MASM's defaults. If you're using MASM, make sure you have that semicolon.

Modifying the command line isn't difficult. You can backspace over the existing command and replace it with a new one, or zap the whole line at once by pressing Ctrl-X. Then, once the command line is empty, you can type in your new command line.

When the changes are the way you want them, press Enter to retain the changes and record them in JED.CFG. If you change your mind after zapping or otherwise altering the existing command line, you can abandon your changes and leave the original command line untouched by simply pressing **Esc.**

You'll notice that while you're editing a command line, a line of periods runs from the end of the command line to the right margin. These periods indicate how large the command line can be. You can type as far as the periods allow. If you try to type further, JED will quite literally reply "uh-uh."—Try it and see!

Changing the link command line is done the same way. TASM's link command line is

TLINK ~

MASM's link command line, on the other hand, requires a semicolon, and for the same reasons mentioned before

LINK ~;

These are the absolute simplest command lines possible and will suffice for simpler learning programs like EAT2.ASM. For more advanced work you may need to use assembler or linker *options,* which are additional commands that provide special information to the assembler or linker about the job at hand.

For example, under MASM you can specify that the assembler write the program's segments to disk in alphabetical order (don't worry for now if you don't know what this means) by using the /A option. This requires that you enter the /A option onto the assemble command line:

MASM /A~ ;

Both TASM and MASM have numerous options of this type. You won't need any of them while working your way through this book. Later, when you move on to larger and more sophisticated assembly language work, you will need to understand and use these options. If you continue to use JED at that stage, you'll have to add the desired options to the assemble and link command lines.

Assembling the Current File

If you're satisfied that the assemble and link command lines are correct, it's time to assemble EAT2. Press function key F9; the following will happen:

1. JED will save the current file to disk as a safety measure. Any time JED transfers control outside of itself (by executing the program under development or one of the utilities) it does this.

2. The screen will clear. JED will invoke your assembler using the assemble command line described in the previous subsection. The assembler will display its copyright notice and certain other information on your screen. (Precisely what it displays depends on the assembler.) This includes error messages if your source code file contains errors.

3. When the assembler is finished, JED saves the contents of the screen onto the heap so you can bring the information (typically error messages) back for later examination. This happens invisibly and takes almost no time.

4. Finally, a prompt reading "Press any key to return to JED" will appear at the center of the bottom line of the screen. JED will wait for any keystroke, allowing you to take your time reading the displayed error messages. When you're ready to resume work, press a key and the editor screen will reappear. An example of the screen at this point is shown in Figure 4.4.

If you recall, you made a change to EAT2.ASM a little earlier by typing the word *FOO* on line 9. This word at this location in the file means nothing,

```
Turbo Assembler Version 1.0  Copyright (c) 1988 by Borland International

Assembling file:    EATZ.ASM
**Error** EATZ.ASM(9) Illegal instruction
Error messages:     1
Warning messages:   None
Remaining memory:   228k

















                Press any key to return to JED...
```

FIGURE 4.4   A TASM error message

and it will generate an assembler error message. You can see this error message as TASM presents it, along with TASM's copyright notice and other information, in Figure 4.4. TASM calls the word *FOO* an "illegal instruction" because no instruction in the '86-family instruction set is named **FOO.** If you misspelled a genuine instruction (say, by fumble-fingering **MOV** into **MVO**) you would most likely see the same error message.

Both MASM and TASM are helpful in that they identify the line where they first noticed an error. (This is not always where the error actually *is,* but we'll return to this matter later in the book.) This time, the error is a pretty obvious one and no assembler should have any trouble telling you that the problem exists in line 9 of the source code file. Once you press a key and return to JED's edit screen, move to line 9 and delete the offending line containing *FOO.* Just press Ctrl-Y and the line will vanish. Save the repaired file by pressing F2. Finally, invoke the assembler again by pressing F9 once more. This time you *won't* see any error messages.

MAKEing an Executable File and Running It

What, exactly, does running the assembler actually accomplish? By itself, not much. Invoking the assembler alone is useful to determine if there are any errors in your source code file. If the file contains no errors, you still won't have a runnable program after the assembler has done its job. What you *do* have is a relocatable object file with the same name as the current file but with a file extension of .OBJ. In our example here, the assembler read in the current file EAT2.ASM and produced the new file EAT2.OBJ.

You can't run EAT2.OBJ, and you can't read it or print it. You can't do much of anything with it, in fact, but *link* it. As I explained in the previous chapter, linking is a process by which one or more .OBJ files are translated into an executable program file with an .EXE extension. It's called *linking* because more than one .OBJ file can be combined into a single .EXE file through the linking process. Even if you only have one .OBJ file (as we do here with EAT2), however, you must still perform the link step on it to create an executable program file.

JED can perform the link step very easily. It does not, however, perform the link step all by itself. Running the assembler alone is useful to identify errors, but running the linker alone is pretty pointless unless you intend to run the executable program file produced by the link step. JED combines the link step with the step of actually running your new assembly language program to see what it does. Furthermore, it performs the assemble step again so that you can do it all in one keystroke: Assemble, link, and away you go!

When you press function key F10, JED will do very much what it did when you pressed F9, and then some:

1. JED saves the current file to disk. The first time you run *any* new assembly language program, you had better be prepared to reboot your machine. It happens to the best of us now and then, and it will happen to you with a disturbing frequency. Because we humans sometimes forget to save the source before running the .EXE file, JED *never* forgets.

2. JED executes the assembler and if there are no errors in the file produces an .OBJ version of the current file. If errors are detected, no .OBJ file is generated and JED immediately takes control from the assembler. The link and go steps are not taken. JED will wait for a keystroke so that you can stare at the error messages for awhile.

3. If there were no assembler errors, JED executes the linker. The .OBJ file is translated into an .EXE file. Again, there is the possibility that linker errors will occur, although they are much less common than assembler errors. If errors are detected, JED takes control back directly from the linker and the .EXE file will not be run. In the event of an error, JED waits for a keystroke so that you can examine the wreckage before pressing a key and going on.

4. The .EXE file produced by the linker is executed. Your fledgling program runs, and when it finishes JED will once again wait for a keystroke so that you can examine your program's output. In our test case of EAT2, this output consists of those two lines of text shown earlier about eating at Joe's.

At this point, I have a confession to make.

What I just told you was the truth, but not the *whole* truth. The F10 command is a little more complicated than just those four steps. Suppose, for example, that you use the F10 command to create and run an .EXE file as we just did. Then suppose that you wanted to see it work again almost immediately, without making any further changes to the program. You press F10, expecting to have to wait through the assemble and link step again.

But no . . .

The second time you press F10, the .EXE file executes *immediately,* with neither the assembler nor the linker doing their thing.

What gives?

JED is pretty clever after all. Since you didn't make any additional changes to the source file, there was no need for JED to reassemble and relink to recreate an .EXE file identical to the one created a few seconds earlier. JED therefore simply executed the .EXE file as it did the first time, without making you wait through the needless assemble and link steps.

Here's what happens: when you press F10, JED looks at two files on disk. The first one is the .EXE file. If no .EXE file exists on disk, JED obviously has to create one by executing both the assembler and the linker. If the .EXE file does exist, however, JED looks at the file's *time stamp* and stores a copy of the time stamp.

A time stamp is DOS's way of knowing when a file was last changed. Every file created under DOS has both a time and a date attached to it. When you execute a DIR command from the DOS command line, the files listed tell you when they were last changed by displaying their time stamps as date and time values:

```
Volume in drive C is DISK1_VOL1
Directory of C:\TURBO\JED

JED   BAK   27659   1-08-89   4:39p
JED   PAS   27633   1-08-89   4:39p
JED   EXE   31920   1-08-89   4:39p
JED   CFG     326   1-08-89   5:25p
        4 File(s) 10803200 bytes free
```

The two rightmost columns are the date and time portions of each file's time stamp.

Once JED stores a copy of the .EXE file's time stamp, it examines the current source code .ASM file and stores a copy of its time stamp. Once JED has both time stamps, it compares them.

If the .ASM file's time stamp shows a time more recent than the .EXE file's time stamp, JED recreates the .EXE file by invoking both the assembler and the linker. If the .ASM file's time stamp says the .ASM file is *older* than the .EXE file, JED simply runs the .EXE file without recreating it.

Think about that for a moment until it makes perfect sense—it's important! If the .ASM file is older than the .EXE file, there is *no* possibility that changes made to the .ASM file have not been reflected in the .EXE file. If the .ASM file is newer than the .EXE file, however, it might mean that changes were made to the .ASM file that have not yet been reflected in the .EXE file. JED therefore updates the .EXE file so that it is guaranteed to reflect all possible changes made in the source code .ASM file.

This process is a common one among software development tools. The name of the process is *MAKE,* meaning that when necessary, JED will choose to *make* the .EXE file from the .ASM file by invoking the assembler and the linker. The MAKE process is efficient because it only happens when it has to. If the .EXE file is found to be up to date, the assemble and link steps are skipped.

As I've hinted before, running a brand new assembly language program is dangerous business, *especially* for new assembly language programmers. High-level languages like Pascal and C protect you to a considerable extent from your own ignorance. Assembly language offers almost no such protection. Until you really *really* know what you're doing, your assembly language programs will crash your machine "hard" more often than they let it live. (This is why most assembly language programmers choose machines with hard-reset buttons on the front panel. Pushing RESET is much gentler on the machine than turning it off and on again.)

Don't get discouraged when you crash. As that old *Desiderata* poem on your Day-Glo '60s psychedelic posters takes pains to point out, "No doubt the universe is unfolding as it should." Crashing is part of the process. What *is* stupid is crashing again and again without knowing why. Figuring out why you're crashing is one of the most difficult and rewarding facets of assembly language programming, as we'll see by and by.

Taking Another Look at Your Error Messages

The assembler won't give you a lot of clues as to where you went wrong when it detects an error, so you have to make the most of the clues you get. The assembler displays error messages during the assemble step. It would be handy to keep those error messages around and refer to them when you're back in JED's editor, staring at your errant source code.

JED can do it. Before JED clears the assembler's error messages from the screen and returns you to the text editor, it saves the screen information in memory. Later on, you can redisplay the screen as it was immediately after the assemble step by pressing F6.

The only time this system fails a little bit is if you have so many errors in the source code file that they begin to scroll off the top of the screen. This means, first of all, that you have some wholesale error hunting to do. But there is a way to avoid losing the first few error messages of a multi-error assemble step. As soon as the first few error messages appear, halt the assemble step by pressing Ctrl-C. It's wise to treat the first error messages first, because error messages sometimes breed other error messages, and getting rid of the first one might purge five or fifteen others farther down the file.

If you try to recall an error message screen before running the assembler, JED will clear the screen and explain the situation.

You should also keep in mind that if an assemble step occurs without errors, you will still be able to recall the assembler's copyright notice and status information by pressing F6. JED is not particular; whether errors occur or not, it saves the screen from the last time the assembler was run.

Running DEBUG

An important part of developing assembly language programs is using the DEBUG utility. JED can run DEBUG for you with a single keystroke. Once you've produced a working EAT2.EXE file, press F3. JED will invoke DEBUG.COM with your current .EXE file as its parameter. DEBUG will execute and in turn load your .EXE file into memory. The screen will clear, and you'll see DEBUG's terse little dash prompt.

Press D, and DEBUG will dump the first 128 bytes of EAT2.EXE as it was loaded into memory. Press R, and debug will show you the current state of the registers. You can actually run EAT2.EXE by pressing G (for Go) at DEBUG's prompt. Finally, you can quit DEBUG by pressing Q. JED will take back control and wait for one final keystroke so you can grab a last look at what DEBUG had displayed.

One additional feature is that the last screenful of information displayed by DEBUG is saved in memory by JED, and can be recalled by pressing F6, just as with assembler error screens. This is handy when you need to refer back to a hex dump of a region of memory while examining a berserk source code file in the editor.

"Ducking Out" to DOS

For all that it does do, JED is a modest program and doesn't try to do everything. I was tempted to build printer support into it so that you could create a printed listing of the current file by pressing a single key, but decided against it. There are a multitude of different kinds of printers out there, each with its own font sizes and setup strings and control sequences. Rather than try to cover all the printer bases, I decided to build a quick trap door into JED so that you can quickly duck out to DOS and run your own listing program, or do anything else that can be done from DOS.

Exiting to DOS is done by pressing F5. To be safe, JED will save the current file out to disk, but then it will clear the screen and drop you back out to the DOS command prompt. It looks very much like JED has terminated and returned control to DOS, but not so—JED is very much alive in memory, waiting patiently for you to finish your business with DOS and come back home.

From DOS you can do things like search the directory for a lost file, make room on your disk by erasing some clutter, or even (in a pinch) run another major program like Turbo Pascal. The only caution here is that JED and your program take up a certain amount of memory that is therefore not available to other programs like Turbo Pascal. Very large programs like Ventura Publisher or Paradox may not run at all if you try to execute them from beneath JED, not because you've done anything wrong but only because such large programs need the memory JED is taking up.

By actual examination using the CHKDSK utility, I've found that JED and its workspace take up about 180K of RAM. That's a lot of RAM, and you have to take its loss into account when you try to do things with JED waiting in memory.

Getting back into JED is easy. Just type the command EXIT at the DOS prompt. JED will instantly take you back with open arms, and you can continue work as though you had never taken a DOS break at all.

One interesting thing to do is to create and run an .EXE file by pressing F10, then duck out to DOS by pressing F5 and *erase* the .EXE file. Once you return to JED, immediately press F10 again. Even though you made no additional changes to the source code file, JED will search for the .EXE file before attempting to run it. If no .EXE file can be found, JED has no choice but to remake it.

4.4　◆　JED's Editor in Detail

As JED's beating heart, the text editor deserves a little space all to itself. JED's editor is the Borland Binary Editor, essentially the same editor that is used in the Turbo languages and Sidekick. Borland disengaged the editor module from its other products and made it available in linkable form (essentially one of those .OBJ files I described a while back) and placed it in the Turbo Pascal Editor Toolbox. If you own the Turbo Pascal Editor Toolbox, you can read up on the Binary Editor's many commands in the Editor Toolbox documentation. I'll describe them all briefly in this section.

Loading Files into the Editor

When you invoke JED and it begins running, it loads either the file you named on the command line or the last file it worked on as recorded in JED.CFG. The file is loaded into an area of memory called the *editor workspace*. The editor workspace is limited to 64K in size, and any file to be loaded must fit into memory in its entirety. If the file is too large to fit in available memory, you will see the message

Insufficient text buffer size

JED will then have no choice but to throw up its hands and return to DOS. You'll have to cut the monster file up into smaller files (which is a good idea anyway) and invoke JED again on only a portion of the oversized file.

Also keep in mind that individual lines within an edit file are limited to 248 characters. Loading a file with longer lines will cause the editor to insert hyphens at the 248-character point.

Moving the Cursor

Apart from the keypad keys and function keys F7 and F8 (used for marking text blocks, as I'll explain below) all editor commands are control keystrokes. That is, you must hold the Ctrl key down while pressing another key or two keys. All of the keys that control cursor movement are grouped together for you in a cluster toward the left hand side of the keyboard:

```
 W  E  R
 A  S  D  F
 Z  X  C
```

This arrangement of cursor command keys will be familiar to anyone who has worked with the WordStar word processor.

One character at a time.

Moving the cursor one character at a time can be done in all four directions:

CTRL-E or **Up Arrow** moves the cursor **Up** one character.

CTRL-X or **Down Arrow** moves the cursor **Down** one character.

CTRL-S or **Left Arrow** moves the cursor **Left** one character.

CTRL-D or **Right Arrow** moves the cursor **Right** one character.

The position of these four keys (E, X, S, and D) provide a hint as to which way they move the cursor. Look at how they are arranged on the keyboard:

```
   E
 S D
   X
```

Until the directions become automatic to your fingers (as they will, if you do enough editing!) thinking of the "magic diamond" will remind you which way the cursor will move for which key pressed.

When you move the cursor to the bottom of the screen and press Ctrl-X one more time, the screen will *scroll.* All the lines on the screen will jump up by one, and the top line will disappear. As long as the cursor is on the bottom line of the screen and you continue to press Ctrl-X, the screen will scroll upward. If you use Ctrl-E to move the cursor back in the opposite direction (upward) until it hits the top of the screen, continuing to press Ctrl-E will scroll the screen downward one line per keystroke.

One word at a time. JED will also move the cursor one word at a time to the left or right:

> **CTRL-A** or **CTRL-Left Arrow** moves the cursor **Left** one word.
>
> **CTRL-F** or **CTRL-Right Arrow** moves the cursor **Right** one word.

More hints are given here, because the A key is on the left side of the magic diamond, and the F key is on the right side of the magic diamond.

One screen at a time. It is also possible to move the cursor up or down through the file one whole screen at a time. Up in this sense means toward the beginning of the file; down means toward the end of the file. A screen is the height of your CRT display (25, 43, or 50 lines, depending on what display adaptor is installed and what font is currently loaded) minus two lines for the editor status line at the top and JED's prompt bar at the bottom.

> **CTRL-R** or **PgUp** moves the cursor **Up** one screen.
>
> **CTRL-C** or **PgDn** moves the cursor **Down** one screen.

Moving the cursor by scrolling the screen. I have described how the screen will scroll when you use the one-character-at-a-time commands to move up (Ctrl-E) from the top line of the screen or down (Ctrl-X) from the bottom line of the screen. You can scroll the screen up or down no matter where the cursor happens to be by using the scrolling commands:

> **CTRL-W** scrolls the screen **Down** one line.
>
> **CTRL-Z** scrolls the screen **Up** one line.

When you scroll the screen with these commands, the cursor rides with the screen as it scrolls up or down, until the cursor hits the top or bottom of the screen. Further scrolling will then make the screen slip past the cursor. The cursor always remains visible.

These are all of the cursor movement commands that may be invoked by one Ctrl keystroke. There are a few more that are accomplished by holding the Ctrl key down and pressing *two* keys in succession. *You must hold the Ctrl key down through both keypresses!*

Moving to the ends of the line. No matter where your cursor is on the screen, it is always within a line, even if that line happens to be empty of characters. There are two commands that will move the cursor either to the beginning (left side) of the line (screen column 1) or to the end of the line, which is the position following the last visible character on the line:

> **CTRL-Q-S** or **Home** sends the cursor to the **Beginning** of the line.
>
> **CTRL-Q-D** or **End** sends the cursor to the **End** of the line.

Moving to the ends of the file. The last set of cursor movement commands we'll describe takes the cursor to the beginning of the file or to the end of the file. If the file you are editing is more than a few screens long, it can save you a great deal of pounding on the keyboard to move one screen at a time.

> **CTRL-Q-R** or **CTRL-PgUp** sends the cursor to the **Beginning** of the file.
>
> **CTRL-Q-C** or **CTRL-PgDn** sends the cursor to the **End** of the file.

Because all of the current file is in memory all of the time, moving between the ends of the file can be done *very* quickly.

The Editor Status Line

At the very top of JED's editor screen is the editor status line; it provides you with some important information while you are editing. A typical instance of the status line looks like this:

> Line 1   Col 1   Insert Indent   C:EAT2.ASM   09:04:45

While you were moving the cursor around, the line and column numbers were continually changing to reflect the location of the cursor in the file. The column number reflects the position of the cursor within its line; the line number indicates which line in the file contains the cursor, counting from the beginning of the file, *not* from the top of the screen. At the other end of the status line is the name of the current file.

The other words (**Insert** and **Indent**) shown as part of the status line merit some explaining. Insert and Indent are the names of two *toggles*. A toggle is a condition that can exist in one of two different states. A toggle is like a switch controlling the lights in a room; the switch can be either on or off.

Insert determines how newly typed characters are added to your work file. When **Insert** is on (that is, when the word **Insert** appears in the status line) characters that you type are *inserted* into the file. The characters appear over the cursor and immediately push the cursor and the rest of the line to the left to make room for themselves. The line becomes one character longer for each character you type. If you press Enter, the cursor moves down one line, carrying with it the part of the line lying to its right.

When **Insert** is off (i.e., the word **Insert** is *not* displayed in the status line), characters that you type will *overwrite* characters that already exist in the file. No new characters are added to the file unless you move the cursor to the end of the line or the end of the file and keep typing. If you press Enter, the cursor will move down to the first character of the next line down, but nothing else will change. A line will only be added to the file if you press Enter with the cursor on the last line of the file.

Turning **Insert** on and off is done with a single control keypress:

CTRL-V toggles **Insert** on and off.

Indent is also a toggle. It indicates whether JED's auto-indent feature is on or off. When **Indent** is on, the cursor will automatically move beneath the first visible character on a new line when you press Enter. In other words (assuming that **Indent** is on) given this little bit of text on your screen:

```
Adjust:
        MOV AX, [BP] + 6
        SUB AX, Increment_      ← Before pressing Enter

        _
      ↑ After pressing Enter
```

The cursor is at the end of the last line of text. When you press Enter, the cursor will move down one line, but it will also space over automatically until it is beneath the S in SUB. This allows you to begin typing the next line of code without having to space the cursor over so that it is beneath the start of the previous line.

Like **Insert, Indent** can be toggled on and off. It takes a double control keystroke:

CTRL-Q-I toggles **Indent** on and off.

Indent is on when the word *Indent* appears in the status line.

Tab Mode

The editor status line also displays the current tab mode. What we call *tabbing* is the automatic spacing to the right upon pressing of the Tab key. On the PC's keyboard, there is no key with the word *Tab* on it; instead, the key is imprinted with two arrows pointing in opposite directions, with a vertical bar at the head of each arrow:

$$|\leftarrow$$
$$\rightarrow|$$

Some clone keyboards do include the word *Tab;* IBM's do not. It is usually positioned directly over the Ctrl key.

There are two kinds of tabs in JED's editor. The default tabs are not tabs as most people knew them prior to the onset of Borland's Turbo Pascal. These "smart" tabs move the cursor to the position beneath the start of the next word on the previous line. In other words, if you had the following line on your screen with the cursor on the line beneath it, the caret marks would show where the cursor would pause at each successive press of the Tab key:

Think of it as evolution in action...

This tabbing is done by inserting spaces, *not* by inserting the ASCII Tab (Ctrl-I) character.

Smart tabs as described above are the default tab mode in the editor. Pressing Ctrl-O-T toggles to the opposite tab mode, which supports true, 8-character fixed tabs that insert Ctrl-I characters at each press of the Tab key. If fixed tabs are in effect, the word **Tab** will be shown on the status line between the word Indent and the filename:

Line 1   Col 1   Insert Indent Tab C:EAT2.ASM   09:45:07

In summary, on tab mode

CTRL-O-T toggles between **Smart Tabs** and **Fixed Tabs.**

Inserts and Deletes

We've already seen how to insert characters into a text file: you make sure **Insert** is on and type away. Each typed character will be inserted into the file at the cursor position.

It is also possible to insert entire blank lines. One way, of course, is to move the cursor to the beginning of a line and press Enter. (**Insert** must be on.) A new blank line will be inserted above the line with the cursor, and the rest of the file will be pushed down. The cursor will ride down with the text.

The other way to insert a line is independent of the Insert toggle. Move the cursor to the beginning of a line and press Ctrl-N. A new line will appear, pushing the rest of the file down, *but the cursor will not move down with the other text.*

> **CTRL-N** inserts a **new line** at the cursor position.

There are also a number of different ways to *delete* text as well. The simplest is to use the Del (Delete) key. Pressing Ctrl-G performs exactly the same delete function.

> **Del** deletes one **Character** to the **Right** of the cursor.
>
> **CTRL-G** deletes one **Character** to the **Right** of the cursor.

The cursor does not move; it swallows the character to its right and the rest of the line to its right moves over to fill in the position left by the deleted character.

The Backspace key can be used to delete characters to the *left* of the cursor; another way the backspace key differs from Del is that the cursor rides to the left on each deletion:

> **Backspace** deletes one **Character** to the **Left** of the cursor.

You can think of backspace as eating one character to the left as it moves the cursor leftward.

To save a few keystrokes, you can also delete one *word* to the right of the cursor:

> **CTRL-T** deletes one **Word** to the **Right** of the cursor.

When you press Ctrl-T, all characters from the cursor position rightward to the end of the current word will be deleted. If the cursor happens to be on a space or group of spaces between words, those spaces will be deleted up to the beginning of the next word. It is possible to delete from the cursor position to the end of the cursor line:

> **CTRL-Q-Y** deletes from the cursor to **the end of the line.**

Finally, it is possible to delete the entire cursor line with a single control keystroke:

> **CTRL-Y** deletes the entire **Line** containing the cursor.

The line beneath the cursor moves up to take the place of the deleted line, pulling up the rest of the file behind it.

A warning here for those of you with thick fingers: the T and Y characters are right next to one another on the keyboard. In a late night frenzy at the keyboard you may find yourself reaching for the Ctrl-T to delete a word and hit Ctrl-Y instead, losing the entire line irretrievably. I've done this often enough that I simply broke myself of the habit of using Ctrl-T at all.

Undoing Changes to a Line

JED's editor keeps a "backup" copy of each line while you're working on it, and retains that copy as long as the cursor remains within the line. Therefore, if you delete a word or some other portion of the line, or add something to a line by mistake, you can undo those changes to the line *as long as you haven't yet left the line.* Once you leave the line, even momentarily, the editor throws away the backup copy, and undoing the error is no longer possible.

> **CTRL-Q/L** restores a line to its condition before you entered it.

One drawback is that the undo feature will *not* restore a line deleted entirely with the Ctrl-Y command. Once a line is deleted, the cursor (by necessity) leaves the line, and so the editor does not retain the backup copy of the line. Be careful how you use Ctrl-Y!

Markers and Blocks

JED's editor supports two different kinds of markers; that is, positions in the file that have a name or number and can be moved around as needed by the programmer. These are *place markers* and *block markers.*

Place markers.

There is no such thing as a page number in an editor file. You can move the cursor to the beginning or end of the file with a single command, but to move to a specific place in the file is more difficult. The best way is to remember a distinctive title, procedure name, or something like that and search for it (see below). You might also make use of the editor's place marker feature.

The editor supports four place markers, numbered 0 to 3. These can be placed at any position in a text file with a single command:

CTRL-K-<n> sets marker <n> within a file. <n> can be 0 to 3.

For example, to set marker 2, you would press Ctrl-K-2.

Once a place marker has been set, you can move the cursor to it with a single command:

CTRL-Q-<n> moves the cursor to marker <n>.

For example, to move to marker 2 you would type Ctrl-Q-2. If you have two or three "construction zones" within a largish source file, you might drop one of the place markers at the start of each zone so you can shuttle between the zones with a single command.

The markers are invisible, and if you forget where they are all you can do is move the cursor to them with the Ctrl-Q-<n> command.

Block markers.

The block marker is used to specify the beginning and end of a text block. There are only two of these markers, and in consequence only one block can be marked within a file at any given time. These are called the block markers, and their names are B and K, after the commands that position them in your file.

The block markers are invisible and do not appear on your screen in any way. If both are present in a file, however, all the text between them (the currently marked block) is shown as highlighted text.

Placing each block marker is a two-character control keystroke:

CTRL-K-B places the **B** marker. The shortcut is **F7.**

CTRL-K-K places the **K** marker. The shortcut is **F8.**

Note the two function key shortcuts, which are extremely convenient and fast.

A marker is placed at the cursor position and remains there until you move it elsewhere. You cannot delete or remove a marker once placed, although you can hide the block of text that lies between the markers, which effectively gets the markers out of the picture. (See below for more on hiding marked blocks.)

Moving the cursor to a block marker.
There are also commands to move the cursor to the block markers, B and K:

CTRL-Q-B moves the cursor to the **B** marker.

CTRL-Q-K moves the cursor to the **K** marker.

Hiding and unhiding blocks of text.
The major advantage of markers, however, is their ability to define a block a text. There are a number of commands available in JED's editor to manipulate the text that lies between the B and K markers.

You probably noticed while experimenting with setting markers that as soon as you positioned *both* the B and K markers in a file, the text between them became highlighted. The highlighted text is a marked text block. As we mentioned before, there is no way to remove a marker completely from a file once it has been set. You can, however, suppress the highlighting of text between the two markers. This is called hiding a block.

CTRL-K-H will **Hide** a **Block** of text.

Remember that the markers are still there. Ctrl-K-H is a toggle. You invoke it once to hide a block, and you can invoke it a second time to *unhide* the block and bring out the highlighting again on the text between the two blocks.

Something else to keep in mind: the other block commands we'll be looking at below work *only* on highlighted blocks. Once a block is hidden, it is hidden from the block commands as well as from your eyes.

Marking a word as a block.
The editor includes a short form of the command sequence for marking a single word as a block. Ordinarily, you'd have to move the cursor to the beginning of the word, press F7, then move to the end of the word and press F8. With one command you can mark a word as a block once you've moved the cursor to any position within that word.

CTRL-K-T marks the **word** containing the cursor as a **block.**

Block commands.   The simplest block command to understand is delete block. Getting rid of big chunks of text that are no longer needed is easy: Mark the text as a block with the two markers, and issue the delete block command:

CTRL-K-Y will **Delete** a **Block** of text.

The markers themselves are not destroyed with the block of text. They close up and occupy the same single cursor position, but they are still there, and you can move the cursor to them with the Ctrl-Q-B or Ctrl-Q-K commands.

The copy block command is useful when you have some standard text construction (a standard boilerplate comment header for procedures, perhaps) that you need to use several times within the same text file. Rather than type it each time, you type it once, mark it as a block, and then copy it from the original into each position where you need it. Simply place the cursor where the first character of the copied text must go, and issue the copy block command:

CTRL-K-C will **Copy** a **Block** of text to the cursor position.

Moving a block of text is similar to copying a block of text. The difference, of course, is that the original block of text that you marked vanishes from its original position and reappears at the cursor position. You must first mark the text you wish to move as a block, then put the cursor where you wish the marked text to go, and issue the move block command:

CTRL-K-V will **Move** a **Block** of text to the cursor position.

The last two block commands allow you to write a block of text to disk or to read a text file from disk into your work file. Writing a block to disk begins by marking the block you want saved as a separate text file. Then issue the write block command

CTRL-K-W will **Write** a **Block** of text to disk:

The editor needs to know the name of the disk file into which you want to write the marked block of text. It prompts you for the file name with a dialog box entitled, "Write block to file." You must type the name of the file with full path if you intend the block to be written outside of the current directory. Once the name is typed and you have pressed Enter, the block is written to disk. The block remains highlighted, and the cursor does not move.

Reading a text file from disk into your work file is also easy. You position the cursor at the point where the first character of the text from the file should go and issue the read block command

CTRL-K-R will **Read** a **Block** of text from disk to the cursor position.

Just as with the write block command, the editor will prompt you for the name of the file that you wish to read from disk with a dialog box entitled "Read block from file."

There is one small gotcha to be aware of in connection with file names. If you enter a file name *without* a period or file extension (that is, a file name like FOO rather than FOO.ASM) JED's editor will first look for a file named FOO. If it does not find one, it will then look for a file named FOO.ASM. If it cannot find a file with the entered name plus the .ASM file extension, it will issue this error message within an alarming red (if you have a color monitor) box:

Unable to open FOO.ASM.   Press <ESC>

Pressing Esc cancels the command entirely, and to enter the name correctly you will need to issue the Ctrl-K-R command again.

The text file will be read and inserted into your work file at the cursor position. It will come in as a marked block, and you will have to issue the hide block command to remove the highlighting. Remember also that reading a block of text from disk will effectively move your two block markers from elsewhere in your file and place them around the text that was read in.

The editor is not especially picky about the type of files you read from disk. Text files need not have been generated by JED's editor. Files need not be text files at all, but remember that reading raw binary data into a text file can cause the file to appear shortened: the first binary 26 (Ctrl-Z) encountered in a text file is assumed to signal the end of the file. Data after that first Ctrl-Z may or may not be accessible. Furthermore, the editor will attempt to display the binary characters as is, and loading (for example) an .EXE file will fill the screen with some pretty lively garbage.

Searching and Replacing

Much of the power of electronic text editing lies in its ability to search for a particular character pattern in a text file. Furthermore, once found, it is a logical extension of the search concept to replace the found text string with a different text string. For example, if you decide to change the name of a variable to something else to avoid conflict with another identifier in a program, you might wish to have the text editor locate every instance of the old variable name in a program and replace each one with the new variable name.

The editor can do both search and search and replace operations with great ease. Simply locating a given text string in a program is often better than having page numbering (which JED's editor does not.) If you wish to work on the part of a program that contains a particular procedure, all you need do is search for that procedure's name and you will move the cursor right to the spot you want.

CTRL-Q-F will **Find** a given text string.

When you issue the Find command, the editor prompts you with a single word:

Find:

You must then type the text string that you wish found, ending it by pressing Enter. The editor then prompts you for command options:

Options:

There are several command options that may be given to both the find and the find/replace commands. These are single letters (or numbers), and can be grouped together in any order without spaces in between,

Options: BWU

for example. We'll discuss each option in detail shortly. Once you press Enter after entering the options (if any) the editor executes the command. For the Find command, the cursor will move to the first character of the found text string. If the editor cannot find any instance of the requested text string in the work file, it displays the message

Search string not found. Press <ESC>

You must then press Esc to continue editing.

Find/replace.   Find/replace goes that extra step. Once the search text is found, it will replace the search text with a replacement text. The options mean everything here; you can replace only the first instance of the search text, or all instances, and you can have the editor ask permission before replacing, or simply go ahead and do the deed to as many instances of the search text as it finds. (This last operation is especially beloved of programmers, who call it *search and destroy.*)

As with Find, the editor prompts for the search text and options. It also must (for find/replace) prompt for the replacement string:

Replace with:

If no options are in force, the editor will locate the first instance of the search string, place the cursor beneath it, and give you the permission prompt:

Replace (Y/N):

If you type a Y here (no Enter required) the editor will perform the replacement. If you type an N, nothing will change.

Search/replace options.

The editor's find/replace options allow you to fine tune a find or find/replace command to cater to specific needs. For example, without any options the Find command is case sensitive. In other words, *FOO*, *foo,* and *Foo* are three distinct text strings, and searching for *FOO* will not discover instances of *foo.* With the U option in force, however, *FOO, foo,* and *Foo* are considered identical and searching for any of the three forms will turn up instances of any of the three that are present. There are several such options to choose from within the editor. In general, they are the same find/replace options used by WordStar.

B is the **Search Backwards** option. Ordinarily, a search will proceed from the cursor position toward the end of the file. If the object of the search is closer to the beginning of the file than the cursor, the search will not find it. With the B option in force, the search proceeds *backwards* through the file, toward the beginning.

G is the **Global Search** option. As mentioned above, searches normally begin at the cursor position and proceed toward one end of the file or the other, depending on whether or not the B option is in force. With the G option in force, searches begin at the beginning of the file and proceed to the end, irrespective of the cursor position. The G option overrides the B option.

N is the **Replace Without Asking** option. Without this option, the editor (during a find/replace) will prompt you for a yes/no response each time it locates an instance of the search text. With N in force, it simply does the replacement. Combining the G and N options means that the editor will search the entire file and replace every instance of the search text with the replacement text without asking. *Make sure you set it up right,* or you can cause wholesale damage to your work file. In general, *don't use G and N together without W.* (See below for details on the W option.)

U is the **Ignore Case** option. Without this option, searches are case sensitive. *FOO* and *foo* are considered distinct and searching for one will not find the other. With the U option in force, corresponding lower and upper case characters are considered identical. *FOO* and *foo* will both be found on a search for either.

W is the **Whole Words** option. Without this option, the search text will be found even when it is embedded in a larger word.

For example, searching for *LOCK* will find both *BLOCK* and *CLOCK*. With W in force, the search text must be bounded by spaces to be found. This option is especially important for global find/replace commands, when (if you omit W) replacing all instances of *LOCK* with *SECURE* will change all instances of *BLOCK* to *BSECURE* and all instances of *CLOCK* to *CSECURE*.

You may also give a number as one of the options. For the find command, this tells the editor to find the *n*th instance of the search text. For find/replace, a number tells the editor to find and replace text *n* times.

Find or find/replace again.   The editor remembers what the last find or find/replace command was—search text, replacement text, options, and all. You can execute that last find or find/replace command again simply by issuing the find or find/replace again command:

CTRL-L will perform the last find or find/replace command **again.**

Ctrl-L can save you some considerable keystroking. Suppose, for example, you wanted to examine the header line of every procedure in a large (perhaps 1000 line) program with 30 or 40 procedures. The way to do it is to search for the string *PROC* with the G, U, and W options in effect. The first invocation of this command will find the first procedure in your program file. To find the next one, simply press Ctrl-L. You need not reenter the search text *PROC* or the options. Each time you press Ctrl-L, the editor will find the next instance of the reserved word *PROC* until it gets to the end of the file or until you issue a new and different find or find/replace command.

Saving Your Work

It is *very* important to keep in mind what is happening while you edit text files with the editor. *You are editing entirely within memory.* Nothing goes out to disk while you are actually doing the edit. You can work on a file for hours, and one power failure will throw it all away. You must develop the discipline of saving your work frequently.

The easiest way to execute a save command from within the editor is with the save shortcut, F2. The "longcut" to saving the file from within the editor is Ctrl-K-S (useful if you have WordStar burned into your synapses) but F2 is easier to type and remember.

>   **F2** or **Ctrl-K-S** will *always* **Save** your work file.

Exiting the Editor

There is more than one way to get out of JED once you're finished with the job at hand. You can get out with any of these commands:

>   **Ctrl-K-D Saves** the current file, and **Exits** to DOS.
>   **Ctrl-K-Q ends** the edit *without* saving, and **Exits** to DOS.
>   **Alt-X Saves** the current file *if necessary* and **Exits** to DOS.

The differences between them are subtle. Ctrl-K-D always saves the current file and exits to DOS whether the file has been modified or not. If the current file is very large, this can mean a delay of several seconds while the file is written out to disk, *especially* if you're working from diskettes.

Ctrl-K-Q, on the other hand, may be used to exit from JED *without* saving the current file, even if the current file has been modified since it was last saved. JED, always the one for safety, will ask you if you want to abandon the changes you've made. You can answer only Y or N; Y will indeed exit to DOS without saving the current file. N, on the other hand, indicates a change of heart on your part and JED will save the current file to disk.

Finally, Alt-X is the smart way out. If you made changes to the current file since the last time it was saved to disk, JED will save the file to disk. If no changes were made, JED will not waste your time with an unnecessary save, but will drop you out to disk immediately.

No matter how you exit to DOS, JED considerately restores the DOS screen that existed just before you invoked JED.

One important use of Ctrl-K-Q is to undo a disastrous search-and-destroy operation that went bad using Ctrl-Q-A. If you've changed every one of the 677 instances of MOV to MUV by accident, *and haven't yet saved the damaged file to disk using F2,* your only course of action is to exit to DOS without saving the damaged file to disk. That done, you can reenter JED and the last undamaged version of the current file will be reloaded and ready for you to try again.

So be careful, huh?

Chapter 5

An Uneasy Alliance

The 8086/8088 CPU and Its Segmented Memory System

As comedian Bill Cosby once said, "I told you that story so I could tell you *this* one. . . ." We're pretty close to half finished with this book, and I haven't even begun describing the principal element in PC assembly language: the 8086/8088 CPU. Most books on assembly language, even those targeted to beginners, assume that the CPU is as good a place as any to start their story, without considering the mass of groundwork that without which most beginning programmers get totally lost and give up. That's why I began at the *real* beginning, and took 144 pages to get to where the other guys start.

Keep in mind that this book was created to supply that essential groundwork. It is *not* a complete course in PC assembly language. Once you finish this book, you'll have one leg up on the other, more advanced books in this series, or on any of the multitude of "beginner" books on assembly language from other publishers.

And it's high time we got right to the heart of things and met the foreman of the PC himself.

5.1 ◆ Through a Glass, with Blinders

Having worked my way up to the good stuff, I find myself faced with a tricky conundrum. Programming involves two major components of the PC: the CPU and memory. Most books begin by choosing one or the other and describing it. My own opinion is that you can't really describe memory and memory addressing without describing the CPU and you can't really describe the CPU without going into memory and memory addressing. So let's do both at once.

The Nature of a Megabyte

The 8086 and 8088 CPUs are identical in most respects, which is why we often refer to them and their cousins as the '86 family. The 8088 is used in IBM's original PC and XT and their ubiquitous clones. The 8086 is used in two of IBM's newer machines, the PS/2 models 25 and 30. Both machines can contain and use up to a megabyte of directly addressable memory. This memory is also called *real memory* or *DOS memory*. There is another kind of memory that you may have heard of, called *expanded memory*, that follows the Lotus-Intel-Microsoft (LIM) expanded memory specification (EMS). We're not speaking of expanded memory at all in this book; I consider it an advanced topic.

As I discussed briefly in Chapter 2, a megabyte of memory is actually not 1,000,000 bytes of memory, but 1,048,576 bytes. It doesn't come out even in our base 10 because computers insist on base 2. Expressed in base 2, 1,048,576 bytes is 100000000000000000000b bytes. (We don't use commas in base 2—that's yet another way to differentiate binary notation from decimal apart from the suffixed *b.*) That's 2^{20}, a fact that we'll return to shortly. The number 100000000000000000000b is so bulky that it's better to express it in the compatible (and much more compact) base 16, which we call hexadecimal. The number 2^{20} is equivalent to 16^5, and may be written in hexadecimal as 100000H. (If the notion of number bases still confounds you, I'd recommend another trip through Chapter 1 if you haven't been through it already, or, perhaps, even if you have.)

Now, here's a tricky and absolutely critical question: in a memory bank containing 100000H bytes, what's the address of the very last byte in the bank? The answer is *not* 100000H. The clue is the flipside to that question: what's the address of the *first* byte in the memory bank? That answer, you might recall, is 0. *Computers always begin counting from 0.* It's a gotcha that will occur again and again in computer programming. The last in a row of four items is item number 3, because the first item in a row of four is item number 0. Count 0, 1, 2, 3.

The address of a byte in a memory bank is just the number of that byte *starting from zero.* This means that the last, or highest address in a memory bank containing 1 megabyte, is 100000H minus one, or 0FFFFFH. (The initial 0, while not mathematically necessary, is there for the convenience of your assembler. Get in the habit of using an initial zero on any hex number beginning with the hex digits A to F.)

The addresses in a megabyte of memory, then, run from 00000H to 0FFFFFH. In binary notation, that is equivalent to the range of 00000000000000000000b to 11111111111111111111b. That's a lot of bits—20, to be exact. If you'll look back to Figure 2.3 in Chapter 2 (page 56 you'll see that a 1-megabyte memory bank has 20 address lines. One of those 20 bits is routed to each of those 20 address lines, so that any address expressed as 20 bits will identify 1 and only 1 of the 1,048,576 bytes contained in the memory bank.

That's what a megabyte of memory is: some arrangement of memory chips within the computer, connected by an address bus of 20 lines. A 20-bit address is fed to those 20 address lines to identify 1 byte out of the megabyte.

16-bit Blinders

The 8088 and 8086 can "see" a full megabyte. That is, the CPU chips have 20 address pins and can pass a full 20-bit address to the memory system.

From that perspective, it seems pretty simple and straightforward. The bulk of all the trouble you're ever likely to have understanding the '86 family CPUs stems from this fact: whereas those CPUs can see a full megabyte of memory, they are constrained to look at that megabyte through 16-bit blinders.

You may call this peculiar. (Later on, you'll probably call it much worse.) But you *must* understand it, and understand it thoroughly.

The blinders metaphor is closer to literal than you might think. Look at Figure 5.1. The long rectangle represents the megabyte of memory that the 8088 can address. The CPU is off to the right. In the middle is a piece of metaphorical cardboard with a slot cut in it. The slot is 1 byte wide and 65,536 bytes long. The CPU can slide that piece of cardboard up and down the full length of its memory system. However, *at any one time,* it can only access 65,536 bytes.

The CPU's view of memory is peculiar. It is constrained to look at memory in chunks, where no chunk is larger than 65,536 bytes in length.

64K is an important number, just as 1MB is. (We call 65,536 "64K" for the same reason that we call 1,048,576 "1MB"—it's just shorthand for what is actually a binary number that comes out even.) In fact, 64K is more important in assembly language programming than 1MB. 64K is the number that circumscribes almost everything that an assembly language programmer needs to do with the '86 family CPUs. It is, for one thing, the largest single number that the CPU can actually count and remember as an integral whole. You'll encounter it again and again and again.

65,536 in binary is 10000000000000000B; that is, 1 followed by 16 zeros; in hex it's 10000H. The important characteristic of 64K is that the number can be expressed in 16 bits. Sixteen bits, being a multiple of 1 byte, carries with it some of the magic quality of the byte as the data atom in our computer universe. The 8088 and 8086 are often called 16-bit computers, because they typically and most efficiently process 16 bits at once crunch. As we begin to discuss CPU registers, you'll come to fully understand just why the magical number 65,536 is as important and all pervasive as it is.

5.2 ◆ "They're Diggin' It up in Choonks!"

That's what Ray Walston shouted jubilantly in the marvelous film version of *Paint Your Wagon.* He was referring to gold being mined somewhere else (of course) but the metaphor to '86 family memory manipulation is apt. As we pointed out in the last section, the 8088 and its siblings dig memory

OFFFFFH

A full megabyte (1,048,576 bytes) of memory is at the 8088's disposal. However...

...the blinders force the 8088 to read and manipulate memory in chunks only 65,536 bytes in size.

8088

00000H

FIGURE 5.1   Seeing a megabyte through 64K blinders *only* in chunks—that's how they're made. Furthermore, it may not be as bad an idea as most programmers think.

To cement my point, let's talk about another type of nugget: native copper. The better part of a mile under the Mesabe range in upper Michigan is an enormous nugget of native copper the size of a freight locomotive. It may even be larger; the mining company that discovered it isn't entirely sure how large it is. This supernugget was discovered before World War II and is still down there at the end of a long tunnel, largely forgotten about.

Why leave a fortune in copper sitting where it was found, you ask? OK, wise guy—how do you get it out? Pure copper is a notoriously intractable metal. While not very hard, it is tough in ways that dull cutting tools and cause them to get stuck in their holes. The truth is that cutting the giant nugget up into manageable pieces would literally cost more than the copper would be worth at today's prices. Hauling out easily crushed copper ore in fist-sized chunks is enormously easier on men and equipment—so the supernugget remains in its hole, a curiosity and nothing more.

The lesson here is twofold: First of all, just as most mining companies do not encounter locomotive-sized nuggets every day (or even every century) most jobs a computer has to do don't involve enormous quantities of memory *at one time.* Second, even on computers without any such set of 64K blinders as the 8088, playing with a megabyte all at once is hard work and costly in machine performance.

It may be that the '86 family's blinders enable it to work more quickly and efficiently within its megabyte of memory. Whether true or not, this notion of seeing memory as a number of chunks, called *segments,* is key to understanding the '86 family CPUs as well.

The Nature of Segments

In '86 parlance, a *segment* is a region of memory that begins on a paragraph boundary and extends for some number of bytes less than or equal to 64K (65,536). We've spoken of the number 64K before, but paragraphs?

Time out for a lesson in '86 family trivia. A *paragraph* is a measure of memory equal to 16 bytes. It is one of numerous technical terms used to describe various quantities of memory. We've spoken of some of them before, and all of them are even multiples of 1 byte. Bytes are data atoms, remember; loose memory bits never exist in the absence of a byte of memory to contain them. These terms are of uneven usefulness, but you should be aware of all of them, which are given in Table 5.1.

Table 5.1 lists two names for each term. One is the technical term that you and I and all the rest of the humans use in speaking. The assembler has

TABLE 5.1　　　Collective terms for memory

NAME		SIZE	
Technical	*Assembler*	*Decimal*	*Hex*
Byte	BYTE	1	01H
Word	WORD	2	02H
Double word	DWORD	4	04H
Quad word	QWORD	8	08H
Ten byte	TBYTE	10	0AH
Paragraph	PARA	16	10H
Page	PAGE	256	100H
Segment	SEGMENT	65,536	10000H

its own names for these terms, which you will have to use when writing assembly language programs. Some of these terms, like ten byte, occur very rarely, and others, like page, occur almost never. The term paragraph is almost never used, *except* in connection with the places where segments may begin.

Any memory address evenly divisible by 16 is called a *paragraph boundary.* The first paragraph boundary is address 0, the second is address 10H, the third is address 20H, and so on. Any paragraph boundary can be considered the start of a segment.

This *doesn't* mean that a segment actually starts every 16 bytes up and down throughout that megabyte of memory. A segment is like a shelf in one of those modern adjustable bookcases. On the back face of the bookcase are a great many little slots spaced one-half inch apart. A shelf bracket can be inserted into any of the little slots. There aren't hundreds of shelves, however, but only four or five. Most of the slots are empty. They exist so that a much smaller number of shelves can be adjusted up and down the height of the bookcase as needed.

In a very similar manner, paragraph boundaries are little slots at which a segment may be begun. An assembly language program can make use of only four or five segments, but each of those segments can begin at any of the 65,536 paragraph boundaries existing in the 8088's megabyte of memory.

There's that number again: 65,536, our beloved 64K. There are 64K different paragraph boundaries where a segment may begin. Each paragraph boundary has a number. As always, the numbers begin from 0 and go to 64K minus 1; in decimal, 65,535; in hex, 0FFFFFH. Because a segment can begin at any paragraph boundary, the number of the paragraph boundary at which a segment begins is called the *segment address* of that particular segment. We rarely, in fact, speak of paragraphs or paragraph boundaries at all. When you see the term "segment address," keep in mind that each segment address is 16 bytes (one paragraph) farther along in memory than the one before it. See Figure 5.2.

FIGURE 5.2   Memory addresses versus segment addresses

In short, segments can begin at any segment address. There are 65,536 segment addresses evenly distributed across the 8088's full megabyte of memory, 16 bytes apart. A segment address is more a permission than a compulsion; for all the 64K possible segment addresses, only five or six are ever actually used to begin segments at any one time. Think of segment addresses as slots where segments may be placed.

So much for segment addresses; now, what of segments themselves? A segment can be up to 64K bytes in size, but it doesn't *have* to be. A segment can be only 1 byte long, or 256 bytes long, or 21,378 bytes long, or any length at all, short of 64K bytes.

A Horizon, Not a Place

You define a segment primarily by stating where it begins. What, then, defines how *long* a segment is? Nothing, really, and we get into some really tricky semantics here. A segment is more a *horizon* than a *place*. Once you define where a segment begins, that segment can encompass any location in memory between that starting place and the horizon, which is 65,536 bytes down the line.

Nothing says, of course, that a segment must use all of that memory. In most cases, when you define a segment to exist at some segment address, you only end up considering the next few hundred bytes as part of that segment, at least until you get into some truly world-class programs. Most beginners read about segments and think of them as some kind of memory allocation, a protected region of memory with walls on both sides, reserved for some specific use.

This is about as far from true as you can get. Nothing is protected within a segment, and segments are not reserved for any specific register or access method. Segments can overlap. Segments don't really exist, in a very real sense, *except* as horizons beyond which a certain type of reference cannot go. It goes back to that set of 64K blinders the CPU wears, as I drew in Figure 4.1. I think of it this way: *A segment is the location in memory at which the CPU's 64K blinders are positioned.* In looking at memory through the blinders, you can see bytes starting at the segment address and going on until the blinders cut you off, 64K bytes down the way.

The key to understanding this admittedly metaphysical definition of a segment is knowing how segments are used. And coming to understand that finally brings us to the subject of registers.

Making 20-Bit Addresses out of 16-Bit Registers

The 8088 and 8086 are often called 16-bit CPUs because their internal registers are almost all 16 bits in size. A *register,* as I've hinted before, is a memory location *inside* the CPU chip rather than outside in a memory bank. The '86 family has a fair number of registers, and these registers are an interesting crew indeed.

Registers do many jobs, but one of their more important jobs is holding addresses of important locations in memory. If you'll recall, the 8088 has 20 address pins, and its megabyte of memory requires addresses 20 bits in size.

How do you put a 20-bit memory address in a 16-bit register?

Easy. You don't.

You put a 20-bit address in *two* 16-bit registers.

What happens is this: all locations within the 8088's megabyte of memory have not one address but *two*. Every byte in memory is assumed to reside within a segment. A byte's complete address, then, consists of the address of its segment, along with the distance of the byte from the start of that segment. The address of the segment is (as we said before) the byte's *segment address*. The byte's distance from the start of the segment is the byte's *offset address*. Both addresses must be specified to completely describe any single byte's location within the full megabyte of memory. When written, the segment address comes first, followed by the offset address; the two are separated by a colon. Segment:offset addresses are always written in hexadecimal. Make sure the colon is there so that people know you're specifying an address and not just a couple of numbers!

I've drawn Figure 5.3 to help make this a little clearer. A byte of data that we'll call **MyByte** exists in memory at the location marked. Its address is given as 0001:001D. This means that **MyByte** falls within segment 0001H and is located 001DH bytes from the start of that segment. Note that when two numbers are used to specify an address with a colon between them, you do *not* end each of the two numbers with the *H* that indicates hexadecimal.

You can omit leading zeroes if you like, i.e., instead of saying 00B2:0004 you could write 0B2:4. (The leading zero is retained in front of the *B* is in keeping with the assembly language policy of never allowing a hex number to begin with the hex digits A through F.) As a good rule of thumb, however, I recommend using all four hex digits in both components of the address *except* when all four digits are zero. In other words, you can abbreviate 0000:0061 to 0:0061 or 0B00:0000 to 0B00:0.

The universe is perverse, however, and clever eyes will perceive that **MyByte** can have two other perfectly legal addresses: 0:002D; and 0002:000D. How so? Keep in mind that a segment may start every 16 bytes throughout the full megabyte of real memory. A segment, once begun, embraces all bytes from its origin to 65,535 bytes farther up in memory. There's nothing wrong with segments overlapping, and in Figure 5.3 we have three

MyByte could have any of three
possible addresses:

0000H : 002DH
0001H : 001DH
0002H : 000DH

FIGURE 5.3   Segments and offsets

overlapping segments. **MyByte** is 2DH bytes into the first segment, which begins at segment address 0000H. **MyByte** is 1DH bytes into the second segment, which begins at segment address 0001H. It's not that **MyByte** is in two or three places at once; it's in only one place, but that one place can be described in any of three ways.

It's a little like Chicago's street number system. Howard Street is 76 blocks from Chicago's origin, Madison Street. Howard Street is, however, only 4 blocks from Touhy Avenue. You can describe Howard Street's location relative to either Madison Street or Touhy Avenue, depending on what you want to do.

An arbitrary byte somewhere in the middle of the 8086's megabyte of memory may fall within literally tens of thousands of different segments. Which segment the byte is *actually* in is strictly a matter of convention.

This problem occurs in real life to confront programmers of the IBM PC. The PC keeps its time and date information in a series of memory bytes that start at address 0040:006C. There is also a series of memory bytes containing PC timer information located at 0000:046C. You guessed it—we're talking about exactly the same starting byte. Different writers speaking of that same byte can give its address in either of those two ways, and they'll all be completely correct.

The way, then, to express a 20-bit address in two 16-bit registers is to put the segment address into one 16-bit register and the offset address into another 16-bit register. The two registers taken together identify one byte among all 1,048,576 bytes in a megabyte.

5.3 ◆ Registers and Memory Addresses

Think of the segment address as the starting position of the 8086/8088's 64K blinders. Typically, you'll move the blinders to encompass the location that you wish to work with, and then leave the blinders in one place while moving around within their 64K limits.

This is exactly how registers tend to be used in 8086/8088 assembly language. There are exactly four *segment registers* specifically designated as holders of segment addresses. Each segment register is a 16-bit memory location existing within the CPU chip itself. No matter what the CPU is doing, if it's addressing some location in memory, the segment address of that location is present in one of the four segment registers.

The segment registers have names that reflect their general functions: **CS, DS, SS,** and **ES.**

◆ **CS** stands for **C**ode **S**egment. Machine instructions exist at some offset into a code segment. The segment address of the code segment of the currently executing instruction is contained in **CS.**

◆ **DS** stands for **D**ata **S**egment. Variables and other data exist at some offset into a data segment. There may be many data segments, but the CPU typically uses only one at a time by placing the segment address of that segment in register **DS.**

◆ **SS** stands for **S**tack **S**egment. The *stack* is a very important component of the CPU used for temporary storage of data and addresses. I'll explain how the stack works a little later; for now simply understand that, like everything else within the 8086/8088's megabyte of memory, the stack has a segment address, which is contained in **SS.**

♦ **ES** stands for **E**xtra **S**egment. The extra segment is exactly that: a spare segment that may be used for specifying a location in memory.

General-Purpose Registers

The segment registers exist only to hold segment addresses. They can be forced to do a few other things, but by and large segment registers should be considered specialists in containing segment addresses. The 8086/8088 CPU has a crew of generalist registers to do the rest of the work of assembly language computing. Among many other things, these *general-purpose registers* are used to hold the offset addresses that must be paired with segment addresses to pin down a location in memory.

Like the segment registers, the general-purpose registers are memory locations existing inside the CPU chip itself. They all have names rather than numeric addresses: **AX, BX, CX, DX, SP, BP, SI,** and **DI.** The general purpose registers really are generalists in that all of them share a large suite of capabilities. However, each of the general-purpose registers also has what I call its "hidden agenda": a task or set of tasks that only it can perform.

I'll explain all these hidden agendas as I go. For now, we'll concentrate on the role of the general purpose registers in addressing memory.

Several of the general-purpose registers (BX, BP, SP, SI, and DI) can contain an offset address. This offset address may be used in combination with any of the segment registers to zero in on any one of the 1,048,576 bytes in the megabyte address space of the 8086/8088. All you need to do is specify which two registers are to be used together, with the segment register first and the general-purpose register second. For example:

```
SS : SP
SS : BP
ES : DI
DS : SI
CS : BX
```

Register halves.   General purpose registers AX, BX, CX, and DX have an important property: they can be cut in half. Actually, assemblers recognize special names for the two halves of these four registers. The A, B, C, and D are retained, but instead of the X, a half is specified with an *H* (for high half) or an *L* (for low half). Each register half is 1 byte (8 bits) in size, allowing the entire register to be 16 bits in size, or word-sized.

Thus, making up word-sized register AX you have byte-sized register halves AH and AL; within BX there is BH and BL, and so on. One nice thing about this arrangement is that you can read and change one half of a 16-bit number without disturbing the other half. This means that if you place the word-sized hexadecimal value 76E9H into register AX, you can read the byte-sized value 76H from register AH, and 0E9H from register AL. Better still, if you then store the value 0AH into register AL and then read back register AX, you'll find that the original value of 76E9H has been changed to 760AH.

Being able to treat the AX, BX, CX, and DX registers as 8-bit halves can be extremely handy in situations where you're manipulating a lot of 8-bit quantities. Each register half can be considered a separate register, leaving you twice the number of places to put things while your program works. As you'll see later on, finding a place to stick a value in a pinch is one of the great challenges facing assembly language programmers.

Keep in mind that this dual nature involves *only* general-purpose registers AX, BX, CX, and DX. The other general-purpose registers SP, BP, SI, and DI, are *not* similarly equipped. There are no SIH and SIL 8-bit registers, for example, as convenient as that would sometimes be.

The Instruction Pointer

Yet another type of register lives inside the 8086/8088 CPU. The *instruction pointer* (usually called **IP**) is in a class by itself. IP is far more of a specialist than are any of the segment registers. It can do only one thing: it contains the offset address of the next machine instruction to be executed.

While executing a program, the CPU uses IP to keep track of where it is. Each time an instruction is executed, IP is *incremented* by some number of bytes. The number of bytes is the size of the instruction just executed. The net result is to bump IP further into memory, so that it points to the start of the next instruction to be executed. Instructions come in different sizes, ranging anywhere from 1 to 6 bytes. The CPU is careful to increment IP by just the right number of bytes, so that it does in fact end up pointing to the start of the next instruction and not merely into the middle of the last instruction.

If IP contains the offset address of the next machine instruction, where is the segment address? The segment address is kept in the code segment register CS. Together, CS and IP contain the full 20-bit address of the next machine instruction to be executed.

> **The full 20-bit address of the next machine instruction to be executed is kept in CS:IP.**

A *code segment* is an area of memory where machine instructions are stored. The steps and tests of which a program is made are contained in code segments. There may be many code segments in a program, but small programs like the ones in this book will most likely have only one. The *current code segment* is that code segment whose segment address is currently stored in code segment register CS. At any given time, the machine instruction currently being executed exists within the current code segment.

Typically, large programs are divided into chunks, with each chunk considered to be part of a separate code segment. Switching from one code segment to another is done with a class of instructions called branching instructions, which I'll be covering in Section 9.3.

IP is notable in being the *only* register that can neither be read nor written to directly. It's possible to obtain the current value of IP, but the method involves some trickery that will have to wait until we discuss branching instructions.

The Flags Register

There is one additional type of register inside the CPU: The flags register. The flags register as a whole is simply called the *flags register*. It is 16 bits in size and most of these 16 bits are single-bit registers called *flags*. Each of these individual flags has a name like **CF, DF, OF,** and so on.

When your program performs a test, what it tests are one or another of the single-bit flags in the flags register. Because a single bit may contain one of only two values, 1 or 0, a test in assembly language is a two-way affair: Either a flag is set to 1 or it isn't. If the flag is set to one, the program takes one action; if the flag is set to 0, the program takes a different action.

We're concentrating on memory addressing at the moment, so for now I'll simply promise to go into flag lore in more detail at more appropriate moments later in the book.

Reading and Changing Registers with DEBUG

The DOS DEBUG utility provides a handy window into the CPU's hidden world of registers. How DEBUG does this is the blackest of all the black arts and I won't begin to explain it. For now, just consider DEBUG a magic box.

Looking at the registers from DEBUG doesn't even require that you load a program into DEBUG. Simply run DEBUG and at the dash prompt type the single-letter command R. The display will look something very close to this:

```
-R
AX=0000   BX=0000   CX=0000   DX=0000   SP=FFEE   BP=0000   SI=0000   DI=0000
DS=1980   ES=1980   SS=1980   CS=1980   IP=0100      NV UP EI PL NZ NA PO NC
1980:0100     389A5409        CMP     [BP+SI+0954],BL                 SS:0954=8A
```

I say "something very close" because details of the display will vary depending on what resident programs you have loaded in memory, which version of DOS you're using, and so on. What will vary will be the values listed as present in the various registers, and the machine instruction shown in the third line of the display. (Here, the machine instruction is **CMP [BP+SI+0954],BL**)

What will *not* vary is the fact that every CPU register has its place in the display, along with its current value shown to the right of an equals sign. The characters *NV UP EI PL NZ NA PO NC* are a summary of the current values of the flags in the flags register.

The display shown above is that of the registers when *no* program has been loaded. All of the general-purpose registers except for SP have been set to 0, and all of the segment registers have been set to the value 1980H. These are the default conditions set up by DEBUG in the CPU when no program has been loaded. (The 1980H value will probably be different for you—it represents the first available segment in memory above DOS and where that segment falls depends on what else exists in memory both above and below DOS.)

Changing a register is done very simply, again using DEBUG's R command. To change the value of AX, type R AX:

```
-R AX
AX:0000
:0A7B
-
```

DEBUG will respond by displaying the current value of AX, and then, on the following line, a colon prompt. It will wait for you to either enter a new numeric value for AX, or else for you to press Enter. If you press Enter, the current value of the register will not be changed. In the example shown above, I typed *0A7B* (you needn't type the H indicating hex) followed by Enter.

Once you do enter a new value and then press Enter, DEBUG does nothing to verify the change. To see the change to register AX, you must display all the registers again using the R command:

```
-R
AX=0A7B  BX=0000  CX=0000  DX=0000  SP=FFEE  BP=0000  SI=0000  DI=0000
DS=1980  ES=1980  SS=1980  CS=1980  IP=0100     NV UP EI PL NZ NA PO NC
1980:0100   389A5409       CMP    [BP+SI+0954],BL                  SS:0954=8A
```

Take a few minutes to practice entering new values for the general purpose registers, then display the registers as a group to verify that the changes were made. While exploring you might find that the IP register can be changed, even though I said earlier that it can't be changed directly. The key word is *directly;* DEBUG knows all the dirty tricks.

Inspecting the Video Refresh Buffer with DEBUG

One good way to help your knowledge of memory addressing sink in is to use DEBUG to take a look at some interesting places in the PC's memory space.

One easy thing to do is look at the video display adapter's refresh buffer. A *video refresh buffer* is a region of memory with a difference: any characters written to this buffer memory are instantly displayed on the computer's screen. This is accomplished electrically through the special use of the information that comes out of the memory data pins. Precisely how it is done is beyond the scope of this book. For now, simply understand that writing a character to your display screen can be done by writing the ASCII code for that character into the correct address in the video refresh buffer portion of memory.

As with any memory location anywhere within the PC, the video refresh buffer has a segment address. What that segment address is depends on the kind of display installed in the PC. There are two separate possibilities, and which is present is easy enough to determine: If your PC has a *color* screen, the segment address of the video refresh buffer is 0B800H. If you have a *monochrome* screen, the segment address is 0B000H.

It takes 2 bytes in the buffer to display a character. The first of the 2 (that is, first in memory) is the ASCII code of the character itself. For example, an *A* would require the ASCII code 41H; a *B* would require the

ASCII code 42H, and so on. (The full ASCII code set is shown in Appendix A). The second of the 2 bytes is the character's *attribute*. Think of it this way: in the display of a character on the screen, the ASCII code says *what* and the attribute says *how*. The attribute dictates the color of a character and its background cell on a color screen. On a monochrome screen, the attribute specifies if a character is underlined or displayed in reverse video. (*Reverse video* is a character display mode in which a dark character is shown on a light background, rather than the traditional light character on a dark or black background.) Every character byte has an attribute byte and every attribute byte has its character byte; neither can ever exist alone.

The very first character/attribute pair in the video refresh buffer corresponds to the character you see in the upper left hand corner of the screen. The next character/attribute pair in the buffer is the character on the second position on the top line of the screen, and so on. I've drawn a diagram of the relationship between characters on the screen and byte values in the video refresh buffer in Figure 5.4.

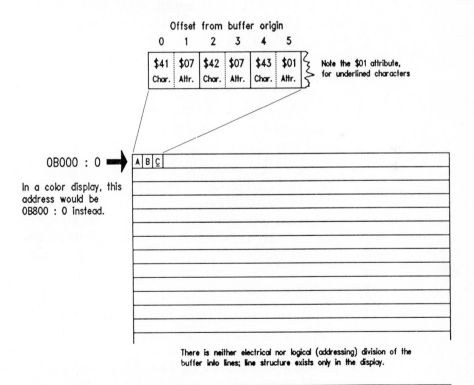

FIGURE 5.4   The PC's video refresh buffer

In Figure 5.4, the three letters *ABC* are displayed in the upper left corner of the screen. Notice that the *C* is underlined. The screen shown in Figure 5.4 is a monochrome screen. The video refresh buffer therefore begins at 0B000:0. The byte located at address 0B000:0 is ASCII code 41H, corresponding to the letter *A.* The byte at address 0B00:0001 is the corresponding attribute value of 07H. 07H as an attribute dictates normal text in both color and monochrome displays, where normal means white characters on a black background.

The byte at 0B000:0005 is also an attribute byte, but its value is 01H. On a monochrome screen, 01H makes the corresponding character underlined. On a color display, 01H makes the character blue on a black background.

There is nothing about the video refresh buffer to divide it into the lines you see on the display. The first 160 characters (80 ASCII codes plus their 80 attribute bytes) are shown as the first line, and each of the subsequent 160 characters is shown on the next line down the screen.

You might rightfully ask what ASCII code is in the video refresh buffer for locations on the screen that show no character at all. The answer, of course, is that there *is* a character in every empty space, the space character, whose ASCII code is 20H.

You can inspect the memory within the video refresh buffer directly through DEBUG. Take the following steps:

1. Clear the screen by entering CLS at the DOS prompt and pressing Return.
2. Invoke DEBUG.
3. Decide where your video refresh buffer is located, and enter the proper segment address into the ES register through the R command. Remember, color screens use the 0B800H segment address, while monochrome screens use the 0B000H segment address. Note from the session dump below that 0B800H must be entered into DEBUG as B800, *without* the leading zero. TASM and MASM *must* have that leading zero, and DEBUG *cannot* have it. Sadly, no one ever said that all parts of this business had to make perfect sense.
4. Dump the first 128 bytes of the video refresh buffer by entering D ES:0.
5. Dump the next 128 bytes of the video refresh buffer simply by entering the D command alone a second time.

What you'll see should look a lot like the session dump shown below:

```
C:\ASM>debug
-r es
ES 1980
```

```
:b800
-d es:0
B800:0000  20 07 20 07 20 07 20 07-20 07 20 07 20 07 20 07   . . . . . . . .
B800:0010  20 07 20 07 20 07 20 07-20 07 20 07 20 07 20 07   . . . . . . . .
B800:0020  20 07 20 07 20 07 20 07-20 07 20 07 20 07 20 07   . . . . . . . .
B800:0030  20 07 20 07 20 07 20 07-20 07 20 07 20 07 20 07   . . . . . . . .
B800:0040  20 07 20 07 20 07 20 07-20 07 20 07 20 07 20 07   . . . . . . . .
B800:0050  20 07 20 07 20 07 20 07-20 07 20 07 20 07 20 07   . . . . . . . .
B800:0060  20 07 20 07 20 07 20 07-20 07 20 07 20 07 20 07   . . . . . . . .
B800:0070  20 07 20 07 20 07 20 07-20 07 20 07 20 07 20 07   . . . . . . . .
-d
B800:0080  20 07 20 07 20 07 20 07-20 07 20 07 20 07 20 07   . . . . . . . .
B800:0090  20 07 20 07 20 07 20 07-20 07 20 07 20 07 20 07   . . . . . . . .
B800:00A0  43 07 3A 07 5C 07 41 07-53 07 4D 07 3E 07 64 07   C. :. \. A. S. M. >. d.
B800:00B0  65 07 62 07 75 07 67 07-20 07 20 07 20 07 20 07   e. b. u. g. . . . .
B800:00C0  20 07 20 07 20 07 20 07-20 07 20 07 20 07 20 07   . . . . . . . .
B800:00D0  20 07 20 07 20 07 20 07-20 07 20 07 20 07 20 07   . . . . . . . .
B800:00E0  20 07 20 07 20 07 20 07-20 07 20 07 20 07 20 07   . . . . . . . .
B800:00F0  20 07 20 07 20 07 20 07-20 07 20 07 20 07 20 07   . . . . . . . .
```

The first 80 character/attribute pairs are the same: 20H/07H, which display as plain ordinary blank space. When you execute the CLS command on most machines, the screen is cleared, and the DOS prompt reappears on the *second* line from the top of the screen, *not* the top line. The top line is typically left blank, as is the case here.

You'll see in the second block of 128 dumped bytes the DOS prompt and the invocation of DEBUG in lower case. Keep in mind when reading DEBUG hex dumps that any character not readily displayed as one of the standard ASCII letters, numbers, or punctuation marks is represented as a period character. This is why the 07H attribute character is shown on the right portion of DEBUG's display as a period character, since the ASCII code 07H has no displayable equivalent.

You can keep dumping further into the video refresh buffer by pressing DEBUG's D command repeatedly.

Reading the BIOS Revision Date

Another interesting item that's easy to locate in your PC is the revision date in the ROM BIOS. *ROM* (Read Only Memory) chips are special memory chips that retain their contents when power to the PC is turned off. The *BIOS* (Basic Input/Output System) is a collection of assembly language routines that perform basic services for the PC: disk handling, video handling, printer handling, etc. The BIOS is kept in ROM at the very top of the PC's megabyte of address space.

   The BIOS contains a date, indicating when it was declared finished by its authors. This date is always at the same address, and can be easily displayed using DEBUG's D command. The address of the date is 0FFFF:0005. The DEBUG session is shown below. Note again that the hex number 0FFFFH must be entered without its leading zero:

```
-d ffff:0005
FFFF:0000                    30 34 2F-33 30 2F 38 37 00 FC B8        04/30/87 . . .
FFFF:0010   00 00 00 00 00 00 00 00-00 00 00 00 00 00 00 00   . . . . . . . . . . . . . . .
FFFF:0020   00 00 00 00 00 00 00 00-00 00 00 00 00 00 00 00   . . . . . . . . . . . . . . .
FFFF:0030   00 00 00 00 00 00 00 00-00 00 00 00 00 00 00 00   . . . . . . . . . . . . . . .
FFFF:0040   00 00 00 00 00 00 00 00-00 00 00 00 00 00 00 00   . . . . . . . . . . . . . . .
FFFF:0050   00 00 00 00 00 00 00 00-00 00 00 00 00 00 00 00   . . . . . . . . . . . . . . .
FFFF:0060   00 00 00 00 00 00 00 00-00 00 00 00 00 00 00 00   . . . . . . . . . . . . . . .
FFFF:0070   00 00 00 00 00 00 00 00-00 00 00 00 00 00 00 00   . . . . . . . . . . . . . . .
FFFF:0080   00 00 00 00 00                                    . . . . .
```

One peculiarity of DEBUG illustrated here is that when you begin a hex dump of memory at an address that is *not* evenly divisible by 16, DEBUG spaces the first byte of the dump over to the right so that paragraph boundaries still fall at the left margin.

   Another rather peculiar thing to keep in mind while looking at the dump shown above is that *only the first line of memory shown in the dump really exists.* The segment 0FFFFH begins only 16 bytes before the end of the 8086/8088's megabyte of memory space. (See Figure 5.2 for a good illustration of this.) The byte at 0FFFF:000F is the *last* byte in memory. Addresses from 0FFFF:0010 to 0FFFF:0FFFF would require more than 20 address bits to express, so they simply don't exist. DEBUG won't tell you that—it'll just give you endless pages of zeroes for memory beyond the 8086/8088 megabyte limit.

Transferring Control to Machine Instructions in ROM

So far we've looked at locations in memory as containers for data. All well and good, but memory contains machine instructions as well. A very effective illustration of a machine instruction at a particular address is also provided by the ROM BIOS, and right next door to the BIOS revision date, at that.

The machine instruction in question is located at address 0FFFF:0. Recall that, by convention, the *next* machine instruction to be executed is the one whose address is stored in CS:IP. Run DEBUG. Load the value 0FFFFH into code segment register CS, and 0 into instruction pointer IP. Then dump memory at 0FFFF:0:

```
-r  cs
CS 1980
:ffff
-r  ip
-r  0100
:0

-r
AX=0000   BX=0000   CX=0000   DX=0000   SP=FFEE   BP=0000   SI=0000   DI=0000
DS=1980   ES=1980   SS=1980   CS=FFFF   IP=0000      NV UP EI PL NZ NA PO NC
FFFF:0000    EA5BE000F0    JMP    F000:E05B
FFFF:0000 EA 5B E0 00 F0 30 34 2F-33 30 2F 38 37 00 FC B8   .[...04/30/87...
FFFF:0010 00 00 00 00 00 00 00 00-00 00 00 00 00 00 00 00   ................
FFFF:0020 00 00 00 00 00 00 00 00-00 00 00 00 00 00 00 00   ................
FFFF:0030 00 00 00 00 00 00 00 00-00 00 00 00 00 00 00 00   ................
FFFF:0040 00 00 00 00 00 00 00 00-00 00 00 00 00 00 00 00   ................
FFFF:0050 00 00 00 00 00 00 00 00-00 00 00 00 00 00 00 00   ................
FFFF:0060 00 00 00 00 00 00 00 00-00 00 00 00 00 00 00 00   ................
FFFF:0070 00 00 00 00 00 00 00 00-00 00 00 00 00 00 00 00   ................
```

Look at the third line of the register display, which we've been ignoring until now. To the right of the address display is this series of five bytes: **EA5BE000F0.**

These 5 bytes make up the machine instruction we want. Notice that the first line of the memory dump begins with the same address, and, sure enough, shows us the same 5 bytes.

Trying to remember what machine instruction **EA5BE000F0** is would try anyone's intellect, so DEBUG is a good sport and translates the 5 bytes into a more readable representation of the machine instruction. We call this process of translating binary machine codes back into human-readable assembly language mnemonics *unassembly* or, more commonly, *disassembly*:

JMP F000:E05B.

What this instruction does, quite simply, is tell the CPU to jump to the address 0F000:0E05B and begin executing the machine instructions located there. If we execute the machine instruction at CS:IP, that's what will happen: the CPU will jump to the address 0F000:0E05B and begin executing whatever machine instructions it finds there.

All PCs have a **JMP** instruction at address 0FFFF:0. The address to where that **JMP** instruction jumps will be different for different makes and models of PC. This is why on your machine you won't necessarily see the exact 5 bytes **EA5BE000F0,** but whatever 5 bytes you find at 0FFFF:0, they will *always* begin with 0EAH. The 0EAH byte specifies that this instruction will be a **JMP** instruction. The remainder of the machine instruction is the address to which the CPU must jump. If that address as given in the machine instruction looks a little scrambled, well, it is . . . but that's the way the '86 family of CPUs do things. We'll return to the issue of funny-looking addresses a little later.

DEBUG has a command, G (for Go) that begins execution at the address stored in CS:IP. If you enter the G command and press Enter, the CPU will jump to the address built into the **JMP** instruction and begin executing machine instructions. What happens then?

Your machine will go into a *cold boot,* just as it would if you powered down and powered up again. (So make sure you're ready for a reboot before you try it!)

This may seem odd, but consider that the CPU chip has to begin execution somewhere. When the CPU wakes up after being off all night with the power removed, it must get a first machine instruction from somewhere and start executing. Built into the silicon of the 8086/8088 CPU chips is the assumption that a legal machine instruction will exist at address 0FFFF:0. When power is applied to the CPU chip, the first thing it does is place 0FFFFH in CS, and 0 in IP. Then it starts fetching instructions from the address in CS:IP and executing them, one at a time, in the manner that CPUs must.

This is why all PCs have a **JMP** instruction at 0FFFF:0, and why this **JMP** instruction always jumps to the routines that bring the PC up from stone cold dead to fully operational.

So go ahead—Load 0FFFFH into CS and 0 into IP, and press G. Feel good?

It's what we call the feeling of *power.*

Chapter 6

Following Your Instructions

Meeting Machine Instructions up Close and Personal

The most visible part of any assembly language program is its set of machine instructions, those atoms of action that are the steps a program must take to get its work done. The collection of instructions supported by a given CPU is that CPU's *instruction set.* The 8086 and 8088 CPUs share the same instruction set, which is why most people consider them the same CPU.

This cannot be said for the 80286 and 80386, both of which offer additional instructions not found in the 8086/8088. By and large, I'll only be introducing instructions in this book that the 8086/8088 understand. Furthermore, I can't cover *all* machine instructions in this book, even if I limit myself to the 8086/8088. Those that I will describe are the most common and most useful.

Nor will I abandon the discussion of memory addressing begun in the last chapter. As I've said before, understanding how the CPU and its instructions address memory is more difficult but probably more important than understanding the instructions themselves. In and around the descriptions of the machine instructions I'll present from this point on, there will be discussions and elaborations on memory addressing. Pay attention! If you don't learn that, memorizing the entire instruction set will do you no good at all.

6.1 ◆ Assembling and Executing Machine Instructions with DEBUG

The most obvious way to experiment with machine instructions is to build a short program out of them and watch it go. This can easily be done (and we'll be doing it a lot in later chapters) but it's far from the fastest way to do things. Editing, assembling, and linking all take time, and when you only want to look at *one* machine instruction in action (rather than a crew of them working together) the full development cycle is overkill.

Once more, we turn to DEBUG.

At the close of the last chapter we got a taste of a DEBUG feature called *unassembly,* which is a peculiar way of saying what most of us call *disassembly.* This is the reverse of the assembly process we looked at in detail in Chapter 3. Disassembly is the process of taking a binary machine instruction like 42H and converting it into its more readable assembly language equivalent, **INC DX.**

In addition to all its other tools, DEBUG also contains a simple assembler, suitable for taking assembly language mnemonics like **INC DX** and converting them to their binary machine code form. Later on we'll use a stand-alone assembler like TASM or MASM to assemble complete assembly language programs. For the time being, we can use DEBUG to do things one or two instructions at a time.

Assembling a MOV Instruction

The single most common activity in assembly language work is getting data from here to there. There are several specialized ways to do this, but only one truly general way: the **MOV** instruction. **MOV** can move a byte or word of data from one register to another, from a register into memory, or from memory into a register. What **MOV** *cannot* do is move data directly from one address in memory to a different address in memory.

The name **MOV** is a bit of a misnomer, because what is actually happening is that data are *copied* from a source to a destination. Once copied to the destination, however, the data do not vanish from the source, but continue to exist in both places. This conflicts a little with our intuitive notion of moving something, which usually means that something disappears from a source and reappears at a destination. Because **MOV** is so general and obvious in its action, it's a good place to start in working with DEBUG's assembler.

Bring up DEBUG and use the R command to display the current state of the registers. You should see something like this:

```
-r
AX=0000  BX=0000  CX=0000  DX=0000  SP=FFEE  BP=0000  SI=0000  DI=0000
DS=1980  ES=1980  SS=1980  CS=1980  IP=0100     NV UP EI PL NZ NA PO NC
1980:0100 701D           JO      011F
```

We ignored the third line of the register display before. Now let's think a little bit more about what it means.

When DEBUG is loaded without a specific file to debug, it simply takes the empty region of memory where a file would have been loaded (had a file been loaded when DEBUG was invoked) and treats it as though a program file were really there. The registers all get default values, most of which are zero. IP, however, starts out with a value of 0100H, and the code segment register CS gets the segment address of DEBUG's workspace, which is theoretically empty.

Memory is never really empty. A byte of memory always contains some value, whether it be true garbage that happened to reside in memory at power-up time or a leftover value remaining from the last time that byte of memory was used. In the above register dump, memory at CS:IP contains a **JO** instruction. This rather obscure instruction (**J**ump on **O**verflow) was not placed there deliberately, but is simply DEBUG's interpretation of the two bytes 701DH that happen to reside at CS:IP. Most likely, the 701D value was part of some data table belonging to the last program to use that area of memory. It could have been part of a word processor file, a spreadsheet, or anything else. Just don't think that some program *necessarily* put a **JO** instruction in memory. Machine instructions are just numbers, after all, and what numbers in memory do depends completely on how you interpret them—and what utility program you feed them to.

DEBUG's internal assembler assembles directly into memory and places instructions one at a time, as you enter them at the keyboard, into memory at CS:IP. Each time you enter an instruction, IP is incremented to the next free location in memory. By continuing to enter instructions, you can actually type an assembly language program directly into memory.

Try it. Type the A command (for **A**ssemble) and press Enter. Debug responds by displaying the current value of CS:IP, and then waits for you to enter an assembly language instruction. Type **MOV AX,1.** Press Enter. DEBUG again displays CS:IP and waits for a second instruction. It will continue waiting for instructions until you press Enter without typing anything. Then you'll see DEBUG's dash prompt again.

Now, use the R command again to display the registers. You should see something like this:

```
-r
AX=0000  BX=0000  CX=0000  DX=0000  SP=FFEE  BP=0000  SI=0000  DI=0000
DS=1980  ES=1980  SS=1980  CS=1980  IP=0100  NV  UP EI  PL NZ NA PO NC
1980:0100  B80100          MOV    AX,0001
```

The registers haven't changed, but now the third line shows that the **JO** instruction is gone and that the **MOV** instruction you entered has taken its place. Notice once again that CS contains 1980H and IP contains 0100H. The address of the **MOV** instruction is shown as 1980:0100; in other words, at CS:IP.

Executing a MOV Instruction with the Trace Command

Note that you haven't *executed* anything. You've simply used DEBUG's assemble command to write a machine instruction into a location in memory.

There are two ways to execute machine instructions from within DE-BUG. One way is to execute a program in memory, starting at CS:IP. This means that DEBUG will simply start the CPU executing whatever sequence of instructions begins at CS:IP. We looked at the G command very briefly at the end of the last chapter, when we found the **JMP** instruction that reboots your PC on power-up, and used G to execute that instruction. The command is quite evocative: **G**o. But don't type G just yet . . .

You haven't entered a program. You've entered *one* instruction, and one instruction does not a program make. The instruction *after* your **MOV** instruction could be anything at all, recalling that DEBUG is simply interpreting garbage values in memory as random machine instructions. A series of random machine instructions could easily go berserk, locking your system into an endless loop or writing zeroes over an entire segment of memory that may contain part of DOS or of DEBUG itself. We'll use DEBUG's G command a little later, once we've constructed a complete program in memory.

> **Go executes programs in memory starting at CS:IP; Trace executes the single instruction at CS:IP.**

For now, consider the mechanism DEBUG has for executing one machine instruction at a time. It's called Trace, and you invoke it by typing T. The Trace command will execute the machine instruction at CS:IP, then give control of the machine back to DEBUG. Trace is generally used to *single-step* a machine-code program one instruction at a time, in order to watch what it's up to every step of the way. For now, it's a fine way to execute a single instruction and examine that instruction's effects.

So type T. DEBUG will execute the **MOV** instruction you entered at CS:IP, and then immediately display the registers before returning to the dash prompt. You'll see this:

```
-r
AX=0001  BX=0000  CX=0000  DX=0000  SP=FFEE  BP=0000  SI=0000  DI=0000
DS=1980  ES=1980  SS=1980  CS=1980  IP=0103    NV  UP EI  PL NZ NA PO NC
1980:0103  6E          DB  6E
```

Look at the first line. DEBUG says AX is now equal to 0001. It held the default value 0000 before; obviously, your **MOV** instruction worked.

Something else to look at here: the third line shows an instruction called **DB** at CS:IP. Not quite true—**DB** is not a machine instruction, but an assembly language *directive* that means **D**efine **B**yte. (We'll return to **DB** later on, in Chapter 7.) It's DEBUG's way of saying that the number

6EH does not correspond to *any* machine instruction. It is truly a garbage byte sitting in memory, doing nothing.

6.2 ◆ Machine Instructions and Their Operands

As we said earlier, **MOV** copies data from a source to a destination. **MOV** is an extremely versatile instruction, and understanding its versatility demands a little study of this notion of source and destination.

Source and Destination Operands

Many machine instructions, **MOV** included, have one or more *operands*. In the machine instruction **MOV AX,1** there are two operands. The first is **AX,** and the second is the number 1.

By convention in assembly language, the first operand belonging to a machine instruction is the *destination operand.* The second operand is the *source operand.*

With the **MOV** instruction the sense of the two operands is pretty literal: the source operand is copied to the destination operand. In **MOV AX,1,** the source operand 1 is copied into the destination operand **AX.** The sense of source and destination is not nearly so literal in other instructions, but a rule of thumb is this: whenever a machine instruction causes a new value to be generated, that new value is placed in the destination operand.

There are three different flavors of data that may be used as operands. These are *immediate data, register data,* and *memory data.* I've blown some example **MOV** instructions up to larger-than-life size in Figure 6.1, to give you a flavor for how the different types of data are specified as operands to the **MOV** instruction.

Immediate data are the easiest to understand. We'll look at this type first.

Immediate Data

The **MOV AX,1** machine instruction that I had you enter into DEBUG was a good example of what we call *immediate data* accessed through an addressing mode called *immediate addressing.* Immediate addressing gets its name from the fact that the item being addressed is immediate data built right into the machine instruction. The CPU does not have to go anywhere to find immediate data. It's not in a register, nor is it stored in

Instruction	Destination operand	Source operand	
MOV	AX,	1	Immediate data
MOV	BX,	CX	16–bit register data
MOV	DL,	BH	8–bit register data
MOV	[BP],	DI	Memory data at SS:BP
MOV	DX,	[SI]	Memory data at DS:SI
MOV	BX,	ES:[BX]	Memory data at ES:BX

FIGURE 6.1   MOV and its operands

a data segment somewhere out in memory. Immediate data is always right inside the instruction being fetched and executed.

Immediate data must be of an appropriate size for the operand. In other words, you can't move a 16-bit immediate value into an 8-bit register half like AH or DL. Neither DEBUG nor the standalone assemblers will allow you to assemble an instruction like this:

```
MOV CL,67EF
```

Because it's built right into a machine instruction, you might think immediate data would be quick to access. This is true only to a point: Fetching *anything* from memory takes more time than fetching anything from a register, and instructions are, after all, stored in memory.

While addressing immediate data is somewhat quicker than addressing ordinary data stored in memory, neither is anywhere near as quick as simply pulling a value from a CPU register.

Also keep in mind that *only* the source operand can be immediate data. The destination operand is the place where data *goes,* not where it comes from. Because immediate data consists of literal constants (numbers like 1, 0, or 7F2BH) trying to copy something *into* immediate data rather than *from* immediate data simply has no meaning.

Register Data

Data stored inside a CPU register are known as *register data,* and accessing register data directly is an addressing mode called *register addressing.* Register addressing is done by simply naming the register we want to work with. Here are some examples of register data and register addressing:

```
MOV AX,BX
MOV BP,SP
MOV BL,CH
MOV ES,DS
ADD DI,AX
AND DX,SI
```

The last two examples point out that we're not speaking *only* of the **MOV** instruction here. Register addressing happens any time data in a register is acted on directly.

The assembler keeps track of certain things that don't make sense, and one such situation is having a 16-bit register and an 8-bit register half within the same instruction. Such operations are not legal—after all, what would it mean to move a 2-byte source into a 1-byte destination? While moving a 1-byte source into a 2-byte destination might seem more reasonable, the CPU does not support it and it cannot be done.

Playing with register addressing is easy using DEBUG. Bring up debug and assemble the following series of instructions:

```
MOV AX,67FE
MOV BX,AX
MOV CL,BH
MOV CH,BL
```

Now, reset the value of IP to 0100 using the R command, then execute the four machine instructions by issuing the T command four times in a row. The session under DEBUG would look like this:

```
-A
333F:0100 MOV AX,67FE
333F:0103 MOV BX,AX
333F:0105 MOV CL,BH
333F:0107 MOV CH,BL
333F:0109
```

```
-R IP
IP 0100
:0100
-R
AX=0000   BX=0000   CX=0000   DX=0000   SP=FFEE   BP=0000  SI=0000   DI=0000
DS=333F   ES=333F   SS=333F   CS=333F   IP=0100    NV UP EI PL NZ NA PO NC
333F:0100   B8FE67          MOV     AX,67FE
-T

AX=67FE   BX=0000   CX=0000   DX=0000   SP=FFEE   BP=0000  SI=0000   DI=0000
DS=333F   ES=333F   SS=333F   CS=333F   IP=0103    NV UP EI PL NZ NA PO NC
333F:0103   89C3            MOV     BX,AX
-T

AX=67FE   BX=67FE   CX=0000   DX=0000   SP=FFEE   BP=0000  SI=0000   DI=0000
DS=333F   ES=333F   SS=333F   CS=333F   IP=0105    NV UP EI PL NZ NA PO NC
333F:0105   88F9            MOV     CL,BH
-T

AX=67FE   BX=67FE   CX=0067   DX=0000   SP=FFEE   BP=0000  SI=0000   DI=0000
DS=333F   ES=333F   SS=333F   CS=333F   IP=0107    NV UP EI PL NZ NA PO NC
333F:0107   88DD            MOV     CH,BL
-T

AX=67FE   BX=67FE   CX=FE67   DX=0000   SP=FFEE   BP=0000  SI=0000   DI=0000
DS=333F   ES=333F   SS=333F   CS=333F   IP=0109    NV UP EI PL NZ NA PO NC
333F:0109   1401            ADC     AL,01
```

Keep in mind that the T command executes the instruction displayed in the third line of the most recent R-command display. The **ADC** instruction in the last register display is yet another garbage instruction; although executing it would not cause any harm, I recommend against executing random instructions just to see what happens. Executing certain jump or interrupt instructions could wipe out sectors on your hard disk or, worse, cause internal damage to DOS that would not show up until later on.

Let's look at what these four instructions accomplished. The first instruction is an example of immediate addressing: the hexadecimal value 067FEH was moved into the AX register. The second instruction used register addressing to move data from AX into BX. Keep in mind that the way the operands are written is slightly contrary to the common sense view of things; the destination operand comes *first*. Moving something from AX to

BX is done by executing **MOV BX,AX.** Assembly language is just like that sometimes.

The third and fourth instructions both move data between register halves rather than full, 16-bit registers. The two instructions accomplish something interesting. Look at the last register display and compare the value of BX and CX. By moving the value from BX into CX a byte at a time, it was possible to reverse the order of the two bytes making up BX. The high half of BX (what we sometimes call the *most significant byte,* or MSB, of BX) was moved into the low half of CX. Then the low half of BX (what we sometimes call the *least significant byte,* or LSB, of BX) was moved into the high half of CX. This is just a sample of the sort of tricks you can play with the general-purpose registers.

Just to disabuse you of the notion that the **MOV** instruction should be used to exchange the two halves of a 16-bit register, do the following: before you exit DEBUG from your previous session, assemble the following instruction and execute it using the T command:

```
XCHG CL,CH
```

The **XCHG** instruction exchanges the value contained in its two operands. What was interchanged before is interchanged again, and the value in CX will match the values already in AX and BX. A good idea while writing your first assembly language programs is to double check the instruction set periodically to see that what you have cobbled together with four or five instructions is not possible using a single instruction. The 8086/8088 instruction set is very good at fooling you in that fashion!

Memory Data

The immediate data type is built right into its own machine instruction. Register data are stored in one of the CPU's limited collection of internal registers. In contrast, *memory data* are stored somewhere in the megabyte vastness of 8086/8088 external memory. Specifying that address is much more complicated than simply reaching into a machine instruction or naming a register.

Recall that a memory location must be specified in two parts: a *segment address,* which is one of 65,536 locations spaced every 16 bytes in memory, and an *offset address,* which is the number of bytes by which the specified byte is offset from the start of the segment. Within the CPU, the segment address is kept in one of the four segment registers, while the offset address (generally just called the offset) may be in one of a select group of general-purpose registers that includes *only* BP, BX, SI, and DI. (Register SP is a special case, and addresses data located on the *stack,* as I'll explain in Section 7.2.) To pin down a single byte within the 8086/8088's megabyte of memory, you need both the segment and the offset components. We generally write them together, specified with a colon to separate them, as either literal constants or register names: 0B00:0167, DS:SI or CS:IP.

BX's hidden agenda. One of the easiest mistakes to make early on is to assume that you can use *any* of the general purpose registers to specify an offset for memory data. Not so! If you try to specify an offset in AX, CX, or DX, the assembler will flag an error.

> **Only BP, BX, SI, and DI can hold an offset for memory data.**

So, general-purpose registers AX, CX, and DX aren't quite so general after all. Why was general-purpose register BX singled out for special treatment? Think of it as the difference between dreams and reality for Intel. In the best of all worlds, every register could be used for all purposes. Unfortunately, when CPU designers get together and argue about what their nascent CPU is supposed to do, they are forced to face the fact that there are only so many transistors on the chip to do the job.

Each chip function is given a budget of transistors (often numbering in the tens or even hundreds of thousands), and if the desired logic cannot be implemented using that number of transistors, the expectations of the designers have to be brought down a notch and some CPU features shaved from the specification.

The 8086 and 8088 are full of such compromises. There were not enough transistors available at design time to allow all general purpose registers to do everything, so in addition to the truly general-purpose ability to hold data, each 8086/8088 register has what I call a "hidden agenda." Each register has some ability that none of the others share. I'll describe each register's hidden agenda at the appropriate point in this book and I'll call it out as such.

Register BX was the X register chosen to address memory data. None of the other X registers can ever be used in that fashion. By convention and because there simply isn't enough horsepower in the CPU to allow *all* registers to do it, addressing memory data is one element of BX's hidden agenda.

Using memory data. With only one or two important exceptions (the string instructions, which I won't be covering in detail in this book) only *one* of an instruction's two operands may specify a memory location. In other words, you can move an immediate value to memory, or a memory value to a register, or perform some other similar combination, but you *can't* move a memory value directly to another memory value. This is just an inherent limitation of the CPU, and we have to live with it, inconvenient as it gets at times.

Specifying a memory address as one of an instruction's operands is a little complicated. The offset address must be resident in one of the general-purpose registers. To specify that we want the data at the memory location contained in the register rather than the data in the register itself, we use square brackets around the name of the register. In other words, to move the word at address DS:BX into register AX, we would use the following instruction:

```
MOV AX,[BX]
```

Similarly, to move a value residing in register DX into the word at address DS:DI, you would use this instruction:

```
MOV [DI],DX
```

Segment register assumptions.

The only problem with these examples is, *where does it say to use DS as the segment register?*

It doesn't. To keep addressing notation simple, the 8086/8088 makes certain assumptions about certain instructions in combinations with certain registers. There is no particular system to these assumptions, and like dates in history or Spanish irregular verbs, you'll just have to memorize them, or at least know where to look them up. (They are listed in Appendix C.)

One of these assumptions is that the **MOV** instruction uses the segment address stored in segment register DS unless you explicitly tell it otherwise. In this case above, we did not tell the **MOV** instruction to use some segment register other than DS, so it fell back on its assumptions and used DS. However, had you specified the offset as residing in register SP, the **MOV** instruction would have assumed the use of segment register SS instead. This assumption involves a memory mechanism known as the *stack,* which we won't really address until the next chapter.

Overriding segment assumptions for memory data.

What if you *want* to use CS as a segment register with the **MOV** instruction? It's not difficult. The instruction set includes what are called *segment override prefixes.* These are not precisely instructions, but are more like the filters that can be snapped in front of a camera lens. The filter is not itself a lens, but it alters the way the lens operates.

There is one segment override prefix for each of the four segment registers: CS, DS, SS, and ES. In assembly language they are written as the name of the segment register followed by a colon:

```
CS:   ; Forces use of code segment register CS
DS:   ; Forces use of the data segment register DS
SS:   ; Forces use of the stack segment register SS
ES:   ; Forces use of the extra segment register ES
```

In use, the segment override prefix is placed immediately in front of the memory data reference whose segment register assumption is to be overridden. For example, to force a MOV instruction to copy a value from the AX register into a location at an offset (contained in SI) into the code segment, you would use this instruction:

```
MOV CS:[SI],AX
```

Without the CS: override prefix, this instruction would move the value of AX into the data segment, at an address specified as DS:SI.

Prefixes in use are very reminiscent of how an address is written; in fact, understanding how prefixes work will help you keep in mind that in *every* reference to memory data within an instruction, there is a ghostly segment register assumption floating in the air. You may not see the ghostly DS assumption in your **MOV** instruction, but if you forget that it is there the whole concept of memory data will begin to seem arbitrary and magical.

> *Every* **reference to memory data includes either an assumed segment register or a segment override prefix to specify a segment register other than the assumed segment register.**

At the machine code level, a segment override prefix is a single binary byte. The prefix byte is placed *in front of,* rather than within, a machine instruction. In other words, if the binary bytes comprising a **MOV AX,[BX]** instruction are 8BH 07H, adding the ES segment override prefix to the instruction (**MOV AX,ES:[BX]**) places a single 26H in front of the actual instruction bytes, giving us 26H 8BH 07H as the full binary equivalent.

Memory data summary.

Memory data consists of a single byte or word in memory, addressed by way of a segment value and an offset value. The register containing the offset address is enclosed in square brackets to indicate that the contents of memory, rather than the contents of the register, are being addressed. The segment register used to address memory data is usually assumed according to a complex set of rules. Optionally, a segment override prefix can be placed in the instruction to specify some segment register other than the default segment register.

Figure 6.2 shows diagrammatically what happens during a **MOV AX,ES:[BX]** instruction. The segment address component of the full 20-bit memory address is contained inside the CPU in segment register ES. Ordinarily, the segment address would be in register DS, but the **MOV** instruction contains the **ES** segment override prefix. The offset address component is specified to reside in the BX register.

The CPU sends out the values in ES and BX side by side to the memory system. Together, the two values pin down one memory location where **MyWord** begins. **MyWord** is actually 2 bytes, but that's fine—the 8086 CPU can bring both bytes into the CPU at once, while the 8088 brings the 2 bytes in separately, one after the other. The CPU handles details like that and you needn't worry about it. Because AX is a 16-bit register, of course, two 8-bit bytes can fit into it quite nicely.

The segment address can reside in any of the four segment registers: CS, DS, SS, or ES. The offset address can reside only in registers BX, BP, SP, SI, or DI, however. AX, CX, and DX can *not* be used to contain an offset address during memory addressing.

Limitations of the MOV Instruction

The **MOV** instruction can move nearly any register to any other register. For reasons probably having to do with the limited budget of transistors on the 8086 and 8088 chips, **MOV** can't quite do every move you can think of. Here is a list of **MOV**'s limitations:

1. **MOV** cannot move memory data to memory data. In other words, an instruction like **MOV [SI],[BX]** is illegal. Either of **MOV**'s two operands can be memory data, but *both* cannot be memory data at once.

2. **MOV** cannot move one segment register into another. Instructions like **MOV CS,SS** are illegal. This would have been handy but it simply can't be done.

3. **MOV** cannot move immediate data into a segment register. Again, it would be handy but you just can't do it.

4. **MOV** cannot move one of the 8-bit register halves into a 16-bit register, or vice versa. There are easy ways around any possible difficulties here, and preventing moves between operands of different sizes can keep you out of numerous kinds of trouble.

MOV AX, ES:[BX]

FIGURE 6.2 How memory data is addressed

These limitations, of course, are over and above those situations that simply don't make sense, i.e., moving a register or memory into immediate data, moving immediate data into immediate data, specifying a general-purpose register as a segment register to contain a segment, or specifying a segment register to contain an offset address. Figure 6.3 shows numerous illegal **MOV** instructions that illustrate these various limitations and nonsense situations.

6.3 ◆ Reading and Using an Assembly Language Reference

Like a medium-sized screwdriver, you'll end up using **MOV** for normal tasks and maybe some abnormal ones, just as I use screwdrivers to pry nails out of boards, club black widow spiders in the garage, discharge

These are all illegal!

MOV 17, 1	Only 1 operand may be immediate data
MOV 17, BX	Only the source operand may be immediate data
MOV CX, DH	Operands must be the same size
MOV [DI], [SI]	Only 1 operand may be memory data
MOV DI, DX:[BX]	DX is not a segment register
MOV ES, 0B800H	Segment registers may not be loaded from immediate data
MOV DS, CS	Only 1 operand may be a segment register
MOV [AX], BP	AX may not address memory data
MOV SI, [SS]	Segment registers may not address memory data

FIGURE 6.3   Rogue MOV instructions

large electrolytic capacitors, and other intriguing things over and above workaday screw-turning. The 8086/8088 instruction set contains dozens of instructions, however, and over the course of the rest of this book I'll be mixing in descriptions of various other instructions with further discussions of memory addressing and program logic and design.

Remembering a host of tiny, tangled details involving dozens of different instructions is brutal and unnecessary. Even the big guys don't try to keep it all between their ears at all times; most keep a "blue card" or some other sort of reference document handy to jog their memories about machine instruction details.

Blue Cards

A blue card is a reference summary printed on a piece of colored card stock. It folds up like a road map and fits in your pocket. The original blue card may actually have been blue, but knowing the perversity of programmers in general, it was probably bright orange. Most assemblers come with a blue card. Guard it with your life.

Blue cards aren't always cards anymore. One of the best is a full sheet of very stiff shiny plastic, sold by Micro Logic Corp. of Hackensack, NJ[1]. The one sold with Microsoft's MASM is actually published by Intel, and has grown to a pocket-sized booklet stapled on the spine.

Blue cards contain very terse summaries of what an instruction does, what operands are legal, what flags it affects, and how many machine cycles it takes to execute. This information, while helpful in the extreme, is often so tersely put that newcomers might not quite fathom which end of the card is up.

An Assembly Language Reference for Beginners

In deference to those just starting out in assembly language, I have put together a beginner's reference to the most common 8086/8088 instructions and called it Appendix A. It contains at least a page on every instruction I'll be covering in this book, plus a few additional instructions that everyone ought to know. It does *not* include descriptions on *every* instruction, but only the most common and most useful. Once you've gotten skillful enough to use the more arcane instructions, you should be able to pick up the blue

---

[1] 8086/8088 Micro Chart, Micro Logic Corp., P.O. Box 174, Hackensack, NJ 07602.

card provided with your assembler and run with it. A sample entry from Appendix A appears on page 185. Refer to it during the following discussion.

The instruction's mnemonic is at the top of the page, highlighted in bold to make it easy to spot while flipping quickly through the appendix. To the mnemonic's right is the name of the instruction, which is a little more descriptive than the naked mnemonic.

Flags.

Immediately beneath the mnemonic is a minichart of machine flags in the flags register. I haven't spoken in detail of flags yet, but the flags register is a collection of one-bit values that retain certain essential information about the state of the machine for short periods of time. Many (but by no means all) 8086/8088 instructions change the values of one or more flags. The flags can then be individually tested by one of the **JMP** instructions, which then change the course of the program depending on the state of the flags.

We'll get into this business of tests and jumps in Chapter 9. For now, simply understand that each of the flags has a name, and that for each flag there is a symbol in the flags minichart. You'll come to know the flags by their two-character symbols in time, but until then the full names of the flags are shown to the right of the minichart. Most of the flags are not used frequently in the beginning assembly language work. Most of what you'll be paying attention to, flags-wise, is the carry flag (**CF**). It's used, as you might imagine, for keeping track of binary arithmetic when an arithmetic operation carries out of a single byte or word.

There will be an asterisk (*) beneath the symbol of any flag affected by the instruction. *How* the flag is affected depends on what the instruction does. You'll have to divine that from the *Notes* section. When an instruction affects no flags at all, the word <none> will appear in the minichart.

In the example page, the minichart indicates that the **NEG** instruction affects the overflow flag, the sign flag, the zero flag, the auxiliary carry flag, the parity flag, and the carry flag. The various ways that the flags are affected depend on the results of the negation operation on the operand specified. These are summarized in the second paragraph of the *Notes* section.

Legal forms.

A given mnemonic represents a single 8086/8088 instruction, but each instruction can include more than one legal form. The form of an instruction varies by the type and order of the operands passed to it.

What the individual forms actually represent are different binary number opcodes. For example, beneath the surface the **POP AX** instruction is the number 58H, whereas the **POP SI** instruction is the number 5EH.

Sometimes there will be special cases of an instruction and its operands that are shorter than the more general cases. For example, the **XCHG**

NEG   Negate (two's complement; i.e. multiply by −1)

Flags affected

O	D	I	T	S	Z	A	P	C
F	F	F	F	F	F	F	F	F
*				*	*	*	*	*

OF: Overflow flag   TF: Trap flag   AF: Aux carry
DF: Direction flag   SF: Sign flag   PF: Parity flag
IF: Interrupt flag   ZF: Zero flag   CF: Carry flag

Legal forms

> NEG r8
> NEG m8
> NEG r16
> NEG m16

Examples

> NEG AL
> NEG CX
> NEG BYTE PTR [BX]   ; Negates byte quantity at DS:BX
> NEG WORD PTR [DI]   ; Negates word quantity at DS:BX

Notes

This is the assembly language equivalent of multiplying a value by −1. Keep in mind that negation is *not* the same as simply inverting each bit in the operand. (Another instruction, NOT, does that.) The process is also known as generating the *two's complement* of a value. The two's complement of a value added to that value yields zero. −1 = $FF; −2 = $FE; −3 = $FD; etc.

If the operand is 0, CF is cleared and ZF is set; otherwise CF is set and ZF is cleared. If the operand contains the maximum negative value (−128 for 8-bit or −32768 for 16-bit) the operand does not change, but OF and CF are set. SF is set if the result is negative, otherwise SF is cleared. PF is set if the low-order 8 bits of the result contain an even number of set (1 bit; otherwise PF is cleared).

NOTE: You *must* use a type override specifier (BYTE PTR or WORD PTR) with memory data!

r8 = AL AH BL BH CL CH DL DH   r16 = AX BX CX DX BP SP SI DI
sr = CS DS SS ES
m8 = 8-bit memory data   m16= 16-bit memory data
i8 = 8-bit immediate data   i16 = 16-bit immediate data
d8 = 8 bit signed displacement   d16 = 16-bit signed displacement

instruction, which exchanges the contents of the two operands, has a special case when one of the operands is register AX. Any **XCHG** instruction with AX as one of the operands is represented by a single-byte opcode. The general forms of **XCHG** (i.e., like **XCHG r16,r16**) are always 2 bytes long. This implies that there are actually two different opcodes that will do the job for a given combination of operands, for example **XCHG AX,DX.** This is true enough, and most assembler programs are smart enough to choose the shortest form possible in any given situation. If you are hand-assembling a sequence of raw opcode bytes, say, for use in a Turbo Pascal **INLINE** statement, you need to be aware of the special cases, and all special cases will be marked as such in the *Legal Forms* section.

When you want to use an instruction with a certain set of operands, make sure you check the *Legal Forms* section of the reference guide for that instruction to make sure that the combination is legal. The **MOV** instruction, for example, cannot move one segment register directly into another, nor can it move immediate data directly into a segment register. Neither combination of operands is a legal form of the **MOV** instruction.

In the example reference page on the **NEG** instruction, you'll see that a segment register cannot be an operand to **NEG.** (If it could, there would be a **NEG sr** item in the *Legal Forms* list.) If you want to negate the value in a segment register, you'll first have to use **MOV** to move the value from the segment register into one of the general-purpose registers before using **NEG.**

Operand symbols. The symbols used to indicate the nature of the operands in the *Legal Forms* section are summarized at the bottom of every page in the reference appendix. They're close to self-explanatory, but I'll take a moment to expand upon them slightly here:

> **r8**—An 8-bit register-half, one of AH, AL, BH, BL, CH, CL, DH, or DL.
>
> **r16**—A 16-bit general-purpose register, one of AX, BX, CX, DX, BP, SP, SI or DI.
>
> **sr**—One of the four segment registers, CS, DS, SS, or ES.
>
> **m8**—An 8-bit byte of memory data.
>
> **m16**—A 16-bit word of memory data.
>
> **i8**—An 8-bit byte of immediate data.
>
> **i16**—A 16-bit word of immediate data.
>
> **d8**—An 8-bit signed displacement. We haven't covered these yet, but a *displacement* is the distance between the current location in the code and another place in the code to which we want to jump. It's *signed* (i.e.,

either negative or positive) because a positive displacement jumps you higher (forward) in memory, whereas a negative displacement jumps you lower (back) in memory. We'll examine this notion in detail in Section 9.3.

d16—A 16-bit signed displacement. Again, for use with jump and call instructions. See Section 9.3.

Examples. Whereas the *Legal Forms* section shows what combinations of operands are legal for a given instruction, the *Examples* section shows examples of the instruction in actual use, just as it would be coded in an assembly language program. I've tried to include a good sampling of examples for each instruction, demonstrating the range of the different possibilities for each instruction. This includes situations that require type override specifiers (which I'll cover in the next section.)

Notes. The *Notes* section of the reference page describes the instruction's action briefly and provides information on how it affects the flags, how it may be limited in use, and any other detail that needs to be remembered, especially things that beginners would overlook or misconstrue.

What's not here. . . . Appendix A differs from most detailed assembly language references in that it does not have the binary opcode encoding information, nor indications of how many machine cycles are used by each form of the instruction.

The binary opcode encoding of an instruction is the actual sequence of binary bytes that the CPU digests as the machine instruction. What we would call **POP AX,** the machine sees as the binary number 58H. What we call **ADD SI,07733H,** the machine sees as 81H 0C6H 33H 77H. Machine instructions are encoded into anywhere from one to four binary bytes, depending on what instruction they are and what their operands are. Laying out the system for determining what the encoding will be for any given instruction is extremely complicated, in that its component bytes must be set up bit-by-bit from several large tables. I've decided that this book is not the place for that particular discussion, and have left encoding information out of the reference appendix.

Finally, I've included nothing anywhere in this book that indicates how many machine cycles are expended by any given machine instruction. A *machine cycle* is one pulse of the master clock that makes the PC perform its magic. Each instruction uses some number of those cycles to do its work, and the number varies all over the map depending on criteria that I won't be explaining in this book.

Furthermore, as Michael Abrash explains in his book *Zen of Assembly Language,* knowing the cycle requirements for individual instructions is rarely sufficient to allow even an expert assembly language programmer to calculate how much time a given series of instructions will take. He and I both agree that it is no fit subject for beginners, and I will let him take it up in his volume, which is far more advanced than mine.

6.4 ◆ Rally 'Round the Flags, Boys!

We haven't studied the flags register as a whole. The flags register is a veritable junkdrawer of disjointed bits of information and it's tough (and perhaps misleading) to just sit down and describe all of them in detail at once. What I'll do is describe the flags as we encounter them in discussing the various instructions in this and future chapters.

The flags register as a whole is a single 16-bit register buried inside the CPU. Of those 16 bits, 9 are actually used as flags. The remaining 7 bits are undefined and ignored. You can neither set them nor read them.

A flag is a single bit of information whose meaning is independent from any other bit. The bit can be set to 1 or cleared to 0 by the CPU, as its needs require. The idea is to tell you, the programmer, the state of certain conditions inside the CPU, so that your program can test for and act on the states of those conditions.

I often imagine a row of country mailboxes, each with its own little red flag on the side. Each flag can be up or down, and if the Smith's flag is up, it tells the mailman that the Smiths have placed mail in their box to be picked up. The mailman looks to see if the Smith's flag is raised (a test) and if so, opens the Smith's mailbox and picks up the waiting mail.

Each of the flags register's nine flags has a two-letter symbol. I'll use those symbols most of the time, and you should become familiar with them. The flags, their symbols, and brief descriptions of what they stand for follows.

OF—The **overflow flag** is set when the result of an operation becomes too large to fit in the operand it originally occupied.

DF—The **direction flag** is an oddball among the flags in that it tells the *CPU* something that you want it to know, rather than the other way around. It dictates the direction that activity moves (up-memory or down-memory) during the execution of string instructions. When **DF** is set, string instructions proceed from high memory toward low memory. When **DF** is cleared, string instructions proceed from low memory toward high memory.

IF—The **interrupt enable flag** is a two-way flag. The CPU sets it under certain conditions, and you can set it yourself using the **STI** and **CLI** instructions. When **IF** is set, interrupts (see Section 7.3) are enabled and can occur when requested. When **IF** is cleared, interrupts are ignored by the CPU.

TF—When set, the **trap flag** allows DEBUG's Trace command to do what it does by forcing the CPU to execute only a single instruction before calling an interrupt routine. This is not an especially useful flag and I won't have anything more to say about it.

SF—The **sign flag** becomes set when the result of an operation forces the operand to become negative. By *negative,* we only mean the highest order bit in the operand becomes 1 during a signed arithmetic operation. Any operation that leaves the sign positive will clear **SF.**

ZF—The **zero flag** becomes set when the results of an operation become zero. If the operand becomes some nonzero value, **ZF** is cleared.

AF—The **auxiliary carry flag** is used only for binary-coded decimal (BCD) arithmetic. BCD arithmetic treats each operand byte as a pair of 4-bit "nybbles" and allows something approximating decimal (base 10) arithmetic to be done directly in the CPU hardware by using one of the BCD arithmetic instructions. It is slow and awkward, however, and I won't be covering BCD arithmetic or **AF** further in this book.

PF—The **parity flag** will seem instantly familiar to anyone who understands serial data communications and utterly bizarre to anyone who doesn't. **PF** indicates whether the number of set (1) bits in the low-order byte of a result is even or odd. For example, if the result is 0F2H, **PF** will be cleared, because 0F2H (11110010) contains an odd number of 1 bits. Similarly, if the result is 3AH (00111100), **PF** will be set because there is an even number of 1 bits in the result. This flag is a carryover from the days when all computer communications were done through a serial port, for which a system of error detection called parity checking depends on knowing whether a count of set bits in a character byte is even or odd. **PF** has no other use and I won't be describing it further.

CF—The **carry flag** is by far the most useful flag in the flags register, and the one you will have to pay attention to most. If the result of an arithmetic or shift operation carries out a bit from the operand, **CF** becomes set. Otherwise, if nothing is carried out, **CF** is cleared.

Check That Reference Page!

What I call *flag etiquette* is the way a given instruction affects the flags in the flags register. You *must* remember that the descriptions of the flags on the previous pages are generalizations *only* and are subject to specific restrictions and special cases imposed by individual instructions. Flag etiquette for individual flags varies widely from instruction to instruction, even though the *sense* of the flag may be the same in every case.

For example, some instructions that cause a zero to appear in an operand set **ZF,** while others do not. Sadly, there's no system to it. When you intend to use the flags in testing by way of conditional jump instructions (see Chapter 9), you have to check each individual instruction to see how the various flags are affected.

Flag etiquette is a highly individual matter. Check the reference for each instruction to see it affects the flags. Assume nothing!

A simple lesson in flag etiquette involves two new instructions, **INC** and **DEC,** and yet another interesting ability of DEBUG.

Adding and Subtracting 1 with INC and DEC

Several instructions come in pairs. Simplest among those are **INC** and **DEC,** which increment and decrement an operand by one, respectively.

Adding one to something or subtracting one from something are actions that happen a lot in computer programming. If you're counting the number of times a program is executing a loop, or counting bytes in a table, or doing something that advances or retreats one count at a time, **INC** or **DEC** can be a very quick way to make the actual addition or subtraction happen.

Both **INC** and **DEC** take only one operand. An error will be flagged by DEBUG or your assembler if you try to use either **INC** or **DEC** with two operands, or without any operands.

Try both by using the assemble command and the trace command under DEBUG. Assemble this short program, display the registers after entering it, and then trace through it:

```
MOV AX, FFFF
MOV BX,002F
DEC BX
INC AX
```

The session should look very much like this:

```
-A
1980:0100 MOV AX,FFFF
1980:0103 MOV BX,002D
1980:0106 INC   AX
1980:0107 DEC   BX
1980:0108
-R
AX=0000  BX=0000  CX=0000  DX=0000  SP=FFEE  BP=0000  SI=0000   DI=0000
DS=1980  ES=1980  SS=1980  CS=1980  IP=0100   NV UP EI PL NZ NA PO NC
1980:0100  B8FFFF          MOV    AX,FFFF
-T

AX=FFFF  BX=0000  CX=0000  DX=0000  SP=FFEE  BP=0000  SI=0000   DI=0000
DS=1980  ES=1980  SS=1980  CS=1980  IP=0103   NV UP EI PL NZ NA PO NC
1980:0103  BB2D00          MOV    BX,002D
-T

AX=FFFF  BX=002D  CX=0000  DX=0000  SP=FFEE  BP=0000  SI=0000   DI=0000
DS=1980  ES=1980  SS=1980  CS=1980  IP=0106   NV UP EI PL NZ NA PO NC
1980:0106  40              INC    AX
-T

AX=0000  BX=002D  CX=0000  DX=0000  SP=FFEE  BP=0000  SI=0000   DI=0000
DS=1980  ES=1980  SS=1980  CS=1980  IP=0107   NV UP EI PL ZR AC PE NC
1980:0107  4B              DEC    BX
-T

AX=0000  BX=002C  CX=0000  DX=0000  SP=FFEE  BP=0000  SI=0000   DI=0000
DS=1980  ES=1980  SS=1980  CS=1980  IP=0108   NV UP EI PL NZ NA PO NC
1980:0108  0F              POP    CS
```

Watch what happens to the registers. Decrementing BX predictably turns the value 2DH into value 2CH. Incrementing 0FFFFH, on the other hand, rolls over the register to 0. 0FFFFH is the largest unsigned value that can be expressed in a 16-bit register. Adding one to it rolls it over to zero, just as adding 1 to 99 rolls the rightmost two digits of the sum to zero in creating the number 100. The difference with **INC** is that *there is no carry.* The carry flag is not affected by **INC,** so don't try to use it to perform multi-digit arithmetic.

Using DEBUG to Watch the Flags

When **INC** rolled AX over to zero, the carry flag was not affected, but the zero flag became set (i.e., equal to 1). The zero flag works that way—when the result of an operation becomes zero, the zero flag is almost always set.

DEC sets the flags in the same way. If you were to execute a **DEC DX** instruction when DX contained 1, DX would become zero and **ZF** would be set.

Apart from looking at a reference guide, how can you tell what flags are affected by a given instruction? DEBUG allows you to see the flags as they change, just as it lets you dump memory and examine the values in the general-purpose and segment registers. The second line of DEBUG's three-line register display contains eight cryptic symbols at its right margin. You've been seeing them, I'm sure, without having a clue as to their meaning.

Eight of the nine 8086/8088 flags are represented by two-character symbols. (The odd flag out is the trap flag, **TF,** which is reserved for exclusive use by DEBUG itself and cannot be examined while DEBUG has control of the machine.) Unfortunately, the symbols DEBUG uses are not the same as the standard flag symbols that programmers use. The difference is that DEBUG's flag symbols do not represent the flags' *names* but rather the flags' *values.* Each flag can be set or cleared, and DEBUG displays the state of each flag by having a unique symbol for each state of each flag, for a total of sixteen distinct symbols in all. The symbols' meanings are summarized in Table 6.1. The best I can say for this symbol set is that it's not obviously obscene. It is, however, nearly impossible to memorize. It's best to keep a reduced copy of this table (perhaps taped to the back of

TABLE 6.1   DEBUG's flag state symbols

Flag		*Set symbol*	*Clear symbol*
OF	Overflow flag	OV	NV
DF	Direction flag	DN	UP
IE	Interrupt enable flag	EI	DI
SF	Sign flag	NG	PL
ZF	Zero flag	ZR	NZ
AF	Auxiliary carry flag	AC	NA
PF	Parity flag	PE	PO
CF	Carry flag	CY	NC

a business card) near your keyboard if you intend to watch the waving of the 8086/8088's flags.

When you first run DEBUG, the flags are set to their default values, which are

NV UP EI PL NZ NA PO NC

You'll note that all these symbols are clear symbols except for EI, which must be set to allow interrupts to happen. Whether you are aware of it or not, interrupts are happening constantly within your PC. Each keystroke you type on the keyboard triggers an interrupt. Every 55 milliseconds, the system clock triggers an interrupt to allow the BIOS software to update the time and date values kept in memory as long as the PC has power. If you disabled the interrupts for any period of time, your real-time clock would stop and your keyboard would freeze up. Needless to say, **IE** must be kept set nearly all the time.

Each time you execute an instruction with the trace command, the flags display will be updated. If the instruction that was executed affected any of the flags, the appropriate symbol will be displayed over the previous symbol.

With Table 6.1 in hand, go back and examine the flags display for the four-instruction DEBUG trace shown a few pages back. The first display shows the default values for all the flags, as no instructions have been executed yet. No change appears for the second and third flags displays, because the **MOV** instruction affects none of the flags.

Look closely at the flags display *after* the **INC AX** instruction executes; three of the flags have changed state. **ZF** has gone from NZ (clear) to ZR (set), indicating that the operand of **INC** went to zero as a result of the increment operation. **AF** has gone from NA to AC. (Let's just skip past that one; explaining what that means would be more confusing than helpful.) Finally, parity flag **PF** has gone from PO to PE. This means that as a result of the increment operation, the number of bits present in the low byte of BX went from odd to even.

Now look at the last flags display, the one shown after the **DEC BX** instruction was executed. Again, **ZF, AF,** and **PF** changed. **ZF** went to NZ, indicating that the **DEC** instruction left a nonzero value in its operand. **PF,** moreover, went from PE to PO, indicating that the number of bits in the low byte of BX was odd after the **DEC BX** instruction.

One thing to keep in mind is that even when a flag doesn't change in state from display to display, it was still *affected* by the previously executed instruction. Five out of nine flags are affected by *every* **INC** and **DEC** instruction that the CPU executes. Not every **DEC** instruction decrements its operand down to zero, but every **DEC** instruction causes some value to be asserted in ZF. The same holds true for the other four affected flags—even if the state of an affected flag doesn't change as a result of an instruction, the state is asserted, even if only the existing value is reasserted.

Thorough understanding of the flags comes with practice and dogged persistence. It's one of the more chaotic aspects of assembly language programming, but as we'll see when we get to conditional branches, flags are what makes the CPU truly come alive to do our work for us.

6.5 ◆ Using Type Overrides

Back on the sample reference appendix page on page 185 notice that the following example uses of the **NEG** instruction:

```
NEG BYTE PTR [BX]   ; Negates byte quantity at DS:BX
NEG WORD PTR [DI]   ; Negates word quantity at DS:BX
```

What indeed is a **BYTE PTR**? Or a **WORD PTR**? Both are what we call *type overrides,* and you literally can't use **NEG** (or numerous other instructions) on memory data without one or the other.

The problem is this: the **NEG** instruction negates its operand. The operand can be either a byte or a word; **NEG** works equally well on both. How does **NEG** know whether to negate a byte or a word? The memory data operand **[BX]** only specifies an address in memory, using DS as the assumed segment register. The address DS:BX points to a byte, but it also points to a word, which is nothing more than two bytes in a row somewhere in memory. So, does **NEG** negate the byte located at address DS:BX? Or does it negate the 2 bytes (a word) that start at address DS:BX?

Unless you tell it somehow, **NEG** has no way to know.

Telling an instruction the size of its operand is what **BYTE PTR** and **WORD PTR** do. Calling them type overrides can be a little misleading sometimes, because **NEG** has no default type to override. Several other instructions that work on single operands only (like **INC, DEC,** and **NOT**) have the same problem.

Types in Assembly Language

So, do type overrides ever override anything? They can, sometimes.

The notion of *type* in assembly language is almost wholly a question of *size.* A word is a type, as is a byte, a double word, a quad word, and so on.

The assembler is unconcerned with what an assembly language variable *means.* (Keeping track of such things is totally up to you.) The assembler only worries about how big it is. The assembler does not want to have to try to fit ten pounds of kitty litter in a five pound bag, which is impossible, nor five pounds of kitty litter in a ten pound bag, which can be confusing and possibly dangerous.

Register data always has a fixed and obvious type because a register's size cannot be changed. BL is 1 byte and BX is 2 bytes. Register types cannot be overridden.

The type of immediate data depends on the magnitude of the immediate value. If the immediate value is too large to fit in a single byte, that immediate value becomes word data and you can't load it into an 8-bit register half. An immediate value that can fit in a single byte may be loaded into either a byte-sized register half or a full word-sized register; its type is thus taken from the context of the instruction in which it exists and matches that of the register data operand into which it is to be loaded.

Memory data is something else again. We've spoken of memory data so far in terms of registers holding offsets, without considering the use of named memory data. I'll be discussing named memory data in the next chapter, but in brief terms, you can define named variables in your assembly language programs using directives like **DB** and **DW.** They look like this:

```
Counter   DB
MixTag    DW
```

Here, **Counter** is a variable allocated as a single byte in memory by the **DB** (define byte) directive. Similarly, **MixTag** is a variable allocated as a word in memory by the **DW** (define word) directive.

By using **DB,** you give the variable **Counter** a type and a size. You must match this type when you use the variable name **Counter** in an instruction to indicate memory data. This, for example, will be accepted by the assembler:

```
MOV BL,Counter
```

This instruction will take the current value located in memory at the address represented by the variable named **Counter** and will load that variable into register-half BL.

What the assembler will refuse to do is load the variable **MixTag** (which is word-sized) into a register-half, like this:

```
MOV BL,MixTag      ; Won't assemble!
```

By using a type override specifier, however, you can force the assembler to do your bidding and put *half* of **MixTag** into register BL:

```
MOV BL,BYTE PTR MixTag
```

The type override specifier **BYTE PTR** forces the assembler to look upon **MixTag** as being one byte in size. **MixTag** is *not* byte-sized, however, so what actually happens is that the least significant (lowermost) byte of **MixTag** will be loaded into BL, with the most significant byte left high and dry.

Is this useful? It can be. Is it dangerous? You bet. It is up to you to decide if overriding the type of memory data makes sense, and it is your responsibility completely to ensure that doing so doesn't sprinkle your code with bugs.

The best use of the type override specifiers is to clear up ambiguous instructions like **INC [DI],** which could specify either a byte or a word as memory data pointed to by a segment register and DI. The other occasions will be rarer and riskier. Use your head, and know what you're doing. That's more important in assembly language than anywhere else in computer programming.

Chapter 7

Our Object All Sublime
Creating Programs That Work

They don't call it "assembly" for nothing. Facing the task of writing an assembly language program brings to mind images of Christmas morning: you've spilled 1,567 small metal parts out of a large box marked *Land Shark HyperBike* (some assembly required) and now you have to somehow put them all together with nothing left over. (In the meantime, the kids seem more than happy playing in the box. . . .)

I've actually explained just about all you absolutely *must* understand to create your first assembly language program. Still, there is a non-trivial leap from here to there; you are faced with many small parts with sharp edges that can fit together in an infinite number of ways, most wrong, some workable, but only a few that are ideal.

So here's the plan: I will present you with the completed and operable Land Shark HyperBike—which I will then tear apart before your eyes. This is the best way to learn to assemble: by pulling apart programs written by those who know what they're doing. Over the rest of this book we'll pull a few more programs apart, in the hope that by the time it's over you'll be able to move in the other direction of putting programs together all by yourself.

7.1 ◆ The Bones of an Assembly Language Program

The listing below is perhaps the simplest correct program that will do anything visible and still be comprehensible and expandable. This issue of comprehensibility is utterly central to quality assembly language programming. With *no* other computer language (not even APL or that old devil FORTH) is there anything even close to the risk of writing code that looks so much like something scraped off the wall of King Tut's tomb.

The program EAT.ASM displays one (short) line of text on your display screen:

    Eat at Joe's!

For that you have to feed 72 lines of text file to the assembler and linker. Many of those 72 lines are unnecessary in the strict sense, but serve instead as commentary to allow you to understand what the program is doing (or more important, *how* it's doing it) six months or a year from now.

One of the aims of assembly language coding is to use as few instructions as possible in getting the job done. This does *not* mean creating as short a source code file as possible. The more comments you put in your file, the better you'll remember how things work inside the program the next time you pick it up. I think you'll find it amazing how quickly the logic of a complicated assembly language file goes cold in your head. After no more than 48 hours of working on other projects, I've come back to assembler projects and had to struggle to get back to flank speed on development.

Comments are neither time nor space wasted. IBM used to say, 'one line of comment per line of code.' That's good—and should be considered a *minimum* for assembly language work. A better course (that I will in fact follow in the more complicated examples later on) is to use one short line of commentary to the right of each line of code, along with a comment block at the start of each sequence of instructions that work together in accomplishing some discrete task.

The program listing appears below; read it carefully.

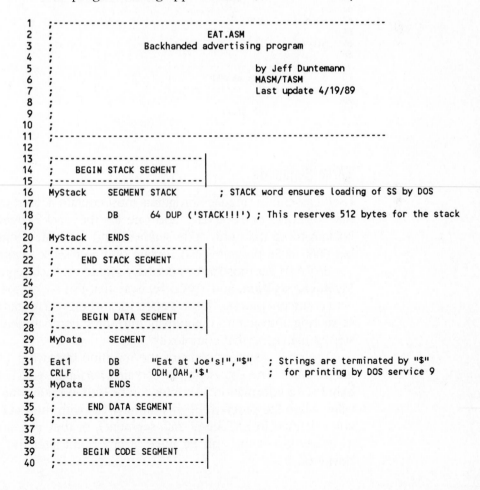

```
 1  ;-----------------------------------------------------------
 2  ;                         EAT.ASM
 3  ;                Backhanded advertising program
 4  ;
 5  ;                                by Jeff Duntemann
 6  ;                                MASM/TASM
 7  ;                                Last update 4/19/89
 8  ;
 9  ;
10  ;
11  ;-----------------------------------------------------------
12
13  ;------------------------------------
14  ;     BEGIN STACK SEGMENT           |
15  ;------------------------------------
16  MyStack    SEGMENT STACK         ; STACK word ensures loading of SS by DOS
17
18             DB      64 DUP ('STACK!!!') ; This reserves 512 bytes for the stack
19
20  MyStack    ENDS
21  ;------------------------------------
22  ;     END STACK SEGMENT             |
23  ;------------------------------------
24
25
26  ;------------------------------------
27  ;     BEGIN DATA SEGMENT            |
28  ;------------------------------------
29  MyData     SEGMENT
30
31  Eat1       DB      "Eat at Joe's!","$"   ; Strings are terminated by "$"
32  CRLF       DB      0DH,0AH,'$'           ;  for printing by DOS service 9
33  MyData     ENDS
34  ;------------------------------------
35  ;     END DATA SEGMENT             |
36  ;------------------------------------
37
38  ;------------------------------------
39  ;     BEGIN CODE SEGMENT           |
40  ;------------------------------------
```

```
41   MyProg     SEGMENT
42
43   Main       PROC
44              ASSUME CS:MyProg,DS:MyData    ; Which segment does which job?
45
46   Start:     ; This is where program execution begins:
47
48              mov  AX,MyData     ; Set up our own data segment address in DS
49              mov  DS,AX         ; Can't load segment reg. directly from memory
50
51              lea  DX,Eat1       ; Load offset of Eat1 message string into DX
52              mov  AH,09H        ; Select DOS service 09H: Print string
53              int  21H           ; Call DOS
54
55              lea  DX,CRLF       ; Load offset of CRLF string into DX
56              mov  AH,09H        ; Select DOS service 09H: Print String
57              int  21H           ; Call DOS
58
59              mov  AH,4CH        ; Terminate process DOS service
60              mov  AL,0          ; Pass this value back to ERRORLEVEL
61              int  21H           ; Control returns to DOS
62
63   Main       ENDP
64
65   MyProg     ENDS
66
67   ;--------------------------------|
68   ;     END CODE SEGMENT           |
69   ;--------------------------------|
70
71              END Start
```

Three Segments

Useful assembly language programs must contain at least three segments—one for code, one for data, and one for the stack. Larger programs may contain more than one code segment and more than one data segment, but 8086/8088 programs can contain only *one* stack segment at a time.

EAT.ASM has those three necessary segments. Each segment has a name: **MyStack, MyData,** and **MyCode.** Note that I've set off the three segments with comment blocks. This is a good idea when you're starting out, because separating a program's complexity into three compartments is a good first step in managing that complexity.

The code segment contains the machine instructions that do the program's work. The data segment contains *variables,* which are storage cubbyholes for information. Variables can be defined as having some particular value when the program begins running (as with the **Eat1** and **CRLF** variables defined in EAT.ASM's data segment), or they can simply be defined as empty boxes that can be filled at any point after the program begins operation.

The stack segment contains the program's stack. I haven't explained stacks just yet, and because you don't really need to understand stacks in order to understand how EAT.ASM works, I'm going to hold off just a little while longer. In short, a stack is simply an ordered place to stash things for the short term, and that will have to do until we cover the concept in depth in Section 7.2.

Labels

A segment is defined in a program by associating a label with the assembler directive **SEGMENT.** Labels are just identifiers that name something, like **MyStack.** The *type* of a label refers to the sort of creature the label identifies. In EAT.ASM, the type of labels **MyStack, MyData,** and **MyCode** is **SEGMENT.** The *value* of a label with a type of **SEGMENT** is the segment address of the named segment. This is why the statement

    MOV AX,MyData

moves the segment address of segment **MyData** into register AX.

Notice that the label **MyData** is used twice in defining the data segment we're naming **MyData.** The **SEGMENT** directive begins the segment, and the **ENDS** (**END S**egment) directive ends the segment. Everything between **MyDATA SEGMENT** and **MyData ENDS** belongs to the segment named **MyData.**

A label can be used to mark a location in the code segment. EAT1.ASM has one such label, **Start:**

    Start: ; This is where program execution begins

Start's value is the offset of its location in the code segment. The way you can spot a label used to mark a code address is by the colon used after the label. The colon, in a sense, is the sign reading "You are here" in the code, where *here* has a name given in the label.

The label **Start** has a special job—it specifies the point in the program where execution is to begin when the program starts running. You'll see in the listing that the label **Start** is repeated in the very last line of the file:

    END Start

The label following the **END** directive is the address of the first instruction to be executed when DOS loads and runs the program. The label used to specify the execution starting point does not have to be **Start,** but there must be *some* label chosen as the starting point, and it must follow the **END** directive for your program to assemble and link without errors.

Later on, we'll see such labels used as the targets of jump instructions. For example, the following machine instruction transfers the flow of instruction execution to the location marked by the label **GoHome:**

```
JNE GoHome
```

Notice that the colon is *not* used here. The colon is placed only where the label is *defined,* not where it is *referenced.* Think of it this way: use the colon when you are *marking* a location, not when you are *going* there.

Variables

The labels **Eat1** and **CRLF** define *variables.* A variable is defined by associating a label with a *data definition directive.* You've seen these used informally earlier in this book, and there are two in EAT.ASM. Data definition directives look like this:

```
MyByte     DB 07H              ; 8 bits in size
MyWord     DW 0FFFFH           ; 16 bits in size
MyDouble   DD 0B8000000H       ; 32 bits in size
MyString   DB "I was born on a pirate ship.","$"
MyData     DB ?                ; Uninitialized storage
MyQuery    DB '?'              ; Contains a question mark
```

Think of the **DB** directive as **D**efine **B**yte. **DB** sets aside one byte of memory for data storage. Think of the **DW** directive as **D**efine **W**ord. **DW** sets aside one word of memory for data storage. Think of the **DD** directive as **D**efine **D**ouble. **DD** sets aside a double word in memory for storage, typically for full 32-bit addresses.

All of the variable definitions shown above except for **MyData** both set aside memory for storage and then place some specific value in storage at that location. **MyData** simply sets aside storage and leaves the storage undefined or empty. This is indicated by the presence of a question mark after the directive itself.

Avoid the mistake of placing the question mark in quotes, if what you really want to do is leave the defined variable empty. If you place the question mark in quotes, what will happen is that the assembler will set aside storage and then place a question mark character (ASCII character 63, or 03FH) in that storage.

You may at some point want to create a variable with a question mark in it, but you need the quotes to do that and to leave the variable empty you must omit the quotes.

String Variables

String variables are an interesting case. A *string* is just that, a sequence or string of characters, all in a row in memory. A string is defined in EAT.ASM:

```
Eat1    DB   "Eat as Joe's!","$"
```

Strings are a slight exception to the rule that a data definition directive sets aside a particular quantity of memory. The **DB** directive ordinarily sets aside 1 byte only. A string may be any length you like, however, as long as it remains on a single line of your source code file. Because there is no data directive that sets aside 16 bytes, or 42, strings are defined simply by associating a label with the place where the string *starts.* The **Eat1** label and its **DB** directive specify 1 byte in memory as the string's starting point. The number of characters in the string is what tells the assembler how many bytes of storage to set aside for that string.

Either single quotes (') or double quotes (") may be used to delineate a string and the choice is up to you, *unless* you are defining a string value that itself contains one or more quote characters. Notice in EAT.ASM the string variable **Eat1** contains a single-quote character used as an apostrophe. Because the string contains a single-quote character, you *must* delineate it with double-quotes. The reverse is also true—if you define a string that contains one or more double-quote characters, you must delineate it with single-quote characters:

```
Yukkh    DB   'He said, "How disgusting!" and threw up.',"$"
```

You may combine several separate substrings into a single string variable by separating the substrings by commas. Both **Eat1** and **Yukkh** do this in that they add a dollar sign ($) in quotes to the end of the main string data. The dollar sign is used to mark the end of the string for the mechanism that displays the string to the screen. More on that mechanism and marking string lengths in Section 7.3.

Directives versus Instruction Mnemonics

Data definition directives look a little like machine instruction mnemonics, but they are emphatically *not* machine instructions. One very common mistake made by beginners is looking for the binary opcode represented by a directive such as **DB** or **DW.** There is no binary opcode for **DW, DB,** and the other directives. Machine instructions, as the name implies, are instructions to the CPU itself. Directives, by contrast, are instructions to the *assembler.*

Understanding directives is easier when you understand the nature of the assembler's job. (Look back to Chapter 3 for a detailed refresher if you've gotten fuzzy on what the assembler and linker do.) The assembler scans your source code text file, and as it scans your source code file it builds an object code file on disk. It builds this object code file step-by-step, one byte at a time, starting at the beginning of the file and working its way through to the end. When it encounters a machine instruction mnemonic, it figures out what binary opcode is represented by that mnemonic and writes that binary opcode (which may be anywhere from 1 to 6 actual bytes) to the object code file.

When the assembler encounters a directive like **DW,** it does not write any opcode to the object code file. If the **DW** directive specifies an empty variable, the assembler just leaves 2 bytes of space in the next available slot in the data segment and moves on. If the **DW** directive specifies an initial value for the variable, the assembler writes the bytes corresponding to that value in the slot it set aside. The assembler writes the address of the allocated space into a table, beside the label that names the variable. Then the assembler moves on to the next directive (if there are further directives) or on to whatever comes next in the source code file.

When you write the following statement in your assembly language program:

```
MyVidOrg DW   0B800H
```

what you are really doing is instructing the assembler to set aside 2 bytes of data (**D**efine **W**ord, remember) and place the value 0B800H in those two bytes. The assembler writes the label **MyVidOrg** and the label's address into a table it builds of labels in the program for later use by the linker.

This is true for all kinds of directives, not simply data definition directives. An assembler directive is just that—your walking orders handed to the assembler. There are numerous assembler directives other than **DB, DW,** and **DD.** The **SEGMENT** and **ENDS** directives are instructions to the assembler to consider the definitions they surround as belonging to a single segment. We'll take up the **PROC** and **ENDP** directives in Section 8.1, and the **ASSUME** directive below.

The Difference Between a Variable's Address and Its Contents

When you use a variable's label in a **MOV** instruction, you are accessing the *value* stored in that variable. Suppose you had defined a variable in the data segment called **MyData** this way:

```
MyData    DW    0744H
```

The label **MyData** represents some address within the data segment, and at that address the assembler places the value 0744H. Now, if you want to copy the value contained in **MyData** to the AX register, you would use the following **MOV** instruction:

```
MOV          AX,MyData
```

After this instruction, AX would contain 0744H.

There are many situations where you need to move the *address* of a variable into a register rather than the *contents* of the variable. In fact, you may find yourself moving the addresses of variables around more than the contents of the variables, especially if you make a lot of calls to DOS and BIOS services. (For more on DOS and BIOS calls, see Section 7.4.) The 8086/8088 instruction set contains an instruction to make moving the address of a variable into a register easy. The instruction is **LEA,** which stands for load effective address. **LEA** is used twice in EAT.ASM. Here's a typical example:

```
LEA          DX,Eat1
```

All this instruction does is take the offset address of the string variable **Eat1** in the data segment and place the offset address into register DX.

If you've used higher-level languages like BASIC and Pascal, this distinction may seem inane. After all, who would mistake the contents of a variable for its location? Well, that's easy for you to say—in BASIC and Pascal you rarely, if ever, even *think* about where a variable is. The language handles all that rigmarole for you. In assembler, knowing where a variable is located is essential in order to do a lot of important things.

The ASSUME Directive

Within the code segment of EAT.ASM, there is another directive, **ASSUME.** The one in EAT.ASM looks like this:

```
ASSUME CS:MyProg,DS:MyData
```

Of all the directives a newcomer is likely to need to make a simple program work, **ASSUME** is almost certainly the toughest to understand. It has to do with labels and the way labels are used by the 8086/8088 CPU.

Recall that all memory addresses have two components, a segment address and an offset address. Furthermore, every label in an assembly language program (with the single exception of labels used before the **SEGMENT** directive) represents some offset address from a segment address.

But which segment address?

Aye, that's the rub. Look at the data segment block named **MyData:**

```
;-----------------------------------|
;      BEGIN DATA SEGMENT           |
;-----------------------------------|
MyData     SEGMENT

Eat1    DB    "Eat at Joe's!","$"      ; Strings are terminated by "$"
CRLF    DB    0DH,0AH,'$'              ;   for printing by DOS service 9

MyData    ENDS
;-----------------------------------|
;      END DATA SEGMENT             |
;-----------------------------------|
```

Everything between the two directives, **SEGMENT** and **ENDS,** is the program's data segment. It says so (as they say) right on the label. But the label (by which I mean the comment blocks) is for *our* eyes only. The assembler ignores comments. *There is nothing in this segment definition to tell the assembler that it is a data segment.* You can define variables in the code segment or in the stack segment if you want, even though it's customary and more correct programming practice to keep variables in the data segment. Segment **MyData** could be just as easily considered a code segment, though not a stack segment. (Stack segments are a special case because, like Tigger, there can only be one. I'll speak of stacks, the stack segment, and the **STACK** directive in Section 7.2.)

We have the problem of indicating to the assembler which segment is the data segment. This might seem like an easy one, but rather than a single problem it is actually two problems—one is that the assembler needs to know which segment address to put into the DS (**D**ata **S**egment) register, and the other problem is which form of memory-addressing machine instructions to use.

The first problem is easily addressed. Notice these two lines in EAT.ASM:

```
mov   AX,MyData      ; Set up our own data segment address in DS
mov   DS,AX          ; Can't load segment reg. directly from memory
```

MyData, if you recall, contains the segment address of a segment defined using the **SEGMENT** and **ENDS** directives. That address is first loaded into AX and then from AX the address is loaded into DS. This roundabout path is necessary because the DS register cannot be loaded with either immediate data or memory data; it *must* be loaded from one of the other registers.

The end result is that the segment address represented by the label **MyData** is loaded into DS. This neatly solves the first problem of specifying the address of the data segment. We simply load the data segment's address into DS. Now **MyData** can be considered a real data segment because its segment address is in the data segment register DS.

That, however, doesn't solve the second problem. Whereas we wrote two instructions that moved the address of our data segment into DS, *the assembler doesn't "know" that this move took place.* Never forget that the assembler follows its orders without "understanding" them. It doesn't make inferences based on what you do to addresses or the segment registers. It must be *told* which segment is to be used as the data segment, the code segment, and the stack segment. Somewhere inside the assembler program is a little table where the assembler "remembers" that segment **MyData** is to be considered the data segment, that segment **MyCode** is to be considered the code segment, and that segment **MyStack** is to be considered the stack segment. It can't remember these relationships, however, unless you first tell the assembler what they are.

This somehow (for the data, code, and extra segments, at least) is the **ASSUME** directive. The **ASSUME** directive in EAT.ASM tidily specifies that **MyData** is the data segment and **MyCode** is the code segment.

Why is this important? It has to do with the way the assembler creates the binary opcodes for a given instruction. When you write an instruction that addresses memory data like this:

```
MOV        AX,MyWord
```

the assembler must put together the series of binary values that will direct the CPU to perform this action. What that series of binary values turns out to be depends on what segment the label **MyWord** resides in. If **MyWord** is in the data segment, the binary opcodes will be one thing, but if **MyWord** resides in the code segment, stack segment, or extra segment, the binary opcodes will be different. The assembler must know whether any label indicates an address within the data segment, code segment, stack segment, or extra segment. The assembler knows that **MyWord** indicates an address within the segment **MyData,** but you must tell the assembler that **MyData** is in fact the data segment.

This is what **ASSUME** is for. As I've said before and will say again, *knowing where things are is the most important part of all your work in assembly language.* If you understand addresses and memory addressing (which includes telling the assembler how to find things as we've done here with **ASSUME**), the rest is easy.

The Main Program as a Procedure

All of the machine instructions in EAT.ASM are bracketed within this pair of assembly language statements:

```
Main PROC
Main ENDP
```

Just as the **SEGMENT** and **ENDS** directives frame a segment, the **PROC** and **ENDP** directives frame what we call a *procedure.* A procedure is just a group of machine instructions that is given a name. This is almost entirely what a procedure is—a name. Unlike Pascal or C, there is no necessary structure to a procedure in assembly language.

Making the main program portion of an assembly language program a procedure is strictly optional, *until* you must begin dividing your program up into modules to keep it manageable. Then, every executable component *must* be a procedure with a name so that the linker can properly link the different modules together into the final executable program. If you're the least bit serious about assembly language, that will happen sooner than later, so I think it's a good idea to get in the habit of considering your main program a procedure at the outset.

In the next chapter I will explain the process of cutting a program up into procedures, and how the procedures work together to comprise a complete assembly language program. Until then I won't have a lot more to say about procedures. The **Main** procedure defined in EAT.ASM is not germane to understanding the program's operation. Consider it a gesture to future expansion of the program, as we'll see in Chapter 8.

Choosing a Starting Point

There are no jumps, loops, or subroutines in EAT.ASM. If you've a smattering of assembly language smarts you may wonder if the **Start:** label following the **ASSUME** directive is unnecessary except for readability purposes. After all, **Start** is not referenced anywhere within the program, so one would think it's an ornament, like **MyStack,** the name of the stack segment. On the contrary—EAT.ASM will not assemble without it.

The issue is this: DOS needs to know at what address to begin execution when it loads and runs the program. You might think DOS could assume that execution would begin at the start of the code segment, but not so—there may be more than one code segment, and under most circumstances the programmer does not specify the order of multiple code segments within a single program. (The linker has its own reasons for arranging them as it does.) It is better to have no doubt about it, and for that reason you the programmer are required to pick a starting point and tell the assembler what it is.

The starting point may be any label that specifies an address within a code segment. Once you choose it, you inform the assembler of your choice by putting the chosen label at the very end of the source code file, following the **END** directive. Note that you must put the colon after the label when you define its location in its code segment, but you *cannot* use the colon when you place the starting point label after **END.**

END does multiple service for the assembler. Its most obvious job is to tell the assembler, that's all, folks—the source code file is finished and no further machine instructions or assembler directives will be forthcoming. Any text placed after the **END** directive will be ignored by the assembler. You can put comment blocks there if you like, but don't forget that any instructions or directives you place after **END** will simply be ignored, and *the assembler will not tell you that it is ignoring them.* Best, I think, not to put anything at all after **END.**

Why specify the starting point after the **END** directive? Very simply: the assembler can, with confidence, assume that the starting point cannot be redefined. There can be more than one of most everything else in an assembly language program (including stack segments—you just can't *use* more than one at a time) but there must be only *one* starting point for execution. Putting the starting label after **END** ensures that this will be the case.

7.2 ◆ First in, First out via the Stack

One problem with assembly language is that it's tough knowing where to put things; there are only so many registers to go around. Having variables in a data segment is helpful, but it isn't the whole story. People who come to assembler from higher-level languages like Pascal and BASIC find this particularly jarring because they're used to being able to create new variables at any time as needed.

The 8086/8088 CPU contains the machinery to create and manage a vital storage area called the *stack*. The name is appropriate, and for a usable metaphor I can go back to my high school days, when I was a dishwasher for Resurrection Hospital on Chicago's northwest side.

Five Hundred Plates an Hour

What I did most of the time was pull clean plates from a moving conveyor belt of little prongs that emerged endlessly from the steaming dragon's mouth of a dishwashing machine. This was hot work, but it was a lot less slimy than stuffing the dirty plates into the other end of the machine.

When you pull five hundred plates an hour out of a dishwashing machine, you had better have some efficient place to stash them. Obviously you could simply stack them on a table, but stacked ceramic plates in a place habituated by rowdy teenage boys is asking for fragments. What the hospital had instead was an army of stainless steel cabinets on wheels equipped with one or more spring-loaded circular plungers that were accessed from the top. When you had a handful of plates, you pushed them down into the plunger. The plunger's spring was adjusted so that the weight of the added plates pushed the whole stack of plates down just enough to make the new top plate flush with the top of the cabinet.

Each plunger held about fifty plates. We rolled one up next to the dragon's mouth, filled it with plates, and then rolled it back into the kitchen where the clean plates were used at the next meal shift.

It is instructive to follow the path of the first plate out of the machine on a given shift. That plate got into the plunger first, and was subsequently shoved down into the bottom of plunger by the remaining 49 plates that the cabinet could hold. After the cabinet was rolled into the kitchen, the kitchen workers pulled plates out of the cabinet one by one as they set trays. The *first* plate out of the cabinet was the *last* plate in. The *last* plate out of the cabinet was the *first* plate in.

The 8086/8088 stack is like that. We call it a **L**ast **I**n, **F**irst **O**ut, or LIFO, stack.

An Upside-Down Segment

Two of the 8086/8088 registers team up to create and maintain the stack. Like everything else in '86-land, the stack must exist within a segment. The SS (**S**tack **S**egment) register holds the segment address of the segment

chosen to be the stack segment, and the SP (**S**tack **P**ointer) register points
to locations within the stack segment. As with all other segments, the stack
segment can be as much as 65,536 bytes long, but it may be any length
less than that as well. You'll find in practice that the stack rarely needs to
be larger than 1000 bytes unless you're doing some really peculiar things.

The stack segment begins at SS:0, but the truly odd thing about it is that
all the stack action happens at the *opposite* end of the stack segment. When
a stack segment is set up, the SS register points to the base, or beginning,
of the stack segment and SP is set to point to the end of the stack segment.
To store something in the stack segment, which is usually called "pushing
something on the stack," we move SP "down the stack" (i.e., closer to SS)
and then copy the item to the memory location pointed to by SS:SP.

This takes some getting used to. Figure 7.1 provides the big picture
of the stack segment and the two pointers that give it life. SS is set to the
base of the stack segment by DOS when the program is loaded and begins
running. SP is set to the far end of the stack segment, again by DOS when
your program is loaded.

You can place data onto the stack in numerous ways, but the most
straightforward involves a pair of related machine instructions, **PUSH** and
PUSHF. The two are identical except that **PUSHF** pushes the flags register
onto the stack, while **PUSH** pushes a register onto the stack that is specified
by you in your source code file

```
PUSHF           ; Push the Flags register

PUSH AX         ; Push the AX register
PUSH [BX]       ; Push the word at DS:BX
PUSH DI         ; Push the DI register
PUSH ES         ; Push the ES register
```

Note that **PUSHF** takes no operands. You'll generate an assembler error if
you try to hand it an operand; **PUSHF** pushes the flags and that's all it is
capable of doing.

Both **PUSH** and **PUSHF** work this way: SP is first decremented by one
word (2 bytes) so that it points to an empty area of the stack segment that
is 2 bytes long. Then, whatever is to be pushed onto the stack is written
to memory in the stack segment at the offset address in SP. Voila! The data
is safe on the stack, and SP has crawled two bytes closer to SS. We call the
word of memory pointed to by SP the *top of the stack*.

All memory between SP's initial position and its current position (the
top of the stack) contains real data that was explicitly pushed on the stack
and will presumably be fetched from the stack (we say "popped" from the

Initial SP

Any data at
or above SP
is "real"

SP moves
up and down
as needed

SP after values
have been pushed
onto the stack

All memory
below SP
is free space

PUSH AX

Moves SP 1 word down the
stack, and then copies the
contents of AX into the word
at the new location of SP

POP AX

Takes the word at SS:SP
and copies it into AX, then
moves SP 1 word up the stack.

SS

The stack segment begins at SS:0
and continues for up to 64K bytes

FIGURE 7.1   The big picture of the 8086/8088 stack

stack) later on. Memory between SS and SP, however, is considered free
and available, and is used to store new data that is to be pushed onto the
stack.

> **All memory between SS:0 and SS:SP is considered free and available for the use of the stack.**

Don't forget one important fact: the 8086/8088 pushes *only* word-sized items onto the stack. You can't push AL or BH or any other of the 8-bit registers, nor can you push immediate data onto the stack. Registers and memory data are legal for pushing onto the stack, but immediate data will generate an assembler error. (There is in fact a variant of PUSH that *will* push immediate data onto the stack, but it's only available on the 80286 and 80386 CPUs. That is a subject for a more advanced book, however.)

Your morbid curiosity may be wondering what happens when SP runs out of room in its downward crawl and collides with SS. Nothing good, certainly; it depends heavily on how your program is laid out, but I would lay money on your program crashing hard and probably taking the system with it. *Stack crashes are serious business,* at least in part because there is only one stack in action at a time in the 8086/8088. Be sure to allocate more than enough memory to serve your stack-pushing needs, and keep an eye on the proximity of SS and SP while you trace a program in DEBUG.

POP Goes the Opcode

In general, what gets pushed must get popped, or you can end up in any of several different kinds of trouble. Getting a word of data *off* the stack is done with another two instructions, **POP** and **POPF.** As you might expect, **POP** is the general purpose popper, while **POPF** is dedicated to popping the flags off of the stack:

```
POPF            ; Pop the top of the stack into Flags

POP SI          ; Pop the top of the stack into SI
POP CS          ; Pop the top of the stack into CS
POP [BX]        ; Pop the top of the stack into memory at DS:BX
```

As with **PUSH, POP** only operates on word-sized operands. Don't try to pop data from the stack into an 8-bit register like AH or CL.

> **The stack instructions PUSH and POP work *only* on word-sized operands.**

POP works pretty much the same way **PUSH** does, but in reverse. First, the word of data at SS:SP is copied from the stack and placed in **POP**'s operand, whatever you specified that to be. Then, SP is decremented by 2 bytes, so that in effect it moves 2 bytes up the stack, away from SS.

It is significant that SP is decremented *before* placing a word on the stack, but *after* removing a word from the stack. Certain other CPUs work in the opposite manner, which is fine—just don't get confused. *Unless the stack is empty, SP points to real data, not empty space.*

Ordinarily, you don't have to remember that fact, as **PUSH** and **POP** handle it all for you and you don't have to manually keep track of what SP is pointing to. If you decide to manipulate the stack pointer directly, it helps to know the sequence of events behind **PUSH** and **POP.**

Figure 7.2 shows the stack's operation in a little more detail. The values of the four "X" registers at some hypothetical point in a program's execution are shown at the top of the figure. AX is pushed first on the stack. Its least significant byte is at SS:SP, and its most significant byte is at SS:SP + 1. (Remember that both bytes are pushed onto the stack at once, as a unit.)

Each time one of the registers is pushed onto the stack, SP is decremented 2 bytes down toward SS. The first three columns show AX, BX, and CX being pushed onto the stack, respectively. Note what happens in the fourth column, however, when the instruction **POP DX** is executed. The stack pointer is incremented by two bytes and moves away from SS. DX now contains a copy of the contents of CX. In effect, CX was pushed onto the stack, and then immediately popped off into DX.

That's a roundabout way to copy the value of CX into DX. The instruction, **MOV DX,CX** is lots faster and more straightforward. However, *MOV will not operate on the flags register.* If you want to load a copy of flags into a register, you must first push the flags register onto the stack with **PUSHF,** then pop the flag word off the stack into the register of your choice. Getting the flags register into BX is done like this:

```
PUSHF        ; Push the flags register onto the stack..
POP BX       ; ..and pop it immediately into BX
```

Storage for the Short Term

The stack should be considered a place to stash things for the short term. Items stored on the stack have no names, and in general must be taken off the stack in the reverse order that they were put on.

One excellent use of the stack allows the all-too-few registers to do multiple duty. If you need a register to temporarily hold some value to be operated on by the CPU and all the registers are in use, push one of the busy registers onto the stack. Its value will remain safe on the stack while you use the register for other things. When you're finished using the

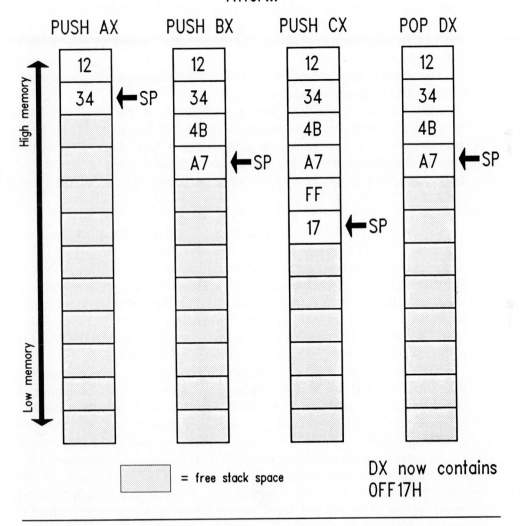

Given these initial register values:

AX = 01234H
BX = 04BA7H
CX = 0FF17H
DX = 034E0H

After...

FIGURE 7.2   How the stack works

register, pop its old value off the stack and you've gained the advantages of an additional register without really having one.

Specifying the Size of the Stack

The size of your program's code segment is dictated by the number of machine instructions you write into your program. Similarly, the size of your data segment is dictated by the number and sizes of the variables you define in your data segment. You might well ask, how do you specify the size of your stack segment when, until the program begins running, there's nothing in it?

The answer, quite simply, is to define the stack segment as one enormous variable without a name.

EAT.ASM (see page 199) has a stack segment allocated this way. Note that the stack segment contains a single **DB** directive with no label associated with it. The stack segment's **DB** is a little different from the ones in the data segment. It contains an additional directive, **DUP** (for **DUP**licate), that is the key to the whole mystery. Here's the **DB** in its entirety:

```
DB  64 DUP ('STACK!!!') ; This reserves 512 bytes for the stack
```

As the comment indicates, this statement allocates 512 bytes for the stack. The **DB** directive by itself ordinarily allocates only a single byte within a segment. **DB,** however, can also mark the first byte of multi-byte strings and buffers. A *buffer* is nothing more than an area of memory set aside for later use with nothing particular inside it. The stack segment in EAT.ASM is really just a buffer without a name, addressed by SS and SP.

The *Eat at Joe's!* string (including the $ at the end) is 14 bytes long, yet is defined by a **DB** directive. Really large variables and most buffers must be allocated with the help of the **DUP** directive. **DUP** must be followed by some sort of expression in parentheses, and preceded by a number indicating how many times that expression is to be duplicated in memory.

An *expression* is a collection of values that ultimately "cooks down" (we say "evaluates") to some specific value. In EAT.ASM, the stack segment's **DB** statement doesn't really contain an expression—its value is already "cooked down" as far as it will go. Later on we'll look at some more complex expressions that will need some cooking.

The stack segment's **DB** takes the short string of characters **'STACK!!!'** from within the parentheses and replicates the string into memory 64 times.

The total size of the buffer is 64 times 8, (which is the length of the string 'STACK!!!' shorn of its parentheses) for a total of 512 bytes. By this we accomplish two things: we set aside a buffer 512 bytes in size for the use of the stack, and we mark this buffer unmistakably so that we can spot it in memory and see how much of the buffer has actually been used by the stack.

The marking is indeed unmistakable. Assemble and link EAT.ASM and then invoke DEBUG on EAT.EXE. Do a memory dump at SS:0. You should see this:

```
-d ss:0
19AA:0000 53 54 41 43 4B 21 21 21-53 54 41 43 4B 21 21 21   STACK!!!STACK!!!
19AA:0010 53 54 41 43 4B 21 21 21-53 54 41 43 4B 21 21 21   STACK!!!STACK!!!
19AA:0020 53 54 41 43 4B 21 21 21-53 54 41 43 4B 21 21 21   STACK!!!STACK!!!
19AA:0030 53 54 41 43 4B 21 21 21-53 54 41 43 4B 21 21 21   STACK!!!STACK!!!
19AA:0040 53 54 41 43 4B 21 21 21-53 54 41 43 4B 21 21 21   STACK!!!STACK!!!
19AA:0050 53 54 41 43 4B 21 21 21-53 54 41 43 4B 21 21 21   STACK!!!STACK!!!
19AA:0060 53 54 41 43 4B 21 21 21-53 54 41 43 4B 21 21 21   STACK!!!STACK!!!
19AA:0070 53 54 41 43 4B 21 21 21-53 54 41 43 4B 21 21 21   STACK!!!STACK!!!
```

There should be four blocks marked like this, as DEBUG's dump routine displays 128 bytes at a time. If any bytes in any of those four blocks get written over, you'll see it immediately. Certainly the last few bytes will be written over during the normal course of the program, but if something else in your program or your machine is clobbering your stack, this is one way to start the search for the alien menace.

Nothing, of course, *requires* that you use the 'STACK!!!' string to allocate space in the stack segment. The simplest way is simply to use **DUP** with the undefined space symbol (?)

```
DB   512 DUP (?)
```

All this statement does is set aside 512 bytes of memory. *Nothing* is stored in that memory initially to mark it as belonging to the stack or anything else. The (?) simply reserves memory but does not otherwise touch it. Note here that the question mark is *not* in quotes. Putting it in quotes will fill your stack segment with 512 questions mark characters, which may be useful but is not the same as undefined space!

7.3 ◆ Using DOS Services through INT

I think of EAT.ASM as something of a Tom Sawyer program. It doesn't do much, and it does what it does in time-honored Tom Sawyer fashion—by getting somebody else to do all the work. All that EAT does is display two character strings on your screen. One is the advertising slogan itself, **Eat at Joes!** The other is the pair of invisible characters we call *newline* or *EOL,* carriage return (0DH) followed by line feed (0AH). (For more on EOL markers and how they interact with text, see Section 3.2.) The EOL marker does nothing more than return the display cursor to the left margin of the next screen line so that any subsequent text displayed will begin at the left margin and not be nipping at the heels of **Eat at Joe's!**

Invisible though it may be, the carriage return–line feed combination is still considered a text string and is sent to the display in exactly the same way, through a *DOS service.*

As I explained in Chapter 3, DOS is both a god and a troll. It controls all the most important elements of the machine in godlike fashion: the disk drives, the printer, and (to some extent) the display. At the same time, DOS is like a troll living under a bridge to all those parts of your machine—you tell the troll what you want done, and the troll will go out and do it for you.

There is another troll guarding the bridges to other components of your machine called BIOS, to which we'll return in a little while. Both DOS and BIOS offer *services,* which are simple tasks that your programs would have to do themselves if the services were not provided. Quite apart from saving you, the programmer, a lot of work, having DOS and BIOS services helps guarantee that certain things will be done in identical fashion on all machines, which (especially in terms of disk storage) is a major reason software written for DOS runs on so many different machines: all the machine-dependent stuff is done the same way.

One of the services DOS provides is simple (far too simple, actually) access to your machine's display. For the purposes of EAT.ASM (which is just a lesson in getting your first assembly language program written and operating) simple services are enough.

So, how do we use DOS and BIOS services? The way is as easy to use as it is tricky to understand—through software interrupts.

An Interrupt That Doesn't Interrupt Anything

As someone new to the 8086/8088 family of processors, the notion of a software interrupt drove me nuts. I kept looking and looking for the interrupter and interruptee. Nothing was getting interrupted.

The name is unfortunate, even though I admit that there was some reason for calling software interrupts what they are. They are, in fact, courteous interrupts—if you can still call an interrupt *an interrupt* when it is so courteous that it does no interrupting at all.

The nature of software interrupts and DOS services is best explained by a real example illustrated twice in EAT.ASM. As I hinted above, DOS keeps little sequences of machine instructions tucked away within itself. Each sequence does something useful like read something from a disk file, display something to the screen, send something to the printer. DOS uses them to do its own work, and it also makes them available (with its troll hat on) to you, the programmer, to access from your programs.

Well, there is the critical question: how do you find something tucked away inside of DOS? All code sequences, of course, have addresses, and Microsoft or IBM could publish a booklet of addresses indicating where all the code is hidden. There are numerous good reasons not to pass out the addresses of the code itself, however. DOS is evolving and (we should hope) being improved on an ongoing basis. Repairing and improving code involves adding, changing, and removing machine instructions, which changes the size of those hidden code sequences and also, in consequence, changes their location. Add a dozen instructions to one sequence, and all the other sequences up-memory from that one sequence will have to shove over to make room. Once they shove over, they'll be at different addresses, so instantly the booklets are obsolete. Even *1 byte* added to or removed from a code sequence in DOS could change *everything.* (What if the first code sequence has a bug that must be repaired?)

The solution is ingenious. At the very start of memory, down at segment 0, offset 0, is a special table with 256 entries. Each entry is a complete address including segment and offset portions for a total of four bytes. The first 1024 bytes of memory in *any* 8086/8088 machine are reserved for this table, and no code or data may be placed there.

Each of the addresses in the table is called an *interrupt vector.* The table as a whole is called the *interrupt vector table.* Each vector has a number, from 0 to 255. The vector occupying bytes 0 to 3 in the table is vector 0. The vector occupying bytes 4 to 7 is vector 1, and so on, as shown in Figure 7.3.

None of the addresses is burned into permanent memory the way BIOS routines are. When your machine starts up, DOS and BIOS fill many of the slots in the interrupt vector table with addresses of certain service routines within themselves. Each version of DOS knows the location of its innermost parts, and when you upgrade to a new version of DOS, that new version will fill the appropriate slots in the vector table with upgraded and accurate addresses.

The bottom of memory

FIGURE 7.3   The interrupt vector table

What *doesn't* change from DOS version to DOS version is the *number* of the interrupt that holds a particular address. In other words, since the PC first began, interrupt 21H has pointed the way into darkest DOS to DOS's *services dispatcher,* a sort of multiple railway switch with spurs heading out to the many (over 50) individual DOS service routines. The address of the dispatcher has changed with every DOS version, but regardless of version, programs can find the address of the dispatcher in slot 21 of the interrupt vector table.

Furthermore, programs don't have to go snooping in the table for the address themselves. The 8086/8088 CPU includes a machine instruction that makes use of the interrupt vector table. The **INT** (**INT**errupt) instruction is used by EAT.ASM to request the services of DOS in displaying two strings on the screen. At two places, EAT.ASM has an **INT 21H** instruction. When an **INT 21H** instruction is executed, the CPU goes down to the interrupt vector table, fetches the address from slot 21H, and then jumps execution to the address stored in slot 21H. Because the DOS services dispatcher lies at the address in slot 21H, the dispatcher gets control of the machine and does the work that it knows how to do.

The process is shown in Figure 7.4. When DOS loads itself at boot time, one of the many things it does to prepare the machine for use is to put correct addresses in several of the vectors in the interrupt vector table. One of these addresses is the address of the dispatcher, which goes into slot 21H.

Later on, when you type the name of your program MYPROG on the DOS command line, DOS loads MYPROG.EXE into memory and gives it control of the machine. MYPROG.EXE does *not* know the address of the DOS dispatcher. MYPROG *does* know that the dispatcher's address will always be in slot 21H of the vector table, so it executes an **INT 21** instruction. The correct address lies in vector 21H, and MYPROG is content to remain ignorant and simply let the **INT 21** instruction and vector 21H take it to where it needs to go.

Back on the northwest side of Chicago, there was a bus that ran along Milwaukee Avenue. All Chicago bus routes had numbers, and the Milwaukee Avenue route was #56. It started somewhere in the tangled streets just north of downtown, and ended up in a forest preserve just inside the city limits. The forest preserve district had a swimming pool called Whelan Pool. Kids all along Milwaukee Avenue could not necessarily have told you the address of Whelan Pool, but come summer, they'd tell you in a second how to get there: just hop bus #56 and take it to the end of the line. It's like that with software interrupts. Find the number of the vector that reliably points to your destination, and ride that vector to the

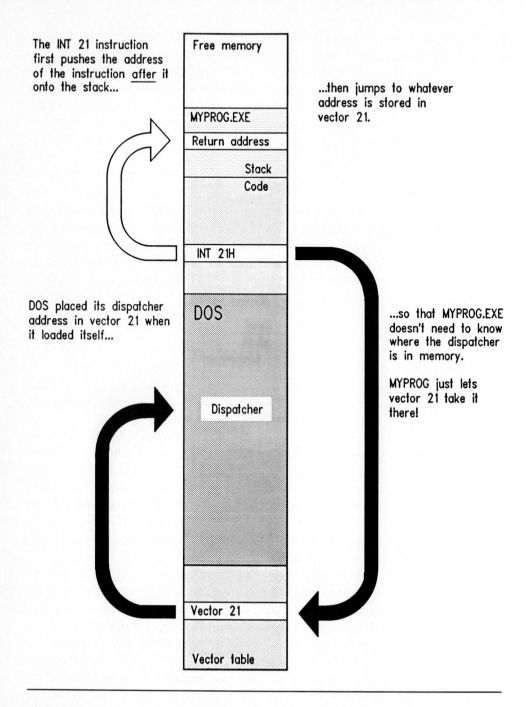

The INT 21 instruction first pushes the address of the instruction <u>after</u> it onto the stack...

...then jumps to whatever address is stored in vector 21.

DOS placed its dispatcher address in vector 21 when it loaded itself...

...so that MYPROG.EXE doesn't need to know where the dispatcher is in memory.

MYPROG just lets vector 21 take it there!

Free memory

MYPROG.EXE

Return address

Stack

Code

INT 21H

DOS

Dispatcher

Vector 21

Vector table

FIGURE 7.4   Riding an interrupt vector into DOS

end of the line, without worrying about the winding route or the address of your destination.

Note that the **INT 21** instruction does something else; it pushes the address of the *next* instruction (that is, the instruction immediately following the **INT 21** instruction) on the stack before it follows vector 21H into the depths of DOS. Like Hansel and Gretel, the **INT 21** was pushing some breadcrumbs to the stack as a way of helping execution find its way back to MYPROG.EXE after the excursion down into DOS. This will be discussed later.

The DOS dispatcher controls access to dozens of individual service routines. How does it know which one to execute? You have to tell the dispatcher which service you need, and you do so by placing the service's number in the 8-bit register AH. The dispatcher may require other information as well, and will expect you to provide that information in the correct place before executing **INT 21.**

Look at the following three lines of code from EAT.ASM.

```
lea   DX,EAT1   ; Load offset of Eat1 message string into DX
mov AH,09H     ; Select DOS service 09H: Print string
int   21H       ; Call DOS
```

This sequence of instructions requests that DOS display a string on the screen. The first line sets up a vital piece of information, which is the offset address of the string to be displayed on the screen. Without the offset address, DOS will not have any way to know what it is that we want to display. The dispatcher expects the offset address to be in DX, and assumes that the segment address will be in DS. The address of the data segment was loaded into DS earlier in the program by these two instructions:

```
mov AX,MyData ; Set up our own data segment address in DS
mov DS,AX     ; Can't load segment reg. directly from memory
```

Once loaded, DS is not disturbed during the full run of the program, so the DOS dispatcher's assumption is valid even though DS is loaded early in the program and not each time we want to display a string.

In moving 09H into register AH, we tell the dispatcher which service we want performed. Service 09H is DOS's *print string* service. This is not the fastest nor in other ways the best way to display a string on the PC's screen, but it is most certainly the *easiest.*

DOS service 09H has a slightly odd requirement: the end of the string must be marked with a dollar sign ($). This is the reason for the dollar signs hung incongruously on the ends of both of EAT.ASM's strings. Because DOS does not ask us to pass it a value indicating how long the string is, the end of the string has to be marked somehow, and the dollar sign is DOS's chosen way. It's a lousy way, unfortunately, because with the dollar sign acting as a marker, *there is no way to display a dollar sign.* If you intend to talk about money on the PC's screen, don't use DOS service 09H! As I said, this is the easiest, but certainly not the best way to display text on the screen.

With the address of the string in DS:DX and the service number 09H in AH, we take a trip to the dispatcher by executing **INT 21H.** The **INT** instruction is all it takes—*boom!* DOS has control, reading the string at DS:DX and sending it to the screen through mechanisms it keeps more or less to itself.

Getting Home Again

So much for getting into DOS. How do we get home again? The address in vector 21H gave control to DOS, but how does DOS know where to go to pass program execution back into EAT.EXE? Half of the cleverness of software interrupts is knowing how to get there, and the other half (just as clever) is knowing how to get back.

To get into DOS, a program looks in a completely reliable place for the address of where it wants to go—the address stored in vector 21H. This address takes execution deep into DOS, leaving the program sitting above DOS. To continue execution where it left off prior to the **INT 21** instruction, DOS has to look in a completely reliable place for the return address, and that completely reliable place is none other than the top of the stack.

I mentioned earlier (without much emphasis) that the **INT 21** instruction pushes an address to the top of the stack before it launches off into the unknown. This address is the address of the *next* instruction in line for execution, the instruction immediately following the **INT 21** instruction. This location is completely reliable because, just as there is only one interrupt vector table in the machine, there is only one stack in operation at any one time. This means that there is only one top of the stack, SS:SP, and DOS can always send execution back to the program that called it by popping the address off the top of the stack and jumping to that address.

The process is shown in Figure 7.5, which is the continuation of Figure 7.4. Just as the **INT** instruction pushes a return address onto the stack and then jumps to the address stored in a particular vector, there is a combination instruction that pops the return address off the stack and then

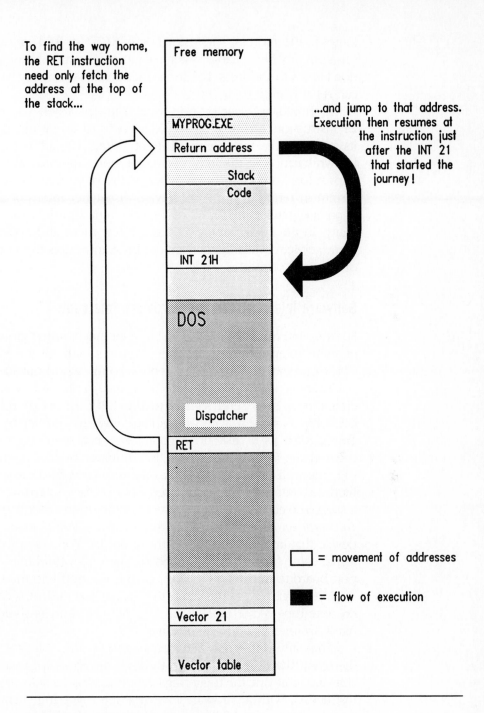

To find the way home, the RET instruction need only fetch the address at the top of the stack...

...and jump to that address. Execution then resumes at the instruction just after the INT 21 that started the journey!

Free memory

MYPROG.EXE

Return address

Stack

Code

INT 21H

DOS

Dispatcher

RET

Vector 21

Vector table

☐ = movement of addresses

■ = flow of execution

FIGURE 7.5   Returning home from an interrupt

jumps to the address. The instruction is **RET** (for **RET**urn) and it completes this complex but reliable system of jumping to an address when you really don't know the address. The trick, once again, is knowing where the address can reliably be found.

It should be clear by now what happens when you execute an **INT 21** instruction. EAT.ASM uses DOS services to save it the trouble of writing its string data to the screen a byte at a time. The address into DOS is at a known location in the interrupt vector table, and the return address is at a known location on the stack. Whereas I've described the software interrupt system in terms of the DOS service dispatcher interrupt 21H, the system is precisely the same for all of the other software interrupts, and there are many. In the next chapter we'll use a few more and explore some of the many services available through the BIOS interrupts that control your video display and printer.

Software Interrupts versus Hardware Interrupts

Software interrupts evolved from an older mechanism that *did* involve some genuine interrupting—hardware interrupts. A hardware interrupt is your CPU's mechanism for paying attention to the world outside itself.

There is a fairly complex electrical system built into your PC that allows circuit boards to send signals to the CPU. An actual metal pin on the CPU chip is moved from one voltage level to another by a circuit board device such as a disk drive controller or a serial port board. Through this pin the CPU is tapped on the shoulder by the external device. The CPU recognizes this tap as a *hardware interrupt*. Like software interrupts, hardware interrupts are numbered, and for each interrupt number there is a slot reserved in the interrupt vector table. In this slot is the address of an *interrupt service routine* (ISR) that performs some action relevant to the device that tapped the CPU on the shoulder. For example, if the interrupt signal came from a serial port board, the CPU would then allow the serial port board to transfer a character byte from itself into the CPU.

Most properly, any routine that lies at the end of a vector address in the interrupt vector table is an ISR, but the term is usually reserved for hardware interrupt service routines.

The only difference between hardware and software interrupts is in the event that triggers the trip through the interrupt vector table. With a software interrupt, the triggering event is part of the software; that is, an **INT** instruction. With a hardware interrupt, the triggering event is an electrical signal applied to the CPU chip itself without any **INT** instruction taking part in the process. The CPU itself pushes the return address on the stack when it recognizes the electrical pulse that triggers the interrupt; however, when the ISR is done, a **RET** instruction sends the program execution home, just as it does for a software interrupt.

Hardware ISRs can be (and usually are) written in assembly language. It's a difficult business, because the negotiations between the hardware and the software must be done just so or the machine may lock up or go berserk. This is no place for beginners, and I would advise you to develop some skill and obtain some considerable knowledge of your hardware setup before attempting to write a hardware ISR.

7.4 ◆ Summary: EAT.ASM on the Dissection Table

Let's recap our disassembly of EAT.ASM by putting it back together again, with commentary. I should point out that this is one way to write an assembly language program, but it isn't by any means the only way. I'm outlining what I feel is an ideal organization for short assembly language programs containing less than 1000 lines or so of source code assembled and linked *as one piece*. Beyond that 1000 lines, an assembly language program must be broken up into modules or the program will collapse into an undecipherable black hole into which any quantity of effort can be poured without any improvement in the program. We'll begin talking about modularizing programs in Chapter 8.

The essential structure of this organization is shown in Figure 7.6.

Segment Definition and Segment Order

An assembly language program of any usefulness must consist of at least three segments: (1) a data segment for variables used by the program, (2) a stack segment containing the program's stack, and (3) a code segment containing the program's machine instructions. These segments are defined by the use of two directives: **SEGMENT** marking the start of the segment and **ENDS** marking the end.

Each segment must have a name, and the name must be used *twice* in the definition of a segment: once before the **SEGMENT** directive and again before the **ENDS** directive. A segment must be named even though the name is not referenced anywhere in the program. Note that in EAT.ASM, the stack segment has a name, **MyStack,** even though nothing in the program ever needs to reference **MyStack** by name.

The stack segment must be defined with the directive **STACK** following

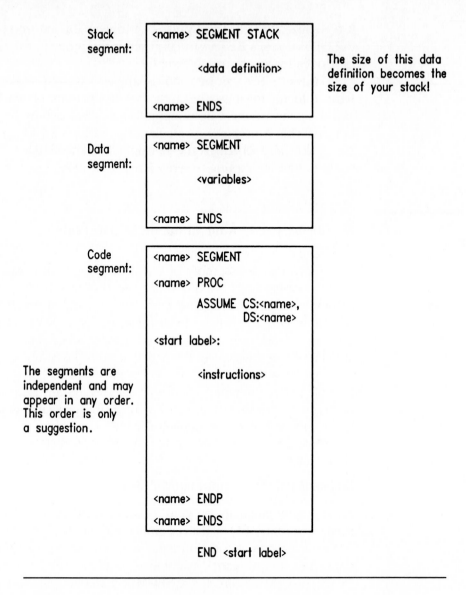

Stack segment:

```
<name>  SEGMENT STACK

          <data definition>

<name>  ENDS
```

The size of this data definition becomes the size of your stack!

Data segment:

```
<name>  SEGMENT

          <variables>

<name>  ENDS
```

Code segment:

```
<name>  SEGMENT

<name>  PROC

          ASSUME CS:<name>,
                 DS:<name>

<start label>:

          <instructions>

<name>  ENDP

<name>  ENDS
```

The segments are independent and may appear in any order. This order is only a suggestion.

```
END <start label>
```

FIGURE 7.6   The structure of a simple program

the directive **SEGMENT.** This tells DOS which segment address to load into the **SS** (**S**tack **S**egment) register.

The size of the stack segment is dictated by the definition of some data within the segment. You must define enough stack space to cover any possible need the program may have. If you don't define enough stack space, you may have a stack crash, which will definitely terminate your program and very possibly crash the machine as well. Decide how much stack space you may realistically need and allocate twice as much. Use the **DB** and **DUP** directives to allocate space, as described below.

The segments are order-independent. You can place the segments in any order without changing the way the segments work together, or without changing the way the assembler treats them. My own custom is to define the stack segment first, followed by the data segment, followed by the code segment.

Data Definitions for Variables and Stack Space

Variables and space for the stack must be allocated during assembly. The **DB, DW, DD** and **DUP** directives are the most common means to do this. **DW** allocates word-sized (16-bit) variables, typically to contain register-sized values. **DD** allocates double-word-sized (32-bit) variables, typically for full addresses containing both segment and offset.

These definitions have a form like the examples shown below.

```
MyWord      DW 0FFFFH
MyAddress   DD 0B8000000H
```

The **DB** directive was designed to allocate byte-sized (8 bit) quantities like characters and register-halves, but it has the special property of being able to allocate strings as well. Elements of the string may be numbers, characters, or quoted strings separated by commas. The following are all legal **DB** variable definitions.

```
MyByte    DB   042H              ; Using hex notation
Counter   DB   17                ; Decimal!
Eat1      DB   "Eat at Joe's!","$"        ; Character string
CRLF      DB   0DH,0AH,'$'   ; Numbers separated by commas
```

If you need to allocate a variable or a buffer without specifying any initial values, use the **DUP** directive with a question mark (?) as the value:

```
MyBuffer   DB   1024 DUP (?)
```

This sets memory aside but stores nothing in it. Do not put the question mark in quotes, or the assembler will store a question mark character (ASCII 3FH) into every byte of the buffer.

The **DUP** directive also can be used to store repeated patterns into larger variables and buffers. This can make the buffers and variables easy to spot in hex dumps from DEBUG.

```
Marked   DB  10 DUP ('Zorro!!!')
Table1   DB  5 DUP (02H,04H,06H,08H)
         DB  64 DUP ('STACK!!!')
```

The last example allocates space for the stack segment in EAT.ASM. It points up the fact that you needn't give a name to a buffer that simply exists to take up space, as in allocating space for the stack segment. In general, however, all variables and buffers should be given names.

Setting up the Code Segment

Like any segment, the code segment must have a name, and the name must be given at the start and at the end of the segment definition, before the **SEGMENT** and **ENDS** directives. The name itself is unimportant and probably won't be referenced anywhere in the code itself. It must be there, however, or an assembler error will result.

An **ASSUME** directive must be included in the program. Its purpose is to tell the assembler which of the segments you have defined is to be used for the code segment and which segment is to be used for the data segment. Unlike the stack segment, which has the directive **STACK** to tell the assembler what sort of segment it is, nothing in the code or data segments specifies which sort of segment they are. It isn't enough that there are variables defined in the data segment or machine instructions in the code segment—the assembler will allow you put variable definitions in the code segment and machine instructions in the data segment, regardless of whether that makes sense or not. (It may make sense in certain advanced techniques.)

In EAT.ASM, the **ASSUME** directive tells the assembler that the code segment will be the segment named **MyCode,** and that the data segment will be named **MyData.**

EAT.ASM has its machine instructions grouped together in a procedure named **Main** with the **PROC** directive. This is not strictly necessary unless you have broken down your program into procedures or modules, and EAT.ASM will assemble and run correctly without the **Main PROC** and **Main ENDP** statements. I would advise you to get in the habit of placing the main program portion of any assembly language program into a procedure called **Main** to help make the program more readable.

What *is* essential, however, is to provide a label that marks the place where program execution is to begin. I recommend the label **Start:** as a convention, but the label can be any legal identifier. Whatever label you choose, mark the main program's starting point with the label and a colon. Then, place the same label *minus* the colon after the **END** directive that marks the end of the source code file itself. This tells the assembler that there is no more source code and that the label is the point at which execution is to begin.

What EAT.ASM's Machine Instructions Do

From the top:

```
mov AX,MyData     ; Set up our data segment address in DS
mov DS,AX         ; Can't load segment reg. directly from memory
```

Before your program can access any of its variables in the data segment, it must have the segment address of the data segment in the DS register. The **ASSUME** directive tells the assembler to assemble any instruction referencing an identifier in the **MyData** segment under the assumption (hence the name of the directive) that **MyData** is to be a data segment. **ASSUME,** however, *does not load the data segment address into DS!*

You must do that yourself, which is the purpose of the two instructions shown above. This seemingly simple operation takes two instructions rather than one because **MOV** cannot move memory data directly into a segment register like DS. To load the address of memory data into a segment register, you must first load the address into one of the general-purpose registers and *then* load the general-purpose register into the segment register.

```
lea   DX,Eat1     ; Load offset of Eat1 message string into DX
mov AH,09H        ; Select DOS service 09H: Print string
int   21H         ; Call DOS
```

Here's where the first real work of EAT.ASM gets done. The **LEA** instruction (**L**oad **E**ffective **A**ddress) puts the offset address of variable **Eat1** into the DX register. Keep in mind that the segment address of **Eat1** is already in DS, loaded by the first two instructions in the program. **MOV AH,09H** loads the number of DOS service 09H (print string) into register half AH. *Print String* is a misnomer, but the term is inherited from an ancient age when video terminals were considered exotic and strings could *only* be printed on (kerchunk-kerchunkity-chunk) Teletype terminals!

Finally, **INT 21H** transfers control to the DOS services dispatcher by way of software interrupt 21H. The dispatcher looks in DS:DX for the address of the string variable to be displayed, and then hands control over to the *print string* service routine somewhere deep within DOS. When the string is displayed, execution returns to the instruction following the **INT 21H** instruction. This is possible because the **INT 21H** instruction pushed the address of the next instruction onto the stack before it passed execution to the DOS services dispatcher. The dispatcher simply popped that return address off the stack and resumed execution at that address. This is how interrupts work, and is explained in detail in the previous section.

```
lea  DX,CRLF    ; Load offset of CRLF string into DX
mov AH,09H      ; Select DOS service 09H: Print String
int  21H        ; Call DOS
```

The previous block of instructions were enough to display the string "Eat at Joe's!" on your video display. DOS leaves the hardware cursor on the character following the last character of the string, however, and any subsequent display output would follow "Eat at Joe's!" immediately. You may want this, and you may not—if you don't, it would be a good idea to return the cursor to the left margin and bump it down to the next screen line. This is what's going on here: the **CRLF** variable contains the EOL or newline code 0DH (ASCII carriage return) and 0AH (ASCII line feed). EAT.ASM passes the string containing these two invisible characters to DOS in exactly the same way it passed the string "Eat at Joe's!" by loading **CRLF**'s address into DS:DX and selecting DOS service 09H before handing control to the DOS services dispatcher through software interrupt 21H.

```
mov AH,4CH      ; Terminate process DOS service
mov AL,0        ; Pass this value back to ERRORLEVEL
int  21H        ; Control returns to DOS
```

Finally, the job is done, Joe's has been properly advertised, and it's time to let DOS have the machine back. Another DOS service, 4CH (*Terminate Process*) handles the mechanics of courteously disentangling the machine from EAT.ASM's clutches. *Terminate Process* doesn't need the address of anything, but it will take whatever value it finds in the AL register and place it in the ERRORLEVEL DOS variable. DOS batch programs can test the value of ERRORLEVEL and branch on it, as I'll demonstrate in the next chapter.

EAT.ASM doesn't do anything worth testing in a batch program, but if ERRORLEVEL will be set anyway, it's a good idea to provide some reliable and harmless value for ERRORLEVEL to take. This is why 0 is loaded into AL prior to ending it all by the final **INT 21** instruction. If you were to test ERRORLEVEL after running EAT.EXE, you would find it set to 0 in every case.

Chapter 8

Dividing and Conquering
Using Procedures and Macros to Battle Complexity

8.1 ◆ Programming in Martian

There is a computer language called APL (an acronym for *A Programming Language*—how clever) that has more than a little Martian in it. APL was the first computer language I learned, (on a major IBM mainframe) and when I learned it I learned a little more than just APL.

APL uses a very compact notation, with dozens of odd little symbols, each of which is capable of some astonishing power like matrix inversion. You can do more in one line of APL than you can in one line of anything else I have learned since. The combination of the strange symbol set and the compact notation make it very hard to read and remember what a line of code in APL actually does.

So it was in 1977. Having mastered (or so I thought) the whole library of symbols, I set out to write a text formatting program. The program would justify right and left, center headers, and do a few other things like those that we take for granted today but that were very exotic in the Seventies.

The program grew over a period of a week to about 600 lines of squirmy little APL symbols. I got it to work, and it worked fine—as long as I didn't try to format a column that was more than 64 characters wide. Then everything came out scrambled.

Whoops. I printed the whole thing out and sat down to do some serious debugging. Then I realized with a feeling of sinking horror that, having finished the last part of the program, *I had no idea how the first part worked.*

The APL symbol set was only part of the problem. I soon came to realize that the most important mistake I had made was writing the whole thing as one 600-line monolithic block of code lines. There were no functional divisions, nothing to indicate what any ten-line portion of the code was trying to accomplish.

The Martians had won. I did the only thing possible: I scrapped it. And I settled for ragged margins in my text.

8.2 ◆ Boxes within Boxes

This sounds like Eastern mysticism, but it's just an observation from life: *within any action is a host of smaller actions.* Look inside your common activities. When you brush your teeth you do the following:

◆ Pick up your toothpaste tube
◆ Unscrew the cap

♦ Place the cap on the sink counter

♦ Pick up your toothbrush

♦ Squeeze toothpaste onto the brush from the middle of the tube

♦ Put your toothbrush into your mouth

♦ Work it back and forth vigorously

and so on. The original list went the entire page. When you brush your teeth, you perform every one of those actions. When you think about the sequence, however, you don't run through the whole list. You bring to mind the simple concept of brushing teeth.

Furthermore, when you think about what's behind the action we call "getting up in the morning," you might assemble a list of activities like this:

♦ Shut off the clock radio

♦ Climb out of bed

♦ Put on your robe

♦ Let the dogs out

♦ Make breakfast

♦ Brush your teeth

♦ Shave

♦ Get dressed

Brushing your teeth is on the list, but within the activity you call brushing your teeth are a whole list of smaller actions, as listed above. The same can be said for most of the activities shown above. How many individual actions, for example, does it take to put a reasonable breakfast together? And yet in one small if sweeping phrase, "getting up in the morning," you embrace that whole host of small and even smaller actions without having to laboriously trace through each one.

What I'm describing is the Chinese boxes method of fighting complexity. Getting up in the morning involves hundreds of little actions, so we divide the mass up into coherent chunks and set the chunks into little conceptual boxes. "Making breakfast" is in one box, "brushing teeth" is in another, and so on. Closer inspection of any box shows that its contents can also be divided into numerous boxes, and those smaller boxes into even smaller boxes.

This process doesn't (and can't) go on forever, but it should go on as long as it needs to in order to satisfy this criterion: *the contents of any one box should be understandable with only a little scrutiny.* No single box should contain anything so subtle or large and involved that it takes hours of hair-pulling to figure it out.

Procedures as Boxes for Code

The mistake I made in writing my APL text formatter is that I threw the whole collection of 600 lines of APL code into one huge box marked "Text formatter."

While I was writing it, I should have been keeping my eyes open for sequences of code statements that worked together at some identifiable task. When I spotted such sequences, I should have set them off as *procedures.* Each sequence would then have a name that would provide a memory tag for the sequence's function. If it took ten statements to justify a line of text, those ten statements should have been named **JustifyLine,** and so on.

Xerox's legendary APL programmer Jim Dunn later told me that I shouldn't ever write a procedure that wouldn't fit on a single 25-line terminal screen. "More than 25 lines and you're doing too much in one procedure. Split it up," he said. Whenever I worked in APL after that, I adhered to that rather sage rule of thumb. The Martians still struck from time to time, but when they did, it was no longer a total loss.

All computer languages have procedures of one sort or another, and assembly language is no exception. You may recall from the previous chapter that the main program is in fact a procedure, and the only thing setting it apart as the main program is the fact that its name is specified after the **END** directive.

Your assembly language program can have numerous procedures. There's no limit to the *number* of procedures, as long as the total number of bytes of code contained by all the procedures together does not exceed 65,535 (one segment). Other complications arise at that point, but nothing that can't be worked around.

But that's a lot of code. You needn't worry for awhile, and certainly not while you're just learning assembly language. (I won't be treating the creation of multiple code segments in this book.) In the meantime, let's take a look at the *Eat at Joe's* program, expanded a little to include a couple of procedures:

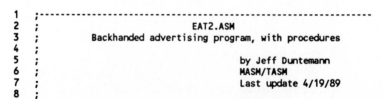

```
1   ;-------------------------------------------------
2   ;                      EAT2.ASM
3   ;          Backhanded advertising program, with procedures
4   ;
5   ;                              by Jeff Duntemann
6   ;                              MASM/TASM
7   ;                              Last update 4/19/89
8   ;
```

```
 9    ;
10    ;
11    ;-------------------------------------------------------------
12    ;
13    ;----------------------------|
14    ;    BEGIN STACK SEGMENT      |
15    ;----------------------------|
16    MyStack    SEGMENT STACK          ; STACK word ensures loading of SS by DOS
17
18               DB      64 DUP ('STACK!!!') ; This reserves 512 bytes for the stack
19
20    MyStack    ENDS
21    ;----------------------------|
22    ;    END STACK SEGMENT        |
23    ;----------------------------|
24
25
26    ;----------------------------|
27    ;    BEGIN DATA SEGMENT       |
28    ;----------------------------|
29    MyData     SEGMENT
30
31    Eat1       DB      "Eat at Joe's...",'$'
32    Eat2       DB      "...ten million flies can't ALL be wrong!",'$'
33    CRLF       DB      0DH,0AH,'$'
34
35    MyData     ENDS
36    ;----------------------------|
37    ;    END DATA SEGMENT         |
38    ;----------------------------|
39
40    ;----------------------------|
41    ;    BEGIN CODE SEGMENT       |
42    ;----------------------------|
43    MyCode     SEGMENT
44
45    Main       PROC
46               assume CS:MyCode,DS:MyData
47
48    Start:     ; This is where program execution begins:
49               mov  AX,MyData  ; Set up our own data segment address in DS
50               mov  DS,AX      ; Can't load segment reg. directly from memory
51
52               lea  DX,Eat1    ; Load offset of Eat1 string into DX
53               call Writeln    ;    and display it
54               lea  DX,Eat2    ; Load offset of Eat2 string into DX
55               call Writeln    ;    and display it
56
57               mov  AH,4CH     ; Terminate process DOS service
58               mov  AL,0       ; Pass this value back to ERRORLEVEL
59               int  21H        ; Control returns to DOS
60
61    ;-----------------------------------------|
62    ;            PROCEDURE SECTION             |
63    ;-----------------------------------------|
64
65    Write      PROC
66               mov AH,09H           ; Select DOS service 9: Print String
67               int 21H              ; Call DOS
68               ret                  ; Return to the caller
69    Write      ENDP
70
71
```

```
72    Writeln    PROC
73               call Write          ; Display the string proper through Write
74               mov DX,OFFSET CRLF  ; Load address of newline string to DS:DX
75               call Write          ; Display the newline string through Write
76               ret                 ; Return to the caller
77    Writeln    ENDP
78
79    ;-------------------------------------------|
80    ;          END PROCEDURE SECTION            |
81    ;-------------------------------------------|
82
83    Main       ENDP
84
85    MyCode     ENDS
86
87    ;------------------------------------------|
88    ;        END CODE SEGMENT                  |
89    ;------------------------------------------|
90
91               END Start    ; The procedure named Start becomes the main program
```

Calling and Returning

EAT2.ASM does about the same thing as EAT.ASM. It prints a two-line slogan and that's all. The way the two lines of the slogan are displayed, however, bears examination:

```
lea DX,Eat1
call Writeln
```

Here's a new instruction: **CALL.** The label **Writeln** refers to a procedure. As you might have gathered, **CALL Writeln** simply tells the CPU to go off and execute a procedure named **Writeln.**

The means by which **CALL** operates may sound familiar: **CALL** first pushes the address of the *next* instruction after itself onto the stack. Then **CALL** transfers the program execution to the address represented by the name of the procedure. The instructions contained in the procedure execute. Finally, the procedure is terminated by **CALL**'s alter ego, **RET** (for **RET**urn). The **RET** instruction pops the address off the top of the stack and transfers execution to that address. Because the address pushed was the address of the first instruction *after* the **CALL** instruction, execution continues as though **CALL** had not changed the flow of instruction execution at all (see Figure 8.1).

This should remind you strongly of how software interrupts work. The main difference is that the caller *does* know the exact address of the routine it wishes to call. Apart from that, it's very much the same process.

Free memory

Stack

SP: Offset of MOV

Data segment

Proc1

RET

Proc2

Main program

CALL Proc1
MOV AX,BX
<etc.>

CS:

The procedure's RET instruction pops the address from the top of the stack, and branches to that address.

The CALL instruction pushes the address of the next instruction onto the stack, and branches to the procedure.

☐ = movement of addresses

■ = flow of execution

FIGURE 8.1   Procedure calling and returning

The structure of a procedure is simple and easy to understand. Look at the **Write** procedure from EAT2.ASM:

```
Write    PROC
         mov AH,09H    ; Select DOS service 9: Print String
         int 21H       ; Call DOS
         ret           ; Return to the caller
Write    ENDP
```

The important points are these: a procedure must be bracketed by the **PROC/ENDP** directives, preceded in both cases by the name of the procedure. Also, somewhere within the procedure, and certainly as the last instruction in the procedure, there must be at least one **RET** instruction.

The **RET** instruction is the only way that the program execution can get back to the caller of the procedure. There can be more than one **RET** instruction in a procedure although your procedures will be easier to read and understand if there is only one. Using more than one **RET** instruction requires the use of **JMP** (**JuMP**) instructions, which I haven't covered yet but will shortly.

Calls within calls.   Within a procedure you can do anything that you can do within the main program. This includes calling other procedures from within a procedure; even something as simple as EAT2.ASM does that. Look at the **Writeln** procedure:

```
Writeln  PROC
         call Write    ; Display the string proper through Write
         lea DX,CRLF    ; Load address of newline string to DS:DX
         call Write    ; Display the newline string through Write
         ret           ; Return to the caller
Writeln  ENDP
```

The **Writeln** procedure displays a string to your screen and then returns the cursor to the left margin of the following screen line. This is actually two distinct activities and **Writeln** very economically uses a mechanism that already exists: the **Write** procedure. The first thing that **Writeln** does is call **Write** to display the string itself to the screen. Remember that the caller loaded the address of the string to be displayed into register DX before calling **Writeln.** Nothing has disturbed DX, so **Writeln** can immediately call **Write,** which will fetch the address from DX and display the string to the screen.

Returning the cursor is done by displaying the newline sequence, which is stored in a string named **CRLF. Writeln** again uses **Write** to display **CRLF.** Once that is done, the work is finished, and **Writeln** executes a **RET** instruction to return execution to the caller.

Calling procedures from within procedures requires you to pay attention to one thing: stack space. Remember that each procedure call pushes a return address onto the stack. This return address is not removed from the stack until the **RET** instruction for that procedure executes. If you execute another **CALL** instruction before returning from a procedure, the second **CALL** instruction pushes another return address onto the stack. If you keep calling procedures from within procedures, one return address will pile up on the stack for each **CALL** until you start returning from all those *nested* procedures.

If you run out of stack space, your program will crash and return to DOS, possibly taking DOS and the machine with it. This is why you should take care to allocate considerably more stack space than you think you might ever conceivably need. EAT2.ASM uses at most 4 bytes of stack space, because it nests procedure calls two deep. (**Writeln** within itself calls **Write.**) Nonetheless, I allocated 512 bytes of stack to get you in the habit of not being stingy with stack space. Obviously you won't always be able to keep a 128 to 1 ratio of need to have, but consider 512 bytes a *minimum* for stack space allocation. If you need more, allocate it.

When to Make Something a Procedure

The single most important purpose of procedures is to manage complexity in your programs by replacing a sequence of machine instructions with a descriptive name. This might hardly seem to the point in the case of the **Write** procedure, which contains only two instructions apart from the structurally necessary **RET** instruction.

True, but—the **Writeln** procedure hides two separate calls to **Write** behind itself: one to display the string, and another to return the cursor to the left margin of the next line. If you look back to EAT.ASM, you'll see that it took six instructions to display both the slogan string and the newline string. What took six instructions now takes two, thanks to **Writeln.** Furthermore, the name **Writeln** is more readable and descriptive of what the sequence of six instructions does than the sequence of six instructions themselves.

Extremely simple procedures like **Write** don't themselves hide a great deal of complexity. They *do* give certain actions descriptive names, which is valuable in itself. They also provide basic building blocks for the creation of larger and more powerful procedures, as we'll see later on.

In general, when looking for some action to turn into a procedure, see what actions tend to happen a lot in a program. Most programs spend a lot of time displaying things to the screen. Procedures like **Write** and **Writeln** become general-purpose tools that may be used all over your programs. Furthermore, once you've written and tested them, they may be reused in future programs as well.

Try to look ahead to your future programming tasks and create procedures of general usefulness. I'll be showing you more of those by way of example as we continue, and tool-building is a very good way to hone your assembly language skills.

On the other hand, a short sequence (five to ten instructions) that is only called once or perhaps twice within a middling program (i.e., over a 100 machine instructions) is a poor candidate for a procedure.

You may find it useful to define *large* procedures that are called only once when your program becomes big enough to require breaking it down into functional chunks. A 1000-line assembly language program might split well into a sequence of nine or ten largish procedures. Each is only called once from the main program, but this allows your main program to be very indicative of what the program is doing:

```
Start:   call Initialize
         call OpenFile
Input:   call GetRec
         call VerifyRec
         call WriteRec
         loop Input
         call CloseFile
         call CleanUp
         call ReturnToDOS
```

This is clean and readable and provides a necessary view from a height when you begin to approach a 1000-line assembly language program. Remember that the Martians are always hiding somewhere close by, anxious to turn your program into unreadable hieroglyphics.

There's no weapon against them with half the power of procedures.

8.3 ◆ Using BIOS Services

In the last chapter we looked closely at DOS services, which are accessed through the DOS services dispatcher. The DOS dispatcher lives at the other end of software interrupt 21H, and offers a tremendous list of services at the disposal of your programs. There's another provider of services in your machine that lives even deeper than DOS: the ROM BIOS. ROM is an acronym for read only memory and it indicates memory chips whose contents are burned into their silicon and do not vanish when the power is turned off. BIOS is an acronym for basic input/output system, and it is just that: a collection of fundamental routines for dealing with your computer's input and output peripherals. These include disk drives, displays, printers, and the like. DOS uses BIOS services as part of some of the services that it provides.

Like DOS, BIOS services are accessed through software interrupts. Unlike DOS, which channels nearly all requests for its services through the single interrupt 21H, BIOS uses numerous interrupts (about 10) and groups similar categories of services beneath the control of different interrupts. For example, video display services are accessed through interrupt 10H, keyboard services come through interrupt 16H, printer services through interrupt 17H, and so on.

The overall method for using BIOS services, however, is very similar to that of DOS. You load a service number and sometimes other initial values into the registers and then execute an **INT** $<$**n**$>$ instruction, where the n depends on the category of services you're requesting.

Nothing difficult about that at all. Let's start building some tools.

Positioning the Hardware Cursor

So far, in writing to the display, we've simply let the text fall where it may. In general, this means one line of text following another and when the screen fills, DOS *scrolls* the screen upward to make room on the bottom line for more text. This makes for dull programs, very similar to programming in the bad old days when everything was done on clunky mechanical printers called teletypes. (Indeed, this kind of screen I/O is called *glass teletype* I/O because of its similarity to a printer scrolling paper up one line at a time.)

Let's leave the glass teletypes behind and take control of the cursor. BIOS service 10H (often nicknamed VIDEO, in upper case, for reasons that are obscure) offers a simple service to position the hardware cursor on the text screen. The service number is loaded into AH. This is a common thread through all BIOS services: the service number is placed into AH. A zero must be placed in BH unless you intend to tinker with multiple display pages. That's a story for another time; while you're learning, assume BH should be set to zero for cursor positioning.

The new position of the cursor must be loaded into the two halves of the DX register. Cursor positions are given as *X,Y* coordinate pairs. The *X* component of the cursor position is the number of character columns to the right of the left margin where we want the cursor to be. The *Y* component is the number of lines down from the top of the screen where we want the cursor to be. The *X* component is loaded into DL, and the *Y* component is loaded into DH. The routine itself is nothing more than this:

```
GotoXY   PROC
         mov AH,02H     ; Select VIDEO service 2: Position cursor
         mov BH,0       ; Stay with display page 0
         int 10H        ; Call VIDEO
         ret            ; Return to the caller
GotoXY   ENDP
```

Don't forget that the *X* and *Y* value must be loaded into DX *by the caller.* Using **GotoXY** is done this way:

```
mov DL,35      ; Pass 35 as X coordinate
mov DH,9       ; Pass 9 as Y coordinate
call GotoXY    ; Position the cursor
```

EAT3.ASM uses **GotoXY** to position the cursor, but it does something else as well: it clears the display. If you're going to be moving the cursor at will around the screen with **GotoXY,** it makes sense to start with a completely empty screen so that the remains of earlier programs and DOS commands don't clutter up the view.

There's another VIDEO service that can do the job. Service 6 is an interesting and powerful one: not only does it clear the screen, it can scroll the screen as well, by any specified number of lines. Furthermore, it can clear or scroll the entire screen, or only a rectangular portion of the screen, leaving the rest of the screen undisturbed.

If the term *scrolling* is unfamiliar to you, just press Enter repeatedly at the DOS prompt and watch what happens when you reach the bottom line of the screen. The displayed text on the screen jumps up by one line, and an empty line appears at the bottom of the screen. The DOS prompt is then redisplayed in the empty line. Scrolling is the process of making the screen jump up by one or more lines and inserting one or more blank lines at the bottom as appropriate.

Using VIDEO Service 6

Understanding VIDEO service 6 involves a fair number of values that need to be passed to the service in registers. The one unchanging item is the service number itself, passed as 6 in register AH (as with all BIOS services).

Service 6 acts upon a rectangular region of the display. This may be the full screen or it may be only part of the screen. You must pass the coordinates of the upper left and lower right corners of the region in registers CX and DX. Because screen coordinates are always smaller than 255 (which is the largest value that can be expressed in eight bits) the register halves of CX and DX are used independently to carry the X and Y values.

The upper left corner's *X* coordinate is passed in CL, and the upper left corner's *Y* coordinate is passed in CH. These are *0-based* coordinates, meaning that they count from 0 rather than 1. Confusion is possible here, because most high-level languages like Turbo Pascal number coordinates on the screen from 1. In other words, the upper left corner of the screen in Turbo Pascal is given by the coordinates 1,1. To BIOS, however, that same corner of the screen is 0,0. The width and height of a typical screen to Turbo Pascal would be 80 × 25; BIOS would say 79 × 24.

Similarly, the lower right corner's *X* coordinate is passed in DL, and the lower right corner's *Y* coordinate is passed in DH, again counting from 0.

Service 6 either scrolls or clears the region. It can scroll the screen upward by any arbitrary number of lines. This number is passed to service 6 in register AL. Clearing the region is a special case of scrolling it: when you specify that 0 lines be scrolled, the entire region is cleared instead.

The full screen is actually a special case of a rectangular region. By passing the coordinates of the upper left and lower right corners of the screen (0,0 and 79,24), the full screen is cleared.

Procedures with Multiple Entry Points

This is a lot of versatility for one service to handle, and it brings up a couple of questions. First of all, how versatile should a single procedure be? Should there be one procedure to clear the whole screen, another procedure to clear part of a screen, and a third procedure to scroll part of the screen?

The answer is that one procedure can do all three and not duplicate any code at all. The method involves writing a single procedure that has four different *entry points*. Each entry point is a label, which may be called with a **CALL** instruction. When a given entry point's label is called, execution begins at the instruction specified by that label. There is only one **RET** instruction, so the procedure is in fact one procedure. It's like a house with three front doors but only one back door; having three front doors does not make it three separate houses.

Here's what such a creature looks like:

```
ClrScr    PROC
          mov CX,0        ; Upper left corner of full screen
          mov DX,LRXY     ; Load lower-right XY coordinates into DX
ClrWin:   mov AL,0        ; 0 specifies clear entire region
ScrlWin:  mov BH,07H      ; Specify "normal" attribute for blanked line(s)
VIDEO6:   mov AH,06H      ; Select VIDEO service 6: Initialize/Scroll
          int 10H         ; call VIDEO
          ret             ; Return to the caller
ClrScr    ENDP
```

There's nothing much to this. What we have here is a collection of **MOV** instructions setting up values in registers before calling VIDEO through interrupt 10H. Note that all of the entry points except the one doing double-duty as the procedure name (**ClrScrn**) must be given with colons. The colon, as I pointed out earlier, is necessary after any label used to mark an address within a code segment.

The multiple entry points exist only to allow you to skip certain portions of the procedure that set up values that you don't want set. All the registers used by service 6 must be set up *somewhere*. However, they can either be set within the procedure or in the caller's code just before the procedure is called. If the procedure sets them, they have to be set to some generally useful configuration (say, clearing the entire screen) whereas if the caller sets them, the registers can be set to serve the caller's needs and make service 6 perform any of its varied combinations.

So it is with procedure **ClrScr.** If you enter **ClrScr** through its main or top entry point, *all* of its internal code will be executed. CX and DX will be set to the upper left and lower right corner coordinates of the full screen, AL is set to 0 to clear the full screen rather than scroll it, and BH is loaded with the normal (i.e., blank, for white text on a black background) text display attribute. Service 6 is then called.

If you wish to clear only a rectangular area of the screen (a *window*) you would use the **ClrWin** entry point. This entry point starts executing the code *after* CX and DX are set to the corners of the full screen. This means that the caller must load CX and DX with the upper left and lower right corners of the screen region to be cleared. Calling **ClrWin** *without* setting CX and DX at all will execute service 6 with whatever leftover garbage values happen to be in CX and DX. Something will happen, for certain; whether it's what you *want* to happen or not is far less certain.

Keeping in mind that for proper operation all of service 6's required registers must be set, calling **ClrWin** would be done this way:

```
mov CX,0422H   ; Set upper left corner to X=22H; Y=04H
mov DX,093AH   ; Set lower right corner to X=3AH; Y=09H
call ClrWin    ; Call the window-clear procedure
```

The two **MOV** instructions are worth a closer look. Rather than use a separate instruction to load each half of DX and CX, the two halves are loaded together by loading a 16-bit immediate data value into the full 16-bit register. Thus, two **MOV** instructions can do the work that at first glance you might think would take four **MOV** instructions. This is a good example of writing tight, efficient assembler code. The trick is to document it (as I've done above) to make sure you understand six weeks from now what the magic number 093AH means!

The first instruction at the label **CrlWin** sets AL to 0, indicating that the region is to be cleared, not scrolled. If in fact you *do* want to scroll the region, you need to skip the **MOV** instruction that loads 0 into AL. This is the purpose of the entry point labeled **ScrlWin.** It gets you into the procedure below the point where you select clearing over scrolling. This means that you not only have to set the corners of the region to be scrolled, but also the number of lines to scroll as well:

```
mov CX,0422H   ; Set upper left corner to X=22H; Y=04H
mov DX,093AH   ; Set lower right corner to X=3AH; Y=09H
mov AL,1       ; Set to scroll by one line
call ScrlWin   ; Call the window-scroll procedure
```

As you can see, more and more of the work is being done by caller and less and less within the procedure. How you arrange the entry points to the procedure depends on what operations get done most frequently. In my programs I tend to clear the whole screen a lot, clear windows less frequently, and scroll windows less frequently still, and this is what I had in mind while arranging the code within **ClrScr.**

Note that there is no entry point to scroll the full screen. To scroll the full screen, you need to load the coordinates of the corners of the full screen into CX and DX, and then call **ClrWin** as though you were clearing just a portion of the screen. If you do a lot of screen scrolling, you might define a separate routine for scrolling the full screen. As an interesting exercise, write such a routine and a program to test it.

As one more entry point, I included a label VIDEO6, which short-circuits all of the register setup apart from loading the service number itself into AH. This allows you to do something odd and infrequently, like scrolling the entire screen by three lines.

Memory Data or Immediate Data?

You may be wondering what the variable identifier **LRXY** is for and where it is defined. What it's for is simply to hold the current *X,Y* coordinates for the lower right corner of the screen. Where it's defined is in the program's data segment, in the usual way variables are defined, as you'll see if you look ahead to the full listing of EAT3.ASM on page 250.

The more interesting question is *why*. Most of the time I've been showing you values loaded into registers from immediate data, and this is often useful. The coordinates of the upper left corner of the full screen, for example, are always going to be 0,0 and nothing will change that. The lower right corner, however, is not necessarily always 79,24.

The original 1981-vintage IBM MDA and CGA graphics adapters are indeed capable of 80 by 25 text screens and no more. However, with an EGA it is possible to have an 80 by either 25 or 43 text screen, and the VGA introduced in 1987 with the PS/2 line can display 25, 43, or 50 line screens, all 80 characters wide. If your program can determine what size screen is in force when it is invoked, it can modify its displays accordingly.

Avoid dropping immediate values into code (we call this *hard-coding*) whenever you can. A better strategy, which I'll be following from now on, uses variables in the data segment initialized with currently correct values when the program begins running.

Use Comment Headers!

As time goes on, you'll find yourself creating dozens or even hundreds of procedures as a means of not recreating the same old wheel. The libraries of available procedures that most high-level language vendors supply with their compilers just don't exist with assembly language. By and large, you create your own.

Keeping such a list of routines straight is no easy task, even when you've written them all yourself. You *must* document the essential facts about each individual procedure or you'll forget them or remember them incorrectly and act on bad information. (The resultant bugs are often very hard to find, because you're *sure* you remember everything there is to know about that procedure! After all, you *wrote* it!)

I recommend adding a comment header to every procedure you write, no matter how simple. Such a header should contain the following information:

♦ The name of the procedure
♦ The date it was last modified
♦ What it does
♦ What data items the caller must pass it to make it work correctly
♦ What other procedures, if any, are called by the procedure
♦ Any *gotchas* that need to be kept in mind while writing code that uses the procedure

A typical workable procedure header is shown below:

```
; ----------------------------------------------------------------
;   WRITELN -- Displays information to the screen via DOS
;                    service 9 and issues a newline
;   Last update 3/5/89
;
;   1 entry point:
;
;   Writeln:
;       Caller must pass:
;       DS: The segment of the string to be displayed
;       DX: The offset of the string to be displayed
;           String must be terminated by "$"
;       Action: Displays the string at DS:DX up to the "$"
;               marker, then issues a newline. Hardware cursor
;               will move to the left margin of the following
;               line. If the display is to the bottom screen
;               line, the screen will scroll.
;       Calls: Write
; ----------------------------------------------------------------
```

A comment header does not relieve you of the responsibility of adding comments to the individual lines of code within the procedure. It's a good idea to put a short comment to the right of every line that contains a machine instruction mnemonic and, in longer procedures, a comment block describing every major functional block within the procedure.

Examine EAT3.ASM, and notice the various commenting conventions. For a very short program such as this, such elaborate internal documentation might seem overkill. Once your programs get serious, however, you'll be very glad you expended the effort.

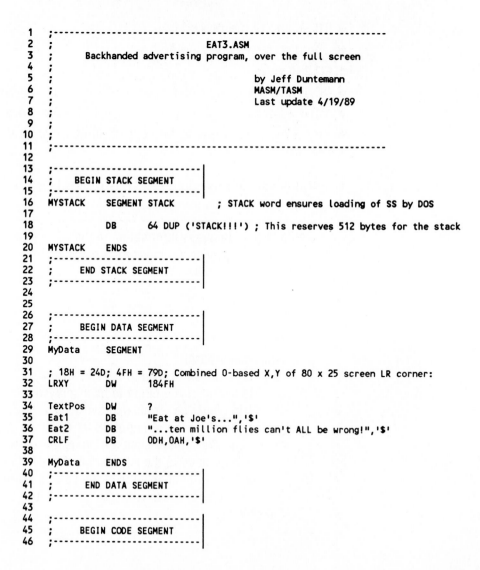

```
 1  ;------------------------------------------------------------
 2  ;                              EAT3.ASM
 3  ;          Backhanded advertising program, over the full screen
 4  ;
 5  ;                                    by Jeff Duntemann
 6  ;                                    MASM/TASM
 7  ;                                    Last update 4/19/89
 8  ;
 9  ;
10  ;
11  ;------------------------------------------------------------
12
13  ;----------------------------|
14  ;    BEGIN STACK SEGMENT      |
15  ;----------------------------|
16  MYSTACK      SEGMENT STACK         ; STACK word ensures loading of SS by DOS
17
18               DB      64 DUP ('STACK!!!') ; This reserves 512 bytes for the stack
19
20  MYSTACK      ENDS
21  ;----------------------------|
22  ;     END STACK SEGMENT       |
23  ;----------------------------|
24
25
26  ;----------------------------|
27  ;    BEGIN DATA SEGMENT       |
28  ;----------------------------|
29  MyData       SEGMENT
30
31  ; 18H = 24D; 4FH = 79D; Combined 0-based X,Y of 80 x 25 screen LR corner:
32  LRXY         DW      184FH
33
34  TextPos      DW      ?
35  Eat1         DB      "Eat at Joe's...",'$'
36  Eat2         DB      "...ten million flies can't ALL be wrong!",'$'
37  CRLF         DB      0DH,0AH,'$'
38
39  MyData       ENDS
40  ;----------------------------|
41  ;      END DATA SEGMENT       |
42  ;----------------------------|
43
44  ;----------------------------|
45  ;    BEGIN CODE SEGMENT       |
46  ;----------------------------|
```

```
47   MyProg     SEGMENT
48
49   Main       PROC
50              assume CS:MyProg,DS:MyData
51
52   Start:     ; This is where program execution begins:
53              mov  AX,MyData   ; Set up our own data segment address in DS
54              mov  DS,AX       ; Can't load segment reg. directly from memory
55
56              call ClrScr      ; Clear the full display
57
58              mov  TextPos, 0914H   ; 0914H = X @ 20, Y @ 9
59
60              mov  DX,TextPos  ; TextPos contains X,Y position values
61              call GotoXY      ; Position cursor
62              lea  DX,Eat1     ; Load offset of Eat1 string into DX
63              call Write       ;    and display it
64
65              mov  DX,TextPos  ; Re-use text position variable
66              mov  DH,10       ; Put new Y value into DH
67              call GotoXY      ; Position cursor
68              lea  DX,Eat2     ; Load offset of Eat2 string into DX
69              call Writeln     ;    and display it
70
71              mov  AH,4CH      ; Terminate process DOS service
72              mov  AL,0        ; Pass this value back to ERRORLEVEL
73              int  21H         ; Control returns to DOS
74
75   ;--------------------------------|
76   ;    PROCEDURE SECTION           |
77   ;--------------------------------|
78
79   ;-------------------------------------------------------------
80   ;    GOTOXY    --  Positions the hardware cursor to X,Y
81   ;    Last update 3/5/89
82   ;
83   ;    1 entry point:
84   ;
85   ;    GotoXY:
86   ;       Caller must pass:
87   ;       DL: X value    These are both 0-based; i.e., they
88   ;       DH: Y value       assume a screen 24 by 79, not 25 by 80
89   ;       Action: Moves the hardware cursor to the X,Y position
90   ;               loaded into DL and H.
91   ;-------------------------------------------------------------
92   GotoXY     PROC
93              mov AH,02H           ; Select VIDEO service 2: Position cursor
94              mov BH,0             ; Stay with display page 0
95              int 10H              ; Call VIDEO
96              ret                  ; Return to the caller
97   GotoXY     ENDP
98
99   ;-------------------------------------------------------------
100  ;    CLRSCR    --  Clears or scrolls screens or windows
101  ;    Last update 3/5/89
102  ;
103  ;    4 entry points:
104  ;
105  ;    ClrScr:
106  ;       No values expected from caller
107  ;       Action: Clears the entire screen to blanks with 07H as
108  ;               the display attribute
```

```
109   ;
110   ;   ClrWin:
111   ;      Caller must pass:
112   ;      CH: Y coordinate, upper left corner of window
113   ;      CL: X coordinate, upper left corner of window
114   ;      DH: Y coordinate, lower right corner of window
115   ;      DL: X coordinate, lower right corner of window
116   ;      Action:  Clears the window specified by the caller to
117   ;                  blanks with 07H as the display attribute
118   ;
119   ;   ScrlWin:
120   ;      Caller must pass:
121   ;      CH: Y coordinate, upper left corner of window
122   ;      CL: X coordinate, upper left corner of window
123   ;      DH: Y coordinate, lower right corner of window
124   ;      DL: X coordinate, lower right corner of window
125   ;      AL: number of lines to scroll window by (0 clears it)
126   ;      Action:  Scrolls the window specified by the caller by
127   ;                  the number of lines passed in AL.  The blank
128   ;                  lines inserted at screen bottom are cleared
129   ;                  to blanks with 07H as the display attribute
130   ;
131   ;   VIDEO6:
132   ;      Caller must pass:
133   ;      CH: Y coordinate, upper left corner of window
134   ;      CL: X coordinate, upper left corner of window
135   ;      DH: Y coordinate, lower right corner of window
136   ;      DL: X coordinate, lower right corner of window
137   ;      AL: number of lines to scroll window by (0 clears it)
138   ;      BH: display attribute for blanked lines (07H is "normal")
139   ;      Action:  Generic access to BIOS VIDEO service 6.  Caller
140   ;                  must pass ALL register parameters as shown above
141   ;---------------------------------------------------------------
142
143   ClrScr    PROC
144             mov CX,0          ; Upper left corner of full screen
145             mov DX,LRXY       ; Load lower-right XY coordinates into DX
146   ClrWin:   mov AL,0          ; 0 specifies clear entire region
147   ScrlWin:  mov BH,07H        ; Specify "normal" attribute for blanked line(s)
148   VIDEO6:   mov AH,06H        ; Select VIDEO service 6: Initialize/Scroll
149             int 10H           ; Call VIDEO
150             ret               ; Return to the caller
151   ClrScr    ENDP
152
153
154   ;---------------------------------------------------------------
155   ;   WRITE    --  Displays information to the screen via DOS
156   ;                  service 9: Print String
157   ;   Last update 3/5/89
158   ;
159   ;   1 entry point:
160   ;
161   ;   Write:
162   ;      Caller must pass:
163   ;      DS: The segment of the string to be displayed
164   ;      DX: The offset of the string to be displayed
165   ;          String must be terminated by "$"
166   ;      Action:  Displays the string at DS:DX up to the "$" marker
167   ;---------------------------------------------------------------
168
169   Write     PROC
170             mov AH,09H        ; Select DOS service 9: Print String
```

```
171                 int 21H          ; Call DOS
172                 ret              ; Return to the caller
173    Write    ENDP
174
175
176    ;-------------------------------------------------------------
177    ;   WRITELN -- Displays information to the screen via DOS
178    ;                  service 9 and issues a newline
179    ;   Last update 3/5/89
180    ;
181    ;   1 entry point:
182    ;
183    ;   Writeln:
184    ;      Caller must pass:
185    ;      DS: The segment of the string to be displayed
186    ;      DX: The offset of the string to be displayed
187    ;          String must be terminated by "$"
188    ;      Action:  Displays the string at DS:DX up to the "$" marker
189    ;               marker, then issues a newline.  Hardware cursor
190    ;               will move to the left margin of the following
191    ;               line.  If the display is to the bottom screen
192    ;               line, the screen will scroll.
193    ;      Calls: Write
194    ;-------------------------------------------------------------
195
196    Writeln    PROC
197               call Write          ; Display the string proper through Write
198               mov DX,OFFSET CRLF   ; Load address of newline string to DS:DX
199               call Write          ; Display the newline string through Write
200               ret                 ; Return to the caller
201    Writeln    ENDP
202
203    ;----------------------------|
204    ;   END PROCEDURE SECTION     |
205    ;----------------------------|
206
207
208    Main     ENDP
209
210    MyProg   ENDS
211
212    ;----------------------------|
213    ;   END CODE SEGMENT          |
214    ;----------------------------|
215
216               END Start    ; The procedure named Start becomes the main program
```

8.4 ◆ Building External Libraries of Procedures

You'll notice that the EAT3.ASM program given at the end of the previous section had most of its bulk devoted to procedures. This is as it should be, with the caution that the procedures it uses are the kind you're likely to use in any and all of your assembly language programs. Keeping cursor movement and screen-clearing routines in source code form in every single program you write is a waste of space and can clutter up the program in a way that makes it less easy to understand.

The answer is to break the utility procedures out into an external library that you assemble only once, and then link into every program that uses its procedures without assembling the library every time you assemble the program. This is called *modular programming,* and it is an extremely effective tool for programming efficiently in any language, assembly language not excluded.

I described this process briefly back in Chapter 3, and showed it pictorially in Figures 3.4 and 3.5. A program might consist of three or four separate .ASM files, each of which is assembled separately to a separate .OBJ file. To produce the final executable .EXE file, the linker weaves all of the .OBJ files together, resolving all of the references from one to the other, finally creating an .EXE file.

Each .ASM file is considered a *module,* and each module contains one or more procedures and possibly some data definitions. When all the declarations are done correctly, all of the modules can freely call one another, and any procedure can refer to any data definition.

The trick, of course, is to get all the declarations right.

Public and External Declarations

If you reference a label in your program (by, say, including a **CALL** instruction to that label) without defining that label anywhere in the program, the assembler will gleefully give you an error message. (You've probably already experienced this if you've begun writing your own programs in assembler.) In modular programming, you're frequently going to be calling procedures that don't exist anywhere in your program. How to get past the assembler's watchdogs?

The answer is to declare a procedure *external.* This works very much like it sounds: the assembler is told that a given label will have to be found outside the program somewhere, in another module. Once told that, that assembler is happy to give you a pass on an undefined label. You've promised the assembler you'll provide it later, and the assembler accepts your promise and keeps going without flagging the undefined label.

The promise looks like this:

```
EXTRN ClrScr : PROC
```

Here, you've told the assembler that the label **ClrScr** represents a procedure, and that it will be found somewhere external to the current module. That's all the assembler needs to know to withhold its error message.

Having done that, the assembler's part is finished. It leaves in place an empty socket in your program where the external procedure can later be plugged in. I sometimes think of it as an eyelet where the external procedure will later hook in.

Over in the other module where procedure **ClrScr** exists, it isn't enough just to define the procedure. An eyelet needs a hook; you have to warn the assembler that **ClrScr** will be referenced from outside the module. The assembler needs to forge the hook that will hook into the eyelet. You forge the hook by declaring the procedure *public,* meaning that other modules may freely reference the procedure. Declaring a procedure public is simplicity itself:

```
PUBLIC ClrScr
```

That done, who actually connects the hook and the eyelet? The linker does that during the link operation. After all, why call it a linker if it doesn't link anything? At link time, the linker takes the two .OBJ files generated by the assembler, one from your program and the other from the module containing **ClrScr,** and combines them into a single .EXE executable file. When the .EXE file is loaded and run, the program can call **ClrScr** as cleanly and quickly as though both had been declared in the same source code file.

This process is summarized in Figure 8.2.

What works for procedures works for data as well, and it can work in either direction. Your program can declare a variable as **PUBLIC,** and that variable may then be used by any module in which the same variable name is declared as external with the **EXTRN** directive.

We sometimes say that a program or module containing procedures or variables declared as public *exports* those items. We also say that a program or module that uses procedures or variables that are external to it *imports* those items.

The Mechanics of Publics and Externals

I've described the source code mechanics of assembly language programs in detail in the last few chapters. EAT1.ASM, EAT2.ASM, and EAT3.ASM are good examples. External modules are similar to programs. There are two major differences, concerning things that external modules lack:

♦ External modules have no main program and hence no start address. That is, no label is given after the **END** directive that concludes the source code file.

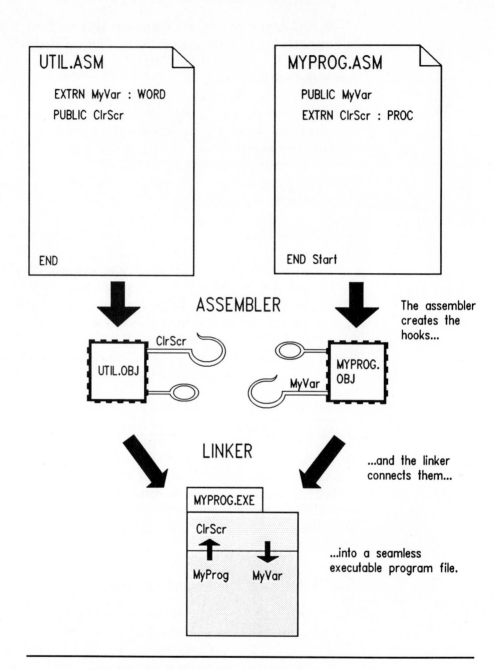

FIGURE 8.2   Connecting publics and externals

♦ External modules are not intended to be run by themselves, so a start address is both unnecessary and (if one were added) a temptation to chaos.

♦ External modules have no stack segment. This is not an absolute requirement (there are few such requirements in assembler work) but for simple assembly language programming it's true enough. Your stack segment should be defined in your main program module. External modules should have none.

External modules can have a data segment. If the external is to define a variable that is to be shared by the main program or by other externals, it obviously must have a data segment for that variable to reside in. But less obviously, if the external is to share a variable with another external or with the main program, it must *still* define a data segment, even if that data segment is empty except for the external declaration.

This is easier to demonstrate than to explain. Take a look at the following external module, which is a library containing all of the simple display control procedures introduced in EAT3.ASM:

```
1    ;--------------------------------------------------------------
2    ;                         VIDLIB.ASM
3    ;                    Video display library
4    ;
5    ;                              by Jeff Duntemann
6    ;                              MASM/TASM
7    ;                              Last update 4/19/89
8    ;
9    ;
10   ;
11   ;--------------------------------------------------------------
12
13   MyData     SEGMENT PUBLIC
14
15              EXTRN  CRLF:BYTE,LRXY:WORD
16
17   MyData     ENDS
18
19
20   MyCode     SEGMENT PUBLIC
21
22              PUBLIC GotoXY,ClrScr,ClrWin,ScrlWin,VIDEO6
23              PUBLIC Write,Writeln
24
25              ASSUME  CS:MyCode,DS:MyData
26
27   ;--------------------------------------------------------------
28   ;   GOTOXY    -- Positions the hardware cursor to X,Y
29   ;   Last update 3/5/89
30   ;
31   ;   1 entry point:
32   ;
```

```
33  ;    GotoXY:
34  ;        Caller must pass:
35  ;        DL: X value      These are both 0-based; i.e., they
36  ;        DH: Y value         assume a screen 24 by 79, not 25 by 80
37  ;        Action:  Moves the hardware cursor to the X,Y position
38  ;                    loaded into DL and H.
39  ;----------------------------------------------------------------
40  GotoXY    PROC
41            mov AH,02H        ; Select VIDEO service 2: Position cursor
42            mov BH,0          ; Stay with display page 0
43            int 10H           ; Call VIDEO
44            ret               ; Return to the caller
45  GotoXY    ENDP
46
47  ;----------------------------------------------------------------
48  ;    CLRSCR    -- Clears or scrolls screens or windows
49  ;    Last update 3/5/89
50  ;
51  ;    4 entry points:
52  ;
53  ;    ClrScr:
54  ;        No values expected from caller
55  ;        Action:  Clears the entire screen to blanks with 07H as
56  ;                    the display attribute
57  ;
58  ;    ClrWin:
59  ;        Caller must pass:
60  ;        CH: Y coordinate, upper left corner of window
61  ;        CL: X coordinate, upper left corner of window
62  ;        DH: Y coordinate, lower right corner of window
63  ;        DL: X coordinate, lower right corner of window
64  ;        Action:  Clears the window specified by the caller to
65  ;                    blanks with 07H as the display attribute
66  ;
67  ;    ScrlWin:
68  ;        Caller must pass:
69  ;        CH: Y coordinate, upper left corner of window
70  ;        CL: X coordinate, upper left corner of window
71  ;        DH: Y coordinate, lower right corner of window
72  ;        DL: X coordinate, lower right corner of window
73  ;        AL: number of lines to scroll window by (0 clears it)
74  ;        Action:  Scrolls the window specified by the caller by
75  ;                    the number of lines passed in AL.  The blank
76  ;                    lines inserted at screen bottom are cleared
77  ;                    to blanks with 07H as the display attribute
78  ;
79  ;    VIDEO6:
80  ;        Caller must pass:
81  ;        CH: Y coordinate, upper left corner of window
82  ;        CL: X coordinate, upper left corner of window
83  ;        DH: Y coordinate, lower right corner of window
84  ;        DL: X coordinate, lower right corner of window
85  ;        AL: number of lines to scroll window by (0 clears it)
86  ;        BH: display attribute for blanked lines (07H is "normal")
87  ;        Action:  Generic access to BIOS VIDEO service 6.  Caller
88  ;                    must pass ALL register parameters as shown above
89  ;----------------------------------------------------------------
90
91  ClrScr    PROC
92            mov CX,0          ; Upper left corner of full screen
93            mov DX,LRXY       ; Load lower-right XY coordinates into DX
```

```
 94   ClrWin:    mov AL,0          ; 0 specifies clear entire region
 95   ScrlWin:   mov BH,07H        ; Specify "normal" attribute for blanked line(s)
 96   VIDEO6:    mov AH,06H        ; Select VIDEO service 6: Initialize/Scroll
 97              int 10H           ; Call VIDEO
 98              ret               ; Return to the caller
 99   ClrScr     ENDP
100
101
102   ;-------------------------------------------------------------
103   ;   WRITE    -- Displays information to the screen via DOS
104   ;                    service 9: Print String
105   ;   Last update 3/5/89
106   ;
107   ;   1 entry point:
108   ;
109   ;   Write:
110   ;      Caller must pass:
111   ;      DS: The segment of the string to be displayed
112   ;      DX: The offset of the string to be displayed
113   ;          String must be terminated by "$"
114   ;      Action:  Displays the string at DS:DX up to the "$" marker
115   ;-------------------------------------------------------------
116
117   Write      PROC
118              mov AH,09H        ; Select DOS service 9: Print String
119              int 21H           ; Call DOS
120              ret               ; Return to the caller
121   Write      ENDP
122
123
124   ;-------------------------------------------------------------
125   ;   WRITELN -- Displays information to the screen via DOS
126   ;                    service 9 and issues a newline
127   ;   Last update 3/5/89
128   ;
129   ;   1 entry point:
130   ;
131   ;   Writeln:
132   ;      Caller must pass:
133   ;      DS: The segment of the string to be displayed
134   ;      DX: The offset of the string to be displayed
135   ;          String must be terminated by "$"
136   ;      Action:  Displays the string at DS:DX up to the "$" marker
137   ;               marker, then issues a newline.  Hardware cursor
138   ;               will move to the left margin of the following
139   ;               line.  If the display is to the bottom screen
140   ;               line, the screen will scroll.
141   ;      Calls: Write
142   ;-------------------------------------------------------------
143
144   Writeln    PROC
145              call Write        ; Display the string proper through Write
146              mov DX,OFFSET CRLF ; Load address of newline string to DS:DX
147              call Write        ; Display the newline string through Write
148              ret               ; Return to the caller
149   Writeln    ENDP
150
151
152   MyCode     ENDS
153
154              END
```

VIDLIB.ASM has both a code segment and a data segment. Note well that both segments are declared with the **PUBLIC** keyword. A common mistake made by beginners is to declare the procedures and variables public, but not the segments that they reside in. Nonobvious it may be, but essential nonetheless: make your module segments public if they contain any public declarations!

The code segment contains all of the procedures. The data segment, on the other hand, contains only the following statement:

```
EXTRN CRLF:BYTE,LRXY:WORD
```

VIDLIB.ASM declares no variables of its own. Instead, it uses two variables declared within the main program module EAT4.ASM. (EAT4.ASM is identical to EAT3.ASM, except that it has had its procedures removed and declared as external and two of its variables declared public. The program's function is exactly the same as that of EAT3.ASM.)

The **EXTRN** statement above indicates that two variables referenced within the module are to be imported from somewhere. *You don't have to specify from where.* The names of the variables, and their types have to be there. The linker and assembler are not case sensitive.

The directives following the colons in the **EXTRN** statement are type specifiers. The assembler builds hooks into the .OBJ file it creates from the external module's source file. These hooks will then mate with the appropriate hooks in the .OBJ file that export the imported variables. To get the hooks right, however, the assembler needs to know what kind of item is being imported. The name of the variable is just a label and gives no information about the type or size of the data being imported. The type specifier must match the definition of the variable being imported. Table 8.1 summarizes what commonly used type specifiers correspond to what data declaration directives.

The most important piece of information contained in the type specifier is the size of the item being imported. Machine instructions assemble to

TABLE 8.1   Type specifiers for external declarations

Specifier	Use with directive	Specifies
PROC	PROC	Procedure
BYTE	DB	Byte or string
WORD	DW	Word-sized data
DWORD	DD	Double word-sized data

different binary opcodes depending on the size of their memory data operands. An opcode that acts on byte-sized data in memory will be different from an opcode that acts on word-sized data. To get the hooks right, then, the assembler has to know the size of the imported item *at assembly time.*

Dividing a Segment Across Module Boundaries

Note that the names of the code segment and data segment in the external module are the same as the names of the code segment and data segment in the main program module. The data segment is **MyData** in both, and the code segment is **MyCode** in both. This is not an absolute requirement, but it simplifies things greatly and is a good way to set things up while you're just learning your way around in assembly language. Regardless of the number of external modules that link with your main program, the program as a whole contains only one code segment and one data segment. Until your data requirements and code size get *very* large, you won't need more than a single code and data segment.

As long as the code and data segments are declared with the **PUBLIC** directive in all the modules sharing the segments, the linker will consider all to be part of the same code and data segments.

It is also necessary to have an **ASSUME** statement in every module sharing segments in this fashion. Furthermore, it should be the same **ASSUME** statement as the one in the main program, with CS associated with your single code segment and DS associated with your single data segment:

ASSUME CS:MyCode,DS:MyData

This ensures that the assembler does not get confused as it puts together references to the two segments in the .OBJ files it builds.

Your Main Program Module

Below is our backhanded advertising program, as modified for use with an external display control module:

```
1   ;-----------------------------------------------------------
2   ;                           EAT4.ASM
3   ;     Backhanded advertising program, with external references
4   ;
5   ;                                   by Jeff Duntemann
6   ;                                   MASM/TASM
```

```
 7   ;                                        Last update 4/17/89
 8   ;
 9   ;
10   ;
11   ;-------------------------------------------------------------
12
13   ;----------------------------|
14   ;    BEGIN STACK SEGMENT      |
15   ;----------------------------|
16   MYSTACK     SEGMENT STACK         ; STACK word ensures loading of SS by DOS
17
18           DB      64 DUP ('STACK!!!') ; This reserves 512 bytes for the stack
19
20   MYSTACK    ENDS
21   ;----------------------------|
22   ;     END STACK SEGMENT       |
23   ;----------------------------|
24
25
26   ;----------------------------|
27   ;    BEGIN DATA SEGMENT       |
28   ;----------------------------|
29   MyData     SEGMENT PUBLIC
30           PUBLIC  LRXY,CRLF     ; These are used by routines in VIDLIB
31
32   LRXY       DW      184FH ; 18H = 24D; 4FH = 79D; 0-based XY or LR screen corner
33
34   TextPos    DW      ?
35   Eat1       DB      "Eat at Joe's...",'$'
36   Eat2       DB      "...ten million flies can't ALL be wrong!",'$'
37   CRLF       DB      0DH,0AH,'$'
38
39   MyData     ENDS
40   ;----------------------------|
41   ;      END DATA SEGMENT       |
42   ;----------------------------|
43
44   ;----------------------------|
45   ;     BEGIN CODE SEGMENT      |
46   ;----------------------------|
47
48   ; Note that the following items are external to EAT4.ASM, and must
49   ;   be linked from the external file VIDLIB.OBJ.  Assemble VIDLIB.ASM
50   ;   first to VIDLIB.OBJ before attempting the link.
51
52           EXTRN GotoXY:PROC,Write:PROC,Writeln:PROC,ClrScr:PROC
53
54   MyCode     SEGMENT PUBLIC
55
56
57   Main       PROC
58           ASSUME CS:MyCode,DS:MyData
59
60   Start:     ; This is where program execution begins:
61           mov  AX,MyData   ; Set up our own data segment address in DS
62           mov  DS,AX       ; Can't load segment reg. directly from memory
63
64           call ClrScr      ; Clear the full display
65
66           mov  TextPos, 0914H   ; 0914H = X a 20, Y a 9
67
68           mov  DX,TextPos  ; TextPos contains X,Y position values
```

```
69                   call GotoXY       ; Position cursor
70                   lea  DX,Eat1      ; Load offset of Eat1 string into DX
71                   call Write        ;   and display it
72
73                   mov  DX,TextPos   ; Re-use text position variable
74                   mov  DH,10        ; Put new Y value into DH
75                   call GotoXY       ; Position cursor
76                   lea  DX,Eat2      ; Load offset of Eat2 string into DX
77                   call Writeln      ;   and display it
78
79                   mov  AH,4CH       ; Terminate process DOS service
80                   mov  AL,0         ; Pass this value back to ERRORLEVEL
81                   int  21H          ; Control returns to DOS
82
83      Main    ENDP
84
85      MyCode  ENDS
86
87      ;---------------------------|
88      ;     END CODE SEGMENT      |
89      ;---------------------------|
90
91              END Start    ; The procedure named Start becomes the main program
```

EAT4.ASM differs in only a few ways from EAT3.ASM. First of all, the data and code segment declarations now include the **PUBLIC** directive:

```
MyData SEGMENT PUBLIC
MyCode SEGMENT PUBLIC
```

This is easy to forget but you must keep it in mind: the segments containing imported or exported items *as well as the imported or exported items themselves* must be declared as public.

Take note of the declaration of two of the variables in the data segment as public:

```
PUBLIC LRXY,CLRF
```

This allows external modules to use these two variables. The other variables declared in the main program, **Eat1, Eat2,** and **TextPos,** are not declared as public and are inaccessible from external modules. We would say that those three variables are *private* to the main program module EAT4.ASM.

EAT4.ASM contains no procedure declarations of its own. All the procedures it uses are imported from VIDLIB.ASM, and all are therefore declared as external in the code segment, using this statement:

```
EXTRN GotoXY:PROC,Write:PROC,Writeln:PROC,ClrScr:PROC
```

Something to keep in mind is that while VIDLIB.ASM exports seven procedures (seven labels, actually, because four are entry points to the **ClrScr** procedure), EAT4.ASM imports only four. The **ClrWin, ScrlWin,** and **VIDEO6** entry points to procedure **ClrScr** are declared as public in VIDLIB.ASM, but they are not declared as external in EAT4.ASM. EAT4.ASM only uses the four it imports. The other three are available, but the EAT4.ASM does not call them and therefore does not bother declaring them as external. If you were to expand EAT4.ASM to use one of the three other entry points to **ClrScr,** you would have to add the entry point to the **EXTRN** list.

Once all the external and public declarations are in place, your machine instructions can reference procedures and variables across module boundaries as though they were all within the same large program. No special qualifiers have to be added to the instructions. **CALL ClrScr** is written the same way, whether **ClrScr** is declared in the main program module or in an external module like VIDLIB.ASM.

Linking Multiple Modules

The linker hasn't had to do much linking so far. Once you have multiple modules, however, the linker begins to earn its keep. To link multiple modules, you must specify the name of the .OBJ file for each module on the linker command line.

Up until now, the linker command line contained only the name of the main program module:

    TLINK EAT3

Now you must add the names of all external modules to the linker command line:

    TLINK EAT4 VIDLIB

If you're using JED, bring up the commands screen with function key F4 and edit the linker command line. For example, to use TASM to link EAT4.OBJ and VIDLIB.OBJ, the linker command line would be the following:

    TLINK˜ VIDLIB

Remember that the tilde character (˜) stands for the currently loaded file in JED.

It is pretty obvious that if you forget to name an external module on the linker command line, the linker will not be able to resolve the external references involving the missing .OBJ file, and you will get linker error messages like the following, one for each unresolved external reference:

Undefined symbol 'CLRSCR' in module EAT4.ASM

External Module Summary

Here are some points to keep in mind when you're faced with splitting a single program up into a main program and one or more external modules:

♦ Declare the code segments public in all modules, and give them all the same name.

♦ Declare the data segments public in all modules, and give them all the same name.

♦ Declare all exported procedures, entry points, and variables as **PUBLIC.** Put the public declaration statement *inside* the segment where the exported items are declared.

♦ Declare all imported procedures, entry points, and variables as **EXTRN.** Put the external declaration statement *inside* the segment where the imported items are to be used. Data are used in the data segment, code is used in the code segment.

♦ Make sure that there is a common **ASSUME** statement in the *code segment* of every module associating the CS register with the shared code segment and the DS register with the shared data segment.

♦ Finally, don't forget to add the names of all external modules to the linker command line in the link step.

If this still seems fuzzy to you, follow VIDLIB.ASM and EAT4.ASM as a model. It would certainly be worth beefing up VIDLIB.ASM by adding more screen control procedures.

8.5 ♦ Creating and Using Macros

There is more than one way to split an assembly language program into more manageable chunks. Procedures are the most obvious way and are certainly the easiest to understand. The mechanism for calling and returning from procedures is built right into the CPU and is independent of any given assembler product.

Today's two major assemblers (Microsoft's MASM and Borland's TASM) provide another complexity-management tool that works a little differently: *macros.* They're hardly a minor feature; their name is built right into Microsoft's product, the Microsoft Macro Assembler.

Macros are a different breed of animal entirely. Whereas procedures are implemented by the use of **CALL** and **RET** instructions built right into the instruction set, macros are a trick of the assembler and do not depend on any particular instruction or group of instructions.

Quite simply, a macro is a label that stands for some sequence of text lines. This sequence of text lines can be (but is not necessarily) a sequence of instructions. When the assembler encounters the macro label in a source code file, it replaces the macro label with the macro's text lines. This is called *expanding* the macro, because the name of the macro (occupying one text line) is replaced by several lines of text that are then assembled just as though they had appeared in the source code file all along.

Macros bear some resemblance to *include files* in high-level languages like Pascal. In Turbo Pascal, an include command might look like this:

```
{$I ENGINE.DEF}
```

When this include command is encountered, the compiler goes out to disk and finds the file named ENGINE.DEF. It then opens the file and starts feeding the text contained in that file into the source code file at the point where the include command was placed. The compiler then processes those lines as though they had always been in the source code file.

You might think of a macro as an include file that's built right into the source code file. It's a sequence of text lines that is defined once, given a name, and then can be dropped into the source code again and again by simply using the name.

This process is shown in Figure 8.3. The source code as stored on disk has a definition of the macro, bracketed between **MACRO** and **ENDM** directives. Later in the file, the name of the macro appears several times. When the assembler processes this file, it copies the macro definition into a buffer somewhere in memory. As it assembles the text read from disk, the assembler drops the statements contained in the macro into the text wherever the macro name appears. The disk file is not affected; the expansion of the macros occurs *only* in memory.

The source code file
presented to the
assembler:

What the assembler
actually assembles:

Macro
definition:

```
ClrScr  MACRO
        MOV
        MOV
        MOV
        INT  10H
        ENDM
```

Macro
invocations:

```
ClrScr
```

```
ClrScr
```

```
ClrScr
```

```
MOV
MOV
MOV
INT  10H
```

```
MOV
MOV
MOV
INT  10H
```

```
MOV
MOV
MOV
INT  10H
```

The original macro
definition is discarded...

...but the instruction
sequence represented
by the macro now
appears three separate
times in the assembled
text.

The actual source code
file on disk is not
modified. Macro
expansion takes place
only within memory.

Each invocation of
the macro is replaced by
all the instructions
contained in the macro.

FIGURE 8.3   How macros work

Macros versus Procedures: Pro and Con

There are advantages to macros over procedures. One of them is speed. It
takes time to execute the **CALL** and **RET** instructions that control entry to
and exit from a procedure. In a macro, neither instruction is used. Only
the instructions that perform the actual work of the macro are executed, so
the macro's work is performed as quickly as possible.

There is a cost to this speed, and the cost is in extra memory used, especially if the macro is called a great many times. Notice in Figure 8.3 that three invocations of the macro generate a total of 12 instructions in memory. If the macro had been set up as a procedure, it would have required the four instructions in the body of the procedure, plus one **RET** instruction and three **CALL** instructions to do the same work. This would give you a total of eight instructions for the procedure and twelve for the macro. If the macro were called five or seven times or more, the difference would grow. *Every time a macro is called, all of its instructions are duplicated in the program.*

In short programs, this may not be a problem and in situations where the code must be as fast as possible, as in graphics drivers, macros have a lot going for them. By and large, think macros for speed and procedures for compactness.

The Mechanics of Macro Definition

A macro definition looks a lot like a procedure definition, with a slightly different pair of directives: **MACRO** and **ENDM.** One other crucial difference is that the name of the macro *cannot* be repeated in front of the **ENDM** directive. I'm not sure why this must be so, but it confuses the assembler to no end. Also, don't put a **RET** instruction at the end of the macro! Executing a **RET** without a previous **CALL** will corrupt your stack and probably crash your program.

One important shortcoming of macros vis-a-vis procedures is that macros can have only *one* entry point. The **ClrScr** procedure described in the last section cannot be converted into a macro without splitting it into four separate invocations of VIDEO interrupt 10H. If the **ClrScr** function (clearing the full screen to blanks for the normal video attribute) alone were written as a macro, it would look like this:

```
ClrScr  MACRO
        mov CX,0        ; Upper left corner of full screen
        mov DX,LRXY     ; Load lower-right XY coordinates into DX
        mov AL,0        ; 0 specifies clear entire region
        mov BH,07H      ; Specify "normal" attribute for blanked line(s)
        mov AH,06H      ; Select VIDEO service 6: Initialize/Scroll
        int 10H         ; Call VIDEO
        ENDM
```

You can see that **ClrScr** has shed its **RET** instruction and its additional entry points, but apart from that it's exactly the same sequence of instructions. Functionally it works the same way, except that every time you clear your screen, **ClrScr**'s six instructions are dropped into the source code.

Macros are called simply by naming them. Don't use the **CALL** instruction! Just place the macro name on a line:

ClrScr

The assembler will handle the rest.

Defining Macros with Parameters

So far, macros may seem useful but perhaps not especially compelling. What makes macros really sing is their ability to mimic high-level language subroutines and take arguments through parameters. For example, if you were to define a macro named **GoToXY** that would position the hardware cursor, you could pass it the *X* and *Y* values as arguments:

GotoXY 17,3   ; Move the cursor to the Name field

You'd have to pinch yourself to be sure you weren't working in BASIC, no?

Macro parameters are, again, artifacts of the assembler. They are not pushed onto the stack or set into COMMON or anything like that. The parameters are simply placeholders for the actual values (called *arguments*) that you pass to the macro through its parameters.

I've converted the **GotoXY** procedure to a macro to show you how this works. Here's the macro:

```
GotoXY   MACRO NewX, NewY
         mov DH,NewY        ; The NewY parameter loads into DH
         mov DL,NewX        ; The NewX parameter loads into DL
         mov AH,02H         ; Select VIDEO service 2: Position cursor
         mov BH,0           ; Stay with display page 0
         int 10H            ; Call VIDEO
         ENDM
```

The two parameters are **NewX** and **NewY.** Parameters are a kind of label and they can be referenced anywhere *within* the macro. Here, the parameters are referenced as operands to a couple of **MOV** instructions.

The arguments passed to the macro in **NewX** and **NewY** are thus loaded into DL and DH.

The actual values passed into the parameters are referred to as *arguments*. Don't confuse the actual values with the parameters. If you understand Pascal, it's *exactly* like the difference between formal parameters and actual parameters. A macro's parameters correspond to Pascal's formal parameters, whereas a macro's arguments correspond to Pascal's actual parameters. The macro's parameters are the labels following the **MACRO** directive where the macro is *defined*. The arguments are the values specified on the line where the macro is *invoked*.

The Mechanics of Macro Parameters

A macro can have as many parameters as will fit on one line. This is a rather arbitrary restriction, leaving you no recourse but to use short parameter names if you need lots of parameters for a single macro.

Arguments are dropped into parameters in order, from left to right. If you pass only two arguments to a macro with three parameters, you're likely to get an error message from the assembler, depending on how you've referenced the unfilled parameter. The assembler is building opcodes depending on the types of operands passed as arguments; if you don't pass an argument for a given parameter, any instructions that reference that parameter won't be constructable by the assembler, hence the errors.

If you pass *more* arguments to a macro than there are parameters to receive the arguments, the extraneous arguments will be ignored.

Local Labels within Macros

I haven't really gone into labels and branches yet, but there's an important problem with labels used inside macros. Labels in assembly language programs must be unique, and yet a macro is essentially duplicated in the source code as many times as it is invoked. This means there will be error messages flagging duplicate labels . . . unless you declare a macro's labels as *local*.

Local labels are declared with the **LOCAL** directive. Here's an example; don't worry if you don't fully understand all of the instructions it uses.

```
UpCase   MACRO Target,Length        ; Target is a string; Length its length
         LOCAL Tester,Bump
         mov  CX,Length             ; CX is acting as length counter for loop
         lea  BX,Target             ; String will be at DS:BX
```

```
Tester:    cmp BYTE PTR [BX],'a'    ; Is string character below 'a'?
           jb Bump                  ; If so, leave character alone
           cmp BYTE PTR [BX],'z'    ; If string character above 'z'?
           ja Bump                  ; If so, leave character alone
           and BYTE PTR [BX],11011111b  ; Char is lc alpha, so force bit 5 to 0
Bump:      inc BX                   ; Bump BX to point to next char in string
           loop Tester              ; And go back and to it again!
           ENDM
```

The important thing is to understand that unless the labels **Tester** and **Bump** were made local to the macro, there would be multiple instances of a label in the program and the assembler would generate a duplicate label error.

The only thing to remember about declaring local labels within macros is that the **LOCAL** statement must be the statement immediately following the macro header. Don't put anything—not even a comment line—between the two.

Macro Libraries

Just as procedures can be gathered in libraries external to your program, so can macros be gathered into *macro libraries*. A macro library is really nothing but a text file that contains the source code for the macros in the library. Unlike procedures gathered into a module, macro libraries are not separately assembled and must be passed through the assembler each time the program is assembled. This is a problem with macros in general, not only with macros that are gathered into libraries. Programs that manage complexity by dividing code up into macros will assemble more slowly than programs that have been divided up into separately assembled modules.

Macro libraries are used by including them into your program's source code file. The means to do this is the **INCLUDE** directive. The **INCLUDE** directive precedes the name of the macro library:

```
INCLUDE MYLIB.MAC
```

This statement can be anywhere in your source code file, but you must keep in mind that all macros must be fully defined before they are invoked. For this reason, it's a good idea to use the **INCLUDE** directive near the top of your source code file, before any possible invocation of one of the library macros could occur.

The following is a macro library containing macro versions of all the procedures we discussed in the previous section:

```
 1    ;--------------------------------------------------------------
 2    ;                         MYLIB.MAC
 3    ;            Macro library from ASSEMBLING FROM SQUARE ONE
 4    ;
 5    ;                              by Jeff Duntemann
 6    ;                              MASM/TASM
 7    ;                              Last update 4/16/89
 8    ;
 9    ;
10    ;
11    ;--------------------------------------------------------------
12
13
14    ;--------------------------------------------------------------
15    ;   CLEAR    --  Clears the entire visible screen buffer
16    ;   Last update 3/16/89
17    ;
18    ;     Caller must pass:
19    ;     In VidAddress:  A FAR pointer to the video refresh buffer
20    ;     In ClearAtom:   A word containing the video attribute to be
21    ;                       used in the high byte, and the fill character
22    ;                       to be used in the low byte.
23    ;     In BufLength:   The size of the refresh buffer in bytes
24    ;     Action:      Blasts copies of ClearAtom into the refresh buffer
25    ;                       until the buffer is filled.
26    ;--------------------------------------------------------------
27    Clear     MACRO VidAddress,ClearAtom,BufLength
28              les   DI,DWORD PTR VidAddress ; Load ES and DI from FAR pointer
29              mov   AX,ClearAtom    ; Load AX with word to blast into memory
30              mov   CX,BufLength    ; Load CX with length of buffer in bytes
31              shr   CX,1            ; Divide size of buffer by 2 for word count
32              rep   stosw           ; Blast away!
33              GotoXY 0,0            ; Move hardware cursor to UL corner of screen
34              ENDM
35
36
37    ;--------------------------------------------------------------
38    ;   GOTOXY    --  Positions the hardware cursor to X,Y
39    ;   Last update 3/5/89
40    ;
41    ;     Caller must pass:
42    ;     In NewX: The new X value
43    ;     In NewY: The new Y value
44    ;       These are both 0-based; i.e., they assume a screen
45    ;       whose dimensions are 24 by 79, not 25 by 80.
46    ;     Action:  Moves the hardware cursor to the X,Y position
47    ;                       passed as NewX and NewY.
48    ;--------------------------------------------------------------
49    GotoXY    MACRO NewX,NewY
50              mov   DH,NewY
51              mov   DL,NewX
52              mov   AH,02H         ; Select VIDEO service 2: Position cursor
53              mov   BH,0           ; Stay with display page 0
54              int   10H            ; Call VIDEO
55              ENDM
56
57
```

```
58    ;--------------------------------------------------------------
59    ;    NEWLINE  --  Sends a newline sequence to DOS Standard Output
60    ;                 via DOS service 40H
61    ;    Last update 3/16/89
62    ;
63    ;       Caller need not pass any parameters.
64    ;       Action:  Sends a newline sequence DOS Standard Output
65    ;--------------------------------------------------------------
66
67    Newline   MACRO
68              Write CRLF,2
69              ENDM
70
71
72    ;--------------------------------------------------------------
73    ;    POKECHAR    --  Inserts a single character into a string
74    ;    Last update 3/16/89
75    ;
76    ;       Caller must pass:
77    ;       In Target:  The name of the string to be poked at
78    ;       In TheChar: The character to be pocked into the string
79    ;       In ToPos:   The 0-based position in the string to poke to
80    ;       Action:     Pokes character passed in TheChar into string
81    ;                   passed in Target to position passed in ToPos.
82    ;                   The first character in the string is 0, etc.
83    ;--------------------------------------------------------------
84    PokeChar  MACRO Target,TheChar,ToPos
85              lea  BX,Target  ; Load the address of target string into BX
86              mov  BYTE PTR [BX+ToPos],TheChar  ; Move char into the string
87              ENDM
88
89
90    ;--------------------------------------------------------------
91    ;    WRITE    --  Displays information to the screen via DOS
92    ;                 service 40: Print String to Standard Output
93    ;    Last update 3/16/89
94    ;
95    ;       Caller must pass:
96    ;       In ShowIt:     The name of the string to be displayed
97    ;       In ShowLength: The length of the string to be displayed
98    ;       Action:  Displays the string to DOS Standard Output
99    ;--------------------------------------------------------------
100   Write     MACRO ShowIt,ShowLength
101             mov BX,1          ; Selects DOS file handle 1: Standard Output
102             mov CX,ShowLength ; Length of string passed in CX
103             lea DX,Showit     ; Offset address of string is passed in DX
104             mov AH,40H        ; Select DOS service 40: Print String
105             int 21H           ; Call DOS
106             ENDM
107
108   ;--------------------------------------------------------------
109   ;    WRITELN  --  Displays information to the screen via DOS
110   ;                 service 40H: Display to Standard Output, then
111   ;                 issues a newline
112   ;    Last update 3/16/89
113   ;
114   ;       Caller must pass:
115   ;       In ShowIt: The name of the string to be displayed
116   ;       In ShowLength: The length of the string to be displayed
117   ;       Action:  Displays the string in ShowIt, then issues a
118   ;                   newline.  Hardware cursor will move to the
119   ;                   left margin of the following line.  If the
```

```
120    ;                    display is to the bottom screen line, the
121    ;                    screen will scroll.
122    ;       Calls: Write
123    ;------------------------------------------------------------
124
125    Writeln    MACRO ShowIt,ShowLength
126               Write ShowIt,ShowLength   ; Display the string proper through Write
127               Write CRLF,2              ; Display the newline string through Write
128               ENDM
129
130
```

Look closely at the four macros that have taken the place of the single procedure **ClrScr.** Recall that macros can have only one entry point, so procedure **ClrScr** had to be pulled apart and its four entry points each given their own macro with its own call to VIDEO interrupt 10H.

And, finally, yet another version of EAT.ASM, this time rearranged to make use of the macros in MYLIB.MAC. The macro library is included by way of the **INCLUDE** statement immediately after the comment header at the top of the file.

```
1     ;------------------------------------------------------------
2     ;                          EAT5.ASM
3     ;       Backhanded advertising program, full screen, with macros
4     ;
5     ;                                by Jeff Duntemann
6     ;                                MASM/TASM
7     ;                                Last update 4/19/89
8     ;
9     ;
10    ;
11    ;------------------------------------------------------------
12
13    INCLUDE MYLIB.MAC                ; Load in screen control macro library
14
15    ;-----------------------------|
16    ;   BEGIN STACK SEGMENT        |
17    ;-----------------------------|
18    MYSTACK    SEGMENT STACK        ; STACK word ensures loading of SS by DOS
19
20               DB     64 DUP ('STACK!!!') ; This reserves 512 bytes for the stack
21
22    MYSTACK    ENDS
23    ;-----------------------------|
24    ;   END STACK SEGMENT          |
25    ;-----------------------------|
26
27    ;-----------------------------|
28    ;   BEGIN DATA SEGMENT         |
29    ;-----------------------------|
30    MyData     SEGMENT
31
32    ; 18H = 24D; 4FH = 79D; Combined 0-based X,Y of 80 x 25 screen LR corner:
33    LRXY       DW     184FH
34
35    VidOrigin  DD     0B8000000H
36
```

```
37   Eat1       DB       "Eat at Joe's..."
38   Eat1Length EQU $-Eat1
39   Eat2       DB        "...ten million flies can't ALL be wrong!"
40   Eat2Length EQU $-Eat2
41   CRLF       DB        0DH,0AH
42
43   MyData     ENDS
44   ;--------------------------|
45   ;     END DATA SEGMENT     |
46   ;--------------------------|
47
48   ;--------------------------|
49   ;     BEGIN CODE SEGMENT   |
50   ;--------------------------|
51   MyProg     SEGMENT
52
53   Main       PROC
54              ASSUME CS:MyProg,DS:MyData
55
56   Start:     ; This is where program execution begins:
57              mov  AX,MyData   ; Set up our own data segment address in DS
58              mov  DS,AX        ; Can't load segment reg. directly from memory
59
60              Clear VidOrigin,07B0H,4000
61
62              GotoXY 14H,09H          ; Position cursor
63              Write Eat1,Eat1Length   ;   and display first text line
64
65              GotoXY 14H,0AH          ; Position cursor
66              Writeln Eat2,eat2Length ;   and display second text line
67
68              mov  AH,4CH      ; Terminate process DOS service
69              mov  AL,0         ; Pass this value back to ERRORLEVEL
70              int  21H          ; Control returns to DOS
71
72   Main       ENDP
73
74   MyProg     ENDS
75
76   ;--------------------------|
77   ;     END CODE SEGMENT     |
78   ;--------------------------|
79
80              END Start    ; The procedure named Start becomes the main program
```

If you look closely at the main program procedure in EAT5.ASM, something odd may occur to you: it's starting to look like something other than an assembly language program. This is true, and it's certainly possible to create so many macros that your programs will begin to look like some odd high-level language.

The danger here is that unless you name your macros carefully and document them both in their macro library files and on the lines where they are invoked, your programs will not be any more comprehensible for their presence. Dividing complexity into numerous compartments is only half the job—labeling the compartments is just as (if not more) important!

Chapter 9

Taking Wing

Building Skills in Assembly Language Programming

You don't take off until *all* your flight checks are made.

That's the reason that we haven't done a lot of instruction arranging in this book up until this, the last chapter. I've found that machine instructions aren't the most important part of assembly language programming. What's most important is understanding your machine and your tools, and how everything fits together. Higher-level languages like Pascal and Modula 2 hide much of those essential details from you. In assembler you must see to them yourself. For some reason, authors of previous "beginner" books on assembly language haven't caught on to this fact.

This fact (in fact) was the major motivation for my writing this book.

If you've digested everything I've said so far, however, you're ready to get in and understand the remainder of the 8086/8088 instruction set. I won't teach it all in this book, but the phrase, "ready to understand" is germane. You can now find yourself a reference and learn on your own what instructions I don't cover. The skills you need to build programming skills are now yours, and if this book has accomplished that much, I'd say it's accomplished a lot.

So let the fun begin.

9.1 ◆ Bits Is Bits (and Bytes Is Bits)

Assembly language is big on bits.

Bits, after all, are what bytes are made of, and one essential assembly language skill is building bytes and taking them apart again. A technique called *bit mapping* is widely used in assembly language. Bit mapping assigns special meanings to individual bits within a byte to save space and squeeze the last little bit of utility out of a given amount of memory.

There is a family of instructions in the 8086/8088 instruction set that allow you to manipulate the bits within the bytes by applying Boolean logical operations to the bytes on a bit-by-bit basis. These are the *bitwise logical instructions:* **AND, OR, XOR,** and **NOT.** Another family of instructions allows you to slide bits back and forth within a single byte. These are the shift/rotate instructions: **ROL, ROR, RCL, RCR, SHL,** and **SHR.** (There's another related instruction, **SAR,** that I will not be discussing in this book.)

Bit Numbering

Dealing with bits requires that we have a way of specifying which bits we're dealing with. By convention, bits in assembly language are numbered, starting from 0 at the *least significant bit* in the byte, word, or other item we're using as a bit map. The least significant bit is the one with the least value in the binary number system. (Return to Chapter 1 and reread the material on base 2 if that seems fuzzy to you.) It's also the bit on the far right, if you write the value down as a binary number.

This works best as a visual metaphor (see Figure 9.1).

> **When you count bits, start with the bit on the right, and number them from 0.**

"It's the Logical Thing to Do, Jim . . ."

Boolean logic sounds arcane and forbidding, but remarkably, it reflects the realities of ordinary thought and action. The Boolean operator AND, for instance, pops up in many of the decisions you make every day of your life. For example, to write a check that doesn't bounce, you must have money in your checking account AND checks in your checkbook. Neither alone will do the job. ("How can I be overdrawn?" goes the classic question, "I still have checks in my checkbook!") You can't write a check you don't have, and a check without money behind it will bounce. People who live out of their checkbooks (and they always end up ahead of me in the supermarket checkout line) must use the AND operator frequently.

Bits are numbered from right to left,
starting from 0:

Byte value:

7	6	5	4	3	2	1	0

Word value:

15	14	13	12	11	10	9	8	7	6	5	4	3	2	1	0

Most significant   Least significant
bit (MSB)   bit (LSB)

FIGURE 9.1   Bit numbering

TABLE 9.1   The AND truth table for formal logic

Condition 1	Operator	Condition 2		Result
False	AND	False	=	False
False	AND	True	=	False
True	AND	False	=	False
True	AND	True	=	True

When mathematicians speak of Boolean logic, they manipulate abstract values called *true* and *false*. The AND operator works like this. Condition 1 AND condition 2 will be considered true if *both* condition 1 and condition 2 are true. If either condition is false, the result will be false.

There are, in fact, four different combinations of the two input values, so logical operations between two values are usually summarized in a form called a *truth table*. The truth table for the AND operator is shown in Table 9.1. There's nothing mysterious about the truth table. It's just a summary of all possibilities of the AND operator as applied to two input conditions. The important thing to remember is that *only* when both input values are true will the result also be true.

That's the way mathematicians see AND. In assembly language terms, the AND operator looks at 2 bits and yields a third bit based on the values of the first 2 bits. By convention, we consider a 1 bit to be true and a 0 bit to be false. The *logic* is identical; we're just using different symbols to represent true and false. Keeping that in mind, we can rewrite AND's truth table to make it more meaningful for assembly language work (see Table 9.2).

The AND Instruction

The **AND** instruction embodies this concept in the 8086/8088 instruction set. The **AND** instruction performs the AND logical operation on 2 bytes or

TABLE 9.2   The AND truth table for assembly language

Bit 1	Operator	Bit 2		Result bit
0	AND	0	=	0
0	AND	1	=	0
1	AND	0	=	0
1	AND	1	=	1

two words (depending on how you write the instruction) and replaces its *first* operand with the result of the operation. (By first I mean the operand closest to the mnemonic.) In other words, if you write this instruction:

AND AL,BL

the CPU will perform a gang of eight bitwise AND operations on the 8 bits in AL and BL. Bit 0 of AL is ANDed with a bit 0 of BL, bit 1 of AL is ANDed with bit 1 of BL, and so on. Each AND operation generates a result bit, and that bit is placed in the first operand (here, AL) *after all eight* AND operations occur. This is a common thread among machine instructions that perform some operation with a result on two operands: the result replaces the first operand.

Masking out Bits

The primary use of the **AND** instruction is to isolate 1 or more bits out of a byte value or a word value. *Isolate* here simply means to set all *unwanted* bits to a reliable 0 value. As an example, suppose we are interested in testing bits 4 and 5 of a value to see what those bits are. To do that, we have to be able to ignore the other bits (bits 0 to 3 and 6 to 7) and the only way to safely ignore bits is to set them to 0.

AND is the way to go. We set up a *bit mask* in which the bit numbers that we want to inspect and test are set to 1, and the bits that we wish to ignore are set to 0. To mask out all bits but bits 4 and 5, we must set up a mask in which bits 4 and 5 are set to 1, with all other bits at 0. This mask in binary is 00110000B, or 30H. (To verify it, count the bits from the right hand end of the binary number, starting with 0.) This bit mask is then ANDed against the value in question. Figure 9.2 shows this operation in action, with the 30H bit mask just described, and an initial value of 9DH. The three binary values involved are shown laid out vertically, with the LSB (i.e., the right-hand end) of each value at the top. You should be able to trace each **AND** operation and verify it by looking at Table 9.2.

The end result is that all but bits 4 and 5 are *guaranteed* to be 0 and can thus be safely ignored. Bits 4 and 5 could be either 0 or 1. (That's why we need to test them; we don't *know* what they are.) With the initial value of 9DH, bit 4 turns out to be a 1, and bit 5 turns out to be a 0. If the initial value were something else, bits 4 and 5 could both be 0, both 1, or some combination of the two.

Don't forget that the result of the **AND** operation replaces the first operand after the operation is complete.

AND AL,BL

AL: 9DH	BL: 30H	The result is placed
10011101B	00110000B	in AL *after* the AND operation is performed.

	Value		Mask		Result

	Value		Mask		Result
LSB	1	AND 0	=	0
	0	AND 0	=	0
	1	AND 0	=	0
	1	AND 0	=	0
	1	AND 1	=	1
	0	AND 1	=	0
	0	AND 0	=	0
MSB	1	AND 0	=	0

(After execution:)   AL: 10H
                                00010000B

FIGURE 9.2   The anatomy of an AND instruction

For an example of the **AND** instruction in operation, isolating bits in a word, see the **Byte2Str** procedure on page 287.

The OR Instruction

Closely related to the AND logical operation is **OR**. Structurally, the **OR** instruction works identically to **AND**; only its truth table is different. While **AND** requires that both its operands be 1 for the result to be 1, **OR** is satisfied that at least *one* operand has a 1 value. The truth table for **OR** is

TABLE 9.3   The OR truth table for assembly language

Bit 1	Operator	Bit 2		Result bit
0	OR	0	=	0
0	OR	1	=	1
1	OR	0	=	1
1	OR	1	=	1

shown in Table 9.3. Because it's unsuitable for isolating bits, **OR** is much more rarely used than **AND.**

The XOR Instruction

In a class by itself is the exclusive **OR** operation embodied in the **XOR** instruction. **XOR,** again, does what **AND** and **OR** do: it performs a logical operation on two operands, and the result replaces the first operand. The logical operation, however, is *exclusive or,* meaning that the result is 1 only if the two operands are *different* (i.e., 1 and 0 or 0 and 1). The truth table for **XOR** should make this slippery notion a little clearer (see Table 9.4). In the first and last cases, where the two operands are the *same,* the result is 0. In the middle two cases, where the two operands are *different,* the result is 1.

Some interesting things can be done with **XOR,** but most of them are a little arcane for a beginners' book. I will show you one handy **XOR** trick, however: **XOR**ing any value against itself yields 0. Furthermore, putting 0 in a register by **XOR**ing the register against itself is *faster* than putting a 0 in the register by **MOV**ing in a 0 as immediate data. Both of these instructions accomplish the same thing:

```
mov AL,0
xor AL,AL
```

TABLE 9.4   The XOR truth table for assembly language

Bit 1	Operator	Bit 2		Result bit
0	XOR	0	=	0
0	XOR	1	=	1
1	XOR	0	=	1
1	XOR	1	=	0

The first instruction uses four machine cycles, however, while the second uses only three. That's not a tremendous difference (though purists will argue that it represents a 25% improvement) but there are times in assembly language where every machine cycle counts! How this trick works should be obvious from reading the truth table, but to drive it home I've laid it out in Figure 9.3.

Follow each of the individual **XOR** operations across the figure to its result value. Because each bit in AL is **XOR**ed against itself, in every case the **XOR** operations happen between two operands that are identical.

XOR AL,AL

AL: 9DH
10011101B

	Value		Mask		Result
LSB	1	XOR	1	=	0
	0	XOR	0	=	0
	1	XOR	1	=	0
	1	XOR	1	=	0
	1	XOR	1	=	0
	0	XOR	0	=	0
	0	XOR	0	=	0
MSB	1	XOR	1	=	0

(After execution)

AL = 0

FIGURE 9.3   Using XOR to zero a register

Sometimes both are 1, sometimes both are 0, but in every case the two are the same. With the **XOR** operation, when the two operands are the same, the result is always 0. Voila! Zero in a register in three cycles flat.

The NOT Instruction

Easiest to understand of all the bitwise logical instructions is **NOT.** The truth table for **NOT** is pretty simple because **NOT** only takes one operand. And what it does is simple as well: **NOT** takes the state of each bit in its single operand and changes it to its opposite state. What was 1 becomes 0 and what was 0 becomes 1 (see Table 9.5).

Segment Registers Don't Respond to Logic!

One limitation of the segment registers CS, DS, SS, and ES is that they cannot be used with any of the bitwise logical instructions. If you try, the assembler will hand you an "illegal use of segment register" error. If you need to perform a logical operation on a segment register, you must first copy the segment register's value into one of the registers AX, BX, CX, DX, BP, SI, and DI; perform the logical operation on the new register, and then copy the result back into the segment register.

9.2 ◆ Shifting Bits

The other way of manipulating bits within a byte is a little more straightforward: you *shift* them to one side or the other. There are a few wrinkles to the process, but the simplest shift instructions are pretty obvious: **SHL** shifts its operand left, whereas **SHR** shifts its operand right.

All of the shift instructions (including the slightly more complex ones I'll describe a little later) have the same general form, illustrated here by the **SHL** instruction:

```
SHL <register/memory>,<count>
```

TABLE 9.5   The NOT truth table

Bit	Operator	Result bit
0	NOT	1
1	NOT	0

The first operand is the target of the shift operation; that is, the value that you're going to be shifting. It can be register data or memory data, but not immediate data. The second operand specifies the number of bits by which to shift.

Shift by What?

The <**count**> operand is a little peculiar. It can be one of two things: the literal digit 1, or else the register CL (*not* CX!). If you specify the count as 1, then the shift will be by 1 bit. If you wish to shift by more than 1 bit at a time, you must load the shift count into register CL. Counting things is CX's (and hence CL's) hidden agenda; it counts shifts, loops, string elements, and a few other things. That's why it's sometimes called the *count register,* and can be remembered by the *C* in *count.*

Although you can load a number as large as 255 into CL, it really only makes sense to use count values up to 16. If you shift any bit in a word by 16, you shift it completely out of the word!

Something to keep in mind: moving an immediate count value into CL takes some time. Furthermore, executing a shift instruction that takes its count value from CL takes more time to execute than executing a shift instruction that uses the literal 1 as its count value. These two facts conspire to make it faster to use successive shift-by-one instructions unless you need to shift by five or more bits.

As an example, consider the following instruction sequence, which is what must be done to use CL to shift a word by 3 bits:

```
MOV CL,3
SHL SI,CL
```

Most remarkably, it is faster to accomplish the same shift this way:

```
SHL SI,1
SHL SI,1
SHL SI,1
```

The rule of thumb is that unless you need to shift by more than 4 bits, use consecutive shift-by-one instructions rather than shift-by-CL instructions.

How Bit Shifting Works

Understanding the shift instructions requires that you think of the numbers being shifted as *binary* numbers, and not hexadecimal or decimal numbers.

(If you're fuzzy on binary notation, again, take another slip through Chapter 1.) A simple example would start with register AX containing a value of 0B76FH. Expressed as a binary number (and hence as a bit pattern) 0B76FH is

1011011101101111

Keep in mind that each digit in a binary number is one bit. If you execute an **SHL AX,1** instruction, what you'd find in AX after the shift is the following:

0110111011011110

A 0 has been inserted at the right-hand end of the number, and the whole shebang has been bumped toward the left by one digit. Notice that a 1 bit has been bumped off the left end of the number into nothingness.

Bumping Bits into the Carry Flag

Well, not exactly nothingness. . . . The last bit shifted out is bumped into a temporary bucket for bits called the *carry flag*. The carry flag is one of those odd bits lumped together as the flags register, which I described in Section 6.4. You can test the state of the carry flag with a branching instruction, as I'll explain in Section 9.3.

Keep in mind when using shift instructions, however, that a *lot* of different instructions use the carry flag as well as the shift instructions. If you bump a bit into the carry flag with the intent of testing that bit to see what it is, test it *before* you execute another instruction that affects the carry flag. This includes all the arithmetic instructions, all the bitwise logical instructions, a few miscellaneous instructions, and of course, the other shift instructions. If you shift a bit into the carry flag and then immediately execute another shift instruction, the first bit *will* be bumped off the end of the world and into nothingness.

Byte2Str: Converting Numbers to Displayable Strings

As we've seen, DOS has a fairly convenient method for displaying text to your screen. The problem is that it only displays *text*—if you want to display a numeric value from a register as a pair of digits, DOS won't help. You first have to convert the numeric value into its string representation, and then display the string representation through DOS.

Converting hexadecimal numbers to hexadecimal digits isn't difficult, and the routine to do the job demonstrates several of the new concepts we're exploring in this chapter. Read **Byte2Str** carefully:

```
; -----------------------------------------------------------------------
;
;   Byte2Str -- Converts a byte passed in AL to a string at
;               DS:SI
;   Last update 3/8/89
;
;
;   1 entry point:
;
;
;   Byte2STr:
;     Caller must pass:
;     AL: Byte to be converted
;     DS: Segment of destination string
;     SI:  Offset of destination string
;
;
;     This routine converts 8-bit values to 2-digit hexadecimal
;     string representations at DS:SI. The "H" specifier is
;     *not* included. Four separate output examples:
;     02  B7  FF  6C
; -----------------------------------------------------------------------

Byte2Str   PROC
           mov  DI,AX               ; Duplicate byte in DI
           and  DI,000FH            ; Mask out high 12 bits of DI
           mov  BX,OFFSET Digits    ; Load offset of Digits into DI
           mov  AH,BYTE PTR [BX+DI] ; Load digit from table into AH
           mov  [SI+1],AH           ;    and store digit into string
           xor  AH,AH               ; Zero out AH
           mov  DI,AX               ; And move byte into DI
           shr  DI,1                ; Shift high nybble of byte to
           shr  DI,1                ;    low nybble
           shr  DI,1
           shr  DI,1
           mov  AH,BYTE PTR [BX+DI] ; Load digit from table into AH
           mov  [SI],AH             ;    and store digit into string
           ret                      ; We're done--go home!
Byte2Str   ENDP
```

To call **Byte2Str** you must pass the value to be converted to a string in AL, and the address of the string into which the string representation is to be stored as DS:SI. Typically, DS will already contain the segment address of your data segment, so you most likely will only need to pass the offset of the start of the string in SI.

In addition to the code shown here, **Byte2Str** requires the presence of a second string in the data segment. This string, whose name must be **Digits,** contains all 16 of the digits used to express hexadecimal numbers. The definition of **Digits** looks like this:

```
Digits DB '0123456789ABCDEF'
```

The important thing to note about **Digits** is that each digit occupies a position in the string whose offset from the start of the string is the value it represents. In other words, *0* is at the start of the string, 0 bytes offset from the string's start. The character *7* lies 7 bytes from the start of the string, and so on. **Digits** is what we call a *look-up table* and it represents (as I'll explain below) an extremely useful method in assembly language.

Splitting a Byte into 2 Nybbles

Displaying the value stored in a byte requires two digits. The bottom 4 bits in a byte are represented by one digit (the least significant, or rightmost digit) and the top 4 bits in the byte are represented by another digit (the most significant, or leftmost digit). Selecting the two digits must be done one at a time, which means that we have to separate the single byte into two 4-bit quantities, which are often called *nybbles.*

To split a byte in two, we need to *mask out* the unwanted half. This is done with an **AND** instruction. Note in **Byte2Str** that the first instruction, **MOV DI,AX** copies the value to be converted (which is in AL) into DI. You don't need to move AH into DI here, but there is no instruction to move an 8-bit register-half like AL into a 16-bit register like DI. AH comes along for the ride, but we really don't need it. The second instruction masks out the high 12 bits of DI. This eliminates what had earlier been in free-rider AH, as well as the high 4 bits of AL. What's left in DI is all we want, the lower 4 bits of what was originally passed to the routine in AL.

Using a Lookup Table

The low nybble of the value to be converted is now in DI. The address of **Digits** is loaded into BX. The appropriate digit character is then copied from **Digits** into AH. The whole trick of using a lookup table lies in the way the character in the table is addressed:

```
mov AH,BYTE PTR [BX+DI]
```

DS:BX points to the start of **Digits,** so [BX] would address the *first* character in **Digits.** To get at the desired digit, we must *index* into the lookup table by adding the offset into the table to BX. There is an 8086/8088 addressing mode intended precisely for use with lookup tables, called *base indexed addressing.* That sounds more arcane than it is; what it means is that instead of specifying a memory location at [BX], we add an index to BX, and address a memory location at [BX+DI].

If you recall, we masked out all of DI but the 4 lowest bits of the byte we are converting. These bits will contain some value from 0 through 0FH. **Digits** contains the hexadecimal digit characters from 0 to F. By using DI as the index, the value in DI will select its corresponding digit character in **Digits.** We are using the value in DI to look up its equivalent hexadecimal digit character in the lookup table **Digits** (see Figure 9.4).

So far, we've read a character from the lookup table into AH. Now, we use yet another addressing mode to move the character from AX back into the second character of the destination string whose address was passed to **Byte2Str** in DS:SI. This addressing mode is called *indirect displacement* addressing, though I question the wisdom of memorizing that term. The mode is nothing more than indirect addressing (i.e., addressing the contents of memory at [SI]) with the addition of a literal displacement:

```
mov [SI+1],AH
```

This looks a lot like base indexed addressing (which is why the jargon may not be all that useful) with the sole exception that what is added to SI is not a *register* but a *literal constant.*

Once this **MOV** is done, the first of the 2 nybbles passed to **Byte2Str** in AL has been converted to its character equivalent and stored in the destination string variable at DS:SI.

Now we have to do it again, this time for the high nybble.

Shifting the High Nybble into the Low Nybble

The high nybble of the value to be converted has been waiting patiently all this time in AL. We didn't mask out the high nybble until we moved AX into DI and did our masking on DI instead of AX. So, AL is still just as it was when **Byte2Str** began.

The first thing to do is clear AH to 0. **Byte2Str** uses the **XOR AH,AH** trick I described in the last section. Then we **MOV** AX into DI.

All that remains to be done is to somehow move the high nybble of the low byte of DI into the position occupied by the low nybble. The fastest way to do this is simply to shift DI to the right, four times in a row. This is

MOV AH,BYTE PTR [BX+DI]

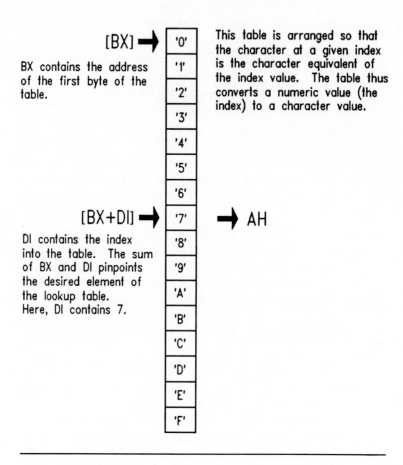

[BX] ➡️

BX contains the address of the first byte of the table.

This table is arranged so that the character at a given index is the character equivalent of the index value. The table thus converts a numeric value (the index) to a character value.

[BX+DI] ➡️

DI contains the index into the table. The sum of BX and DI pinpoints the desired element of the lookup table. Here, DI contains 7.

➡️ AH

FIGURE 9.4   Using a lookup table

what the four **SHR** instructions in **Byte2Str** do. The low nybble is simply shifted off the edge of DI, into the carry flag, and then out into nothingness After the four shifts, what was the high nybble is now the low nybble and, once again, DI can be used as an index into the **Digits** lookup table to **MOV** the appropriate digit into AH.

Finally, there is the matter of storing the digit into the target string at DS:SI. Notice that *this* time, there is no +1 in the **MOV** instruction:

```
mov [SI],AH
```

Why not? The high nybble is the digit on the left, so it must be moved into the first byte in the target string. Earlier, we moved the low nybble into the byte on the right. String indexing begins at the left and works toward the right, so if the left digit is at index 0 of the string, the right digit must be at index 0+1.

Byte2Str does a fair amount of data-fiddling in only a few lines. Read it over a few times while following the above discussion through its course until the whole thing makes sense to you.

Converting Words to Their String Form

Having converted a byte-sized value to a string, it's a snap to convert 16-bit words to their string forms. Not much more difficult than calling **Byte2Str** twice:

```
; --------------------------------------------------------------------
;   Word2Str -- Converts a word passed in AX to a string at
;               DS:SI
;   Last update 3/8/89
;
;   1 entry point:
;
;   Word2Str:
;       Caller must pass:
;       AX : Word to be converted
;       DS : Segment of destination string
;       SI : Offset of destination string
; --------------------------------------------------------------------

Word2Str   PROC
           mov    CX,AX     ; Save a copy of convertee in CX
           xchg   AH,AL     ; Swap high and low AX bytes to do high first
           call   Byte2Str  ; Convert AL to string at DS:SI
           add    SI,2      ; Bump SI to point second 2 characters
           mov    AX,CX     ; Reload convertee into AX
           call   Byte2Str  ; Convert AL to string at DS:SI
           ret              ; And we're done!
Word2Str   ENDP
```

The logic here is fairly simple, if you understand how **Byte2Str** works. Moving AX into CX simply saves an unmodified copy of the word to be converted in CX. Something to watch out for here: if **Byte2Str** were to use

CX for something, this saved copy would be mangled and you might be caught wondering why things weren't working correctly. This is a common enough bug for the following reason: you create **Byte2Str,** and then create **Word2Str** to call **Byte2Str.** The first version of **Byte2Str** does not make use of CX, so it's safe to use CX as a storage bucket.

However, later on you beef up **Byte2Str** somehow, and in the process add some instructions that use CX. You plum fergot that **Word2Str** stored a value in CX *while **Word2Str** was calling **Byte2Str.*** It's pointless arguing whether the bug is that **Byte2Str** uses CX, or that **Word2Str** assumes that no one else is using CX. To make things work again, you would have to stash the value somewhere other than in CX. Pushing it onto the stack is your best bet if you run out of registers.

Virtually everything that **Word2Str** does involves getting the converted digits into the proper positions in the target string. A word requires four digits altogether. In a string representation, the high byte occupies the left two digits and the low byte occupies the right two digits. Because strings are indexed from the left to the right, it makes a certain amount of sense to convert the left end of the string first.

This is the reason for the **XCHG** instruction. It swaps the high and low bytes of AX so that the *first* time **Byte2Str** is called, the high byte is actually in AL instead of AH. (Remember that **Byte2Str** converts the value passed in AL.) **Byte2Str** does the conversion and stores the two converted digits in the first two bytes of the string at DS:SI.

For the second call to **Byte2Str,** AH and AL are not exchanged. Therefore, the low byte will be the one converted. Notice the following instruction:

```
add SI,2
```

This is not heavy-duty math, but it's a good example of how to add a constant to a register in assembly language. The idea is to pass the address of the *second* 2 bytes of the string to **Byte2Str** as though they were actually the start of the string. This means that when **Byte2Str** converts the low byte of AX, it stores the two equivalent digits into the second two bytes of the string.

For example, if the high byte was 0C7H, the digits C and 7 would be stored in the first 2 bytes of the string, counting from the left. Then, if the low byte were 042H, the digits 4 and 2 would be stored at the third and fourth bytes of the string, respectively. The whole string would look like this when the conversion was complete:

```
C742
```

As I've said numerous times before—understand memory addressing and you've got the greater part of assembly language in your hip pocket. Most of the trick of **Byte2Str** and **Word2Str** lies in the different ways they address memory. If you study them, study the machinery behind the lookup table and target string addressing. The logic and shift instructions are obvious and easy to figure out by comparison.

9.3 ◆ Flags, Tests, and Branches

Those assembler-knowledgeable folk who have stuck with me this long may be wondering why I haven't covered conditional jumps until this late in the book. I mean, we've explained procedures already, and haven't even gotten to jumps yet.

Indeed—that's the whole point. I explained procedures before jumps because when people learn those two concepts the other way around, they have a tendency to use jumps for *everything,* even when procedures are called for. Unlike some high-level languages like Pascal and Modula 2, there is no way around jumps—what they so derisively call *GOTOs*—in assembly language. Sadly, some people then assume that jumps are *It* and don't bother imposing any structure at all on their assembly language programs. By teaching procedures first, I feel that I've at least made possible a more balanced approach on the part of the learner.

Besides, I felt it wise to teach how to *manage* complexity before teaching the number one means of *creating* complexity.

Unconditional Jumps

A *jump* is just that: an abrupt change in the flow of instruction execution. Ordinarily, instructions are executed one after the other, in order, moving from low memory toward high memory. There are instructions that alter this smooth sequential flow. *Jump instructions* alter the address of the next instruction to be executed. Execute a jump instruction, and *zap!*—all of a sudden you're somewhere else in the code segment. A jump instruction can move execution forward or backward in memory. It can bend execution back into a loop—and it can tie your program logic in knots . . .

There are two kinds of jumps: *conditional* and *unconditional.* An unconditional jump is a jump that *always* happens. It takes this form:

```
jmp <label>
```

When this instruction executes, the sequence of execution moves to the instruction located at the label specified by **<label>.** It's just that simple.

The unconditional **JMP** instruction is of limited use by itself. It almost always works in conjunction with the conditional jump instructions that test the state of the various 8086/8088 flags.

Conditional Jumps

A conditional jump instruction is one of those fabled tests I introduced in Chapter 0. When executed, a conditional jump tests something, usually one of the 8086/8088 flags. If the flag being tested happens to be in a particular state, execution can jump to a label somewhere else in the code segment, or it may simply fall through to the next instruction in sequence.

This two-way nature is important. A conditional jump instruction either jumps or it falls through. Jump or no jump. It can't jump to one of two or three places. Whether it jumps or not depends on the current value of a single bit within the CPU.

For example, there is a flag that is set to 1 by certain instructions when the result of that instruction is zero. The **DEC** (**DEC**rement) instruction is a good example. **DEC** subtracts one from its operand. If by that subtraction the operand becomes zero, the zero flag (ZF) is set to 1. One of the conditional jump instructions, **JZ** (**J**ump If **Z**ero) tests ZF. If ZF is found set to 1, a jump happens to a label. If ZF is found to be 0, execution falls through to the next instruction in line.

Here's a simple (and nonoptimal) example, using instructions you should already understand:

```
            mov  Counter,17   ; We're going to do this 17 times
WorkLoop: call DoWork         ; Process the data
            dec  Counter       ; Subtract 1 from the counter
            jz   AllDone       ; If the counter is zero, we're done!
            jmp  WorkLoop      ; Otherwise, go back and execute the loop
                                 again
```

The label **AllDone** isn't shown in the example because it's somewhere else in the program, maybe a long way off. The important thing is that the **JZ** instruction is a two-way switch. If ZF is equal to 1, execution moves to the location marked by the label **AllDone.** If ZF is equal to 0, execution falls through to the next instruction in sequence. Here, that would be the unconditional jump instruction **JMP WorkLoop.**

This simple loop is one way to perform a call to a procedure some set number of times. A count value is stored in a variable named **Counter,** and the procedure is called. After control returns from the procedure, **Counter** is decremented by one. If that drops the counter to 0, the procedure has been called the full number of times, and the loop sends execution elsewhere. If the counter still has a value in it, execution loops back to the procedure call and begins the loop again.

Note the use of an unconditional jump instruction to close the loop.

Beware of Endless Loops!

This is a good place to warn you of a common sort of bug that produces the dreaded *endless loop,* which locks up your machine and forces you to reboot to get out. Suppose the above code snippet were done in the following way:

```
WorkLoop: mov   Counter,17  ; We're going to do this 17 times
          call  DoWork      ; Process the data
          dec   Counter     ; Subtract 1 from the counter
          jz    AllDone     ; If the counter is zero, we're done!
          jmp   WorkLoop    ; Otherwise, go back and execute the loop again
```

This becomes a pretty obvious endless loop; however, you'll be appalled at how often such an obvious bug will dance in your face for hours without being recognized as such. . . . The key point is that the instruction that loads the initial value to the counter is *inside* the loop! Every time the loop happens, the counter is counted down by one, and then immediately reloaded with the original count value. Thus, the count value never gets smaller than the original value minus one, and the loop (which is waiting for the counter to become zero) never ends.

You're unlikely to do something like this deliberately, of course. But it's *very* easy to type a label at the wrong place, or (easier still) to type the name of the wrong label, a label that might be at or before the point where a counter is loaded with its initial value.

Assembly language programming requires concentration and endless attention to detail. If you pay attention to what you're doing, you'll make fewer "stupid" errors like the one above.

But I can promise you that you'll still make a few.

Jumping on the Absence of a Condition

There are a fair number of conditional jump instructions, of which I'll discuss only the most common in this book. Their number is increased by the fact that every conditional jump instruction has an alter ego: a jump when the specified condition is *not* set to 1.

The **JZ** instruction provides a good example. **JZ** jumps to a new location in the code segment if the zero flag (ZF) is set to 1. **JZ**'s alter ego is **JNZ** (**J**ump **I**f **N**ot **Z**ero). **JNZ** jumps to a label if ZF is 0 and falls through if ZF is 1.

This may be confusing at first, because **JNZ** jumps when ZF is equal to 0. Keep in mind that the name of the instruction applies to the *condition* being tested and not necessarily the bit value of the flag. In the previous code example, **JZ** jumped when the **DEC** instruction decremented a counter to zero. The condition being tested is something connected with an earlier instruction, *not* simply the state of ZF.

Think of it this way: a condition raises a flag. *Raising a flag* means setting the flag to 1. When one of numerous instructions forces an operand to a value of zero (which is the condition), the zero flag is raised. The logic of the instruction refers to the condition, *not* to the flag.

As an example, let's improve the little loop shown on page 294. I should caution you that its first implementation on page 294, while correct and workable in the strictest sense, is awkward and not the best way to code that kind of task. It can be improved in several ways. Here's one:

```
          mov    Counter,17   ; We're going to do this 17 times
WorkLoop: call   DoWork       ; Process the data
          dec    Counter      ; Subtract 1 from the counter
          jnz    WorkLoop     ; If the counter is zero, we're done!
          < more code >
```

The **JZ** instruction has been replaced with a **JNZ** instruction. That makes much more sense, because to close the loop we have to jump, and we only close the loop while the counter is greater than 0. The jump back to label **WorkLoop** will happen only while the counter is greater than 0.

Once the counter decrements to 0, the loop is considered finished. **JNZ** falls through and the code that follows the loop (which I don't show here) executes. The next instruction could be a **JMP** to label **AllDone,** as shown earlier, or it could be the next bit of work that the assembly language program has to do. The point is that if you can position the program's next task immediately after the **JNZ** instruction, you don't need to use the **JMP** instruction at all. The instruction execution will just flow naturally into the next task that needs performing. The program will have a more natural and less tangled top-to-bottom flow, and will be easier to read and understand.

Flags

Back in Section 6.4 I explained the flags register and briefly described the purposes of all the flags it contains. Most flags are not terribly useful, especially when you're first starting out as a programmer. The carry flag (CF) and the zero flag (ZF) will be 90% of your involvement in flags as a beginner, with the direction flag (DF), sign flag (SF), and overflow flag (OF) together making up the final 10%. It might be a good idea to reread Section 6.4 now, just in case your grasp of flag etiquette has gotten a little rusty.

As explained a few pages ago, **JZ** jumps when ZF is 1, whereas **JNZ** jumps when ZF is 0. Most instructions that perform some operation on an operand (like **AND, OR, XOR, INC, DEC** and all arithmetic instructions) set ZF according to the results of the operation. On the other hand, instructions that simply move data around (such as **MOV, XCHG, PUSH,** and **POP**) do not affect ZF or any other flags. (Obviously, **POPF** affects the flags by popping the top-of-stack value into them.) One slightly irritating exception is the **NOT** instruction, which performs a logical operation on its operand but does not set any flags. Before you write code that depends on flags, *check your instruction reference* (one is almost certainly provided with your assembler) to make sure you have the flag etiquette down correctly.

Comparisons with CMP

One major use of flags is in controlling loops; another is in comparisons between two values. Your programs will often need to know whether a value in a register or memory is equal to some other value. Further, you may want to know if a value is greater than a value or less than a value if it is not equal to that value. There is a jump instruction to satisfy every need, but something has to set the flags for the benefit of the jump instruction. The **CMP** (**C**o**MP**are) instruction is what sets the flags for comparison tasks.

CMP's use is straightforward and intuitive. The second operand is compared with the first, and several flags are set accordingly:

```
cmp <op1>,<op2>      ; Sets OF, SF, ZF, AF, PF, and CF
```

The sense of the comparison can be remembered if you simply recast the comparison in arithmetic terms:

```
Result = <op1> − <op2>
```

The second operand is subtracted from the first. Based on the results of the subtraction, the other flags are set to appropriate values.

After a **CMP** instruction, you can jump based on several arithmetic conditions. People who have a fair grounding in math, and FORTRAN or Pascal programmers will recognize the conditions: *equal, not equal, greater than, less than, greater than or equal to,* and *less than or equal to.* The sense of these operators follows from their names and is exactly like the sense of the equivalent operators in most high-level languages.

A Jungle of Jump Instructions

There is a bewildering array of jump instruction mnemonics, but those dealing with arithmetic relationships sort out well into just six categories, one category for each of the six conditions listed above. Complication arises out of the fact that there are *two* mnemonics for each machine instruction, for example, **JLE** (**J**ump **I**f **L**ess than or **E**qual) and **JNG** (**J**ump **I**f **N**ot **G**reater than). These two mnemonics are *synonyms,* in that the assembler generates the identical binary opcode when it encounters either mnemonic. The synonyms are a convenience to you, the programmer, in that they provide two alternate ways to think about a given jump instruction. In the above example, *jump if less than or equal to* is logically identical to *jump if not greater than.* (Think about it!) If the importance of the preceding compare was to see if one value is less than or equal to another, you'd use the **JLE** mnemonic. On the other hand, if you were testing to be sure one quantity was not greater than another, you'd use **JNG.** The choice is yours.

Another complication is that there is a separate set of instructions for signed and unsigned comparisons. I haven't spoken much about assembly language math in this book, and thus haven't said much about the difference between signed and unsigned quantities. A *signed* quantity is one in which the high bit of the quantity is considered a built-in flag indicating whether or not the quantity is negative. If that bit is 1, the quantity is considered negative. If that bit is 0, the quantity is considered positive.

Signed arithmetic in assembly language is complex and subtle, and not as useful as you might immediately think. I won't be covering it in detail in this book, though most all assembly language books treat it to some extent. All you need to know to get a high-level understanding of signed arithmetic is that in signed arithmetic, negative quantities are legal. Unsigned arithmetic, on the other hand, does not recognize negative numbers.

Greater Than versus Above

To tell the signed jumps apart from the unsigned jumps, the mnemonics use two different expressions for the relationships between two values:

♦ *Signed values* are thought of as being *greater than* or *less than.* For example, to test whether one signed operand is greater than another, you would use the **JG** (**J**ump If **G**reater) mnemonic after a **CMP** instruction.

♦ *Unsigned values* are thought of as being *above* or *below.* For example, to tell whether one unsigned operand is greater (above) another, you would use the **JA** (**J**ump If **A**bove) mnemonic after a **CMP** instruction.

Table 9.6 summarizes the arithmetic jump mnemonics and their synonyms. Any mnemonics containing the words *above* or *below* are for unsigned values, while any mnemonics containing the words *greater* or *less* are for signed values. Compare the mnemonics with their synonyms and see how the two represent opposite viewpoints from which to look at identical instructions.

Table 9.6 simply serves to expand the mnemonics into a more comprehensible form and associate a mnemonic with its synonym. Table 9.7, on the other hand, sorts the mnemonics out by logical condition and according to their use with signed and unsigned values. Also listed in Table 9.7 are the flags whose values are considered in each jump instruction. Notice that some of the jump instructions require one of two possible flag values in order to take the jump, while others require both of two flag values.

TABLE 9.6   Arithmetic jump mnemonics and their synonyms

Mnemonics		*Synonyms*	
JA	Jump If Above	JNBE	Jump If Not Below or Equal
JAE	Jump If Above or Equal	JNB	Jump If Not Below
JB	Jump If Below	JNAE	Jump If Not Above or Equal
JBE	Jump If Below or Equal	JNA	Jump If Not Above
JE	Jump If Equal	\<none\>	
JNE	Jump If Not Equal	\<none\>	
JG	Jump If Greater	JNLE	Jump If Not Less Than or Equal
JGE	Jump If Greater or Equal	JNL	Jump If Not Less
JL	Jump If Less	JNGE	Jump If Not Greater or Equal
JLE	Jump If Less or Equal	JNG	Jump If Not Greater

TABLE 9.7   Arithmetic tests useful after a CMP instruction

Condition	Pascal operator	Unsigned values	Jumps when	Signed values	Jumps when
Equal	=	JE	ZF=1	JE	ZF=1
Not Equal	<>	JNE	ZF=0	JNE	ZF=0
Greater than	>	JA	CF=0 and	JG	ZF=0 or
Not Less than or equal to		JNBE	ZF=0	JNLE	SF=OF
Less than	<	JB	CF=1	JL	SF<>OF
Not Greater than or equal to		JNAE		JNGE	
Greater than or equal to	>=	JAE	CF=0	JGE	SF=OF
Not Less than		JNB		JNL	
Less than or equal to	<=	JBE	CF=1 or ZF=1	JLE	ZF=1 and SF<>OF
Not Greater than		JNA		JNG	

Several of the signed jumps compare two of the flags against one another. **JG,** for example, will jump when either ZF is 0 or when the sign flag (SF) is equal to the overflow flag (OF). I won't spend any further time explaining the nature of the sign flag or overflow flag. As long as you have the sense of each instruction under your belt, understanding exactly how the instructions test the flags can wait until you've gained some programming experience.

Although not listed as synonyms in Table 9.6, the **JE** and **JZ** mnemonics are synonyms, as are **JNE** and **JNZ.** Think again of the way a comparison is done within the CPU: the second operand is subtracted from the first, and if the result is 0 (indicating that the two operands were in fact equal), the zero flag is set to 1. That's why **JE** and **JZ** are synonyms: both are simply testing the state of the zero flag.

Detecting the Installed Display Adapter

A useful example of **CMP** and the conditional jump instructions in action involves detecting the installed display adapter. As of early 1989, there were five different IBM display adapters that can be installed in a PC, from the first generation introduced with the original PC in 1981 to the VGA and MCGA introduced with the PS/2 series in 1987. Each adapter has certain unique features, and if you intend to use some of this rather nifty hardware assistance offered by the more advanced video boards like the EGA and VGA, you had better be prepared to tell which board is in a given machine. Your program must then decide what special features can and cannot be used.

It isn't quite enough to know which board is installed in a given machine. The way a certain board operates can change drastically depending on whether a monochrome or color monitor is attached to the board. The most obvious difference (and the one of most interest to the programmer) is that the memory address of the video display buffer is one address for the color monitor and a different address for the monochrome monitor. This schizophrenic quality of the EGA, VGA, and MCGA is so pronounced that it makes sense to consider the EGA/color monitor combination an entirely separate display adapter from the EGA/monochrome monitor combination.

In my method, I use a separate numeric code to represent each legal adapter/monitor combination. There are nine possibilities in all, summarized in Table 9.8. The codes are not consecutive; note that there is no code 3, 6 or 9. I didn't make these codes up arbitrarily. They are, in fact, the display adapter/monitor combination codes returned by one of the VGA/MCGA BIOS services.

The procedure **DispID** given below determines which display adapter is installed in the machine upon which **DispID** is running. **DispID** then returns one of the codes listed in Table 9.8. I recommend that your programs define a byte-sized variable in their data segments where this code can be stored throughout the program's duration. If you detect the adapter with **DispID** immediately on program startup, your program can

TABLE 9.8   Legal PC display adapter/monitor combinations

Code	*Adapter/monitor*	*Segment of display buffer*
00	None	None
01H	MDA/monochrome	0B000H
02H	CGA/color	0B800H
04H	EGA/color	0B800H
05H	EGA/monochrome	0B000H
07H	VGA/monochrome	0B000H
08H	VGA/color	0B800H
0AH	MCGA/color (digital)	0B800H
0BH	MCGA/monochrome	0B000H
0CH	MCGA/color (analog)	0B800H

inspect the code any time it needs to make a decision as to which video features to use.

Given what I've told you about **CMP** and conditional jump instructions so far, see if you can follow the logic in **DispID** before we go through it blow-by-blow:

```
; --------------------------------------------------------------------------------
;  DispID -- Identifies the installed display adapter
;  Last update 3/8/89
;
;
;  1 entry point:
;
;
;  DispID:
;     Caller passes no parameters
;     Routine returns a code value in AX.
;     The codes are these:
;     0 : Adapter is unknown; recommend aborting
;     1 : MDA (Monochrome Display Adapter)
;     2 : CGA (Color Graphics Adapter)
;
;
; --------------------------------------------------------------------------------


DispID    PROC
          mov   AH,1AH     ; Select PS/2 Identify Adapter Service
          xor   AL,AL      ; Select Get Combination Code Subservice (AL=0)
          int   10H        ; Call VIDEO
          cmp   AL,1AH     ; If AL comes back with 1AH, we have a PS/2
          jne   TryEGA     ; If not, jump down to test for the EGA
          mov   AL,BL      ; Put Combination Code into AL
          ret              ;   and go home!
TryEGA:   mov   AH,12H     ; Select EGA Alternate Function
          mov   BX,10H     ; Select Get Configuration Information subservice
          int   10H        ; Call VIDEO
          cmp   BX,10H     ; If BX comes back unchanged, EGA is *not* there
          je    OldBords   ; Go see whether it's an MDA or CGA
          cmp   BH,0       ; If BH = 0, it's an EGA/color combo
          je    EGAColor   ; otherwise it's EGA/mono
          mov   AL,5       ; Store code 5 for EGA mono
          ret              ;   and go home!
EGAColor: mov   AL,4       ; Store code 4 for EGA color
          ret              ;   and go home!
```

```
OldBords:  int    11H          ; Call Equipment Configuration interrupt
           test   AL,30H        ; If bits 4 & 5 are both =1, it's an MDA
           jne    CGA           ;   otherwise it's a CGA
           mov    AL,1          ; Store code 1 for MDA
           ret                  ;   and go home!
CGA:       mov    AL,2          ; Store code 2 for CGA
           ret                  ;   and go home!
DispID     ENDP
```

DispID is the most complex piece of code shown so far in this book. The overall strategy is not obvious and bears some attention.

IBM's standard display boards appeared in three generations. The first generation consisted of the original Color Graphics Adapter (CGA) and Monochrome Display Adapter (MDA). The second generation consisted of the Enhanced Graphics Adapter (EGA). Finally, the third generation came in with the PS/2 in April 1987 and provided the Video Graphics Array (VGA) and Multi-Color Graphics Array (MCGA).

The simplest way to find out what display board is installed in a machine is to ask the machine by querying BIOS services. There are BIOS services specific to each generation of display board, and by some quirk of fate all such services are well behaved, by which I mean that querying a service that doesn't exist (because an older generation of video board is installed) will not crash the system. (IBM's BIOS standard is extremely downward compatible in that newer generations all contain everything the older generations do.) Furthermore, if a BIOS service specific to a generation of boards is found *not* to exist, that tells us that the installed board is not a member of that generation or a newer generation.

Assuming that the target machine could have any of the standard IBM display boards in it, it makes sense to test for the presence of the newest boards first. Then, through a process of elimination, we move to the older and older boards.

The first test that **DispID** makes, then, is for the VGA or MCGA generation. The PS/2 machines contain in their ROM BIOS a service (VIDEO Service 1AH) specifically to identify the installed display adapter. **DispID** calls VIDEO service 1AH, having cleared AL to 0 via **XOR**. As it happens, if a PS/2 BIOS is present on the bus, the 1AH service number is returned in register AL. On return from the **INT 10H** call, we test AL for 1AH using **CMP.** If 1AH is *not* found in AL, we know up front that there is no PS/2 BIOS in the system, and therefore no VGA or MCGA.

After the **CMP** instruction is the **JNE TryEGA** conditional branch. If the **CMP** finds that AL is *not* equal to 1AH, then control jumps down to the code that tests for the next older generation of video boards: the EGA. If AL *is* equal to 1AH, then the PS/2 BIOS has placed the display adapter code in BL. **DispID** then copies BL into AL (which is where **DispID** returns the display code) and executes a **RET** instruction to pass control back to the caller. .

Testing for the EGA is done a little differently, but the same general idea holds: we call an EGA-specific VIDEO service not present in the oldest generation of boards. The key test, again, is whether a certain register comes back unchanged. There is a twist, however: if BX comes back with the *same* value it held when the VIDEO call was made (here, 10H) then an EGA BIOS does *not* exist in the machine (isn't the PC wonderful?). Here, after the **CMP BX,10H** instruction, we do a **JE OldBords** and not a **JNE** as we did when testing for the PS/2 generation. If BX comes back in an altered state, we assume an EGA is present and that BX contains information on the display configuration.

If an EGA BIOS is found, a value in BH tells us whether the EGA is connected to a monochrome or color monitor. (Remember, there is a different code for each.) The value in BH is not the code itself as it was with the PS/2 BIOS, so we have to do a little more testing to get the right code into AL. If BH contains 0, then the attached monitor is color. Any other value in BH indicates a monochrome system. The following sequence of instructions from **DispID** takes care of loading the proper EGA-specific code into AL:

```
              cmp  BH,0      ; If BH = 0, it's an EGA/color combo
              je   EGAColor  ;  otherwise it's EGA/mono
              mov  AL,5      ; Store code 5 for EGA mono
              ret            ;  and go home!
   EGAColor:  mov  AL,4      ; Store code 4 for EGA color
              ret            ;  and go home!
```

You'll find yourself writing sequences like this a lot, when a single test decides between one of two courses of action. One course here is to load the value 5 into AL and the other course is to load 4 into AL. Notice that after the appropriate **MOV** instruction is executed, a **RET** takes care of passing execution back to the caller. If **DispID** were not a procedure but a simple sequence coded into the main line of instructions, you would need an unconditional jump (**JMP**) after each **MOV** to continue on with instruction execution somewhere else in the program. Using **RET** is much neater, which is yet another reason to wrap up small tasks like display adapter identification in a procedure wrapper.

Finally, if neither PS/2 nor EGA are present, **DispID** realizes that, by default, one of the original generation of display boards is on the bus. Telling MDA from CGA is not done with a BIOS call at all because the first generation BIOS did not know which display board was present. (That was a feature instituted with the EGA in 1984.) Instead, there is a separate software interrupt, 11H, that returns machine configuration information.

Testing Bits with TEST

Service 11H returns a word's worth of bits in AX. Singly or in twos or threes, the bits tell a tale about specific hardware options on the installed PC. These hardware options are summarized in Figure 9.5.

The bits we need to examine are bits 4 and 5. If both are set to 1, then we know we have a Monochrome Display Adapter. If the 2 bits are set to any other combination, the adapter must be a Color Graphics Adapter; all other alternatives have by this time been eliminated.

Testing for two 1 bits in a byte could be done this way, using instructions I've explained in this chapter:

```
and AL,30H        ; Mask out all bits in AL but 4 & 5 to 0
cmp AL,30H        ; See if AL now contains 30H; i.e., both 4 & 5 = 1
jne CGA           ; If not, we've got a CGA
```

This works correctly, but it's one more instruction than we need. The 8086/8088 instruction set recognizes that bit testing is done a lot in assembly language and bundles the **AND** masking task and the **CMP** testing task into one instruction: **TEST.**

TEST performs an **AND** logical operation between two operands, and then sets the flags as the **CMP** instruction would:

```
TEST <operand>,<bit mask>
```

The bit mask should contain a 1 bit in each position where a 1 bit is to be sought in the operand. *TEST is only useful for finding 1 bits.* If you need to identify 0 bits, you must first flip each bit to its opposite state with the logical **NOT** instruction, as I explained in Section 9.1. **NOT** changes all 1 bits to 0 bits, and all 0 bits to 1 bits. Once all 0 bits are flipped to 1 bits, you can test for a 1 bit where you need to find a 0 bit. (Sometimes it helps to map it out on paper to keep it all straight.)

In **DispID** we're looking for the monochrome code in bits 4 and 5,

FIGURE 9.5   Interrupt 11H configuration information

which is 11 (i.e., both bits 4 and 5 set to 1). Thus, we can use this method to spot 11 in bits 4 and 5:

```
test AL,30H     ; If bits 4 & 5 are both =1, it's an MDA
jne CGA         ;   otherwise it's a CGA
```

This is simple and readable, as long as all of the bits you need to spot are 1 bits.

When Not to Use TEST

Unfortunately, if you need to find a pattern consisting of a mixture of 1 bits and 0 bits, *you can't use **TEST**.* Instead, mask out all but the bits in question with **AND,** and then compare the bits against a value representing the numeric equivalent of the bit pattern you're looking for.

You might ask how this is different from **TEST,** because **TEST** bundles the **AND** and the **CMP** functions into one instruction. The answer is that **TEST** uses the same value for both the **AND** and **CMP** functions. When you test for a mixed-bit pattern, you must use one value to mask out all but the important bits, and a *different* value to compare against the result of the masking operation.

A simple example: suppose you wished to test specifically for the presence of a CGA set to 40-column mode. (Such machines may or may not still exist; I assume they don't, but you may have other feelings.) The pattern you'd need to spot in the interrupt 11H configuration bitmap would be 01 in bits 4 and 5. Don't make the mistake of assuming you could simply test for a 1 bit in bit 4; that would ignore the possibility of there also being a 1 bit in bit 5, which would indicate a monochrome display. When you mask out a bit, you *ignore* it; you do *not* test it for a value of 0!

Assuming the configuration word is in register AL, this is the code you'd use to spot the 1-bit pattern in bits 4 and 5:

```
and AL,30H      ; Mask out all bits 4 and 5
cmp AL,10H      ; Bit 4 = 1 and bit 5 = 0 means test for 10H
je got40col     ; If AL = 10H, we have a 40 column CGA!
```

Once again, **TEST** performs the equivalent of an **AND** and a **CMP,** but with the *same* mask each time. This only works for 1 bits. To test for a pattern of mixed 1 bits and 0 bits, you must use separate **AND** and **CMP** operations with a different mask.

9.4 ◆ Assembler Odds 'n Ends

Practice is the word.

You can do a lot with what you've learned so far, and you've certainly learned enough to be able to figure out the rest with the help of an assembly language reference and the more advanced books in this series. For the remainder of this chapter we're going to do some practicing, flexing some assembly language muscles and picking up a last few instructions in the process.

Yet Another Lookup Table

The lookup table named **Digits** (used by **Byte2Str** and **Word2Str** in the previous section) is so obvious that it didn't need much in the line of comments or explanations. **Digits** simply converted the table's index into the ASCII character equivalent to the value of the index. **Digits** is only sixteen bytes long, and its contents pretty much indicate what it's for:

```
Digits   DB   '0123456789ABCDEF'
```

Most of the time, your lookup tables will be a little less obvious. A lookup table does *not* have to be one single **DB** variable definition. You can define it pretty much as you need to, either with all table elements defined on a single line (as with **Digits**) or with each table element on its own line.

Consider the following lookup table:

```
OriginTbl   DW   0B000H   ; Code 0: No adapter identified
            DW   0B000H   ; Code 1: MDA
            DW   0B800H   ; Code 2: CGA
            DW   0B000H   ; Undefined
            DW   0B800H   ; Code 4: EGA/color
            DW   0B000H   ; Code 5: EGA/mono
            DW   0B000H   ; Undefined
            DW   0B000H   ; Code 7: VGA/mono
            DW   0B800H   ; Code 8: VGA/color
            DW   0B000H   ; Undefined
            DW   0B800H   ; Code 0AH: MCGA/color (digital)
            DW   0B000H   ; Code 0BH: MCGA/mono
            DW   0B800H   ; Code 0CH: MCGA/color (analog)
```

Here's a table where each table element has its own **DW** definition statement on its own line. This table treats a problem connected with the numerous different kinds of display adapters installable in a PC. There are two different addresses where the video refresh buffer begins. On boards connected to color monitors, the address is B800:0000, whereas on monochrome monitors the address is B000:0000. (Refer back to Figure 5.4 and the accompanying text if you've forgotten what the video refresh buffer is.)

If you intend to address video memory directly (and doing so is much faster than working through DOS as we have been) then you have to know at which address the video refresh buffer lies. Knowing which display adapter is installed is the hardest part, and the **DispID** procedure described in the previous section answers that question. Each of the nine codes returned by **DispID** has a video refresh buffer address associated with it—but which goes with which? You could use a long and interwoven series of **CMP** and **JE** tests, but that's the hard road, and grossly wasteful of memory and machine cycles. A lookup table is simpler, faster in execution, and much easier to read.

The routine below returns the segment portion of the video refresh buffer address in AX. The display adapter code must be passed to **VidOrg** in AL:

```
; --------------------------------------------------------------------------------
;
;   VidOrg -- Returns origin segment of video buffer
;   Last update 3/8/89
;
;
;   1 entry point:
;
;
;   VidOrg:
;       Caller must pass:
;       AL : Code specifying display adapter type
;       VidOrg returns the buffer origin segment in AX
;
; --------------------------------------------------------------------------------

VidOrg   PROC
         xor    AH,AH         ; Zero AH
         mov    DI,AX         ; Copy AX (with code in AL) into DI
         shl    DI,1          ; Multiply code by 2 to act as word index
         lea    BX,OriginTbl  ; Load address of origin table into BX
         mov    AX,[BX+DI]    ; Index into table using code as index
         ret                  ; Done; go home!
VidOrg   ENDP
```

This works a lot like the lookup table mechanism in **Byte2Str.** There's an important difference, however: each entry in the **OriginTbl** lookup table is *2* bytes in size, whereas each entry in **Digits** was *1* byte in size.

Using Shift Instructions to Multiply by Powers of 2

To use the **Digits** lookup table, we simply used the value to be converted as the index into the table. Because each element in the table was one byte in size, this worked. When table elements are more than one byte long, you have to multiply the index by the number of bytes in each table element or the lookup won't work.

OriginTbl is a good working example. Suppose you get a code 2 back from **DispID,** indicating that you have a CGA in the system. Adding the 2 code to the starting address of the table (as we did with **Digits**) takes us to the start of the second element in the table. Read across to the comment at the right of that second element and see which code it applies to—code 1, the MDA! Not cool. . . .

If you scan down to find the table element associated with the CGA, you'll find that it starts at an offset of *4* from the start of the table. To index into the table correctly, you have to add 4, not 2, to the address of the start of the table. This is where multiplication comes in.

There is a general-purpose multiply instruction in the 8086/8088 CPU, but **MUL** is outrageously slow as machine instructions go. Even in its fastest case (multiplying an 8-bit register by some value), **MUL** takes 77 machine cycles to do its work. Considering that most of the instructions we've discussed complete their jobs in 4 to 10 cycles, that's slow indeed.

There's a better way—in some cases. When you need to multiply a value by some power of 2 (that is, 2, 4, 8, 16, 32, and so on) you can do it by using the shift left instruction, **SHL.** Shifting a value to the left by 1 bit multiplies the value by 2. Shifting a value to the left by 2 bits multiplies the value by 4. Shifting a value to the left by three bits multiplies the value by 8, and so on.

Magic? Not at all. Work it out on paper by expressing a number as a bit pattern (i.e., in binary form), shifting the bit pattern 1 bit to the right, and then converting the binary form back to decimal or hex, like so:

00110101	Binary equivalent of 35H, 53 decimal
← by one bit yields	
01101010	Binary equivalent of 6AH, 106 decimal

Sharp readers may have guessed that shifting to the right *divides* by powers of two, and that's also correct. Shifting right by 1 bit divides by 2; shifting right by 2 bits divides by 4, and so on.

The advantage to multiplying with shift instructions is that it's *fast.* Shifting a byte-sized value in a register to the left by one bit *takes only two machine cycles*—two as opposed to 77 with **MUL.**

As we say, no contest.

Once the index is multiplied by two with **SHL,** the index is added to the starting address of the table, just as with **Digits.** A word-sized **MOV** then copies the correct segment address from the table into AX, for return to the caller.

This illustrates how you can realize enormous speed advantages by structuring your tables properly. Even if it means leaving some wasted space at the end of each element, do your best to make the length of your table elements equal to some power of two. That means making each element 1, 2, 4, 8, 16, 32, or some larger power of 2 in size, but not 3, 7, 12, 20, or 25 bytes in size.

Tables within Tables

Tables are about the handiest means at your disposal for grouping data together and organizing them. Sometimes tables can be as simple as those I've just shown you, which are simply sequences of single values.

In most cases, you'll need something a little more sophisticated. Sometimes you'll need a table of tables, and (surprise!) the 8086/8088 has some built-in machinery to handle such nested tables quickly and easily.

Let's continue on with the issue of video support. In the previous section we looked at a table containing the display buffer addresses for each of the display adapters identified by **DispID.** This is good, but not enough: each adapter has a name, a display buffer address, and a screen size dictated by the size of the current character font. These items comprise a table of information about a display adapter and if you wanted to put together a summary of all that information about all legal display adapters, you'd have to create such a table of tables.

Below is such a two-level table:

```
; ---------------------------------------------------------------------------
;
; DISPLAY ADAPTER INFORMATION LOOKUP TABLE
;
;
; This is the lookup table containing information on all legal
; display adapters. The first field in each element is a 26-
; character string containing a brief description of the
; adapter. The next field is the segment of the video refresh
; buffer. The last three fields are the number of screen lines
; an adapter displays when the 8-pixel, 14-pixel, and 16-pixel
```

```
; fonts are loaded, respectively. Note that not all adapters
; support all fonts, but a screen line count is given for all
; three fonts for all adapter types. Illegal combinations will
; not be accessed.
; ------------------------------------------------------------------------------------

VidInfoTbl  DB      'No adapter identified        '  ; Code 0
            DW      0B000H
            DB      25,25,25
            DB      'Monochrome Display Adapter '  ; Code 1
            DW      0B000H
            DB      25,25,25
            DB      'Color Graphics Adapter       '  ; Code 2
            DW      0B800H
            DB      25,25,25
            DB      'Code 3: Undefined            '  ; Code 3
            DW      0B000H
            DB      25,25,25
            DB      'EGA with color monitor       '  ; Code 4
            DW      0B800H
            DB      43,25,25
            DB      'EGA with mono monitor        '  ; Code 5
            DW      0B000H
            DB      43,25,25
            DB      'Code 6: Undefined            '  ; Code 6
            DW      0B000H
            DB      25,25,25
            DB      'VGA with mono monitor        '  ; Code 7
            DW      0B000H
            DB      50,27,25
            DB      'VGA with color monitor       '  ; Code 8
            DW      0B800H
            DB      50,27,25
            DB      'Code 9: Undefined            '  ; Code 9
            DW      0B000H
            DB      25,25,25
            DB      'MCGA with digital color      '  ; Code 0AH
            DW      0B800H
            DB      25,25,25
            DB      'MCGA with monochrome         '  ; Code 0BH
            DW      0B000H
```

```
DB      25,25,25
DB      'MCGA with analog color        '  ; Code 0CH
DW      0B800H
DB      25,25,25
```

The table consists of twelve subtables, one for each possible code returned by **DispID** as well as a subtable for several undefined codes. Why a subtable for undefined codes? We're going to follow the same general strategy of indexing into the table based on the value of the code. In other words, to get the information for code 4 we have to look at the fifth table (counting from zero), which requires that tables 0 to 4 already exist. Code 3 is undefined, yet something must hold its place in the table for our indexing scheme to work.

For clarity's sake, each subtable occupies three lines. Here's a typical subtable:

```
DB      'EGA with color monitor        '  ; Code 4
DW      0B800H
DB      43,25,25
```

The first line is a quoted string containing the name of the display adapter. The second line is a word-sized address, the segment address of the visible display buffer corresponding to that name. The third line contains three numeric values. These are screen sizes, in lines, relating to the font sizes currently in force. The first value is the number of lines on the screen with the 8-pixel font in force. The second value is the number of lines on the screen with the 14-pixel font in force. The third value is the number of lines on the screen with the 16-pixel font in force. The items stored in the subtables give you just about everything you'd really need to know about a given display adapter to do useful work with it.

When your assembly language programs begin executing, they should inspect such a table and extract the values pertinent to the currently installed display adapter. These extracted values should be ordinary variables in the data segment, easily accessible without further table searching. These variables should be defined together, as a block, with comments explaining how they are related:

```
;------------------------------------------------------------------------------
; DISPLAY INFORMATION VARIABLES
;
; The following block of variables all relate to the video
```

```
; system and are initialized by the VidCheck Procedure:
;----------------------------------------------------------------------------------

DispType     DB     0          ; Code for display adapter type
VidOrigin    DW     0          ; Offset for FAR pointer to refresh buffer
VidSegment   DW     0B000H     ; Segment of installed display buffer
VisibleX     DB     80         ; Number of columns on screen
VisibleY     DB     25         ; Number of lines on screen
VidBufSize   DW     4000       ; Default to 25 X 80 X 2 (char & attribute)
FontSize     DB     8          ; Either 8, 14, or 16; default to 8
BordName     DW     ?          ; NEAR pointer to name string of installed board
; 18H = 24D;  4FH = 79D;  Combined 0-based X, Y of 80 x 25 screen LR corner:
LRXY         DW     184FH
```

As the comments indicate, a single routine named **VidCheck** reads values from the two-level lookup table **VidInfoTbl** and loads those values into the variables shown above.

VidCheck is an interesting creature and it demonstrates the way of dealing with two-level tables.

```
;----------------------------------------------------------------------------------
;   VidCheck -- Identifies display board & display parameters
;   Last update 3/16/89
;   
;   1 entry point:
;   
;   VidCheck:
;     Caller need pass no parameters.
;     VidCheck identifies the installed display board by
;     calling DispID. It then calculates numerous display
;     information values, which it then stores in the block
;     of display information variables in the data segment.
;----------------------------------------------------------------------------------

VidCheck   PROC
           ; First task is to figure out which board is on the bus:
           call   DispID        ; Ask BIOS for adapter code; returns in AL
           mov    DispType,AL   ; Store display adapter code in DispType

           ; Next we determine the font size currently in force:
           cmp    AL,0AH        ; See if board is an MCGA
```

```
            jl    TryOld        ; If less than code 0AH, it's not an MCGA
            mov   FontSize, 16  ; MCGA supports *only* 16 pixel text font
            jmp   GetName       ; Jump ahead to look up adapter name string
TryOld:     cmp   DispType,1    ; Is the display adapter code 1, for MDA?
            jne   TryCGA        ; If not, go test for CGA code 2
            mov   FontSize,14   ; MDA uses *only* 14-pixel text font
            jmp   GetName       ; Jump ahead to look up adapter name string
TryCGA:     cmp   DispType,2    ; Is the display adapter code 2, for CGA?
            jne   TryVGA        ; If not, go test for EGA/VGA font size
            mov   FontSize, 8   ; CGA uses *only* 8-pixel text font
            jmp   GetName       ; Jump ahead to look up adapter name string
TryVGA:     mov   AH,11H        ; Select VIDEO Get Font Information subservice
            mov   AL,30H        ;    requires AH = 11H and AL = 30H
            mov   BH,0          ; 0 = Get info about current font
            int   10H           ; Call VIDEO
            mov   FontSize,CL   ; Font size in pixels is returned in CL

            ; Next we get the name string for the board from the info table:
GetName:    mov   AL,DispType   ; Load display adapter code into AL
            xor   AH,AH         ; Zero AH so we don't copy trash into DI
            mov   DI,AX         ; Copy AX (with code in AL) into DI
            mov   CL,5          ; We must shift the code 5 bits to mult. by 32
            shl   DI,CL         ; Multiply code by 32 to act as table index
            lea   BX,VidInfoTbl ; Load address of info. table into BX
            mov   BordName,BX   ; Save pointer to video info. table in BordName
            add   Bordname,DI   ; Add offset into table to right element

            ; Next we get the refresh buffer segment from the table:
            mov   AX,[BX+DI+27] ; Index into table pass name string to segment
            mov   VidSegment,AX ; Store segment from table to VidSegment variable

            ; Here we calculate the number of lines on-screen from font size:
            xor   AH,AH         ; Make sure AH has no trash in it
            mov   AL,FontSize   ; Load the font size in pixels into AL
            cmp   AL,8          ; Is it the 8-pixel font?
            jne   Try14         ; If not, try the 14-pixel font
            mov   AL,1          ; The 8-pixel font is table offset 1
            jmp   ReadLns       ; Jump ahead to read screen lines from table
Try14:      cmp   AL,14         ; Is it the 14-pixel font?
            jne   Do16          ; If not, it has to be the 16-pixel font
            mov   AL,2          ; The 14-pixel font is table offset 2
```

```
            jmp    ReadLns         ; Jump ahead to read screen lines from table
Do16:       mov    AL,3            ; The 16-pixel font is table offset 3
ReadLns:    add    DI,AX           ; Add font size offset to table element offset
            mov    AL,[BX+DI+28]   ; Load the screen lines value from the table
            mov    VisibleY,AL     ;    and store it in the VisibleY variable
            mov    AH,VisibleX     ; Load the screen columns value to AH
            xchg   AH,AL           ; Exchange AH & AL for 0-basing
            dec    AL              ; Subtract one from column count for 0-basing
            dec    AH              ; Subtract one from line count for zero-basing
            mov    LRXY,AX         ; And store 0-based X,Y word in LRXY variable

; Finally, we calculate the size of the refresh buffer in bytes:
            mov    AL,VisibleY     ; We multiply screen lines time screen columns
            mul    VisibleX        ;    times 2 (for attributes) to get buffer size
            shl    AX,1            ; Multiply lines * columes by 2
            mov    VidBufSize,AX   ; Store refresh buffer size in VidBufSize

            ret                    ; Return to caller
VidCheck    ENDP
```

The first thing **VidCheck** does is call **DispID** to determine the installed display adapter. Build on your own tools—there's no need to duplicate logic if you can avoid it. The adapter ID code is stored in the variable **DispType.**

It's possible to use the table to look up the number of lines on the screen from the current text font size, but to do that you have to determine the font size. Determining the font size is a good exercise in the use of the **CMP** instruction and conditional jumps. Certain adapters support only one font size. The MCGA has only the 16-pixel font. The CGA has only the 8-pixel font. The MDA has only the 14-pixel font. A series of compares and jumps selects a font size based on the display adapter ID code. The trickiness comes in with the EGA and VGA, versatile gentlemen capable of using more than one font. Fortunately, BIOS has a service that reports the size in pixels of the text font currently being used, and this service is used to query the font size. Whatever it turns out to be, the font size is stored in the **FontSize** variable in the data segment.

Based-Indexed-Displacement Memory Addressing

So far, we haven't dealt with the **VidInfoTbl** table at all. This changes when we want to look up the string containing the English-language description of the installed display adapter. There are three general steps to reading *any* two-level lookup table:

1. Derive the offset of the subtable from the beginning of the larger table;
2. Derive the offset of the desired information within the subtable; and
3. Read the information from the subtable.

Each of the subtables is exactly 32 bytes in size. To move from the start of the **VidInfoTbl** to a desired subtable, we multiply the index of the subtable by 32, just as we did in the previous section, in reading one single value from **OriginTbl.** The index here is the display adapter ID code. We multiply the index by 32 by loading it into register DI, and then shifting DI to the left by 5 bits. (Shifting left by 5 bits multiplies the shifted quantity by 32.) We use the form

```
mov CL,5
shl  DI,CL
```

because it is shorter and faster to shift by CL than to shift by using five **SHL DI,1** opcodes in sequence.

Because the display adapter description is the first item in every subtable, no offset into the subtable is necessary. (The offset, if you must think of an offset, is 0.) The shifted quantity in DI is added to the address of the larger table, and the sum becomes a 16-bit pointer to the display adapter description string. This pointer is saved in the **BordName** variable.

At this point within **VidCheck,** we have the address of the **VidInfoTbl** table itself in BX, and the offset of the desired subtable in DI. Now we want to fetch the segment address of the display buffer from the middle of the subtable. The segment address is at some fixed offset from the start of the subtable. I say *fixed* because it never changes, and will be the same regardless of which subtable is selected by the adapter ID code. In the case of the segment address, the offset is 27 because the segment address is 27 bytes from the start of the subtable.

Expressed as a sum, the segment address is at the following offset from the start of **VidInfoTbl:** DI+27. Because BX contains the offset of **VidInfoTbl** from the start of the data segment, we can pin down the segment address in the data segment with this sum: BX+DI +27.

Is there a way to address memory using this three-part sum?

There is indeed, and it is the most complex of the numerous 8086/8088 addressing modes: *based-indexed-displacement addressing,* a term you probably can't memorize and shouldn't try. Specifically to serve two-level lookup tables like this one, the CPU understands **MOV** statements like the following:

```
mov AX,[BX+DI+27]
```

Here, the *base* is the address of the larger table in BX; the *index* is the offset of the subtable within the larger table stored in DI, and the *displacement* is the fixed distance between the start of the subtable and the data that we wish to address.

You can't just use any registers in building a memory address using based-indexed-displacement addressing. The base register may be *only* BP or BX. (Think of general-purpose register BX's hidden agenda as that of *base register;* the B is your memory hook.) The index register may be *only* SI or DI. These registers' names: *source index* and *destination index,* should provide you with their own memory hooks.

Finally, the displacement may not be a register at all, but may be only a literal value like 27 or 14 or 3.

Finding the Number of Lines in the Screen

Reading the screen line count from the subtable is the trickiest part of the whole process. In one sense, the list of three different line count values is a table within a table within a table, but 8086/8088 addressing only goes down two levels. What we must do is point BX and DI plus a displacement to the first of the three values, and then add a second index to DI that selects one of the three line counts.

This second index is placed into AL, which is eventually (as part of AX) added to DI. The line count is read from the table with the following instruction

```
mov AL,[BX+DI+28]
```

with the second index already built into DI.

The rest of **VidCheck** fills a few other video-related variables like **LRXY,** which bundles the *X,Y* position of the lower right corner of the screen into a single 16-bit quantity. The size of the video buffer in bytes is calculated as the *X* size of the screen times the *Y* size of the screen times 2, and stored in **VidBufSize.**

A Program to Report on the Current Display Adapter

To make **VidCheck** show its stuff, I've written a short program called INFO.ASM that reports certain facts about the installed display controller.

As a program, INFO.ASM doesn't present anything we haven't used before, except one: string lengths.

To display a string, you have to tell DOS just how long the string is, in characters. Counting characters is difficult, and if you get it wrong you'll either display too much string or not enough.

The solution is simple: the assembler can do the counting. Here's the notation:

```
VidIDStr  DB    ' The installed video board is: '
LVidIDStr EQU  $-VidIDStr
```

The first statement is nothing more than a simple string constant definition that we've been using all along. The second statement is a new kind of statement, an *equate,* which looks a lot like a data definition but is not.

A data definition sets aside and optionally initializes an area of memory to some value. An equate, by contrast, generates a value similar to a simple constant in languages like Pascal. An equate allocates no memory, but instead generates a value that is stored in the assembler's symbol table. This value can then be used anywhere a literal constant of that type may be used.

Here, we're using an equate to generate a value giving us the length of the string defined immediately before the equate. The expression **$-VidIDStr** resolves to the difference between two addresses: one is the address of the first byte of the string variable **VidIDStr,** and the other is the *current location counter,* the assembler's way of keeping track of the code and data it's generating. When the assembler is generating information (either code or data) inside a segment, it begins with a counter set to zero for the start of the segment. As it works its way through the segment, generating code or allocating data, it increments this value past the generated code or allocated data.

The expression **$-VidIDStr** is evaluated immediately after the string **VidIDStr** is allocated. This means that the assembler's current location counter is pointing to the first byte *after* **VidIDStr.** Because the variable name **VidIDStr** itself resolves to the address of **VidIDStr,** and **$** resolves to the location counter immediately after **VidIDStr** is allocated, **$-VidIDStr** evaluates to the length of **VidIDStr.** Even if you add or delete characters to the contents of **VidIDStr,** the length count will always come out correct because the calculation always subtracts the address of the beginning of the string from the address just past the end of the string.

```
 1   ;---------------------------------------------------------------
 2   ;                          INFO.ASM
 3   ;         Utility to determine and report video system parameters
 4   ;
 5   ;                                    by Jeff Duntemann
 6   ;                                    MASM/TASM
 7   ;                                    Last update 4/16/89
 8   ;
 9   ;
10   ;
11   ;---------------------------------------------------------------
12
13   INCLUDE MYLIB.MAC                  ; Load in macro library
14
15   ;----------------------------|
16   ;    BEGIN STACK SEGMENT      |
17   ;----------------------------|
18   MYSTACK     SEGMENT STACK         ; STACK word ensures loading of SS by DOS
19
20               DB        64 DUP ('STACK!!!') ; This reserves 512 bytes for the stack
21
22   MYSTACK     ENDS
23   ;----------------------------|
24   ;    END STACK SEGMENT        |
25   ;----------------------------|
26
27   ;----------------------------|
28   ;    BEGIN DATA SEGMENT       |
29   ;----------------------------|
30   MyData      SEGMENT
31
32   ;---------------------------------------------------------------
33   ; DISPLAY INFORMATION VARIABLES
34   ;
35   ; The following block of variables all relate to the video
36   ; system and are initialized by the VidCheck procedure:
37   ;---------------------------------------------------------------
38   DispType    DB     0        ; Code for display adapter type
39   VidOrigin   DW     0        ; Offset for FAR pointer to refresh buffer
40   VidSegment  DW     0B000H   ; Segment of installed display buffer
41   VisibleX    DB     80       ; Number of columns on screen
42   VisibleY    DB     25       ; Number of lines on screen
43   VidBufSize  DW     4000     ; Default to 25 X 80 X 2 (char & attribute)
44   FontSize    DB     8        ; Either 8, 14, or 16; default to 8
45   BordName    DW     ?        ; NEAR pointer to name string of installed board
46   ; 18H = 24D; 4FH = 79D; Combined 0-based X,Y of 80 x 25 screen LR corner:
47   LRXY        DW     184FH
48
49   ;---------------------------------------------------------------
50   ; DISPLAY ADAPTER INFORMATION LOOKUP TABLE
51   ;
52   ; This is the lookup table containing information on all legal
53   ; display adapters.  The first field in each element is a 26-
54   ; character string containing a brief description of the
```

```
55    ; adapter.  The next field is the segment of the video refresh
56    ; buffer.  The last three fields are the number of screen lines
57    ; an adapter displays when the 8-pixel, 14-pixel, and 16-pixel
58    ; fonts are loaded, respectively.  Note that not all adapters
59    ; support all fonts, but a screen line count is given for all
60    ; three fonts for all adapter types.  Illegal combinations will
61    ; not be accessed.
62    ;-------------------------------------------------------------
63    VidInfoTbl DB      'No adapter identified     '    ; Code 0
64            DW      0B000H
65            DB      25,25,25
66            DB      'Monochrome Display Adapter '    ; Code 1
67            DW      0B000H
68            DB      25,25,25
69            DB      'Color Graphics Adapter     '    ; Code 2
70            DW      0B800H
71            DB      25,25,25
72            DB      'Code 3: Undefined          '    ; Code 3
73            DW      0B000H
74            DB      25,25,25
75            DB      'EGA with color monitor     '    ; Code 4
76            DW      0B800H
77            DB      43,25,25
78            DB      'EGA with mono monitor      '    ; Code 5
79            DW      0B000H
80            DB      43,25,25
81            DB      'Code 6: Undefined          '    ; Code 6
82            DW      0B000H
83            DB      25,25,25
84            DB      'VGA with mono monitor      '    ; Code 7
85            DW      0B000H
86            DB      50,27,25
87            DB      'VGA with color monitor     '    ; Code 8
88            DW      0B800H
89            DB      50,27,25
90            DB      'Code 9: Undefined          '    ; Code 9
91            DW      0B000H
92            DB      25,25,25
93            DB      'MCGA with digital color    '    ; Code 0AH
94            DW      0B800H
95            DB      25,25,25
96            DB      'MCGA with monochrome       '    ; Code 0BH
97            DW      0B000H
98            DB      25,25,25
99            DB      'MCGA with analog color     '    ; Code 0CH
100           DW      0B800H
101           DB      25,25,25
102
103   Digits    DB      '0123456789ABCDEF' ; Lookup table for numeric/string conv.
104
105   ;-------------------------------------------------------------
106   ; These two variables are screen-clear "atoms" useable by the
107   ; Clear macro.  The high byte is the display attribute, while
108   ; the low byte is the character with which Clear fills the
109   ; video refresh buffer to clear the screen.
110   ;-------------------------------------------------------------
111   HToneAtom DW      07B0H            ; Clears screen to halftone pattern
112   ClearAtom DW      0720H            ; Clears screen to blanks
113
114   ;-------------------------------------------------------------
115   ; This is where all predefined string variables are stored.
116   ;-------------------------------------------------------------
```

```
117   CRLF       DB       0DH,0AH        ; Newline string
118   IDString   DB       '>>>INFO V1.0'
119   LIDString  EQU      $-IDString
120   AuthorStr  DB       '   by Jeff Duntemann'
121   LAuthorStr EQU      $-AuthorStr
122   VidIDStr   DB       '   The installed video board is: '
123   LVidIDStr  EQU      $-VidIDStr
124   OrgIDStr   DB       '   The segment of the video refresh buffer is: '
125   LOrgIDStr  EQU      $-OrgIDStr
126   FontSzStr  DB       '   The size of the current text font is: '
127   LFontSzStr EQU      $-FontSzStr
128   ScrnLnStr  DB       '   The number of lines currently on the screen is: '
129   LScrnLnStr EQU      $-ScrnLnStr
130   BufSizStr  DB       '   The size of the refresh buffer in bytes is: '
131   LBufSizStr EQU      $-BufSizStr
132   DigitStr   DB       '     '
133   LDigitStr  EQU      $-DigitStr
134
135   MyData     ENDS
136   ;--------------------------|
137   ;     END DATA SEGMENT     |
138   ;--------------------------|
139
140   ;--------------------------|
141   ;     BEGIN CODE SEGMENT   |
142   ;--------------------------|
143   MyProg     SEGMENT
144
145   Main       PROC
146              ASSUME CS:MyProg,DS:MyData
147
148   Start:     ; This is where program execution begins:
149              mov  AX,MyData     ; Set up our own data segment address in DS
150              mov  DS,AX         ; Can't load segment reg. directly from memory
151
152              call VidCheck      ; Initialize all video information variables
153
154              Clear VidOrigin,ClearAtom,VidBufSize  ; Clear the screen
155
156              ; Here we display the name of the program and its author:
157              Writeln IDString,LIDString       ; Display the program name
158              Writeln AuthorStr,LAuthorStr     ; display the author name
159              Newline
160
161              ; Here we display the name of the installed video board:
162              Write VidIDStr,LVidIDStr         ; Display the intro string
163              mov  BX,1          ; Select DOS file handle 1: Standard Output
164              mov  CX,27         ; The name strings are 27 bytes long
165              mov  DX,BordName   ; The string address is stored in BordName
166              mov  AH,40H        ; Service 40H: Write string to file
167              int  21H           ; Call DOS to display to Standard Output
168              Newline
169
170              ; Here we display the segment address of the refresh buffer:
171              Write OrgIDStr,LOrgIDStr         ; Display the intro string
172              mov  AX,VidSegment ; AX gets the value to convert to a string
173              lea  SI,DigitStr   ; String equivalent is written to DigitStr
174              call Word2Str      ; Do the actual string conversion
175              PokeChar DigitStr,'H',4  ; Append 'H' on the end of the string
176              Writeln DigitStr,5 ;  and display the string equivalent
177
178              ; Here we display the size of the current text font:
```

```
179                   Write FontSzStr,LFontSzStr    ; Display the intro string
180                   mov  AL,FontSize   ; AL gets the value to convert to a string
181                   lea  SI,DigitStr   ; String equivalent is written to DigitStr
182                   call Byte2Str      ; Do the actual string conversion
183                   PokeChar DigitStr,'H',2  ; Append 'H' on the end of the string
184                   Writeln DigitStr,3 ;  and display the string equivalent
185
186                   ; Here we display the number of lines on the screen:
187                   Write ScrnLnStr,LScrnLnStr
188                   mov  AL,VisibleY   ; AL gets the value to convert to a string
189                   lea  SI,DigitStr   ; String equivalent is written to DigitStr
190                   call Byte2Str      ; Do the actual string conversion
191                   PokeChar DigitStr,'H',2   ; Append 'H' on the end of the string
192                   Writeln DigitStr,3 ;  and display the string equivalent
193
194                   ;Finally, we display the size of the video refresh buffer:
195                   Write BufSizStr,LBufSizStr    ; Display the intro string
196                   mov  AX,VidBufSize ; AX gets the value to convert to a string
197                   lea  SI,DigitStr   ; String equivalent is written to DigitStr
198                   call Word2Str      ; Do the actual string conversion
199                   PokeChar DigitStr,'H',4   ; Append 'H' on the end of the string
200                   Writeln DigitStr,5 ;  and display the string equivalent
201                   Newline
202
203                   mov  AH,4CH        ; Terminate process DOS service
204                   mov  AL,0          ; Pass this value back to ERRORLEVEL
205                   int  21H           ; Control returns to DOS
206
207     Main      ENDP
208
209
210     ;----------------------------------------------------------------
211     ;   Byte2Str  --   Converts a byte passed in AL to a string at
212     ;                  DS:SI
213     ;   Last update 3/8/89
214     ;
215     ;   1 entry point:
216     ;
217     ;   Byte2Str:
218     ;      Caller must pass:
219     ;      AL : Byte to be converted
220     ;      DS : Segment of destination string
221     ;      SI : Offset of destination string
222     ;
223     ;      This routine converts 8-bit values to 2-digit hexadecimal
224     ;      string representations at DS:SI.
225     ;----------------------------------------------------------------
226
227     Byte2Str  PROC
228                   mov  DI,AX                  ; Duplicate byte in DI
229                   and  DI,000FH               ; Mask out high 12 bits of DI
230                   mov  BX,OFFSET Digits       ; Load offset of Digits into DI
231                   mov  AH,BYTE PTR [BX+DI]     ; Load digit from table into AH
232                   mov  [SI+1],AH              ;    and store digit into string
233                   xor  AH,AH                  ; Zero out AH
234                   mov  DI,AX                  ; And move byte into DI
235                   shr  DI,1                   ; Shift high nybble of byte to
236                   shr  DI,1                   ;    low nybble
237                   shr  DI,1
238                   shr  DI,1
239                   mov  AH,BYTE PTR [BX+DI]     ; Load digit from table into AH
240                   mov  [SI],AH                ;    and store digit into string
```

```
241                 ret                             ; We're done--go home!
242      Byte2Str   ENDP
243
244
245      ;----------------------------------------------------------------
246      ;   Word2Str  --  Converts a word passed in AX to a string at
247      ;                         DS:SI
248      ;   Last update 3/8/89
249      ;
250      ;   1 entry point:
251      ;
252      ;   Word2Str:
253      ;      Caller must pass:
254      ;      AX : Word to be converted
255      ;      DS : Segment of destination string
256      ;      SI : Offset of destination string
257      ;----------------------------------------------------------------
258
259      Word2Str   PROC
260                 mov  CX,AX       ; Save a copy of convertee in CX
261                 xchg AH,AL       ; Swap high and low AX bytes to do high first
262                 call Byte2Str    ; Convert AL to string at DS:SI
263                 add  SI,2        ; Bump SI to point to second 2 characters
264                 mov  AX,CX       ; Reload convertee into AX
265                 call Byte2Str    ; Convert AL to string at DS:SI
266                 ret              ; And we're done!
267      Word2Str   ENDP
268
269
270      ;----------------------------------------------------------------
271      ;   VidCheck  --  Identifies display board & display parameters
272      ;   Last update 3/16/89
273      ;
274      ;   1 entry point:
275      ;
276      ;   VidCheck:
277      ;      Caller need pass no parameters.
278      ;      VidCheck identifies the installed display board by
279      ;      calling DispID.  It then calculates numerous display
280      ;      information values, which it then stores in the block
281      ;      of display information variables in the data segment.
282      ;----------------------------------------------------------------
283
284      VidCheck   PROC
285                 ; First task is to figure out which board is on the bus:
286                 call DispID       ; Ask BIOS for adapter code; returns in AL
287                 mov  DispType,AL  ; Store display adapter code in DispType
288
289                 ; Next we determine the font size currently in force:
290                 cmp  AL,0AH       ; See if board is an MCGA
291                 jl   TryOld       ; If less than code 0AH, it's not an MCGA
292                 mov  FontSize,16  ; MCGA supports *only* 16 pixel text font
293                 jmp  GetName      ; Jump ahead to look up adapter name string
294      TryOld:    cmp  DispType,1   ; Is the display adapter code 1, for MDA?
295                 jne  TryCGA       ; If not, go test for CGA code 2
296                 mov  FontSize,14  ; MDA uses *only* 14-pixel text font
297                 jmp  GetName      ; Jump ahead to look up adapter name string
298      TryCGA:    cmp  DispType,2   ; Is the display adapter code 2, for CGA?
299                 jne  TryVGA       ; If not, go test for EGA/VGA font size
300                 mov  FontSize,8   ; CGA uses *only* 8-pixel text font
301                 jmp  GetName      ; Jump ahead to look up adapter name string
302      TryVGA:    mov  AH,11H       ; Select VIDEO Get Font Information subservice
```

```
303              mov   AL,30H         ;   requires AH = 11H and AL = 30H
304              mov   BH,0           ; 0 = Get info about current font
305              int   10H            ; Call VIDEO
306              mov   FontSize,CL     ; Font size in pixels is returned in CL
307
308              ; Next we get the name string for the board from the info table:
309   GetName:   mov   AL,DispType     ; Load display adapter code into AL
310              xor   AH,AH          ; Zero AH so we don't copy trash into DI
311              mov   DI,AX          ; Copy AX (with code in AL) into DI
312              mov   CL,5           ; We must shift the code 5 bits to mult. by 32
313              shl   DI,CL          ; Multiply code by 32 to act as table index
314              lea   BX,VidInfoTbl  ; Load address of info. table into BX
315              mov   BordName,BX    ; Save pointer to video info. table in BordName
316              add   Bordname,DI    ; Add offset into table to right element
317
318              ; Next we get the refresh buffer segment from the table:
319              mov   AX,[BX+DI+27]  ; Index into table past name string to segment
320              mov   VidSegment,AX  ; Store segment from table to VidSegment variable
321
322              ; Here we calculate the number of lines on-screen from font size:
323              xor   AH,AH          ; Make sure AH has no trash in it
324              mov   AL,FontSize     ; Load the font size in pixels into AL
325              cmp   AL,8           ; Is it the 8-pixel font?
326              jne   Try14          ; If not, try the 14-pixel font
327              mov   AL,1           ; The 8-pixel font is table offset 1
328              jmp   ReadLns        ; Jump ahead to read screen lines from table
329   Try14:     cmp   AL,14          ; Is it the 14-pixel font?
330              jne   Do16           ; If not, it has to be the 16-pixel font
331              mov   AL,2           ; The 14-pixel font is table offset 2
332              jmp   ReadLns        ; Jump ahead to read screen lines from table
333   Do16:      mov   AL,3           ; The 16-pixel font is table offset 3
334   ReadLns:   add   DI,AX          ; Add font size offset to table element offset
335              mov   AL,[BX+DI+28]  ; Load the screen lines value from the table
336              mov   VisibleY,AL    ;  and store it in the VisibleY variable
337              mov   AH,VisibleX    ; Load the screen columns value to AH
338              xchg  AH,AL          ; Exchange AH & AL for 0-basing
339              dec   AL             ; Subtract one from column count for 0-basing
340              dec   AH             ; Subtract one from line count for zero-basing
341              mov   LRXY,AX        ; And store 0-based X,Y word into LRXY variable
342
343              ; Finally, we calculate the size of the refresh buffer in bytes:
344              mov   AL,VisibleY     ; We multiply screen lines time screen columns
345              mul   VisibleX       ;  times 2 (for attributes) to get buffer size
346              shl   AX,1           ; Multiply lines * columns by 2
347              mov   VidBufSize,AX  ; Store refresh buffer size in VidBufSize
348
349              ret                  ; Return to caller
350   VidCheck   ENDP
351
352
353   ;--------------------------------------------------------------
354   ;   DispID  --   Identifies the installed display adapter
355   ;   Last update 3/8/89
356   ;
357   ;   1 entry point:
358   ;
359   ;   DispID:
360   ;       Caller passes no parameters
361   ;       Routine returns a code value in AX.
362   ;       The codes are these:
363   ;       0 : Adapter is unknown; recommend aborting
364   ;       1 : MDA (Monochrome Display Adapter)
```

```
365   ;      2 : CGA (Color Graphics Adapter)
366   ;      4 : EGA/color
367   ;      5 : EGA/monochrome
368   ;      7 : VGA/mono
369   ;      8 : VGA/color
370   ;     0A : MCGA/digital color
371   ;     0B : MCGA/mono
372   ;     0C : MCGA/analog color
373   ;--------------------------------------------------------------
374
375   DispID    PROC
376             mov  AH,1AH       ; Select PS/2 Identify Adapter Service
377             xor  AL,AL        ; Select Get Combination Code Subservice (AL=0)
378             int  10H          ; Call VIDEO
379             cmp  AL,1AH       ; If AL comes back with 1AH, we have a PS/2
380             jne  TryEGA       ; If not, jump down to test for the EGA
381             mov  AL,BL        ; Put Combination Code into AL
382             ret               ;    and go home!
383   TryEGA:   mov  AH,12H       ; Select EGA Alternate Function
384             mov  BX,10H       ; Select Get Configuration Information subservice
385             int  10H          ; Call VIDEO
386             cmp  BX,10H       ; If BX comes back unchanged, EGA is *not* there
387             je   OldBords     ; Go see whether it's an MDA or CGA
388             cmp  BH,0         ; If BH = 0, it's an EGA/color combo
389             je   EGAColor     ;    otherwise it's EGA/mono
390             mov  AL,5         ; Store code 5 for EGA mono
391             ret               ;    and go home!
392   EGAColor: mov  AL,4         ; Store code 4 for EGA color
393             ret               ;    and go home!
394   OldBords: int  11H          ; Call Equipment Configuration interrupt
395             and  AL,30H       ; Mask out all but bits 4 & 5
396             cmp  AL,30H       ; If bits 4 & 5 are both =1, it's an MDA
397             jne  CGA          ;    otherwise it's a CGA
398             mov  AL,1         ; Store code 1 for MDA
399             ret               ;    and go home!
400   CGA:      mov  AL,2         ; Store code 2 for CGA
401             ret               ;    and go home!
402   DispID    ENDP
403
404
405   MyProg    ENDS
406
407   ;---------------------------|
408   ;     END CODE SEGMENT      |
409   ;---------------------------|
410
411             END Start    ; The procedure named Start becomes the main program
```

Machine-Gunning the Screen with REP STOSW

Most people, having learned a little assembly language, grumble about the seemingly huge number of instructions it takes to do anything useful. By and large, this is a legitimate gripe—and the major reason there are languages like Turbo Pascal and Microsoft BASIC.

The 8086/8088 instruction set, on the other hand, is full of surprises, and before I put the wrapper on this book I wanted to show you one more of them.

There is a class of instructions I haven't touched on yet, the *string instructions,* so called because they alone of all the instructions in the 8086/8088 instruction set have the power to deal with long sequences of bytes or words at one time. (In assembly language, any contiguous sequence of bytes or words in memory can be considered a string.) The string instructions as a group are complicated and subtle and I don't have the room in this very elementary book to explain them as they would have to be explained to beginners.

We do have enough room left to deal with the simplest string instruction, **STOSW.** Simply put, **STOSW** is a software machine gun that can blast a single word value into as many as 32,767 locations in memory *with a single instruction.*

Good trick? You bet. Useful, too . . . so let's consider the problem of clearing a video refresh buffer.

The **ClrScr** procedure we discussed earlier relied on BIOS to handle the actual clearing of the screen. BIOS is very much a black box, and we're not expected to know how it works. (IBM would rather we didn't, in fact.) The trouble with BIOS is that it only knows how to clear the screen to blanks. Some programs (Ashton-Tate's *Framework* comes to mind) give themselves a stylish, sculpted look by clearing the screen to one of the PC's halftone characters, which are character codes 176 to 178. BIOS can't do this. If you want the halftone look, you'll have to do it yourself. It doesn't involve anything more complex than replicating a single word value into every position in your video refresh buffer.

Such things should always be done in tight loops. The obvious way is to put the refresh buffer segment into the extra segment register ES, the refresh buffer offset into DI, the number of words in your refresh buffer into CX, the word value to clear the buffer into AX, and then code up a tight loop this way:

```
Clear:  mov  ES:[DI],AX  ; Copy AX to ES:DI
        inc  DI          ; Bump DI to next *word* in buffer
        inc  DI
        dec  CX          ; Decrement CX by one position
        jnz  Clear       ; And loop again until CX is 0
```

This will work. It's even tolerably fast. But *all* of the above code is equivalent to this one single instruction:

```
rep stosw
```

Really.

There's two parts to this instruction, actually. **REP** is a new type of critter, called a *prefix*. We'll get back to it. Right now let's look at **STOSW.** The mnemonic means **STO**re **S**tring by **W**ord. Like all the string instructions, **STOSW** is more complicated than most instructions. It expects certain registers be set up in certain ways with certain values before it's executed. To wit:

1. ES must be loaded with the segment address of the string into which data will be stored.
2. DI must be loaded with the offset address of the string into which data will be stored.
3. CX must be loaded with the number of times the copy of AX is to be stored into the string. Note that this does *not* mean the size of the string in bytes!
4. AX must be loaded with the word value to be stored into the string.

Once you set up these four registers, you can safely execute a **STOSW** instruction. When you do, this is what happens:

1. The word value in AX is copied to the word at ES:DI.
2. DI is incremented by 2, to point to the next word in memory.
3. CX is decremented by 1.

Note that we're not machine-gunning here. *One* copy of AX gets copied to *one* word in memory. The DI and CX registers are adjusted so that they'll be ready for the next time **STOSW** is executed.

However, if you like, you can execute other instructions before executing another **STOSW.** As long as you don't disturb ES, DI, or CX, you can do whatever you wish. Then when you execute **STOSW** again, another copy of AX will go out to the location pointed to by ES:DI, and DI and CX will be adjusted yet again. Note that you can change AX if you like, but the changed value will be copied into memory. (You may want to do that—there's no law saying you have to fill a string with only one single value.)

However, this is like the difference between a semiautomatic weapon (which fires one round every time you press and release the trigger) and a fully automatic weapon, which fires rounds continually as long as you hold the trigger down. To make **STOSW** fully automatic, just hang the **REP** prefix ahead of it. What **REP** does is beautifully simple: it sets up the tightest of all tight loops completely *inside* the CPU, and fires copies of AX into memory repeatedly (hence its name), incrementing DI by 2 each time and decrementing CX by 1, until CX is decremented down to 0. Then it stops, and amidst the smoke you'll see that your whole string, however large, has been filled with copies of AX.

Man, now *that's* programming!

The following macro sets up and triggers **REP STOSW** to clear the video refresh buffer. **Clear** was designed to be used with the block of video information variables initialized by the **VidCheck** procedure I described earlier in this section. It needs to be passed a FAR pointer to the video refresh buffer, the word value to be blasted into the buffer, and the size of the buffer in bytes.

```
;---------------------------------------------------------------------------
;  CLEAR  --  Clears the entire visible screen buffer
;  Last update 3/16/89
;
;    Caller must pass:
;    In VidAddress:   A FAR pointer in the video refresh buffer
;    In ClearAtom:    A word containing the video attribute to be
;                     used in the high byte, and the fill character
;                     to be used in the low byte.
;    In BufLength:    The size of the refresh buffer in bytes
;    Action:     Blasts copes of ClearAtom into the refresh buffer
;                until the buffer is filled.
;
;---------------------------------------------------------------------------

Clear   MACRO   VidAddress,ClearAtom,BufLength
        les     DI,DWORD PTR VidAddress   ; Load ES and DI from FAR pointer
        mov     AX,ClearAtom    ; Load AX with word to blast into memory
        mov     CX,BufLength    ; Load CX with length of buffer in bytes
        shr     CX,1            ; Divide size of buffer by 2 for word count
        rep     stosw           ; Blast away!
        GotoXy  0,0             ; Move hardware cursor to UL corner of screen
        ENDM
```

Building Your Video Toolkit

Video is important—it's the fundamental way your programs communicate with their users. *Fast* video is essential, and BIOS-based video fails in that regard. The **Clear** macro is a good example of just how fast a video routine can be made with solid knowledge of assembly language.

You have the fundamentals of a really good and extremely fast toolkit of video routines for your assembly language programs. Now that we're at the end of this book, it's up to you to fill that toolkit out, and in the process demonstrate that you're ready to strike off on your own.

Here's a list of some of the new routines you should design and perfect for your video toolkit:

♦ **WriteFast** A routine to move a string of characters from your data segment to the visible display buffer. You can do this easily using the instructions we've discussed. A suggestion: research the **LOOP** instruction for an easy time of it, or the **MOVSW** instruction for a trickier—but much faster—routine.

♦ **WritelnFast** Like **WriteFast,** but move the hardware cursor to the beginning of the following line after the write. If the write is to the bottom line on the screen, scroll the screen.

♦ **WriteDown** A routine to move a string of characters from the data segment to the visible display buffer, only *vertically.* This is useful for displaying boxes for menus and other screen forms, using the PC's line drawing characters.

♦ **DrawBox** using **WriteFast** and **WriteDown,** create a routine that draws a box on the screen. Allow the programmer to specify whether it is made of single or double line-drawing characters.

♦ **GetString** A delimited field-entry routine. Delineate a field somehow, by highlighting the background or framing a portion of a line with vertical bar characters, and allow the user to move the cursor and enter characters within the bounds of the field. When the user presses Enter, return the entered characters to a buffer somewhere in the data segment. This is ambitious and might require seventy of eighty instructions, but it's likely to be a lot of fun.

Getting your video tools in order will allow you to move on to other, more involved subjects like file I/O and interface to the serial and parallel ports. *Real* assembly language programs require all these things, and you should strive to create them as small, easily read and understood toolkit-style procedures and macros. Create them so that they call one another rather than duplicating a function—assembly language is difficult enough without creating routines that do the same old things over and over again.

Conclusion
Not the End, but Only the Beginning

You never really *learn* assembly language.

You can improve your skills over time by reading good books on the subject, by reading good code that others have written, and most of all, by writing lots and lots of code yourself. But at no point will you be able to stand up and say, I *know* it.

You shouldn't feel bad about this. In fact, I take some encouragement from occasionally hearing that Michael Abrash, author of *Zen of Assembly Language,* has learned something new about assembly language. Michael has been writing high-performance assembler code for about six years, and has evolved into one of the five or six best assembly language programmers in the Western Hemisphere.

If Michael is still learning, is there hope for the rest of us?

Wrong question. *Silly* question. If Michael is still learning, it means that *all* of us are students and will always be students. It means that the journey is the goal, and as long as we continue to probe and hack and fiddle and try things we never tried before, that over time we will advance the state of the art, and create programs that would have made the pioneers in our field catch their breath in 1977.

For the point is not to conquer the subject, but to live with it, and grow with your knowledge of it. Remember, the journey *is* the goal, and with this book I've tried hard to help those people who have been frozen with fear at the thought of starting the journey, staring at the complexity of it all and wondering where the first brick in that Yellow Brick Road might be.

It's *here,* Square One, with nothing more than the conviction that you can do it.

I got out of school in recession year 1974 with a B.A. in English, Summa Cum Laude, and not much in reliable prospects outside of driving a cab. I finessed my way into a job with the Xerox Corporation, repairing copy machines. Books were fun, but paperwork makes money—so I picked up a toolbag and had a fine old time for several years before finessing my way into a computer programming position.

But I'll never forget that first awful moment, when I looked over the shoulder of an accomplished technician at a model 660 copier with its panels off, to see what looked like a bottomless pit of little cams and gears and drums and sprocket chains turning and flipping and knocking switch actuators back and forth. Mesmermized by the complexity, I forgot to notice that a sheet of paper had been fed through the machine and turned into a copy of the original document. I was terrified of never learning what all the little cams did, and missed the comforting simplicity of the Big Picture—that a copy machine makes copies.

That's Square One—discover the Big Picture. Ignore the cams and gears for a bit; you can do it. Find out what's important in holding the Big Picture together (ask someone if it's not obvious) and study that before getting down to the cams and gears. Locate the processes that happen. Divide the Big Picture into subpictures. See how things flow. Only then should you focus on something as small and as lost in the mess as an individual cam or switch.

That's how you conquer complexity, and that's how I've presented assembly language in this book. Some might say I've shorted the instruction set, but covering the instruction set was never the real goal here.

The real goal was to conquer your fear of the complexity of the subject, with some metaphors and some pictures and some funny stories to bleed the tension away.

Did it work? You tell me. I'd really like to know.

Where to Now?

If you've followed me so far, you've probably lost your fear of assembly language, picked up some skills and a good part of the instruction set, and are ready to move on. I'd recommend you pick up the next book in this series, *Assembly Language Magic,* by Bill Murray and Chris Pappas. They cover the instructions I've skirted, and techniques that are way too advanced for a book like this. You've taken your first steps; Bill and Chris will keep you on the road.

While you're reading *Assembly Language Magic,* strike out on your own a little. Set yourself a goal, and try to achieve it: something *tough*—say, an assembly language utility that locates all files anywhere on a hard disk drive with a given ambiguous file name. That's ambitious, and will take some research and study and (perhaps) a few false starts. But you can do it, and once you do it you'll be a real journeyman assembly language programmer.

Becoming a master takes work and time. Michael Abrash's two-volume *Zen of Assembly Language* is a compilation of the "secret" knowledge of a programming master. Those two fat volumes are not easy reading, but they will give you a good idea where your mind has to be to consider yourself an expert assembly language programmer.

Keep programming. Michael can show you things that would have taken you years to discover on your own, but they won't stick in your mind unless you *use* them. Set yourself a real challenge, something that has to be both correct and *fast:* rotate graphic objects in 3-D, transfer data through a serial port at 19,200 bits per second, things like that.

You can do it.

Coming to believe the truth in that statement is the essence of stepping away from Square One.

Appendix A

Partial 8086/8088 Instruction Set Reference

Notes on the Instruction Set Reference

Instruction Operands

When an instruction takes two operands, the destination operand is the one on the *left*, and the source operand is the one on the *right*. In general, when a result is produced by an instruction, the result replaces the destination operand. For example, in this instruction:

    ADD BX,SI

the BX register is added to the SI register, and the sum is then placed in the BX register, overwriting whatever was in BX before the addition.

Flag Results

Each instruction contains a flag summary that looks like this (the asterisks will vary from instruction to instruction):

O D I T S Z A P C	OF: Overflow flag	TF: Trap flag	AF: Aux carry
F F F F F F F F F	DF: Direction flag	SF: Sign flag	PF: Parity flag
* * * * * *	IF: Interrupt flag	ZF: Zero flag	CF: Carry flag

The nine flags are all represented here. An asterisk indicates that the instruction on that page affects that flag. If a flag is affected at all (that is, if it has an asterisk beneath it) it will be affected according to these rules:

OF: Set if the result is too large to fit in the destination operand.

DF: Set by the STD instruction; cleared by CLD.

IF: Set by the STI instruction; cleared by CLI.

TF: For debuggers; not used in normal programming and may be ignored.

SF: Set when the sign of the result forces the destination operand to become negative.

ZF: Set if the result of an operation is zero. If the result is non-zero, ZF is cleared.

AF: "Auxiliary carry" used for 4-bit BCD math. Set when an operation causes a carry out of a 4-bit BCD quantity.

PF: Set if the number of 1 bits in the low byte of the result is even, cleared if the number of 1 bits in the low byte of the result is odd. Used in data communications applications but little else.

CF: Set if the result of an add or shift operation "carries out" a bit beyond the destination operand; otherwise cleared. May be manually set by STC and manually cleared by CLC when CF must be in a known state before an operation begins.

Some instructions force certain flags to become undefined. When this is the case, it will be noted under *Notes*. *Undefined* means *don't count on it being in any particular state.*

ADC Arithmetic Addition with Carry

Flags Affected

O	D	I	T	S	Z	A	P	C
F	F	F	F	F	F	F	F	F
*				*	*	*	*	*

OF: Overflow flag   TF: Trap flag   AF: Aux carry
DF: Direction flag   SF: Sign flag   PF: Parity flag
IF: Interrupt flag   ZF: Zero flag   CF: Carry flag

Legal Forms

ADC r8,r8	ADC m8,i8
ADC m8,r8	ADC r16,i16
ADC r8,m8	ADC m16,i16
ADC r16,r16	ADC r16,i8
ADC m16,r16	ADC m16,i8
ADC r16,m16	ADC AL,i8
ADC r8,i8	ADC AX,i16

Examples

```
ADC BX,DI
ADC AX,OFFFFH                    ;Uses single-byte opcode
ADC AL,42H                       ;Uses single-byte opcode
ADC BP,17H
ADC WORD PTR [BX+SI+Inset],5
ADC WORD PTR ES:[BX],0B800H
```

Notes

ADC adds the source operand and the carry flag to the destination operand, and after the operation the result replaces the destination operand. The add is an arithmetic add, and the carry allows multiple precision additions across several registers or memory locations. (To add without taking the carry flag into account, use the ADD instruction. All affected flags are set according to the operation. Most important, if the result does not fit into the destination operand, the carry flag is set to 1.

r8 = AL AH BL BH CL CH DL DH	r16 = AX BX CX DX BP SP SI DI
sr = CS DS SS ES	
m8 = 8-bit memory data	m16 = 16-bit memory data
i8 = 8-bit immediate data	i16 = 16-bit immediate data
d8 = 8-bit signed displacement	d16 = 16-bit signed displacement

ADD   Arithmetic Addition

Flags Affected

O	D	I	T	S	Z	A	P	C
F	F	F	F	F	F	F	F	F
*				*	*	*	*	*

OF: Overflow flag   TF: Trap flag   AF: Aux carry
DF: Direction flag   SF: Sign flag   PF: Parity flag
IF: Interrupt flag   ZF: Zero flag   CF: Carry flag

Legal Forms

ADD r8,r8	ADD m8,i8
ADD m8,r8	ADD r16,i16
ADD r8,m8	ADD m16,i16
ADD r16,r16	ADD r16,i8
ADD m16,r16	ADD m16,i8
ADD r16,m16	ADD AL,i8
ADD r8,i8	ADD AX,i16

Examples

```
ADD BX,DI
ADD AX,OFFFFH              ;Uses single-byte opcode
ADD AL,42H                 ;Uses single-byte opcode
ADD BP,17H
ADD WORD PTR [BX+SI+Inset],5
ADD WORD PTR ES:[BX],0B800H
```

Notes

ADD adds the source operand to the destination operand, and after the operation the result replaces the destination operand. The add is an arithmetic add, and does *not* take the carry flag into account. (To add using the carry flag, use the ADC [add with carry] instruction.) All affected flags are set according to the operation. Most importantly, if the result does not fit into the destination operand, the carry flag is set to 1.

r8 = AL AH BL BH CL CH DL DH	r16 = AX BX CX DX BP SP SI DI
sr = CS DS SS ES	
m8 = 8-bit memory data	m16 = 16-bit memory data
i8 = 8-bit immediate data	i16 = 16-bit immediate data
d8 = 8-bit signed displacement	d16 = 16-bit signed displacement

AND   Logical AND

Flags Affected

O	D	I	T	S	Z	A	P	C
F	F	F	F	F	F	F	F	F
*				*	*	*	*	*

OF: Overflow flag   TF: Trap flag   AF: Aux carry
DF: Direction flag   SF: Sign flag   PF: Parity flag
IF: Interrupt flag   ZF: Zero flag   CF: Carry flag

Legal Forms

AND r8,r8	AND r8,i8
AND m8,r8	AND m8,i8
AND r8,m8	AND r16,i16
AND r16,r16	AND m16,i16
AND m16,r16	AND AL,i8
AND r16,m16	AND AX,i16

Examples

```
AND  BX,DI
AND  AX,OFFFFH           ;Uses single-byte opcode
AND  AL,42H              ;Uses single-byte opcode
AND  ES:[BX],0B800H
AND  [BP+SI],DX
```

Notes

AND performs the AND logical operation on its two operands. Once the operation is complete, the result replaces the destination operand. AND is performed on a bit-by-bit basis, such that bit 0 of the source is ANDed with bit 0 of the destination, bit 1 of the source is ANDed with bit 1 of the destination, and so on. The AND operation yields a 1 if *both* of the operands are 1, and a 0 only if *either* operand is 0. Note that the operation makes the Auxiliary Carry flag undefined. CF and OF are cleared to 0, and the other affected flags are set according to the operation's results.

r8	= AL AH BL BH CL CH DL DH	r16	= AX BX CX DX BP SP SI DI
sr	= CS DS SS ES		
m8	= 8-bit memory data	m16	= 16-bit memory data
i8	= 8-bit immediate data	i16	= 16-bit immediate data
d8	= 8-bit signed displacement	d16	= 16-bit signed displacement

CALL   Call Procedure

Flags Affected

O D I T S Z A P C   OF: Overflow flag   TF: Trap flag   AF: Aux carry
F F F F F F F F F   DF: Direction flag   SF: Sign flag   PF: Parity flag
    \<none\>   IF: Interrupt flag   ZF: Zero flag   CF: Carry flag

Legal Forms

CALL \<near label\>   CALL m16

CALL \<far label\>   CALL m32

CALL r16

Examples

CALL InsideMySegment   ; InsideMySegment is a Near label

CALL OutsideMySegment   ; OutsideMySegment is a Far label

CALL BX

CALL [BX+DI+17]   ; Calls Near address at [BX+DI+17]

CALL DWORD PTR   ; Calls full 32-bit address at

  [BX+DI+17]   [BX+DI+17]

Notes

CALL transfers control to a procedure address. Before transferring control, CALL pushes the address of the instruction immediately after itself onto the stack. This allows a RET instruction (see also) to pop the return address into either CS:IP or IP only (depending on whether it is a Near or Far call) and thus returns control to the instruction immediately after the CALL instruction.

In addition to the obvious CALL to a defined label, CALL can transfer control to a Near address within a 16-bit general-purpose register, and also to an address located in memory. These are shown in the Legal Forms column as m16 and m32. m32 is simply a full 32-bit address stored at a location in memory that may be addressed through any legal 8086/8088 memory addressing mode. CALL m16 and CALL m32 are useful for creating jump tables of procedure addresses.

r8	= AL AH BL BH CL CH DL DH	r16	= AX BX CX DX BP SP SI DI
sr	= CS DS SS ES	m32	= 32-bit memory data
m8	= 8-bit memory data	m16	= 16-bit memory data
i8	= 8-bit immediate data	i16	= 16-bit immediate data
d8	= 8-bit signed displacement	d16	= 16-bit signed displacement

CLC   Clear Carry Flag (CF)

Flags Affected

O D I T S Z A P C
F F F F F F F F F
*　　　* * * * *

OF: Overflow flag　TF: Trap flag　AF: Aux carry
DF: Direction flag　SF: Sign flag　PF: Parity flag
IF:　Interrupt flag　ZF: Zero flag　CF: Carry flag

Legal Forms

CLC <none>

Examples

CLC

Notes

CLC simply sets the carry flag (CF) to the cleared (0) state. Use CLC in situations where the carry flag *must* be in a known cleared state before work begins, as when you are rotating a series of words or bytes using the rotate instructions RCL and RCR.

r8	= AL AH BL BH CL CH DL DH	r16	= AX BX CX DX BP SP SI DI
sr	= CS DS SS ES		
m8	= 8-bit memory data	m16	= 16-bit memory data
i8	= 8-bit immediate data	i16	= 16-bit immediate data
d8	= 8-bit signed displacement	d16	= 16-bit signed displacement

CLD   Clear Direction Flag (DF)

Flags Affected

```
O D I T S Z A P C
F F F F F F F F F
    *
```

OF: Overflow flag   TF: Trap flag   AF: Aux carry
DF: Direction flag   SF: Sign flag   PF: Parity flag
IF: Interrupt flag   ZF: Zero flag   CF: Carry flag

Legal Forms

CLD <none>

Examples

CLD

Notes

CLD simply sets the direction flag (DF) to the cleared (0) state. This affects the adjustment performed by repeated string instructions like STOS, SCAS, and MOVS. Typically, when DF=0, the destination pointer is increased, and decreased with DF=1. DF is set to one with the STD instruction.

r8 = AL AH BL BH CL CH DL DH   r16 = AX BX CX DX BP SP SI DI
sr = CS DS SS ES
m8 = 8-bit memory data   m16 = 16-bit memory data
i8 = 8-bit immediate data   i16 = 16-bit immediate data
d8 = 8-bit signed displacement   d16 = 16-bit signed displacement

CMP   Arithmetic Subtraction

Flags Affected

O	D	I	T	S	Z	A	P	C
F	F	F	F	F	F	F	F	F
*				*	*	*	*	*

OF: Overflow flag   TF: Trap flag   AF: Aux carry
DF: Direction flag   SF: Sign flag   PF: Parity flag
IF: Interrupt flag   ZF: Zero flag   CF: Carry flag

Legal Forms

CMP r8,r8	CMP m8,i8
CMP m8,r8	CMP r16,i16
CMP r8,m8	CMP m16,i16
CMP r16,r16	CMP r16,i8
CMP m16,r16	CMP m16,i8
CMP r16,m16	CMP AL,i8
CMP r8,i8	CMP AX,i16

Examples

    CMP BX,DI
    CMP AX,OFFFFH   ;Uses single-byte opcode
    CMP AL,42H   ;Uses single-byte opcode
    CMP BP,17H
    CMP WORD PTR [BX+SI+Inset],5
    CMP WORD PTR ES:[BX],0B800H

Notes

CMP compares its two operations and sets the flags to indicate the results of the comparison. *The destination operand is not affected.* The operation itself is identical to subtraction of the source from the destination without borrow (SUB) save that the result does not replace the destination. Typically, CMP is followed by one of the conditional jump instructions (i.e., JE to jump if the operands were equal; JNE if they were unequal; etc.).

r8	= AL AH BL BH CL CH DL DH	r16	= AX BX CX DX BP SP SI DI
sr	= CS DS SS ES		
m8	= 8-bit memory data	m16	= 16-bit memory data
i8	= 8-bit immediate data	i16	= 16-bit immediate data
d8	= 8-bit signed displacement	d16	= 16-bit signed displacement

DEC   Decrement Operand

Flags Affected

O	D	I	T	S	Z	A	P	C
F	F	F	F	F	F	F	F	F
*				*	*	*	*	

OF: Overflow flag   TF: Trap flag   AF: Aux carry
DF: Direction flag   SF: Sign flag   PF: Parity flag
IF: Interrupt flag   ZF: Zero flag   CF: Carry flag

Legal Forms

DEC m8	DEC BH
DEC m16	DEC AX
DEC AL	DEC BX
DEC CL	DEC CX
DEC DL	DEC DX
DEC BL	DEC SP
DEC AH	DEC BP
DEC DH	DEC SI
DEC CH	DEC DI

Examples

    DEC BYTE PTR [BP]   ; Decrements the BYTE at [BP]
    DEC AL
    DEC BX
    DEC WORD PTR [BX]   ; Decrements the WORD at [BX]

Notes

Remember that segment registers *cannot* be decremented with DEC. All register-half opcodes are *two* bytes in length, but all 16-bit register opcodes are *one* byte in length. If you can decrement an entire register, of which only the lower half contains data, use the 16-bit opcode and save a byte.

Memory data forms *must* be used with BYTE PTR or WORD PTR!

r8 = AL AH BL BH CL CH DL DH	r16 = AX BX CX DX BP SP SI DI
sr = CS DS SS ES	
m8 = 8-bit memory data	m16 = 16-bit memory data
i8 = 8-bit immediate data	i16 = 16-bit immediate data
d8 = 8-bit signed displacement	d16 = 16-bit signed displacement

INC   Increment Operand

Flags Affected

O	D	I	T	S	Z	A	P	C
F	F	F	F	F	F	F	F	F
*				*	*	*	*	

OF: Overflow flag   TF: Trap flag   AF: Aux carry
DF: Direction flag   SF: Sign flag   PF: Parity flag
IF: Interrupt flag   ZF: Zero flag   CF: Carry flag

Legal Forms

INC m8	INC BH
INC m16	INC AX
INC AL	INC BX
INC CL	INC CX
INC DL	INC DX
INC BL	INC SP
INC AH	INC BP
INC DH	INC SI
INC CH	INC DI

Examples

    INC BYTE PTR [BP]   ; Increments the BYTE at [BP]
    INC AL
    INC BX
    INC WORD PTR [BX]   ; Increments the WORD at [BX]

Notes

Remember that segment registers *cannot* be incremented with INC. All register-half opcodes are *two* bytes in length, but all 16-bit register opcodes are *one* byte in length. If you can increment an entire register, of which only the lower half contains data, use the 16-bit opcode and save a byte.

Memory data forms *must* be used with BYTE PTR or WORD PTR!

r8 = AL AH BL BH CL CH DL DH		r16 = AX BX CX DX BP SP SI DI
sr = CS DS SS ES		
m8 = 8-bit memory data		m16 = 16-bit memory data
i8 = 8-bit immediate data		i16 = 16-bit immediate data
d8 = 8-bit signed displacement		d16 = 16-bit signed displacement

INT   Software Interrupt

Flags Affected

```
O D I T S Z A P C        OF: Overflow flag   TF: Trap flag   AF: Aux carry
F F F F F F F F F        DF: Direction flag   SF: Sign flag   PF: Parity flag
      * *                IF:  Interrupt flag   ZF: Zero flag   CF: Carry flag
```

Legal Forms

INT 3

INT i8

Examples

INT 3   ; Uses single-byte opcode

INT 10H

Notes

INT triggers a software interrupt to one of 256 vectors in the first 102 bytes of memory. The operand specifies which vector, from 0 to 255. When an interrupt is called, the flags register is pushed on the stack along with the return address. The IF flag is cleared, which prevents further interrupts (either hardware or software) from being recognized until IF is set again. TF is also cleared.

A special form of the instruction allows calling Interrupt 3 with a single-byte instruction. Debuggers use Interrupt 3 to set breakpoints in code by replacing an instruction with the single-byte opcode for calling Interrupt 3. Virtually all cases will use the other form, which takes an 8-bit immediate numeric value.

Always return from a software interrupt service routine with the IRET instruction. IRET restores the flags that were pushed onto the stack by INT, and in doing so clears IF, allowing further interrupts.

```
r8  = AL AH BL BH CL CH DL DH        r16  = AX BX CX DX BP SP SI DI
sr  = CS DS SS ES
m8  = 8-bit memory data              m16 = 16-bit memory data
i8  = 8-bit immediate data           i16  = 16-bit immediate data
d8  = 8-bit signed displacement      d16  = 16-bit signed displacement
```

IRET   Return from Interrupt

Flags Affected

```
O D I T S Z A P C
F F F F F F F F F
* * * * * * * * *
```

OF: Overflow flag   TF: Trap flag   AF: Aux carry
DF: Direction flag   SF: Sign flag   PF: Parity flag
IF: Interrupt flag   ZF: Zero flag   CF: Carry flag

Legal Forms

IRET

Examples

IRET

Notes

IRET *must* be used to exit from interrupt service routines called through INT or through interrupt hardware such as serial ports, etc. IRET pops the return address from the top of the stack into CS and IP, and then pops the next word from the stack into the flags register. *All flags are affected.*

If the interrupt was triggered by hardware, there may be additional step to be taken to prepare the hardware for another interrupt before IRET is executed. Consult your hardware documentation.

```
r8  = AL AH BL BH CL CH DL DH        r16  = AX BX CX DX BP SP SI DI
sr  = CS DS SS ES
m8 = 8-bit memory data               m16 = 16-bit memory data
i8  = 8-bit immediate data           i16  = 16-bit immediate data
d8 = 8-bit signed displacement       d16 = 16-bit signed displacement
```

J?   Jump On Condition

Flags Affected

O D I T S Z A P C	OF: Overflow flag	TF: Trap flag	AF: Aux carry
F F F F F F F F F	DF: Direction flag	SF: Sign flag	PF: Parity flag
<none>	IF: Interrupt flag	ZF: Zero flag	CF: Carry flag

Legal Forms	Descriptions	Jump if flags are
JA/JNBE d	(Jump If Above/Jump If not Below or Equal)	CF=0 AND ZF=0
JAE/JNB d	(Jump If Above or Equal/Jump If Not Below)	CF=0
JB/JNAE d	(Jump If Below/Jump If Not Above or Equal)	CF=1
JBE/JNA d	(Jump If Below or Equal/Jump If Not Above)	CF=1 OR ZF=1
JE/JZ d	(Jump If Equal/Jump If Zero)	ZF=1
JNE/JNZ d	(Jump If Not Equal/Jump If Not Zero)	ZF=0
JG/JNLE d	(Jump If Greater/Jump If Not Less or Equal)	ZF=0 OR SF=OF
JGE/JNL d	(Jump If Greater or Equal/Jump If Not Less)	SF=OF
JL/JNGE d	(Jump If Less/Jump If Not Greater or Equal	SF<>OF
JLE/JNG d	(Jump If Less or Equal/Jump If Not Greater)	ZF=1 OR SF<>OF
JC d	(Jump If Carry flag set)	CF=1
JNC d	(Jump If Carry flag Not set)	CF=0
JO d	(Jump If Overflow flag set)	OF=1
JNO d	(Jump If Overflow flag Not set)	OF=0
JP/JPE d	(Jump If PF set/Jump if Parity Even)	PF=1
JNP/JPO d	(Jump If PF Not set/Jump if Parity Odd)	PF=0
JS d	(Jump If Sign flag set)	SF=1
JNS d	(Jump If Sign flag Not set)	SF=0

Examples

```
JB  HalfSplit    ; Jumps if CF=1
JLE  TooLow      ; Jumps if either ZF=1 or SF<>OF
```

Notes

All these instructions make a short jump (127 bytes forward or 128 bytes back) if some condition is true, or fall through if the condition is not true. The conditions all involve flags, and the flag conditions in question are given to the right of the mnemonic and its description.

The mnemonics incorporating *above* or *below* are for use after unsigned comparisons, whereas the mnemonics incorporating *less* or *greater* are for use after signed comparisons. *Equal* and *Zero* can be used after unsigned or signed comparisons.

r8 = AL AH BL BH CL CH DL DH	r16 = AX BX CX DX BP SP SI DI
sr = CS DS SS ES	d = short displacement; −128/+127 byte
m8 = 8-bit memory data	m16 = 16-bit memory data
i8 = 8-bit immediate data	i16 = 16-bit immediate data
d8 = 8-bit signed displacement	d16 = 16-bit signed displacement

JCXZ   Jump If CX = 0

Flags Affected

```
O D I T S Z A P C
F F F F F F F F F
    <none>
```

OF: Overflow flag   TF: Trap flag   AF: Aux carry
DF: Direction flag   SF: Sign flag   PF: Parity flag
IF: Interrupt flag   ZF: Zero flag   CF: Carry flag

Legal Forms

JCXZ <short displacement>

Examples

JCXZ AllDone

Notes

Many instructions use CX as a counter register, and JCXZ allows you to test and jump to see if CX has become 0. The jump may only be a short jump (that is, no more than 127 bytes forward or 128 bytes back), and will be taken if CX = 0 at the time the instruction is executed. If CX is any other value than 0, execution falls through to the next instruction. See also the **Jump on Condition** instructions.

```
r8  = AL AH BL BH CL CH DL DH        r16 = AX BX CX DX BP SP SI DI
sr  = CS DS SS ES
m8  = 8-bit memory data              m16 = 16-bit memory data
i8  = 8-bit immediate data           i16 = 16-bit immediate data
d8  = 8-bit signed displacement      d16 = 16-bit signed displacement
```

JMP   Unconditional Jump

Flags Affected

```
O D I T S Z A P C        OF: Overflow flag    TF: Trap flag    AF: Aux carry
F F F F F F F F F        DF: Direction flag   SF: Sign flag    PF: Parity flag
      <none>             IF:  Interrupt flag  ZF: Zero flag    CF: Carry flag
```

Legal Forms

JMP <short displacement>   JMP r16

JMP <near label>   JMP m16

JMP <far label>   JMP m32

Examples

JMP RightCloseBy	; Plus or minus 128 bytes
JMP InsideMySegment	; To 16-bit offset from CS
JMP OutsideMySegment	; To immediate 32-bit address
JMP DX	; To 16-bit offset stored in GP register
JMP [BX+DI+17]	; To Near address stored at [BX+DI+17]

JMP DWORD PTR
  [BX+DI+17]
	; To full 32-bit address stored at
	    [BX+DI+17]

Notes

JMP transfers control unconditionally to the distination given as the single operand. In addition to defined labels, JMP can transfer control to a 16-bit offset from CS stored in a general-purpose register, or to an address (either Near or Far) stored in memory and accessed through any legal 8086/8088 addressing mode. These m16 and m32 forms are useful for creating jump tables in memory, where a jump table is an array of addresses. For example, JMP [BX+DI+17] would transfer control to the 16 bit offset into CS found at the based-indexed-displacement address [BX+DI+17].

No flags are affected, and unlike CALL, no return address is pushed onto the stack.

r8	= AL AH BL BH CL CH DL DH	r16	= AX BX CX DX BP SP SI DI
sr	= CS DS SS ES	m32	= 32-bit memory data
m8	= 8-bit memory data	m16	= 16-bit memory data
i8	= 8-bit immediate data	i16	= 16-bit immediate data
d8	= 8-bit signed displacement	d16	= 16-bit signed displacement

LEA   Load Affective Address

Flags Affected

O D I T S Z A P C			
F F F F F F F F F	OF: Overflow flag	TF: Trap flag	AF: Aux carry
<none>	DF: Direction flag	SF: Sign flag	PF: Parity flag
	IF: Interrupt flag	ZF: Zero flag	CF: Carry flag

Legal Forms

LEA r16,m<any size>

Examples

LEA BX,MyByteVar   ; Loads offset of MyByteVar to BX

LEA BP,MyWordVar   ; Loads offset of MyWordVar to BP

Notes

LEA derives the offset of the source operand from the start of its segment and loads that offset into the destination operand. The destination operand must be a 16-bit register and *cannot* be memory. The source operand must be a memory operand, but it can be any size. The address stored in the destination operand is the address of the first byte of the source in memory, and the size of the source in memory is unimportant.

   This is a good, clean way to place the address of a variable into a register prior to a procedure or interrupt call.

r8	= AL AH BL BH CL CH DL DH	r16	= AX BX CX DX BP SP SI DI
sr	= CS DS SS ES		
m8	= 8-bit memory data	m16	= 16-bit memory data
i8	= 8-bit immediate data	i16	= 16-bit immediate data
d8	= 8-bit signed displacement	d16	= 16-bit signed displacement

LOOP   Loop until CX = 0

Flags Affected
```
O D I T S Z A P C
F F F F F F F F F
    <none>
```

OF: Overflow flag   TF: Trap flag   AF: Aux carry
DF: Direction flag   SF: Sign flag   PF: Parity flag
IF: Interrupt flag   ZF: Zero flag   CF: Carry flag

Legal Forms
LOOP <short displacement>

Examples
LOOP PokeValue

Notes
LOOP is a combination decrement counter, test, and jump instruction. It simplifies code by acting as a DEC CX instruction, a CMP CX,0 instruction, and JZ instruction all at once. A repeat count must be initially loaded into CX. When the LOOP instruction is executed, it first decrements CX. Then it tests to see if CX = 0. If CX is *not* 0, LOOP transfers control to the displacement specified as its operand:

```
        MOV  CX,17
DoIt:   CALL CrunchIT
        CALL StuffIt
        LOOP DoIt
```

Here, the two procedure CALLs will be made 17 times. The first 16 times through, CX will still be nonzero and LOOP will transfer control to DoIt. On the 17th pass, however, LOOP will decrement CX to 0, and then fall through to the next instruction in sequence when it tests CX.

LOOP does not alter any flags, even when CX is decremented to 0. *Warning:* If CX is initially 0, LOOP will decrement it to 65,535 (0FFFFH) and then perform the loop 65,535 times, which might take long enough to appear to be a system lockup.

r8 = AL AH BL BH CL CH DL DH	r16 = AX BX CX DX BP SP SI DI
sr = CS DS SS ES	
m8 = 8-bit memory data	m16 = 16-bit memory data
i8 = 8-bit immediate data	i16 = 16-bit immediate data
d8 = 8-bit signed displacement	d16 = 16-bit signed displacement

MOV Move (Copy) Right Operand into Left Operand

Flags Affected

O	D	I	T	S	Z	A	P	C
F	F	F	F	F	F	F	F	F

<none>

OF: Overflow flag   TF: Trap flag   AF: Aux carry
DF: Direction flag   SF: Sign flag   PF: Parity flag
IF: Interrupt flag   ZF: Zero flag   CF: Carry flag

Legal Forms

MOV r8,r8

MOV M8,i8

MOV m16,i16

MOV m8,r8

MOV r16,r16

MOV m16,r16

MOV r8,m8

MOV r16,m16

MOV sr,r16

MOV sr,m16

MOV r16,sr

MOV m16,sr

MOV AL,a16

MOV AX,a16

MOV a16,AL

MOV a16,AX

MOV AL,i8

MOV CL,i8

MOV DL,i8

MOV BL,i8

MOV AH,i8

MOV CH,i8   — Single-byte opcodes

MOV DH,i8

MOV BH,i8

MOV AX,i16

MOV CX,i16

MOV DX,i16

MOV BX,i16

MOV SP,i16

MOV BP,i16

MOV SI,i16

MOV DI,i16

Examples

MOV AL,BH

MOV BX,DI

MOV BP,ES

MOV ES,AX

MOV AX,0B800H

MOV ES:[BX],0FFFFH

MOV CX,[SI+Inset]

Notes

This is perhaps the most used of all instructions. Note the large number of register-specific forms that resolve to single-byte opcodes. Use them when you can; smaller opcodes aid both speed and memory efficiency. The flags are not affected.

r8 = AL AH BL BH CL CH DL DH	r16 = AX BX CX DX BP SP SI DI
sr = CS DS SS ES	
m8 = 8-bit memory data	m16 = 16-bit memory data
i8 = 8-bit immediate data	i16 = 16-bit immediate data
d8 = 8-bit signed displacement	d16 = 16-bit signed displacement

NEG   Negate (Two's Complement; i.e. Multiply By −1)

Flags Affected

```
O D I T S Z A P C      OF: Overflow flag   TF: Trap flag    AF: Aux carry
F F F F F F F F F      DF: Direction flag   SF: Sign flag     PF: Parity flag
*       * * * * *      IF:  Interrupt flag   ZF: Zero flag     CF: Carry flag
```

Legal Forms

NEG r8

NEG m8

NEG r16

NEG m16

Examples

NEG AL

NEG CX

NEG BYTE PTR [BX]   ; Negates byte quantity at DS:BX

NEG WORD PTR [DI]   ; Negates word quantity at DS:BX

Notes

This is the assembly language equivalent of multiplying a value by −1. Keep in mind that negation is *not* the same as simply inverting each bit in the operand. (Another instruction, NOT, does that.) The process is also known as generating the *two's complement* of a value. The two's complement of a value added to that value yields zero. −1 = $FF; −2 = $FE; −3 = $FD; etc.

If the operand is 0, CF is cleared and ZF is set; otherwise CF is set and ZF is cleared. If the operand contains the maximum negative value (−128 for 8-bit or −32778 for 16-bit) the operand does not change, but OF and CF are set. SF is set if the result is negative, else SF is cleared. PF is set if the low-order 8 bits of the result contain an even number of set (1) bits; otherwise PF is cleared.

NOTE: You *must* use a type override specifier (BYTE PTR or WORD PTR) with memory data!

```
r8  = AL AH BL BH CL CH DL DH        r16 = AX BX CX DX BP SP SI DI
sr  = CS DS SS ES
m8  = 8-bit memory data              m16 = 16-bit memory data
i8  = 8-bit immediate data           i16 = 16-bit immediate data
d8  = 8-bit signed displacement      d16 = 16-bit signed displacement
```

NOP   No Operation

Flags Affected

O	D	I	T	S	Z	A	P	C
F	F	F	F	F	F	F	F	F

<none>

OF: Overflow flag   TF: Trap flag   AF: Aux carry
DF: Direction flag   SF: Sign flag   PF: Parity flag
IF: Interrupt flag   ZF: Zero flag   CF: Carry flag

Legal Forms

NOP <none>

Examples

NOP

Notes

This, the easiest-to-understand of all '86 family machine instructions, simply does nothing. Its job is to take up space in sequences of instructions. When fetched by the CPU, NOP is simply ignored. IP is incremented by one, and the next instruction is fetched. NOP is used for "NOPping out" machine instructions during debugging, leaving space for future procedure or interrupt calls, or padding time loops.

r8 = AL AH BL BH CL CH DL DH	r16 = AX BX CX DX BP SP SI DI
sr = CS DS SS ES	
m8 = 8-bit memory data	m16 = 16-bit memory data
i8 = 8-bit immediate data	i16 = 16-bit immediate data
d8 = 8-bit signed displacement	d16 = 16-bit signed displacement

NOT Logical NOT (One's Complement)

Flags Affected

O D I T S Z A P C			
F F F F F F F F F	OF: Overflow flag	TF: Trap flag	AF: Aux carry
<none>	DF: Direction flag	SF: Sign flag	PF: Parity flag
	IF: Interrupt flag	ZF: Zero flag	CF: Carry flag

Legal Forms

NOT r8

NOT m8

NOT r16

NOT m16

Examples

NOT CL

NOT DX

NOT WORD PTR [SI]

Notes

NOT inverts each individual bit within the operand separately (i.e., every bit that was 1 becomes 0, and every bit that was 0 becomes 1). This is the "logical NOT" or "one's complement" operation. See also the NEG instruction for the negation or "two's complement" operation.

The value FFH would become 0; the value AAH would become 55H.

r8	= AL AH BL BH CL CH DL DH		r16	= AX BX CX DX BP SP SI DI
sr	= CS DS SS ES			
m8	= 8-bit memory data		m16	= 16-bit memory data
i8	= 8-bit immediate data		i16	= 16-bit immediate data
d8	= 8-bit signed displacement		d16	= 16-bit signed displacement

OR   Logical OR

Flags Affected

O	D	I	T	S	Z	A	P	C
F	F	F	F	F	F	F	F	F
*				*	*	*	*	*

OF: Overflow flag   TF: Trap flag   AF: Aux carry
DF: Direction flag   SF: Sign flag   PF: Parity flag
IF: Interrupt flag   ZF: Zero flag   CF: Carry flag

Legal Forms

OR r8,r8   OR r8,i8

OR m8,r8   OR m8,i8

OR r8,m8   OR r16,i16

OR r16,r16   OR m16,i16

OR m16,r16   OR AL,i8

OR r16,m16   OR AX,i16

Examples

OR BX,DI

OR AX,0FFFFH   ; Uses single-byte opcode

OR AL,42H   ; Uses single-byte opcode

OR ES:[BX],0B800H

OR [BP+SI],DX

Notes

OR performs the OR logical operation between its two operands. Once the operation is complete, the result replaces the destination operand. OR is performed on a bit-by-bit basis, such that bit 0 of the source is ORed with bit 0 of the destination, bit 1 of the source is ORed with bit 1 of the destination, and so on. The OR operation yields a 1 if one of the operands is 1, and a 0 only if both operands are 0. Note that the operation makes the Auxiliary Carry flag undefined. CF and OF are cleared to 0, and the other affected flags are set according to the operation's results.

r8 = AL AH BL BH CL CH DL DH   r16 = AX BX CX DX BP SP SI DI
sr = CS DS SS ES
m8 = 8-bit memory data   m16 = 16-bit memory data
i8 = 8-bit immediate data   i16 = 16-bit immediate data
d8 = 8-bit signed displacement   d16 = 16-bit signed displacement

POP   Pop Top of Stack into Operand; Increment SP by 2

Flags Affected

```
O D I T S Z A P C        OF: Overflow flag   TF: Trap flag   AF: Aux carry
F F F F F F F F F        DF: Direction flag  SF: Sign flag   PF: Parity flag
     <none>              IF:  Interrupt flag  ZF: Zero flag   CF: Carry flag
```

Legal Forms

POP m16   POP SI

POP AX   POP DI

POP BX   POP CS

POP CX   POP DS

POP DX   POP SS

POP BP   POP ES

POP SP

Examples

POP [BX]

POP AX

POP ES

Notes

Note that it is impossible to pop a byte-sized item from the stack. It's words or nothing. Also remember that "the top of the stack" is defined as the word at address SS:SP, and there's no way to override that using prefixes. There is a separate pair of instructions, PUSHF and POPF, for pushing and popping the flags register.

All register forms are single-byte opcodes.

```
r8  = AL AH BL BH CL CH DL DH        r16 = AX BX CX DX BP SP SI DI
sr  = CS DS SS ES
m8  = 8-bit memory data              m16 = 16-bit memory data
i8  = 8-bit immediate data           i16 = 16-bit immediate data
d8  = 8-bit signed displacement      d16 = 16-bit signed displacement
```

POPF   Pop Top of Stack into Flags Reg; Increment SP by 2

Flags Affected

```
O D I T S Z A P C        OF: Overflow flag    TF: Trap flag    AF: Aux carry
F F F F F F F F F        DF: Direction flag   SF: Sign flag    PF: Parity flag
* * * * * * * * *        IF:  Interrupt flag  ZF: Zero flag    CF: Carry flag
```

Legal Forms

POPF <none>

Examples

POPF

Notes

POPF pops the word at the top of the stack into the flags register. "The top of the stack" is defined as the word at SS:SP, and there is no way to override that with prefixes.

SP is incremented *after* the word comes off the stack. Remember that SP always points to either an empty stack or else real data. There is a separate pair of instructions, PUSH and POP, for pushing and popping other register data and memory data.

PUSHF and POPF are most used in writing interrupt service routines, where you must be able to save and restore the environment (i.e., all machine registers) to avoid disrupting machine operations while servicing the interrupt.

```
r8  = AL AH BL BH CL CH DL DH          r16  = AX BX CX DX BP SP SI DI
sr  = CS DS SS ES
m8  = 8-bit memory data                m16  = 16-bit memory data
i8  = 8-bit immediate data             i16  = 16-bit immediate data
d8  = 8-bit signed displacement        d16  = 16-bit signed displacement
```

PUSH   Push Operand onto Top of Stack; Decrement SP by 2

Flags Affected

O D I T S Z A P C			
F F F F F F F F F	OF: Overflow flag	TF: Trap flag	AF: Aux carry
<none>	DF: Direction flag	SF: Sign flag	PF: Parity flag
	IF: Interrupt flag	ZF: Zero flag	CF: Carry flag

Legal Forms

POP m16	POP SI
POP AX	POP DI
POP BX	POP CS
POP CX	POP DS
POP DX	POP SS
POP BP	POP ES
POP SP	

Examples

POP [BX]

POP AX

POP ES

Notes

Note that it is impossible to push a byte-sized item onto the stack. It's words or nothing. Also remember that the top of the stack is defined as the word at address SS:SP+1 and that there's no way to override that using prefixes. There is a seprate pair of instructions, PUSHF and POPF, for pushing and popping the flags register.

Also remember that SP is decremented *before* the push takes place; SP points to either an empty stack or else real data.

r8 = AL AH BL BH CL CH DL DH		r16 = AX BX CX DX BP SP SI DI
sr = CS DS SS ES		
m8 = 8-bit memory data		m16 = 16-bit memory data
i8 = 8-bit immediate data		i16 = 16-bit immediate data
d8 = 8-bit signed displacement		d16 = 16-bit signed displacement

PUSHF   Push Flags onto Top of Stack: Decrement SP by 2

Flags Affected

O D I T S Z A P C   OF: Overflow flag   TF: Trap flag   AF: Aux carry

F F F F F F F F F   DF: Direction flag   SF: Sign flag   PF: Parity flag

    <none>   IF: Interrupt flag   ZF: Zero flag   CF: Carry flag

Legal Forms

PUSHF <none>

Examples

PUSHF

Notes

PUSHF simply pushes the current contents of the Flags register onto the top of the stack. The top of the stack is defined as the word at SS:SP and there is no way to override that with prefixes.

SP is decremented *before* the word goes onto the stack. Remember that SP always points to either an empty stack or else real data. There is a separate pair of instructions, PUSH and POP, for pushing and popping other register data and memory data.

The flags register is not affected when you *push* the flags, only when you pop them back with POPF.

PUSHF and POPF are most used in writing interrupt service routines, where you must be able to save and restore the environment (i.e., all machine registers) to avoid disrupting machine operations while servicing the interrupt.

r8 = AL AH BL BH CL CH DL DH	r16 = AX BX CX DX BP SP SI DI
sr = CS DS SS ES	
m8 = 8-bit memory data	m16 = 16-bit memory data
i8 = 8-bit immediate data	i16 = 16-bit immediate data
d8 = 8-bit signed displacement	d16 = 16-bit signed displacement

RET   Return From Procedure

Flags Affected

O D I T S Z A P C	OF: Overflow flag	TF: Trap flag	AF: Aux carry
F F F F F F F F F	DF: Direction flag	SF: Sign flag	PF: Parity flag
<none>	IF: Interrupt flag	ZF: Zero flag	CF: Carry flag

Legal Forms

RET

RETN

RETF

RET i8

RETN i8

RET i16

RETF i16

Examples

RET

RET 12H

RETN

RETF 117H

Notes

The RETF and RETN forms are *not* available in MASM prior to version 5.0!

There are two kinds of returns: Near and Far, where Near is within the current code segment and Far is to some other code segment. Ordinarily the RET form is used, and the assembler resolves it to a Near or Far return opcode to match the procedure definition's use of the NEAR or FAR specifier. Specifying RETF or RETN may be done when necessary

RET may take an operand indicating how many bytes of stack space are to be released on returning from the procedure. This figure is subtracted from the stack pointer to erase data items that had been pushed onto the stack for the procedure's use immediately prior to the procedure call.

r8	= AL AH BL BH CL CH DL DH	r16	= AX BX CX DX BP SP SI DI
sr	= CS DS SS ES		
m8	= 8-bit memory data	m16	= 16-bit memory data
i8	= 8-bit immediate data	i16	= 16-bit immediate data
d8	= 8-bit signed displacement	d16	= 16-bit signed displacement

ROL Rotate Left

Flags Affected

```
O D I T S Z A P C      OF: Overflow flag   TF: Trap flag   AF: Aux carry
F F F F F F F F F      DF: Direction flag  SF: Sign flag   PF: Parity flag
*               *      IF:  Interrupt flag  ZF: Zero flag   CF: Carry flag
```

Legal Forms

ROL r8,1	ROL r8,CL
ROL m8,1	ROL m8,CL
ROL r16,1	ROL r16,CL
ROL m16,1	ROL m16,CL

Examples

ROL AL,1

ROL WORD PTR [BX+SI],CL

ROL BP,1

ROL BP,CL

Notes

ROL rotates the bits within the destination operand to the left, where left is toward the most significant bit (MSB). A rotate is a shift (see SHL and SHR) that wrap around; the leftmost bit of the operand is shifted into the rightmost bit, and all intermediate bits are shifted one bit to the left. Except for the direction the shift operation takes, ROL is identical to ROR.

The number of bit positions shifted can either be specified as the literal 1, or by the value in CL. (*Not* CX!) It is usually faster to perform sequential shift-by-one instructions unless the number of bits shifted-by exceeds four. Note that while CL may accept a value up to 255, it is meaningless to shift by any value larger than 16, *even though the shifts are actually performed on the 8086 and 8088.*

The leftmost bit is copied into the carry flag on each shift operation. OF is modified *only* by the shift-by-one forms of ROL; after shift-by-CL forms, OF becomes undefined.

r8	= AL AH BL BH CL CH DL DH	r16	= AX BX CX DX BP SP SI DI
sr	= CS DS SS ES		
m8	= 8-bit memory data	m16	= 16-bit memory data
i8	= 8-bit immediate data	i16	= 16-bit immediate data
d8	= 8-bit signed displacement	d16	= 16-bit signed displacement

ROR　Rotate Right

Flags Affected

```
O D I T S Z A P C
F F F F F F F F F
*               *
```

OF: Overflow flag	TF: Trap flag	AF: Aux carry
DF: Direction flag	SF: Sign flag	PF: Parity flag
IF: Interrupt flag	ZF: Zero flag	CF: Carry flag

Legal Forms

ROR r8,1	ROR r8,CL
ROR m8,1	ROR m8,CL
ROR r16,1	ROR r16,CL
ROR m16,1	ROR m16,CL

Examples

```
ROR  AL,1
ROR  WORD PTR [BX+SI],CL
ROR  BP,1
ROR  BP,CL
```

Notes

ROR rotates the bits within the destination operand to the right, where right is toward the least significant bit (LSB). A rotate is a shift (see SHL and SHR) that wraps around; the rightmost bit of the operand is shifted into the leftmost bit, and all intermediate bits are shifted one bit to the right. Except for the direction the shift operation takes, ROR is identical to ROL.

The number of bit positions shifted can be specified either as the literal 1, or by the value in CL. (*Not* CX!) It is usually faster to perform sequential shift-by-one instructions unless the number of bits shifted-by exceeds four. Note that while CL can accept a value up to 255, it is meaningless to shift by any value larger than 16, *even though the shifts are actually performed on the 8086 and 8088.*

The rightmost bit is copied into the carry flag on each shift operation. OF is modified *only* by the shift-by-one forms of ROR; after shift-by-CL forms, OF becomes undefined.

r8	= AL AH BL BH CL CH DL DH	r16　= AX BX CX DX BP SP SI DI
sr	= CS DS SS ES	
m8	= 8-bit memory data	m16　= 16-bit memory data
i8	= 8-bit immediate data	i16　= 16-bit immediate data
d8	= 8-bit signed displacement	d16　= 16-bit signed displacement

SBB   Arithmetic Subtraction with Borrow

Flags Affected

O	D	I	T	S	Z	A	P	C
F	F	F	F	F	F	F	F	F
*				*	*	*	*	*

OF: Overflow flag   TF: Trap flag   AF: Aux carry
DF: Direction flag   SF: Sign flag   PF: Parity flag
IF: Interrupt flag   ZF: Zero flag   CF: Carry flag

Legal Forms

SBB r8,r8   SBB m8,i8
SBB m8,r8   SBB r16,i16
SBB r8,m8   SBB m16,i16
SBB r16,r16   SBB r16,i8
SBB m16,r16   SBB m16,i8
SBB r16,m16   SBB AL,i8
SBB r8,i8   SBB AX,i16

Examples

SBB BX,DI
SBB AX,OFFFFH   ; Uses single-byte opcode
SBB AL,42H   ; Uses single-byte opcode
SBB BP,17H
SBB WORD PTR [BX+SI+Inset],5
SBB WORD PTR ES:[BX],0B800H

Notes

SBB performs a subtraction with borrow, where the source is subtracted from the destination and then the carry flag is subtracted from the result. The result then replaces the destination. If the result is negative, the carry flag is set. To subtract without taking the carry flag into account (i.e., without borrowing) use the SUB instruction.

r8 = AL AH BL BH CL CH DL DH	r16 = AX BX CX DX BP SP SI DI
sr = CS DS SS ES	
m8 = 8-bit memory data	m16 = 16-bit memory data
i8 = 8-bit immediate data	i16 = 16-bit immediate data
d8 = 8-bit signed displacement	d16 = 16-bit signed displacement

SHL   Shift Left

Flags Affected

O	D	I	T	S	Z	A	P	C
F	F	F	F	F	F	F	F	F
*				*	*	*	*	*

OF: Overflow flag   TF: Trap flag   AF: Aux carry
DF: Direction flag   SF: Sign flag   PF: Parity flag
IF: Interrupt flag   ZF: Zero flag   CF: Carry flag

Legal Forms

    SHL r8,1   SHL r8,CL

    SHL m8,1   SHL m8,CL

    SHL r16,1   SHL r16,CL

    SHL m16,1   SHL m16,CL

Examples

    SHL AL,1

    SHL WORD PTR [BX+SI],CL

    SHL BP,1

    SHL BP,CL

Notes

SHL shifts the bits within the destination operand to the left, where left is toward the most significant bit (MSB). The number of bit positions shifted may either be specified as the literal 1, or by the value in CL. (*Not* CX!) It is usually faster to perform sequential shift-by-one instructions unless the number of bits shifted-by exceeds four. Note that while CL may accept a value up to 255, it is meaningless to shift by any value larger than 16, *even though the shifts are actually performed on the 8086 and 8088.*

   The leftmost bit of the operand is shifted into the carry flag; the rightmost bit is cleared to 0. The auxiliary carry flag (AF) becomes defined after this instruction. OF is modified *only* by the shift-by-one forms of SHL; after shift-by-CL forms, OF becomes undefined.

   Except for the direction the shift operation takes, SHL is identical to SHR.

r8	= AL AH BL BH CL CH DL DH	r16	= AX BX CX DX BP SP SI DI
sr	= CS DS SS ES		
m8	= 8-bit memory data	m16	= 16-bit memory data
i8	= 8-bit immediate data	i16	= 16-bit immediate data
d8	= 8-bit signed displacement	d16	= 16-bit signed displacement

SHR   Shift Right

Flags Affected

O	D	I	T	S	Z	A	P	C
F	F	F	F	F	F	F	F	F
*				*	*	*	*	*

OF: Overflow flag   TF: Trap flag   AF: Aux carry
DF: Direction flag   SF: Sign flag   PF: Parity flag
IF: Interrupt flag   ZF: Zero flag   CF: Carry flag

Legal Forms

SHR r8,1	SHR r8,CL
SHR m8,1	SHR m8,CL
SHR r16,1	SHR r16,CL
SHR m16,1	SHR m16,CL

Examples

SHR AL,1

SHR WORD PTR [BX+SI],CL

SHR BP,1

SHR BP,CL

Notes

SHR shifts the bits within the destination operand to the right, where right is toward the least significant bit (LSB). The number of bit positions shifted can be specified either as the literal 1, or by the value in CL. (*Not* CX!) It is usually faster to perform sequential shift-by-one instructions unless the number of bits shifted-by exceeds four. Note that while CL may accept a value up to 255, it is meaningless to shift by any value larger than 16, *even though the shifts are actually performed on the 8086 and 8088.*

The rightmost bit of the operand is shifted into the carry flag; the leftmost bit is cleared to 0. The auxiliary carry flag (AF) becomes undefined after this instruction. OF is modified *only* by the shift-by-one forms of SHR; after shift-by-CL forms, OF becomes undefined.

Except for the direction the shift takes, SHR is identical to SHL.

r8	= AL AH BL BH CL CH DL DH		r16	= AX BX CX DX BP SP SI DI
sr	= CS DS SS ES			
m8	= 8-bit memory data		m16	= 16-bit memory data
i8	= 8-bit immediate data		i16	= 16-bit immediate data
d8	= 8-bit signed displacement		d16	= 16-bit signed displacement

STC   Set Carry Flag (CF)

Flags Affected

```
O D I T S Z A P C
F F F F F F F F F
              *
```

OF: Overflow flag   TF: Trap flag   AF: Aux carry
DF: Direction flag   SF: Sign flag   PF: Parity flag
IF: Interrupt flag   ZF: Zero flag   CF: Carry flag

Legal Forms

STC <none>

Examples

STC

Notes

STC asserts the Carry flag (CF) to a known set state (1). Use it prior to some task that needs a bit in the Carry flag.

r8   = AL AH BL BH CL CH DL DH   r16 = AX BX CX DX BP SP SI DI
sr   = CS DS SS ES
m8   = 8-bit memory data   m16 = 16-bit memory data
i8   = 8-bit immediate data   i16 = 16-bit immediate data
d8   = 8-bit signed displacement   d16 = 16-bit signed displacement

STD   Set Direction Flag (DF)

Flags Affected

```
O D I T S Z A P C        OF: Overflow flag   TF: Trap flag   AF: Aux carry
F F F F F F F F F        DF: Direction flag  SF: Sign flag   PF: Parity flag
      *                  IF: Interrupt flag  ZF: Zero flag   CF: Carry flag
```

Legal Forms

STD <none>

Examples

STD

Notes

STD simply asserts the direction flag (DF) to the set (1) state. This affects the adjustment performed by repeated string instructions like STOS, SCAS, and MOVS. Typically, when DF = 0, the destination pointer is increased, and decreased when DF = 1. DF is set to 0 with CLD instruction.

r8 = AL AH BL BH CL CH DL DH   r16 = AX BX CX DX BP SP SI DI
sr = CS DS SS ES
m8 = 8-bit memory data   m16 = 16-bit memory data
i8 = 8-bit immediate data   i16 = 16-bit immediate data
d8 = 8-bit signed displacement   d16 = 16-bit signed displacement

STOS   Store String

Flags Affected

```
O D I T S Z A P C
F F F F F F F F F
     <none>
```

OF: Overflow flag   TF: Trap flag   AF: Aux carry
DF: Direction flag   SF: Sign flag   PF: Parity flag
IF: Interrupt flag   ZF: Zero flag   CF: Carry flag

Legal Forms

STOS ES:m8

STOS ES:m16

STOSB

STOSW

Examples

STOS ES:MyWordVar	;Stores AX to ES:DI
STOS ES:MyByteVar	;Stores AL to ES:DI
STOSB	;Stores AL to ES:DI
STOSW	;Stores AX to ES:DI
REP STOSW	;Stores AX to ES:DI and following, for CX repeats

Notes

Stores either AL (for 8-bit store operations) or AX to the location at ES:DI. ES must be the segment of the destination and cannot be overridden. Similarly, DI must always be the destination offset.

By placing an operation repeat count (not a byte or word count!) in CX and preceding the mnemonic with the REP prefix, STOS can do an automatic "machine-gun" store of AL/AX into successive memory locations beginning at the initial ES:DI. After each store, DI is adjusted (see next paragraph) by either 1 (for 8-bit store operations) or 2, and CX is decremented by 1.

Adjusting means incrementing if the direction flag is cleared (by CLD) or decrementing if the direction flag has been set.

r8	= AL AH BL BH CL CH DL DH	r16	= AX BX CX DX BP SP SI DI
sr	= CS DS SS ES		
m8	= 8-bit memory data	m16	= 16-bit memory data
i8	= 8-bit immediate data	i16	= 16-bit immediate data
d8	= 8-bit signed displacement	d16	= 16-bit signed displacement

SUB   Arithmetic Subtraction

Flags Affected

O	D	I	T	S	Z	A	P	C
F	F	F	F	F	F	F	F	F
*				*	*	*	*	*

OF: Overflow flag   TF: Trap flag   AF: Aux carry
DF: Direction flag   SF: Sign flag   PF: Parity flag
IF: Interrupt flag   ZF: Zero flag   CF: Carry flag

Legal Forms

SUB r8,r8	SUB m8,i8
SUB m8,r8	SUB r16,i16
SUB r8,m8	SUB m16,i16
SUB r16,r16	SUB r16,i8
SUB m16,r16	SUB m16,i8
SUB r16,m16	SUB AL,i8
SUB r8,i8	SUB AX,i16

Examples

SUB BX,DI
SUB AX,OFFFFH   ;Uses single-byte opcode
SUB AL,42H   ;Uses single-byte opcode
SUB BP,17H
SUB WORD PTR [BX+SI+Inset],5
SUB WORD PTR ES:[BX],0B800H

Notes

SUB performs a subtraction without borrow, where the source is subtracted from the destination and the result replaces the destination. If the result is negative, the carry flag is set. Multiple-precision subtraction can be performed by following SUB with SBB (subtract with borrow), which takes the carry flag into account as a borrow.

r8	= AL AH BL BH CL CH DL DH	r16	= AX BX CX DX BP SP SI DI
sr	= CS DS SS ES		
m8	= 8-bit memory data	m16	= 16-bit memory data
i8	= 8-bit immediate data	i16	= 16-bit immediate data
d8	= 8-bit signed displacement	d16	= 16-bit signed displacement

XCHG   Exchange Operands

Flags Affected

```
O D I T S Z A P C      OF: Overflow flag   TF: Trap flag   AF: Aux  carry
F F F F F F F F F      DF: Direction flag   SF: Sign flag   PF: Parity flag
      <none>           IF:  Interrupt flag   ZF: Zero flag   CF: Carry  flag
```

Legal Forms

```
XCHG  r8,r8        XCHG  AX,CX  ⎤
XCHG  r8,m8        XCHG  AX,DX  ⎥
XCHG  r16,r16      XCHG  AX,BX  ⎥   Single-byte
XCHG  r16,m16      XCHG  AX,SP  ⎥     special cases
                   XCHG  AX,BP  ⎥
                   XCHG  AX,SI  ⎥
                   XCHG  AX,DI  ⎦
```

Examples

```
XCHG  AL,DH
XCHG  BH,[SI]
XCHG  SP,BP
XCHG  DX,[DI]
XCHG  AX,BX        ; Uses single-byte opcode
```

Notes

XCHG exchanges the contents of its two operands. This is why there is no form of XCHG for identical operands (i.e., XCHG AX,AX is not a legal form) because exchanging a register with itself makes no logical sense.

Exchanging an operand with AX may be accomplished with a single-byte opcode, saving fetch time and code space. All good assemblers recognize these cases and optimize for them, but if you are hand-assembling INLINE statements for Turbo Pascal or some other language, keep the single-byte special cases in mind.

```
r8  = AL AH BL BH CL CH DL DH      r16 = AX BX CX DX BP SP SI DI
sr  = CS DS SS  ES
m8  = 8-bit memory data            m16 = 16-bit memory data
i8  = 8-bit immediate data         i16 = 16-bit immediate data
d8  = 8-bit signed displacement    d16 = 16-bit signed displacement
```

XOR Exclusive Or

Flags Affected

```
O D I T S Z A P C        OF: Overflow flag   TF: Trap flag    AF: Aux carry
F F F F F F F F F         DF: Direction flag  SF: Sign flag    PF: Parity flag
*       * * * * *         IF:  Interrupt flag ZF: Zero flag    CF: Carry flag
```

Legal Forms

XOR r8,r8	XOR r8,i8
XOR m8,r8	XOR m8,i8
XOR r8,m8	XOR r16,i16
XOR r16,r16	XOR m16,i16
XOR m16,r16	XOR AL,i8
XOR r16,m16	XOR AX,i16

Examples

```
XOR  BX,DI
XOR  AX,OFFFFH           ;Uses single-byte opcode
XOR  AL,42H              ;Uses single-byte opcode
XOR  ES:[BX],0B800H
XOR  [BP+SI],DX
```

Notes

XOR performs the exclusive OR logical operation between its two operands. Once the operation is complete, the result replaces the destination operand. XOR is performed on a bit-by-bit basis, such that bit 0 of the source is XORed with bit 0 of the destination, bit 1 of the source is XORed with bit 1 of the destination, and so on. The XOR operation yields a 1 if the operands are different and a 0 if the operands are the same. Note that the operation makes the auxiliary carry flag undefined. CF and OF are cleared to 0, and the other affected flags are set according to the operation's results.

r8 = AL AH BL BH CL CH DL DH	r16 = AX BX CX DX BP SP SI DI
sr = CS DS SS ES	
m8 = 8-bit memory data	m16 = 16-bit memory data
i8 = 8-bit immediate data	i16 = 16-bit immediate data
d8 = 8-bit signed displacement	d16 = 16-bit signed displacement

Appendix B

◆◆

The Extended ASCII Code and Symbol Set

Dec	Hex	Binary	Symbol		Dec	Hex	Binary	Symbol
0	00	00000000			32	20	00100000	
1	01	00000001	☺		33	21	00100001	!
2	02	00000010	●		34	22	00100010	"
3	03	00000011	♥		35	23	00100011	#
4	04	00000100	♦		36	24	00100100	$
5	05	00000101	♣		37	25	00100101	%
6	06	00000110	♠		38	26	00100110	&
7	07	00000111	•		39	27	00100111	'
8	08	00001000	◘		40	28	00101000	(
9	09	00001001	○		41	29	00101001	)
10	0A	00001010	◙		42	2A	00101010	*
11	0B	00001011	♂		43	2B	00101011	+
12	0C	00001100	♀		44	2C	00101100	,
13	0D	00001101	♪		45	2D	00101101	−
14	0E	00001110	♫		46	2E	00101110	.
15	0F	00001111	☼		47	2F	00101111	/
16	10	00010000	►		48	30	00110000	0
17	11	00010001	◄		49	31	00110001	1
18	12	00010010	↕		50	32	00110010	2
19	13	00010011	‼		51	33	00110011	3
20	14	00010100	¶		52	34	00110100	4
21	15	00010101	§		53	35	00110101	5
22	16	00010110	▬		54	36	00110110	6
23	17	00010111	↨		55	37	00110111	7
24	18	00011000	↑		56	38	00111000	8
25	19	00011001	↓		57	39	00111001	9
26	1A	00011010	→		58	3A	00111010	:
27	1B	00011011	←		59	3B	00111011	;
28	1C	00011100	∟		60	3C	00111100	<
29	1D	00011101	↔		61	3D	00111101	=
30	1E	00011110	▲		62	3E	00111110	>
31	1F	00011111	▼		63	3F	00111111	?

Dec	Hex	Binary	Symbol	Dec	Hex	Binary	Symbol
64	40	01000000	@	106	6A	01101010	j
65	41	01000001	A	107	6B	01101011	k
66	42	01000010	B	108	6C	01101100	l
67	43	01000011	C	109	6D	01101101	m
68	44	01000100	D	110	6E	01101110	n
69	45	01000101	E	111	6F	01101111	o
70	46	01000110	F	112	70	01110000	p
71	47	01000111	G	113	71	01110001	q
72	48	01001000	H	114	72	01110010	r
73	49	01001001	I	115	73	01110011	s
74	4A	01001010	J	116	74	01110100	t
75	4B	01001011	K	117	75	01110101	u
76	4C	01001100	L	118	76	01110110	v
77	4D	01001101	M	119	77	01110111	w
78	4E	01001110	N	120	78	01111000	x
79	4F	01001111	O	121	79	01111001	y
80	50	01010000	P	122	7A	01111010	z
81	51	01010001	Q	123	7B	01111011	{
82	52	01010010	R	124	7C	01111100	|
83	53	01010011	S	125	7D	01111101	}
84	54	01010100	T	126	7E	01111110	~
85	55	01010101	U	127	7F	01111111	✳
86	56	01010110	V	128	80	10000000	Ç
87	57	01010111	W	129	81	10000001	ü
88	58	01011000	X	130	82	10000010	é
89	59	01011001	Y	131	83	10000011	â
90	5A	01011010	Z	132	84	10000100	ä
91	5B	01011011	[	133	85	10000101	à
92	5C	01011100	\	134	86	10000110	å
93	5D	01011101	]	135	87	10000111	ç
94	5E	01011110	^	136	88	10001000	ê
95	5F	01011111	_	137	89	10001001	ë
96	60	01100000	`	138	8A	10001010	è
97	61	01100001	a	139	8B	10001011	ï
98	62	01100010	b	140	8C	10001100	î
99	63	01100011	c	141	8D	10001101	ì
100	64	01100100	d	142	8E	10001110	Ä
101	65	01100101	e	143	8F	10001111	Å
102	66	01100110	f	144	90	10010000	É
103	67	01100111	g	145	91	10010001	æ
104	68	01101000	h	146	92	10010010	Æ
105	69	01101001	i	147	93	10010011	ô

Dec	Hex	Binary	Symbol	Dec	Hex	Binary	Symbol
148	94	10010100	ö	190	BE	10111110	⌐
149	95	10010101	ò	191	BF	10111111	┐
150	96	10010110	û	192	C0	11000000	└
151	97	10010111	ù	193	C1	11000001	┴
152	98	10011000	ÿ	194	C2	11000010	┬
153	99	10011001	Ö	195	C3	11000011	├
154	9A	10011010	Ü	196	C4	11000100	─
155	9B	10011011	¢	197	C5	11000101	┼
156	9C	10011100	£	198	C6	11000110	╞
157	9D	10011101	¥	199	C7	11000111	╟
158	9E	10011110	₧	200	C8	11001000	╚
159	9F	10011111	ƒ	201	C9	11001001	╔
160	A0	10100000	á	202	CA	11001010	╩
161	A1	10100001	í	203	CB	11001011	╦
162	A2	10100010	ó	204	CC	11001100	╠
163	A3	10100011	ú	205	CD	11001101	═
164	A4	10100100	ñ	206	CE	11001110	╬
165	A5	10100101	Ñ	207	CF	11001111	╧
166	A6	10100110	ª	208	D0	11010000	╨
167	A7	10100111	º	209	D1	11010001	╤
168	A8	10101000	¿	210	D2	11010010	╥
169	A9	10101001	⌐	211	D3	11010011	╙
170	AA	10101010	¬	212	D4	11010100	╘
171	AB	10101011	½	213	D5	11010101	╒
172	AC	10101100	¼	214	D6	11010110	╓
173	AD	10101101	¡	215	D7	11010111	╫
174	AE	10101110	«	216	D8	11011000	╪
175	AF	10101111	»	217	D9	11011001	┘
176	B0	10110000		218	DA	11011010	┌
177	B1	10110001	▒	219	DB	11011011	█
178	B2	10110010	▓	220	DC	11011100	▄
179	B3	10110011	│	221	DD	11011101	▌
180	B4	10110100	┤	222	DE	11011110	▐
181	B5	10110101	╡	223	DF	11011111	▀
182	B6	10110110	╢	224	E0	11100000	α
183	B7	10110111	╖	225	E1	11100001	β
184	B8	10111000	╕	226	E2	11100010	Γ
185	B9	10111001	╣	227	E3	11100011	π
186	BA	10111010	║	228	E4	11100100	Σ
187	BB	10111011	╗	229	E5	11100101	σ
188	BC	10111100	╝	230	E6	11100110	µ
189	BD	10111101	╜	231	E7	11100111	τ

Dec	Hex	Binary	Symbol		Dec	Hex	Binary	Symbol
232	E8	11101000	Φ		244	F4	11110100	∫
233	E9	11101001	Θ		245	F5	11110101	⌡
234	EA	11101010	Ω		246	F6	11110110	÷
235	EB	11101011	δ		247	F7	11110111	≈
236	EC	11101100	∞		248	F8	11111000	°
237	ED	11101101	φ		249	F9	11111001	∙
238	EE	11101110	∈		250	FA	11111010	·
239	EF	11101111	∩		251	FB	11111011	√
240	F0	11110000	≡		252	FC	11111100	η
241	F1	11110001	±		253	FD	11111101	²
242	F2	11110010	≥		254	FE	11111110	∙
243	F3	11110011	≤		255	FF	11111111	

Appendix C

◆◆

Segment Register Assumptions

Where allowed, segment assumptions can be overriden with the segment override prefixes. These are DS: SS: CS: and ES:. For example:

    mov ES:[BX],AX

The assumptions are these:

1. When the offset is specified in BX, SI, or DI, the assumed segment register is DS.
2. When the offset is specified in SP, the assumed segment register is SS. CAN NOT BE OVERRIDDEN.
3. When the offset is specified in BP, the assumed segment register is SS.
4. For string instruction LODS, the assumed segment is DS and the assumed offset is SI. CAN NOT BE OVERRIDDEN.
5. For string instructions STOS and SCAS, the assumed segment is ES and the assumed offset is DI. CAN NOT BE OVERRIDDEN.
6. For string instructions MOVS, the source must be pointed to be DS:SI and the destination must be pointed to by ES:DI. CAN NOT BE OVERRIDDEN.

Index

Attention Developers

Learn to Create User-Friendly User Manuals with
WRITING PERFECT SOFTWARE DOCUMENTATION
by Patricia A. Williams and Pamela S. Beason

Here's a plain-English guide to planning, organizing, and writing all kinds of user manuals, including on-line documentation. Comprehensive enough for both novice and experienced writers, this book offers clear, specific instructions, examples, and illustrations to help you manage each stage of the documentation project. Fill-in forms show exactly the right information to include to help you produce a manual that your users will appreciate.

[ ] Yes! Send me:

_____ Copies of Writing Perfect Software Documentation
        Code number 46163-7

[ ] I have enclosed a check or money order for $27.95
[ ] I will pay by credit card, see information below

Name _____   [ ] Visa   [ ] MasterCard
Address _____   _____
City _____   Account Number
State _____ Zip _____   _____
Phone (   ) _____   Expiration Date
                                       _____
                                                          Signature

Mail to:

Scott, Foresman and Company
Professional Books Group
1900 East Lake Avenue
Glenview, Illinois 60025
(312) 729-3000

Allow 4-6 weeks for delivery
Price and availability subject to change without notice

PBG889

Read the magazine that Jeff Duntemann built!

PC TECHNIQUES

Building Skills in PC Software Development

**The hardheadedly practical
magazine for
PC programmers,
in the spirit of Turbo Technix**

Published by

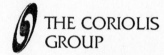

THE CORIOLIS
GROUP

For years, Jeff Duntemann has been known for his crystal-clear, slightly-bemused explanations of programming technology. He's one of the few in computer publishing who's never forgotten that English is the one language we all have in common. Now he's created a magazine to bring you a selection of readable, practical technical articles six times a year, written by himself and a crew of the very best programming writers working today. Keith Weiskamp, Michael Abrash, Tom Swan, David Gerrold, Michael Covington, Scott Robert Ladd, Peter Aitken, Marty Franz, and many more will perform their DOS magic before your eyes, then explain how it works in language you can understand.

If you program in Pascal, C, Assembler, or BASIC, you'll find code you can use in every issue. You'll also find essential debugging techniques, programming tricks and tips, detailed product reviews, and practical advice on how to get the most from your programming workstation—whether it's an 8088 or a 486!

Don't miss another issue--subscribe today!

- -

Enter my subscription to *PC Techniques* for ☐ 1 year at $21.95   ☐ 2 years at $37.95
(US funds. Overseas add $8.00)

Enclosed: ☐ Check   ☐ Money order   ☐ MasterCard/Visa

Card Number: _____   Expires: _____

_____

Last Name   First Name   Initial

_____

Address   City   State   ZIP

Signature: (for charge orders only)

Mail to:

PC Techniques
Subscriptions
3202 E. Greenway,
Suite 1307-302
Phoenix AZ 85032

BC001